AN ASSOCIATION WITH SOCCER

The NZFA celebrates its first 100 years

AN ASSOCIATION WITH SOCCER

The NZFA celebrates its first 100 years

Published in association with

Winfield

94'S THE AIM

First Published in 1991
New Zealand Football Association
Produced on behalf of the NZFA by
The Sporting Press Ltd, 67 View Road,
Glenfield, Auckland.

ISBN 0-473-01291-X

Layout, typesetting, finished art by Sportz Graphics Ltd,
67 View Road, Glenfield, Auckland.

CONTENTS

INTRODUCTION

This is clearly Warwick Gendall's fault. Apart from being, in 1991, the Chairman of the New Zealand Football Association, he is also a steward of the Wellington Racing Club. As I pursue a career as Racing Editor of Wellington's *Dominion* newspaper our paths cross often at the track, even more so when we gather with others to cheer the fortunes or otherwise of our local National League team Hutt Valley United. Some years ago I compiled a history of the Wellington Racing Club and I guess that compelled the Chairman to discuss the possibility of another publication - this one about football. What follows is the end result of those early discussions.

There are one or two points that must be made right from the start. The publication is clearly divided into two sections. The first is text, the other a statistical history, made possible because the New Zealand Football Association's historian Barry Smith has updated all that is relevant in the changing face of the game here. Without Barry's support and his tireless enthusiasm over the years, this publication would not have been possible, in fact not even attempted.

In preparing a work to commemorate 100 years of football in New Zealand, I have taken two very deliberate steps. It would have been easy to go through the records and write from day one a hundred years ago but I have opted for a lighter tone and in many cases have sought to include those who have participated and ultimately shaped the modern day game here.

For those seeking sensations in these pages I can only apologise. There are none. To suggest that football politics did and do not exist in the history of the game would be naive in the extreme. Of course there have been battles around the NZFA tables, in local associations, clubs and on the pitches. The passion that is the love for football has generated more heat than almost any other single subject I have been associated with. But this is a time to reflect and to enjoy a unique milestone in the game. To stir up old wounds and battles now, to my mind, would serve no purpose whatsoever.

New Zealand football has been richly served by thousands of men and women. Just a handful are mentioned here but our unsung heroes at all levels should not be forgotten.

It must also be said that I was given a completely free hand. Not one single restriction was placed on me in the planning and compilation of this work. With the exception of the direct interviews and Vic Deverill's history of the National League all the comments made are mine. Those thoughts come from a playing career cut short by the pursuit of journalism which began in the field of sports writing before the thoroughbred world took over.

Yet as the soccer writer for Wellington's *Evening Post* and the *Saturday Sports Post* in the 60s, there were a good number of years chronicling the deeds for the New Zealand Football Association. With a colleague, the *Dominion's* Al Flett, I used to attend council meetings of the New Zealand Football Association. An uncle Otto Hilton was on the council; so was Warwick Gendall's father, Ian.

Jim Kershaw was an amiable chairman, Steuart Goodman a part-time secretary and the council was made up of strong-willed characters like Bob and Jim Smith, Jack Cowie, George Jackson, Gordon Whyte, Ernie Harris, Charles Wilkins and Syd Guppy. Did I say strong will - some of those nights used to go on forever with their share of heat but all those men had one thing in common - the love and the prosperity of the game.

Having an uncle on the council did have its advantages. I was able to break the story of Lou Brocic's arrival as the National coach and also the team that set off for its ill-judged world tour in 1964.

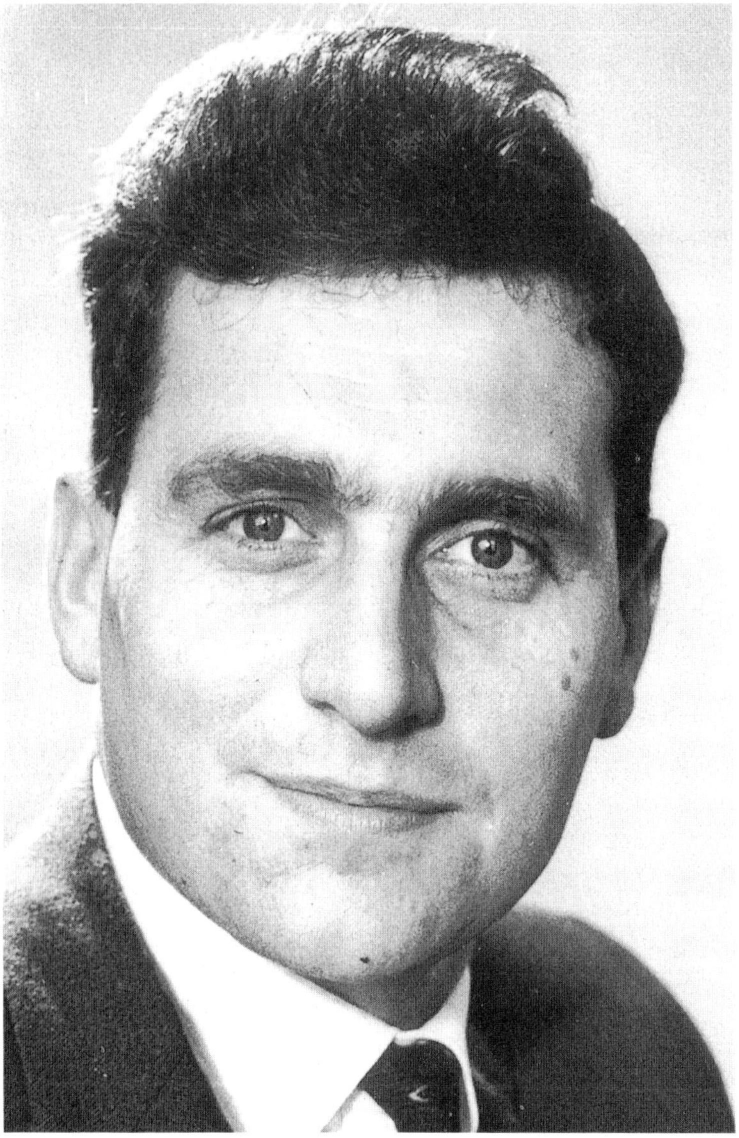
Steuart Goodman. Long serving NZFA secretary before the job became a full-time affair. Tony Hilton collection

There was, I recall, a trial played at Masterton and the team announced a fortnight later. The National selectors had the tourists picked pretty much straight after the Masterton weekend. I had, for the *Evening Post*, to select a side that I thought might tour. There was a major problem - I knew the team. My published "selection" was diplomatically one out. Then again this was long before the days of public bylines. I was just the *Post* Soccer Writer.

My journalistic colleagues these days have a pretty good time when it comes to covering matches. It's a far cry from the days of heading into the wilds of Wellington, Porirua or the Hutt Valley to cover a match for the *Sports Post* and then having to knock on the nearest house door in search of a telephone to dictate an overdue match report back in. The *Sports Post* covered all winter sports; rugby, league and hockey and I recall one Saturday night picking up a copy to see in print a 9-3 scoreline published for a local club match yet only four goal scorers were listed. A check later revealed that the reporter recorded three points for each goal scored.

There was down the years service for both the Wellington and Canterbury Football Associations, the editing of a host of weekly and monthly publications including the *New Zealand Referee* and a seemingly lifelong association with the Petone Club. My admiration for this outfit is clearly reflected in the pages that follow. I make no apology for that. If there is one football moment to treasure it came on Chatham Cup final day 1990 when Petone's place as that season's Central League Division One champions was confirmed. The result was unexpected, the club had finished its programme and while there was a three point lead there was seemingly no way that bottom placed and already relegated Havelock North was going to stop a Nelson United win and a League triumph albeit on goal difference. Well, they did. The 0-0 scoreline at Nelson triggered a run of celebrations that seemingly went on forever.

As rewarding as anything in football has been the comradeship through the years and with it a growing personal philosophy that the game and the players are far more important than those who administer or write about it. My introduction to football was early with the principal influences my father Arthur Hilton, who also served as NZFA council member, and his brother Otto mentioned earlier.

During the 50s and 60s New Zealand football had few heroes but there was one man who in my opinion stood out like a shining beacon. It is a major regret that his early passing meant that the thoughts of Ken Armstrong could not be recalled along with others. Armstrong arrived in 1957 after more than 500 first and second English Division one games with Chelsea. He played for England B and had one game for the full England team at Wembley. The result was a 7-2 win over the auld enemy Scotland. Armstrong arrived in New Zealand in 1957 to play for the Eastern Union club in Gisborne. Not long after Armstrong joined North Shore and guided them and later Eastern Suburbs and Mount Wellington to a series of Chatham Cup, Auckland and National League triumphs. He coached the Auckland province to wins over FK Austria, Stoke City and FC Zurich. He played for New Zealand and coached the national team at a difficult time.

New Zealand in recent times has been blessed with a host of talented players. Full England internationals like Mick Channon, Trevor Brooking, John Fashanu and Paul Mariner spent brief periods here playing National League football yet in the 1960s Ken Armstrong was a pioneer who, whether writing a weekly football column, playing, or as national director of coaching, performed every task with a true professional stamp which was way ahead of its time and foreign to a willing but amateur group of administrators.

The success of the 1982 World Cup takes up its share of space within these pages. As the single-most successful on-field campaign, the run-up and lead-in to Spain captured the public imagination like nothing before or since. Spain 1982 produced a rash of publications at the time but even so much of it has been recalled here.

But if there has been something of a hiatus since, the second century of the New Zealand Football Association has begun with encouragement through

Ken Armstrong of North Shore in familiar pose. Tony Hilton collection

the deeds of not only the age-restricted national teams, but also the full national squad under Ian Marshall of Christchurch who in 1990 not only shared a series with Moscow Lokomotiv but went on to beat the Peoples Republic of China in two home internationals. As a fresh World Cup campaign looms, New Zealand can look to one of its strongest teams in years. Wynton Rufer is recognised as a class international performer in Europe; Ceri Evans and Perry Cotton are playing regularly in the fickle world of English League Football while close to home Robert Ironside and the talented Michael McGarry suggest that in the immediate future there is a degree of high expectation.

Finally, Barry Smith and I would like to acknowledge a host of people who have assisted in this work. Vic Deverill was involved in the early discussions when this book was mooted. It now seems ages ago. He has already published a history of the National League and I gather another is due shortly. His enthusiasm for Soccer and its national media association has been proven many times. He has not been afraid to ripple a few ponds at national level.

Executive Director Noel Robinson was a constant source of help and I thank him for his continuing encouragement. And to the many members of my "squad" of former players, coaches and administrators who gave me so much time and help I also add my thanks as I do to my employers at Wellington Newspapers who willingly allowed me to use their Atex computer system in the preparation of this book.

Tony Hilton
Wellington, May 1991

FOREWORD

Football is a simple, child-like game which achieves its great strength through its simplicity. One only needs a ball, an open area and something to act as goal posts. Its rules, which over 100 years have remained largely unchanged except for the off-side rule, are simple and easily understood. Its world-wide popularity, with over 350 thousand registered clubs, 55 million registered players, 600 thousand referees, and 168 national associations affiliated to FIFA, is due to its simplicity and no other sport is so easily available nor crosses all frontiers so effortlessly.

And within this simple game that delights so many, there are features of a theatrical performance, a social drum, a religious ceremony, a status display, a stylised battle, and a ritual hunt. These are all the "faces" of football which were so perceptively identified by Desmond Morris in his classic book "The Soccer Tribe".

Over the century of organised football in New Zealand, which was born in 1891, there have been changes. These have been made in the continuous endeavour to propel a round ball between the opponents' posts. When the NZFA was created in 1891 the referee as we know it today did not exist. There were two umpires with flags who operated from within the field whilst the referee stood on the sideline to arbitrate or act on matters "referred" to him by the umpires. It was in 1891 that the umpires were sent to the touchlines with their flags and from that time the referee, within the field of play, solely controlled the game. In those days players enjoyed a right of appeal to the referee. They could point out an irregularity shouldering "How's that" or by calling "Foul". The referee did not interfere unless or until the player made such an appeal. Elements of a cricket match existed but over the following decades players gambled away this unusual privilege. It was in June 1891 that the International Football Association Board introduced the penalty kick. The early settlers who brought their game to New Zealand in the 19th century were "the dribblers" because during the mid 19th century there was no deliberate passing of the ball. Rather one player would endeavour to dribble the ball the length of the field until it was lost to an opponent, who would then set off on his return dribble. The tactical formation was, therefore, a goal keeper, one defender and nine attackers. During the 1870s the tactic of deliberate passing was devised by Queen's Park in Scotland and it was not until around the turn of the century that Preston North End invented a centre half. Upon the offside rule being refined in 1925 the Arsenal Football Club developed the famous 1-3-2-5 system, comprising of 2 fullbacks and a centre half, 2 halfbacks, 2 wingers and 2 inside forwards and a centre forward. For 60 years this system was used in New Zealand until Brazil invented the 4-2-4 system in 1958 and which was brought to New Zealand by our first English professional coaches. Later came the 4-3-3 and 4-4-2 in the late 1960s all of which changes, including the recent defensive use of a sweeper introduced by Italy, have led to differing styles and strategies in our game. But the game still remains beautifully simple in design and purpose.

I grew up in a football and sport mad family, with my father's family having lived in Seatoun, a strong soccer suburb in Wellington. As with thousands of youngsters during the 1940s, my brothers and I, together with my father played for hours on the front lawn, on the road, on back lawns, on pitches that tilted at angles or ran uphill, on clay heaps covered with pine needles to soak up mud and water. Indoor games in narrow halls, with a rolled up pair of socks for a ball, were resorted to when the weather was at its worst. Goals were rubbish bins, sticks or jerseys, and imaginary cup finals, with mother's silver egg cup being presented to the winner, were regular events.

Blanford Park, 1936 and a Wellington goal coming up against Auckland. The scorer is Ian Gendall, father of current chairman Warwick. Warwick Gendall collection

My brothers and I graduated to building our own goalposts - of reduced size - and purloined the parents' fine lace double bedspread for nets, the ultimate luxury. Soccer was played on frosty Hutt Valley grounds early on Saturday mornings but rugby was played for primary school teams on Wednesday afternoons because at some schools, the authorities regarded rugby as the "acceptable" game. Saturday afternoons were spent at the Basin Reserve watching the curtain raiser on the eastern pitch, along with large numbers of supporters who would be gingered up by a liquid lunch at the adjacent Caledonian Hotel. Crowds of 3000 to 4000 were common. At the end of the match the crowd would stream around to the opposite side of the Basin Reserve to watch the big match. Local players became our heroes because out of town teams only came to Wellington for the Chatham Cup final, the soccer event of the year. Players such as Bert Hiddlestone, the Yeoman brothers, Keith Gibson, Dave McKissock and Alf Longbottom, were household names. The post-war era saw the rise of the Petone Settlers and I remember being part of a massive crowd which saw that remarkable team win the 1949 Chatham Cup final.

Clubs such as Hospital, Seatoun, Petone and Marist, reigned supreme in Wellington during the early 1950s and I can recollect watching Hospital defeat Seatoun in the final match of the 1952 season at their ground located within the confines of the Porirua Psychiatric Hospital. Those were the days of baggy shorts, bulky shin pads and heavy spun cotton jerseys, usually laced at the neck with a black or white bootlace, of the type worn by rugby players. For some reason soccer boots were brown with hard toes and a leather strap across the instep with leather studs nailed to the soles and we all would remember the heavy brown leather balls which became sodden when wet and were fearsome to head particularly if you happened to hit the laced section. All centres in New Zealand only saw local teams except where there were the North Island and South Island Chatham Cup finals and of course the event of the year was the Chatham Cup final in Wellington.

I remember clearly the dominance which Eastern Suburbs from Auckland and Northern from Dunedin seemed to achieve in the early 1950s but joy unbounded occurred when my father's team, Seatoun, won successive Cup finals in 1957 and 1958. The image of sandy-haired John Donovan scoring six goals in the 1958 Cup final against Christchurch City on a sunny Saturday afternoon in Wellington remains firmly imprinted in my mind. The news media gave extensive coverage of football in the days before television. It is sad this does not continue in the same informative and detailed way as occurred then. The commentary from the Basin Reserve of the match every Saturday by Gordon Whyte, and later Trevor Rigby, together with the extensive summaries of major matches on the evening sports news were regular fare. If Northern, Eastern Suburbs and Seatoun were the teams of the 50s, Blockhouse Bay, North Shore, Eastern Suburbs, Christchurch and Stop Out were the teams of the 60s.

As the National Administration strengthened under the leadership of men such as Jim Kershaw and Jack Cowie the move to bring to New Zealand the best teams from other areas saw the creation of the National Soccer League in 1970. Had it not been for the Rothmans Soccer League the rapid progress football underwent during the 1970's and 80's would not have occurred. I can vividly remember being at Te Whiti Park on Saturday, April 11, 1970 to watch the first Rothman's Soccer League match ever played in Wellington when Stop Out, thanks to a last minute headed goal by Geoff Brand - the super-talented, bow-legged policeman - drew with Gisborne City 1-1. With the added exposure of players from eight teams to the sporting public in four centres, new stars became household names. The seventies were largely dominated by Mt. Wellington and Christchurch United although Blockhouse Bay, Eastern Suburbs and North Shore United were rightfully regarded as giants from Auckland. Names such as John Wrathall, Ray Mears, Grahame Bilby, Graham Griffiths, Vic Pollard, Peter Whiting, Earle Thomas, John Houghton, Alan Vest, Keith Nelson, Maurice Tillotson, Bill de Graaf, Iain Ormond, Brian Turner, Ken France, John Staines and many others brought a new dimension to the game in New Zealand. Our progress to technical, strategical and tactical excellence received enormous impetus by the arrival of coaches such as Ken Armstrong and Barrie Truman. In international matches we were still subject to substantial defeats by overseas national and club sides but by the late 1970s the fruits of the Rothmans Soccer League competition were about to be harvested. I first became a member of the Council of the NZFA in May of 1979 with the intention of "helping out" for six months in order to fill a gap. Twelve years later I remain on the Council, such are the addictive powers of love for football! During 1979 three things of real significance occurred in New Zealand football. The first was the appointment of John Adshead in April to coach the New Zealand National team in games against Norwich City and Australia. We were defeated 4-1 by Norwich but the second significant event was to come when on June 13, 1979, a 25 year drought in international matches against Australia was broken when the New Zealand team defeated Australia 1-0 at Newmarket Park. It was a night when Duncan Cole, then but a youth with a full head of hair, showed his outstanding potential and I shared the after match euphoria and optimism with my friend Sam Malcolmson at his home. He spoke of aiming for the World Cup and we honestly felt that that mountain could be climbed. The third event of 1979 of significance was the appointment of Allan Jones as the National Director of coaching succeeding Barrie Truman who had laid some solid foundations for our integrated coaching schemes.

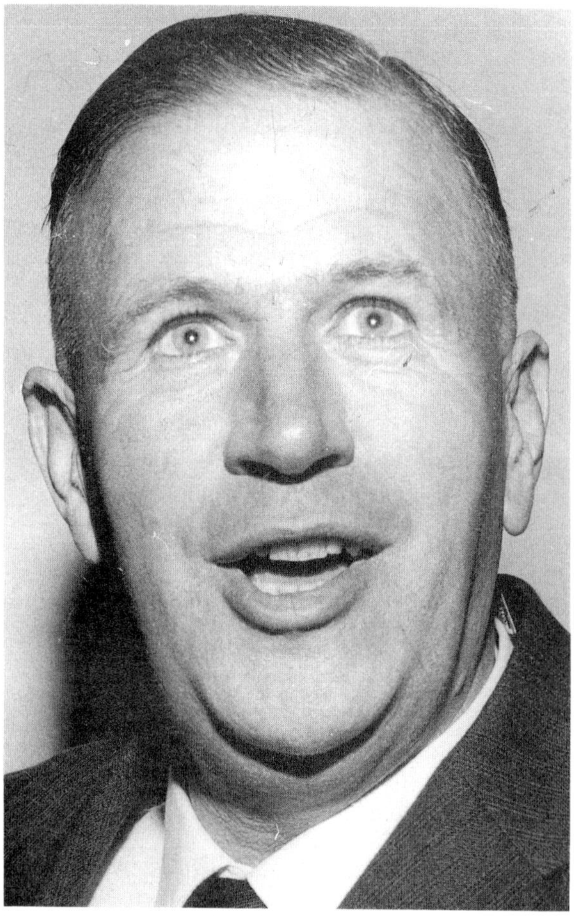

Jack Cowie was a grand fast bowler who represented his country at the summer sport, but as a player and then administrator he gave long and faithful service to soccer here. Tony Hilton collection

The 1980s saw New Zealand come of age on the international front. While it began with the defeat of Australia in 1979 it blossomed in 1980 in the World Youth Cup championships when the New Zealand under-twenty side not only won the Oceania region but defeated Israel in the play offs in South America. That was the only team from New Zealand to have ever played on South American soil and although beaten by Argentina (coached by Cesar Menotti) it nevertheless performed superbly. The team contained youngsters such as Malcolm Dunford, Ceri Evans, Billy Harris, Ian Masson, Martin Felton, Rudi Feitsma and of course Wynton Rufer who was then aged 17 years and two months. One year later at the age of 18 years Wynton was scoring goals against Kuwait, Saudi Arabia and PR China in the glorious World Cup campaign of 1981. The rewards of the NZFA's emphasis on youth coaching are still felt when one views the positions now held by players such as Dunford, Evans and Rufer. They are all stars in their own right.

The remarkable achievement of the national team qualifying for the 1982 World Cup Finals in Spain has been well documented but it was without doubt the high point in our first hundred years of football. It showed that New Zealand can compete on the international stage at the highest level and rates as a major football force in Asia and the Pacific. Whilst the 1970's may have been dominated by the Auckland and Christchurch clubs, apart from Wellington Diamond United's remarkable success in the 1976 Air New Zealand Soccer League, the 1980's were highlighted in domestic football by the growth and success of provincial clubs such as Gisborne City and Napier City Rovers together with further successes of Wellington Diamond United in 1981 and 1985. In fact, the feats of Barrie Truman in winning the league on three occasions, and in 1985 with a squad of entirely New Zealand born players with an average age of 23, were remarkable. It could no longer be said that soccer carried a label of a game of "imports". International successes continued both at home and overseas and our senior national team showed once and for all that it could consistently do best in Asia. Successes over Saudi Arabia, PR China, Indonesia and China Taipei in the 1982 World Cup Campaign, and later successes over Japan, Malaysia and South Korea in the Merdeka Tournament were sufficient evidence of this. I had the honour of being the manager of the 1981 New Zealand side which went to the Merdeka tournament before huge crowds of enthusiastic Asians. I recollect a match against Malaysia under floodlights in the middle of a stadium in Kuala Lumpur when huge butterflies the size of bats - would flutter down in the evening lights and land on the players' heads and shoulders. For some of our players the distraction and fright occasioned by this exceeded any fear of opponents. On another occasion, in torrential rain, the stadium surface was awash with large green frogs which, whilst not exactly participating in the game, leapt enthusiastically around every the time the ball or a player landed nearby. I had one experience in 1981 in Malaysia with the New Zealand side which I hope will never be repeated. Allan Jones was taking the squad for a training session at a suburban Kuala Lumpur ground in torrential rain. Many locals were huddled under trees and in a nearby pavilion watching in awe at the brave strapping kiwis enduring the elements. The anxiety went unnoticed, but became significant when a massive lightning bolt struck a goal post on the practice pitch and a electrical charge was transmitted across the water-laden surface of the ground. Sandy Davie and others were thrown to the ground and the entire squad, led by the manager, fled from the field at alarming speed. We later learned that many are killed each year by lightning strikes and the locals were genuinely frightened for the safety of the squad. Thereafter the practice ground was known as "lightning ground" and I reflected pensively that night and gave thanks that I was not having to cable back to New Zealand that some or all of the National team had been killed in action.

After the marvellous achievement of reaching Spain, the World Cup side, or those who had not retired, undertook a major tour of Fiji and England in late 1984 and I again was honoured with being their manager. The new coaches were Allan Jones and Kevin Fallon. This was an experienced side including players such as Steve Sumner, Richard Wilson, Ricki Herbert, Grant Turner, Alan Boath, Colin Walker, Bill McClure, Keith McKay and Peter Simonsen and had players seeking their first full caps in Clint Gosling, Malcolm Dunford and Keith Garland. It was a very arduous tour which produced riots by spectators and opponents at both games in Fiji. The night match against Fiji in Lautoka was watched by the All Blacks who were in Lautoka to play a rugby test. They reported to the soccer team management after the game that they had never seen violence like it and were glad that they played rugby against Fiji and not soccer! The team's performances in England were of the highest order and New Zealand obtained its first, and it remains its only, success on English soil by defeating Reading 2-1 on October 29, 1984 with goals from Grant Turner and Colin Walker. Invited players who appeared as guests of the Reading club included Martin Peters and George Best who, if a little below their highest form, were nevertheless outstanding opponents. The experience in Britain, which involved six matches, and intensive travel and training, was invaluable for our development and from it emerged Clint Gosling, Malcom Dunford and Colin Walker who went on to become firmly established All White stars. The match against England B at Nottingham produced an outstanding performance with New Zealand being 0-1 behind after 91 minutes at which time Colin Walker hit the cross bar. At that point the crowd were roundly booing the England team but in the 94th minute a snatched goal gave it a 2-0 victory. The quality of the England B side can be illustrated in that it contained players such as Gary Stevens, Steve McMahon, Graham Roberts, Garry Mabbutt, Luther Blissett, Peter Davenport, Steve Hodge and Nigel Callaghan. In other matches New Zealand faced Peter Beardsley, Chris Waddle, Allie McCoist and Gary Lineker. It was a shame that Steve Wooddin, one of the greats in our World Cup campaigns, was passed his best due to injury and that Allan Boath was also in the twilight of his career. But there were many very positive aspects of this tour which are now being reaped through the performances of Gosling and Dunford and the coaching abilities of Sumner and Garland. As in any overseas tour there are many events and happenings which are humorous or noteworthy and some are not suitable for repetition. However, I recollect the team arriving in Ipswich after a nine hour coach ride from Glasgow at about 11pm at night and finding the Victorian style hotel set out in the dark countryside some distance from the city. The hotel was a sports centre and was totally booked by the New Zealand team for use of its facilities and superb adjoining training pitches. It resembled something akin to a cross between Fawlty Towers and a haunted house as it sat in the Suffolk countryside lit only by a pale moon on that dark night. As the squad trudged inside and climbed creaking stairs one of its members, whose initials were GT, began to bay and howl like a coyote crying to the moon. This provoked great merriment amongst the tired team but I did not notice the same reaction from the proprietor. That same individual was even less amused when said player emerged from his rather small bedroom in a state of high irritation stating "I'm not sleeping in here, there's no bloody blankets". An inspection of his room revealed that the beds were furnished with beautiful, thick duvets!

The years from 1985-1990 produced outstanding Rothmans Soccer League and later Air New Zealand Soccer League competitions, as well as our share of successes in the international arena, but there were inevitable disappointments in Olympic and World Cup competitions. Nevertheless, some superb matches were played and results achieved, none greater than the 3-1 defeat of Israel in Auckland and the 2-0 and 1-0 defeats of Australia in Auckland and Hutt Valley. We have progressed in leaps and bounds in the area of sponsorship and media coverage and also have achieved coaching, junior and youth development programmes which are unequalled throughout the world. Particular emphasis has been placed upon the development of our youngest players in the age group 12-16 with programmes such as the Guardian Royal Exchange Centres of Excellence and the NZ Soccer Academy for elite young players. The fruits of these policies have been recently shown in the performance of the Junior All White team in the Oceania qualifying competition and I am sure we will continue to make great progress in this area. It is today's 16-year-olds who will be our World Cup stars in eight years' time. In recent years the NZFA has been ably served by secretaries and chief executive officers who are dedicated to football, understand players and their needs and have a sense of commercial reality. The services given to the game by Gwyn Evans, Paul Cunningham and at present by Noel Robinson deserve the highest recognition and I am fortunate to be able to count each of those men as my personal friends. Football has brought me many blessings not the least of which is the contact and friendship and hundreds if not thousands of players at all levels of the game. Administrators give of their time and talents without monetary gain or reimbursement and always at great expense to their financial, personal and private interests. But the joys and intangible rewards that they received through their involvement in our sport cannot be measured in terms of identifiable or tangible monetary rewards. The reward comes through the pleasure of being part of a great game.

Gwyn Evans. A previous New Zealand FA general-secretary via Crystal Palace and Christchurch United. He's now the proud dad of the 80s and 90s All White Ceri. Tony Hilton collection

The progress of refereeing in New Zealand has been enormous, in particular over the last 20 years. Names such as Tom Delahunty, Ron Harries, Les Coffman, John Cameron, Bill Munro, Ken Wallace, Lennox Sharp and Barry Tasker have all placed New Zealand on the international scene as having officials of the highest standard and the time must surely come when a New Zealand referee will be appointed to officiate at the FIFA World Cup finals. I have greatly appreciated my friendships and administrative contacts with referees and have learnt to understand and appreciate the phenomenal task that they perform for the sake of our game.

Our participation in the Oceania Football Confederation has been total with representation on executive, technical, coaching and referees' committees as well as having Charles Dempsey as the Confederation President, a position he fills with tireless vigour. The efforts of Charles, as well as our senior coaches, referees and administrators, in developing football in the Pacific nations, deserve recognition and reflect the wider part played by the NZFA in the growth of the game.

We reach the end of one hundred years with, I believe, every reason to be satisfied and proud of what has been achieved but all who love football in New Zealand must not see this as the end of a hundred years but the beginning of the next century. The growth in the game over the last 20 years at all levels whether international, domestic, womens or juniors, has been sensational and every indication is that this will continue.

There will be further great successes in the international arena by those who now are juniors or even babies. There will be memorable matches, at all levels. There will be disappointments. But the beauty and allure of our simple game will live on bringing enjoyment and excitement to these and future generations. We can only hope that those who celebrate our next 100 years will be able to look back to see that the progress and pleasures of the first century of football in New Zealand have been doubled in the 21st century. But as we head into the next century we must never forget that football is basically a game and it must remain so, to serve society and not the other way round.

Warwick Gendall
Chairman NZFA
February 1991.

THE KICK OFF

First meeting of the council of the New Zealand Football Association at the office of the Colonial Mutual Assurance Co, Wellington October 2nd, 1891.
Present: L. Tripp (Canterbury) in the chair, P.D. Leslie (Otago), J.R. Gibbons (Auckland) and A. Henderson (Wellington)
1. Proposed by Mr Gibbons, seconded by Mr Henderson that an association be formed to be called the New Zealand Football Association.
2. Proposed by Mr Gibbons and seconded by Mr Tripp that Messrs Leslie and Henderson draw up rules to be submitted at the next meeting about one month hence.

THE FIRST HALF

And so a New Zealand council had met for the first time. Soccer was already here - alive and active in the provinces. Clubs were competing in Auckland, Wellington, Dunedin and Christchurch. New Zealand's two main islands and the difficult nature of early travel made it hard for national gatherings but the initial seeds had been sown. The first faltering steps of a national body had been taken. On October 21, 1891 the quartet met again in the Wellington offices of the Colonial company. The minutes were brief. The one item noted that the rules as drawn up by Leslie and Henderson were to be adopted. The next set of minutes were not dated but one of the association's life members George Cox wrote in pencil that the date might well have been November of 1891. Already the rules of a Trophy competition were being proposed. In 1892 a couple of council meetings were held in Christchurch under the secretaryship of a "local" Tom Maude. The minutes note that the NZFA was able to secure Lancaster Park for the use of a football tournament but a limit on spending was 25 pounds. The possible use of a charge ground was one of the main reasons to shift headquarters from Wellington. The lack of financial success of the tournament is noted. There was a "small attendance of spectators" and total receipts came to £19/4/1. The ball cost 15 shillings and the total percentage to the Rugby Union totalled a princely £21/19/5. That tournament is the major event of the what could well have been the first annual meeting of the association which was held in Hereford Street, Christchurch. It started on April 29 and was adjourned until June 20 but no reason is given. Wellington, after defeating Canterbury 9-2 in the semi-final beat Otago 6-2 in the final. Otago had earlier dealt to Auckland 1-0.

George Cox . . . NZFA life member of the 50s and 60s. Tony Hilton collection

Lancaster Park may have been used but even with the charge of one shilling per head there was a shortfall of ten pounds. George Rhodes, who had played in the very first representative fixture made up the deficit by way of a donation. A year later the Canterbury Association was in the dogbox. It had failed to affiliate to the New Zealand Football Association and had committed the cardinal sin of not putting a single team on the field. The minutes note that a Harry Hill made the trek from Timaru to help financially the Cantabs but he had to return home without achieving his objective. Auckland were the second winners of the provincial tournament played at Petone which now carried with it "Mr Brown's Trophy".

The representative fixtures of 1892 were not the first. On August 16, 1890, Canterbury hosted a team from Wellington and won 2-0 with a brace of goals by Coglan, one in each half. This match is generally regarded as being the country's first representative fixture. The Wellington players, it was noted, had suffered from "a malady to which landsmen are liable at sea", the *Christchurch Press* published. A year later (June 20, 1891) at Wellington's Newtown Park, Wellington gained revenge with a 1-0 triumph. Among those who witnessed the second game was a Mr Robert Brown and he together with the visitors attended a smoke concert on the evening of the fixture. At the concert Mr Brown said he would present a shield for competition among the provinces. The shield, worth twenty five pounds, arrived and in November 1891 a set of rules was drawn up. The Brown Shield was for 23 years the supreme trophy for competition among the provinces until the arrival of the FA Trophy, played for the first time in 1926. Up to 1908 the shield was determined as part of a tournament and then from 1908 to 1909 was played for on a challenge system. From before the war the trophy became the symbol for the minor associations. The Brown Shield still exists and as the oldest trophy certainly holds a high place in New Zealand football. In 1990 the New Zealand Football Association was seeking to reinstate the competition which, not for the first time, had lapsed. The minutes of the second annual meeting end on a positive note. Canterbury, though not an affiliated association formally until 1903, was continuing to function, being referred to either as a club or association while the footballing natives were stirring in the most unlikely venues - Oamaru and Woodville.

Early in 1905 the New Zealand Football Association held three meetings in Christchurch and at one of those a resolution was passed that NZFA headquarters should shift back to Wellington. The city, it was deemed, was the hub of the country. In 1982 the office was finally shifted to Auckland. The first balance sheet shows its receipts, apart from the tournament, to have been £24/14/6. Expenditure is shown at nil, a record not since equalled - and unlikely to be.

In those early days from 1891 to 1898 the name of Alex Henderson appears often in the minutes. He was one of the prime movers in getting the association on the right road. On May 17, 1898 the annual meeting of the Association was held. The report was prepared by the treasurer Arthur Gibbs. In

New Zealand's very first football trophy, "Mr Brown's shield." NZFA collection

The wonders of modern technology. Frank John Edward Smallbone (1878-1937) kept goal for New Zealand in the trendsetting team of 1904. Barry Smith collection

The 1926-27 NZFA Council: Back row: J.A. Milburn, P. Rose, A.J. Hyder, W.G. Bryce, F. Sanders. Front row: B.L. Salmon, F. Campbell (Vice-Chairman), A. Varney (Chairman), L.O. Atkinson (Secretary), H.L. Graves (Hon. Treasurer). Absent: J.J. Roberts. Crown Studios photo

the New Zealand Times the following day Mr Gibbs paid tribute to Mr Henderson. "First mention should be made of the enormous loss which the Association and indeed association football in the country has sustained through Mr Henderson's premature decease. His heart and soul were in the game and he gave his time and his best work ungrudgingly to promote its interests. How difficult it will be to find a successor who can and will devote the time to worthily take up the role of following him as secretary, only those who were intimately associated with him can guess".

And if the minutes in the first minute book were brief, the end is downright depressing. On May 28, 1901 at 5pm the annual meeting was due to be held. An Auckland delegate was present and so was the hon secretary Mr M.J. Courtenay. And that was the total attendance. The meeting lapsed for want of a quorum. It was just as well that future delegates and officials showed a little more interest as the 20th century developed.

Minutes record little at the best of times though in the early days of the country at about the time of the formation of the New Zealand Football Association shorthand was certainly in vogue. As the century progressed newspapers were the only form of communication. Meetings of local councils and other distinguished organisations used to carry reports of those verbatim. Soccer, sorry, association football, was not covered to the same extent. But in this case that is hardly the question in hand. The start of the game in New Zealand prior to the advent of the first council in 1891 is hazy. There are a couple of published references. Al Flett, a leading journalist, author, newspaperman and a grand friend to a budding football writer named Hilton in the early 1960s, wrote in volume one of an *Encylopaedia of New Zealand* (1966) that the future of the code in New Zealand was probably easier to forecast than its beginnings are to define.

"It was inevitable that settlers and crews of ships trading to the colony should play some sort of football during leisure hours, but soccer began to be organised as a sport only in the eighties of the last century. A Reverend J.S. Hill has been credited with starting the game in this country", Flett wrote. He suggests that Northern may have been the first club formed in the country but this honour may also belong to North Shore which, according to club sources, began life as Devonport 1887. North Shore has used this date and in 1987 became the first New Zealand football club to celebrate a centenary. Northern in recent times joined forces with Maori Hill to become North End, a Dunedin regional side. Soccer's early days, Flett notes, were not helped by the death when playing football in 1891 of 31-year-old Thomas M Sibbin at Potters Paddock in Epsom, Auckland. The press in those days noted the development of football and already in those days it was fighting a losing battle. A Canterbury journal of the 90s noted that no matter how strongly the association branch of football became entrenched it would never displace rugby in the affections of the local population. Flett then offers speculation as to why, in a country settled mainly by people from Britain, the oval ball code would have so quickly and decisively established itself as the popular winter sports code. His answers are numerous. They point to the better education of those who arrived to settle in the colony. The advent of the professional game seemingly put soccer somewhat beyond the pale. The association game was the opiate of the masses, the unwashed, the cloth cap and muffler brigade.

The North Shore club, bless it, has produced its own publication (*90 Seasons - A history of the club* by Brian Bond). It traces football back to earlier pastimes in the case of football to Japan as long ago as 1004 BC. The game probably arrived in Britain via Roman, Saxon, Danish and Norman invaders. While football was deemed to be popular, early problems did surface. In 1314 Edward II was hardly complimentary about the "great noise in the city caused by hustling over large balls". The playing of such a game in the city may bring down periods of imprisonment. March on to Scotland and 1491. "In na place of this realme be used futeball, golfe or other sik unprofitable sports". Come forward then to Manchester in 1608 and those today who follow the fortunes of United or

Wellington host the MCC in a match at the Basin Reserve in 1936. Warwick Gendall collection

City would be horrified to learn that football was prohibited under a penalty of 20 pence because of "ye glasse windows broken yearely and spoyled by a company of lewd and disordered persons using that unlarfull exercise".

North Shore have a proud history in New Zealand football. That they have won the Chatham Cup six times from 11 attempts makes them the most successful and busiest side in this grand competition. And they can probably lay claim to one of their own being a leader in setting a trial for players in this country. In England in December 1863 a set of rules governing "football for dribblers" was agreed on. At the time of their introduction, a 16-year-old Charles Craven Dacre, was competing for his school Clapham Grammar as well as for London Athletic and Clapham Rovers - obviously not all at the same time. In one of these matches, not played under the association rules, he was so badly hurt internally that he was not expected to last the night. That he did was a blessing not only for himself and his family but also in the course of time for North Shore, Auckland and New Zealand. The first game under the modern day rules, if they can be called that, was played between Middlesex and Surrey. The rules were designed to suit the so-called "dribblers". Dacre played for Surrey and the game ended in a scoreless draw - surely a forerunner of things to come.

Having played in that historic fixture the attention of Dacre was now firmly headed towards the code in New Zealand, in particular Auckland. The family traces back to the time of the Norman conquests and C C Dacre's father Captain Randulph sailed up the Waitemata Harbour in 1827 which makes him one of the first white men to set foot in Auckland as it was soon to become. Young Dacre was born in Sydney in 1848 and 11 years later travelled by barque to Auckland. He was sent to England for his education and at that time showed skill not only at football but also at cricket. He captained the South of England XI against All England and competed for the Gentlemen against the Players. As an aside it is noted that in one match he took 10 wickets for six in an innings total of 17 and then scored 97 not out. Before he left England en route to Auckland he was one-time secretary of the Football Association and also for the Surrey county. C C Dacre took up farming when he returned to New Zealand but he never lost his interest in the sport and though the code of association football had not yet been introduced he was quick to associate himself with the game of "football" played at the time. In July 1870 he met with others with the object of forming an Auckland football club. The first thing that was required was a football shipped over from Melbourne. The rules of Westminster under which the Middlesex v Surrey fixture had been conducted were adopted.

An Auckland team was soon coached into something like form and the first match was played by the Auckland team against a team from HMS Rosario at the old Albert Barracks, now Albert Park. The final rules were a mixture. No picking up of the ball, no offside and no holding although some shoving was permissible. The teams were of 15-a-side and a report of the match notes that Auckland got home by a goal

1904 New Zealand representative side. Back row: R. Riley, H. Morrison, A. Clapham, A. Stark. Middle row: W.J. Taylor, R. Farquharson, D. McMillan (captain), L. White, P. Smallbone. Front row: W. Kilgour, W. Morrison. Barry Smith collection

to nothing. The match did arouse some interest in football in Auckland and the game continued, though at times the rules it is believed were a mixture of both rugby and soccer. An account of a fixture in 1872 notes clearly that goals were scored by sending the ball between the opponents goal posts. Charles Dacre and his brother Life (not a nickname but one that had appeared years before in a family tree) continued to excel at "both" sets of rules. C C Dacre did play in the first interprovincial rugby match for Auckland against Canterbury and he scored the first try and points for an Auckland rugby team. That was in 1876. Two years later C C Dacre broke his leg playing rugby and the sport was suddenly abandoned. Although little is known, there was obviously progress made in football around the country particularly in Auckland. Dacre continue to arrange games on the North Shore and they were played mainly against visiting ships' teams. During 1885 games were arranged on the shore at the old Devonport Domain and two years later the Reverend Joseph Sidney Hill joined a group that used to kick a football about in the old Beer Garden section of Devonport. Auckland at least was up and running in the guise of North Shore. Dunedin's Northern Club was formed in 1898 and a year later Petone arrived in the lower half of the North Island as Wellington's second club, but now the oldest surviving club in the area. Wellington's first recorded game took place in 1889 when the Petone Wanderers beat the Wellington Rovers 2-0. Jock Houston's 1952 Jubilee Yearbook "*Association Football in New Zealand*" states that the Auckland FA was formed in 1886 and Otago in 1889, after nine years of some form of football activity. The Canterbury FA came into being officially in 1903. While there was also football in Wellington, the local FA was not founded until in 1891 which happens to be the same year that the first New Zealand Football Council met for the first time.

The Brown Shield was well established and football was growing. And not long after the turn of the century New Zealand turned to its near neighbour Australia. In 1904 a team from New South Wales made the sea trip across the Tasman and in the space of a month was able to play nine fixtures in both the North and South Island. The first NSW match was played at Auckland on June 29 1904 and NSW and a team from the North Island shared the spoils at 1-1. The goals came in the second half of the match which the *New Zealand Referee* noted was played before a satisfactory attendance. A heavy ground and some determined defence it seemed helped the local cause for New South Wales were dominant. On July 2 NSW overcame Auckland 3-2 but five days later a team from Wellington was successful 2-1 to become the first "local" team to beat a set of tourists. *The Referee* notes that the game was played in miserable weather. Wellington took full advantage of the conditions to lead 2-0 and then was able to hold on for an historic win.

The big day for a New Zealand representative team came on July 23 at Dunedin when a New Zealand team fronted up to New South Wales. The result was hardly good news for the home side as NSW won by the only goal of the game. The first half of the game was scoreless but a second half strike by Waddell was enough for New South Wales to take the match. New South Wales gave an excellent display of teamwork. New Zealand attempted to spoil the combination of the visitors and the end result reflected credit not only on New Zealand but also its goalkeeper Smallbone. A week later at Wellington the honours were shared 3-3. *The Referee* noted that "better matched teams had never been brought together before". New Zealand was able to gain a two goal lead but by half time the score was 2-2. New South Wales scored first in the second spell but New Zealand drew level before the finish. The match report in the *Referee* is entertaining to say the least. The reporter noted the first two goals but by report's end the "goals" had become 'tries" and the New Zealanders were Maorilanders. New South Wales' first tour had brought five wins, two losses and two draws.

1905 as a sporting year is generally associated with another code of football and the great All Black side which toured Britain. In that same year a New Zealand soccer team travelled to New South Wales for a tour of 11 matches. The team won six, lost three and drew two and while they lost the first match of the tour to a team named Metropolitan they were able to square the three match series. New Zealand won the first "test" 6-4 after being down 3-1 at half time. The Kiwis lost the second 2-0 to a goal in each half and the third was drawn 1-1 in what was called the best game of the tour with New Zealand coming back from a 1-0 half time deficit. Two tours in two years - was this to be a forerunner of things to come? Hardly! It was 17 years later when a full Australian team came to this country. The team won nine of 14 matches drew one and lost four. Wellington and Canterbury were the provincial winners but on this first true international tour New Zealand knew success for the first time. On June 17, 1922 New Zealand beat Australia 3-1 at Dunedin. The game was played at Carisbrook and the *Weekly Press* and *NZ Referee* noted that a crowd of 10,000 was present to see the fixture. Light rain fell and both teams were at full strength. New Zealand's first goal came from a "lineout". Campbell found Cook who drove in a hot

Trendsetters. The 1905 New Zealand soccer team who went to New South Wales - the first national Association side to leave these shores. Barry Smith collection

New Zealand touring party to Australia, 1933. Back row: A. Graham, D.A. Crabbe, W.H. Zuill, J.P. Gerrard, J.I. Kershaw, R.H. Stone, J.P. Baker, G.M. Kay. Sitting: B.L. Salmon (selector), E.J. Barton, J. Christie (captain), H.L. Godber (manager), W.A. Chapman (vice-captain), F.S. Blackie, N. McArthur (assistant manager). In front: A. Stenhouse, C.E. Ives, L. Groves.
Crown Studios photo

shot which entered the net amid applause. Before half-time Maunder had levelled for Australia even though the visitors were having trouble on the greasy surface. In the second spell Knott first and then Cook with his second goal sent New Zealand to its success and win which even the Australian management deemed was deserved. Another 10,000 were at Wellington for the second test which ended 1-1. Cook for New Zealand and then Bratten for Australia did the scoring in the first half and though New Zealand pressed hard in the second spell the game ended level pegging. New Zealand were able to secure a series win 3-1 at Carlaw Park. They scored two first half goals and were able to hold on. *The Referee* notes that the attendance of 15,000 was a record for an association match played in New Zealand. A year later New Zealand went back to Australia. The team recorded seven wins, seven losses and two draws from its 16 matches. On the surface the tour was hardly a raging success, but New Zealand won the test series 2-1. The Australians won the first test 2-1 but the Kiwis won the second 3-2 helped by a hat-trick from Campbell and the third by a convincing scoreline of 4-1. As it transpired Australia had led 1-0 at half-time but the second half belonged entirely to Campbell who in the space of 45 minutes scored all the tourists' goals. The match report notes that the socks worn by Campbell were in demand as souvenirs.

George Campbell played for the Thistle Club in Wellington and was a gifted player who would have been a headline hogger had he played in modern times. The success of the team can best be gauged by a report that appeared in the July 18 edition of the 1923 *New Zealand Times*. "All Black Return" said the headline. "The team brings home the Ashes. They were irresistible." It was quite a glowing tribute to the team that report in the *Times* which was then a daily. It is reproduced in full here:-

"The New Zealand soccer team, which arrived in Wellington by the ss Manuka yesterday afternoon from Sydney, was entertained at the Carlton Hotel last evening by the council for the New Zealand Football Association. Among those present were Messrs. A. Varney, acting chairman, B L Salmon, hon sec, F. Sanders, F Campbell, H Yeoman (NZFA), Messrs A E Wells, Chairman WFA, A Williams hon sec, H L Godber, and also members of the referees association. The whole of the team, with the manager Mr H.G. Mayer and assistant manager Mr H.J. Graves were present.

"The whole party looked exceedingly fit and well with the exception of N McArthur, whose ankle is still causing trouble and it is unlikely that he will play further this season. The tour has been a great success from every point of view and the ashes were literally brought home by the manager, contained in a silver-plated razor blade box. The box was presented for the purpose by Mr W Fisher, secretary of the Queensland

The New Zealand side which beat Canada 1-0 in the third test of the 1927 series. Back row: D. Jones, G. Anderson, W. Cooper, J. McDougall, J. Campbell, H. Spencer. Sitting: W. Nicolle, L. McGirr, C. Ballard (captain), W. Hooper, B.l. Salmond (selector). In front: J. Burke, E. Newman, T. MacCormack. Crown Studios photo

FA. It accompanied the first boat which made the landing on Gallipoli and made the name Anzac known throughout the world and it was thought that this would further cement the link that bound Australia and New Zealand together.

"The box contains the ashes of the cigars smoked by the captains of the Australian and New Zealand test teams at the reception in Queensland. The box is to be sealed and placed in a casket made of Australian and New Zealand woods. The box will be mounted with the fernleaf and kangaroo and will be the trophy for which Australian and New Zealand teams will compete in future years.

"Australian grounds can not compare with New Zealand grounds as they are dry and sandy and in the coal district of Newcastle are covered in coaldust. The hotel accommodation was quite satisfactory and no complaints were made in this respect although they were not any better than the provision made in New Zealand and which was complained of by Mr A. Storey, secretary of the New South Wales Association in his annual report. The party has had almost a surfeit of entertainment, the hospitality of the public everywhere being of the heartiest character. The Australian team took its defeat as good sports and the tour has done a great deal to popularise the game in Australia.

"Mr Varney welcomed the team back and congratulated the players on their splendid victories and upon winning the ashes, also upon having left such a good name behind them as gentlemen both on and off the field. He hoped the players would carry those good qualities back to the clubs to which they belong. Mr Wells spoke on behalf of the WFA and said he was glad to know that New Zealand grounds and referees were not the only ones to be complained of. He heartily congratulated them on their success.

"The toast of the team, manager and assistant manager was received with musical honours.

"Mr Mayer replied that the team behaved splendidly on and off the field and no team travelling in another country had left greater respect although the Sydney Cricket Ground was the finest in the world but beyond that the grounds did not compare with those of the Dominion. Their thanks were particularly due to Mr Langridge for his training and attention to the team in Sydney, and to him they owe a large measure of their success.

"Mr George Campbell, captain of the New Zealand team, also paid splendid tribute to the very fine work of Mr Langridge and asked that the New Zealand Council should send him a letter of

The Basin Reserve in 1936 and joy for the locals as Wellington score against Australia. Bad luck though, the okkers got nine. Warwick Gendall collection

appreciation for what he did for them. (Hear hear). The test games were played in the best of spirit and the Australians took their defeat like men (applause).

"Mr Graves said the smallest of the grounds militated against the New Zealand team whose short passing game quite captivated the public over there. The Australians played a spoiling game and he thought they would make it more attractive by playing more like the New Zealand methods. He hoped the boys who had been on the tour would return to their clubs and help to strongly entrench the game throughout New Zealand.

"Mr F. Campbell proposed the toast of the sole selector Mr B. L. Salmon and congratulated him upon the success which had been achieved by the two teams selected by him. Mr Salmon briefly acknowledged the compliment saying that although he may have made mistakes, he asked for the best and did what he considered was his duty.

"Kissock, centre half for the Hospital, has returned with the team and will play for Hospital against Waterside at the Basin Reserve on Saturday. He has received a tempting offer in Australia and has not yet decided if he will accept it.

"Mr George Campbell said to a *Times* reporter last night: "We were delighted to win the ashes. The boys shaped magnificently and concentrated on the test matches. In the second half of the last test they played like one man. I never saw anything like it and I don't know any combination that could have stood up to it. We simply ran the Australians off their legs. The team played in a manner which was irresistible". Mr Graves added that the New Zealand forwards were "the best combination he had ever seen", this comment ended a glowing newspaper tribute to a fine team.

It seemed that New Zealand football was coming of age and this feeling was probably reinforced when in 1924 a team representing the Chinese Universities visited these shores. The visitors lost to Wellington as all previous tourists had done and won only four of the 22 matches played. Twelve games were lost and New Zealand succeeded in the first test 2-1, the third 5-3 and the fourth 4-2. The second test was drawn 2-2. New Zealand soccer was on the way up or was it? From now until the 1980s New Zealand soccer went on the backfoot as tourists of genuine class and quality arrived in this country. Canada toured in 1927 and when they beat Wellington 2-0 the writing was firmly on the wall. The first test was drawn 2-2, but the second was won 2-1. The New Zealanders came back to win the third 1-0 but Canada won the series with a 4-1 success. Canada won 20 of the 23 games. Two tour games were lost; the other reflected the strength of the West Coast of New Zealand. In one of the most unusual results Canada lost 1-0 to Westland. The tourists scored 116 goals in 23 games and conceded only 16. Only three more tours involving New Zealand would take place before the second World War. The first two involved Australian teams. In 1933 a team from New Zealand visited Australia but the early success of the first matches had gone. New Zealand won only three games in 13. The best win was a 5-1 victory over Queensland. The three tests were lost 4-2, 6-4 and 4-2. Australia won all 12 matches, including the three tests. They scored

Hey ref! Offside? Not quite - the 1933 New Zealand team is about to play Australia in Sydney and the Kiwis are at the end of their haka. Barry Smith collection

100 goals. The test scores were 7-1, 10-0 and 4-1. And if the Kiwis were still reeling 12 months later, the last pre-war tour involved a team of English amateurs led by Bernard Joy. This team won all of its nine matches, scored 84 goals and won the three tests 12-0, 6-0 and 12-1. Just six goals were conceded and four of them by a combined Auckland and South Auckland team. The Englishmen netted eight. With the world about to be plunged into global conflict, it would be another 10 years before New Zealand would again do battle on an international stage.

At the outbreak of the war domestic football was alive and well. The Chatham Cup was certainly a huge success and the Football Association Trophy was firmly established. The trophy, a most handsome ornament, had been donated in 1925 by the Football Association and up to the time of the National League was played for on first a tournament basis and then under a challenge system. The first games were played in 1926 and won by Auckland. The northern province did not lose until Otago was successful in 1931. Canterbury won for the first time in 1936 and Wellington gained its triumph in 1940.

POST WAR

While a number of FA Trophy matches had been played during the war years the first Chatham Cup matches after the cessation of hostilities were staged in the 1945 season. In 1947 a South African team toured Australia and New Zealand. A Springbok tour had been planned to the Southern Hemisphere in 1939 but like a host of other sporting fixtures the visit was canned. The Springboks won eight of the 10 matches they played. They had 3-3 draws in two matches with Auckland and they won the test series 4-0. The first test brought a thrilling 6-5 success followed by 6-0, 8-3 and 4-1 wins. There were even less crumbs a year later, when the 1948 Australians won each of their 12 fixtures scoring 82 goals in 12 games. Of those, 25 came in the four tests with the third test win of 4-0 the closest contest. New Zealand's first post-war "test" win came against the Victorians; a 3-1 success at the

All mates together, but not for long. On the hallowed rugby surface of Christchurch's Lancaster Park Australia (at back) and New Zealand prepare to do battle in a soccer test on August 28, 1948. Bad news though, Australia won 7-0. **Barry Smith collection**

The class of 1947 - New Zealand prepare to meet South Africa in a test at Lancaster Park. Barry Smith collection

Basin Reserve in 1951 while the first post war trip brought with it a tour of New Caledonia and Fiji at the end of the domestic season. New Caledonia won the first game 2-0 but the Kiwis won the next three 6-4, 6-2 and 3-1 before going on to beat Fiji 6-4. A year later the New Zealanders were back in the Islands beating Fiji 3-0 in the series and winning, then drawing with Tahiti. The emphasis on international football was secondary in the early part of football after the war.

Captain, my captain. M D Butts of New Zealand and A Barr of Victoria before the 1951 Basin Reserve test which New Zealand won 3-1. Barry Smith collection

Club and representative football was a staple diet with the Chatham Cup competition the highlight. The early period after the war brought New Zealand one of its most glamorous periods, 1949, the year the Petone Settlers won the Chatham Cup. At the Basin Reserve that year some 12,000 saw Petone beat Northern 1-0 in the final after surviving two Wellington and then two North Island finals. To suggest that Petone could win the Chatham Cup that season was highly optimistic. Two years earlier one of the club's officials, Andy Leslie, had written to the local Wellington Football Association stating that the club would only be fielding a couple of junior teams. For two seasons Petone, Wellington's oldest surviving club, would field no senior teams. The name Leslie may sound familiar. It should, Leslie, a Scot, came to this country in 1927. He joined Petone in time to collect a couple of Chatham Cup medals. His performances brought him a professional contract with Hibernian in the early 30s but he then returned to Petone to play for the club and the three games against Bernard Joy's amateurs in 1937. A son, also Andy, captained the New Zealand rugby team. Leslie, along with other club stalwarts and life members Peter McVean and Jim Campbell visited the Fort Dorset Immigrants Hostel and recruited enough players to field not one but four sides. Whatever form the team showed in pre-season games the Wellington Football Association of that year deemed that the side would, in effect, play in its third division. The first team went on to win its grade and also the Cup. The WFA, with some reluctance, promoted the team two grades to its first division. Petone have these days been modern pioneers. The active seeking of players in 1949 may have made the club the first to pursue a professional approach. Petone these days has its own full-time club manager; the use of a floodlit pitch, is part of the Hutt Valley National League organisation, and its depth is such that in 1990 they were able to win the Central League first division. In the late 60s Petone made headlines again- when it was revealed they were paying players $6 per win and $3 per a draw. In 1966 the club paid 80 pounds to secure the Hungarian Lotsy Polyanszky from the Sydney Club St George Budapest.

New Zealand had to wait two years after 1952 for its next taste of international football and it brought a true international win over Australia. New Zealand, led by Jock Hunter, tripped to Australia. It was a visit that brought with it success; a 2-1 win in the first international, but unlike the 1923 outcome the home side won the rubber with a brace of 4-1 wins. While Victoria also beat the Kiwis, original international foes New South Wales were dumped 4-1 in the next best success on tour, though the tourists did come from a half-time deficit of 1-0 to beat an Australian X1 3-1 at Adelaide. An AAP report called that win an international but New Zealand still had to wait a week for a test success. On August 16 at the Melbourne Showgrounds New Zealand won 2-1 in the 17th International between the countries. The match reports notes that New Zealand made a sensational start scoring twice inside the first seven minutes. King rose high to head in a Steele corner. That goal came after five minutes and two minutes

The 1958 New Zealand touring team to New Caledonia. Back row: F. Poelman, T.H. Vandebroek, W. Hume. Middle row: R.C. Kearns, R.E. Reid, K.W. Hough, A.J. Laffey, C. Steele. Front row: G.S. McLaren, P.A. McFarlane (vice-captain), R.A. Speed (manager). K. Armstrong (captain), D.J. Lapwood. Seated: G. McI. Cuthill, T.G. McCabe. Crown Studios photo

later Steele himself netted. Australia's goal came 15 minutes before the end amidst immense pressure. New Zealand then had the misfortune to lose King, an Eastern Suburbs club player, with a severe knee injury. He had collected a hat-trick against the Australian XI the previous week. Tour manager Jim Kershaw noted that New Zealand could continue to improve and when New South Wales was despatched 4-1 and the record became four wins from five games, his prediction looked like coming true. However, after a 2-2 draw with Queensland, Australia won 4-1 at Brisbane. In that test Australia established a 3-0 lead before New Zealand scored. At no time, the match report notes, did the Kiwis show any of the form that had brought them the success in the Melbourne test. After that showing it came as no surprise that Australia confirmed its second test form with a 4-1 decider in Sydney on September 4. A report published in the *Dominion* notes that goalkeeper Bert Hiddlestone played with a strapped dislocated finger. Australia led 2-0 at half-time. Steele pulled one back after the break but as the Kiwi attack tired Australia scored twice more.

At least New Zealand was opening up. Air travel now made it much easier to reach these shores. In 1960 New Zealand made separate visits to New Caledonia and Tahiti and won all of the five test

Australia didn't lose many games on its 1958 tour to New Zealand, the last before the FIFA ban on that country. But Auckland beat them 2-1 and Bill Hume's goal helped. Tony Hilton collection

The 1960 New Zealand touring team to Tahiti. Back row: J. Wrathall, J. Raat, J. Kemp K. Armstrong. Middle row: J. Middleton, D. McVey, J. Callaghan, W. Rodger, E. Charlton. Front row: G. Smith (manager), J. Bell, P. McFarlane (vice-captain), J. Warrender (captain), A. Moynihan, C. Steele, J. Brown (masseur). Crown Studios photo

matches that were played. As well club teams started to arrive. In 1955 a team from South China played three games. The first brought a 1-1 draw but after that the goals flowed as New Zealand won the next 7-4 and the Chinese the third 5-3. In 1957 a team from Hong Kong arrived and New Zealand won one match and drew the other. In 1959 Saprissa of Costa Rica arrived and lost the only "test" 3-2. But of all the tourists who arrived here in the 50s none was more significant than the men from FK Austria. The tour here involved two tests and if the Austrians had been enjoying the trip in the so-called minor matches they simply flowed in the big games winning both 7-1. The football was rich in character and if it did nothing else, the tour showed that the gap between Europe and even Australasia was vast indeed. The tour by FK Austria however had a damning effect on football in the Oceania region as it is now known. The team also played in Australia. It lost the first test 3-2, but won the next two 5-2 and 8-3. Australia, as New Zealand had been, was captivated by Baumgartner, Tamandl, Jaros and a host of others. Leo Baumgartner was a super striker. He was rated by the Sydney press as one of the most brilliant players ever seen in Australia. Within a year of the tour Baumgartner and Jaros were

A thrilling Wellington goal netted by Ron Moore at the Basin Reserve against the German club side Karlsruhe. Hard lines for Wellington, it lost 7-2. Tony Hilton collection

May 1969. Yes, it is in New Zealand, that is Jimmy Armfield of Blackpool and England and isn't Brett Warman of Auckland as pleased as punch. Barry Smith collection

back in Australia as migrants playing for the leading Sydney club Prague. Jaros had played a full international for Austria against Brazil. Baumgartner was the second rated centre forward in his native country. Austrian officials were far from happy. Neither was FIFA, world football's controlling body. Australia was booted out for what was in effect the poaching of players. The ban didn't stop a host of immigrants arriving, but for potential football teams, whether they were club or national sides, the cost of a tour to New Zealand only was horrendous. Not only did New Zealand not have any direct contact with Australia they were starved of literally all European outfits. There was time in 1958 for a competent and successful Australian side to visit New Zealand before the ban was put in place. New Zealand and Australia did not compete again until a fixture in Auckland in February 1976. By that time Tom Finney had led his team to New Zealand, the Kiwis had taken part in a World Cup and our own National League was well and truly up and running.

MODERN ERA

It would be nice to record that New Zealand football history is garnished with a host of memorable moments of magic on the football pitch. What it would be to have a list of international wins to savour! Moments of high drama; a heritage to rival the giants of South American and Europe as club and national sides bestride the stage of international competition. Sadly no such joy. But if the results are missing the effort certainly is not. As air transport has flourished so has the progress of New

Wellington's excellent goalkeeper Peter Whiting in action for his city against Auckland in a 60s Campbell Rosebowl match at Wellington's Basin Reserve on a "nice" Saturday afternoon. Barry Smith collection

The 1964 World Tour didn't have many highlights but Kiwis to get to Dulwich Hamlet in the South of London for an amateur international when Bert Ormond (right) and England captain J Martin exchanged pennants. New Zealand had a goal after two minutes but when rain deluged the park the match was abandoned with England ahead 4-1. Tony Hilton collection

The 1964 World Cup tour is done and skipper Bert Ormond is quite happy to give an interview at the Auckland Airport. Tony Hilton collection

Zealand football. No longer is the country an international soccer wilderness. Now kiwis get the chance to mix it with some of the best players here at home. And overseas! Who among us will ever forget the end of 1981 and 1982 when a humble 3-3 draw at home with Australia began a journey which ended with the All White heroes in Spain doing battle with arguably the best in the world - Brazil. With the help of television all New Zealand watched, wondered and admired. And if the silky skills were missing those New Zealand sides were never lacking in endeavour. As the World Cup competition continues, future New Zealand teams now have a goal at which to aim. So as the modern day - let's call it the air travel era - has progressed so has New Zealand's involvement on the international stage. There have been literally hundreds of matches played involving not only New Zealand selections but also regional sides against visiting sides. Some of the more "interesting" are recalled by those who took part. It will come as little surprise to find much in here of the Spanish campaign - but in our short history was there ever a time like it before or since?

Before turning over to the professionals it must be noted that New Zealand soccer only came of age in the late 1970s. While the effort in the 1969 World Cup qualifiers was indeed stout, regular success is hard to find. That most determined of strikers Keith Nelson did score twice when New Zealand beat Luton Town 3-2 in 1971 and when Duncan Ormond scored the only goal for New Zealand against Australia in 1979 it was our first win over the Transtasman neighbour in 25 years. But there was one enterprise that has to be recalled and that is the 1964 World Tour.

A team of three officials, a doctor, a coach and 18 players took on a venture that even by today's standards was ambitious to say the least. The tour in the end comprised 15 games and 14 defeats. There were two matches in Hong Kong, two in Thailand, a match against Iran, two in Germany, two in Switzerland, four in England and two in the United States. Only right at the end did the side manage to secure a win. It was a 5-2 triumph over San Francisco. The team scored 17 goals and conceded 59. At times New Zealand looked likely to win, especially in Hong Kong, Germany and in Switzerland but each time they ran out of puff. And in the full amateur international against England they were a goal up in two minutes but with 20 minutes to play the game was called off when the score was 1-4. The difference between world football and New Zealand became apparent when the Kiwis crashed 8-0 to the English first division side Nottingham Forest.

Jim Kershaw was the manager of the side and in 1990 he was reluctant to discuss the tour. The coach was Ken Armstrong and the captain the lovable character Bert Ormond, whose sons Iain and Duncan

A chip off the old block. Bert Ormond's skill on the field made him captain of New Zealand. One son, Iain, was hardly a slouch as some visitors found out. Vic Deverill collection

went on to serve football at both club and international level with great distinction and not a little skill. The tour was extreme, tiring and in hindsight long before its time. But at a time when communications were poor, New Zealand soccer had to climb back. There were a few scattered Press Association tour reports mainly from England and Hong Kong, but there was neither radio nor television. It didn't help in the terms of results. Neither did the superb one off occasion when Manchester United went to English Park and beat New Zealand 11-0. That was in May of 1969 and United had in its ranks gifted players like Bobby Charlton and George Best. Manchester United were here for only a short time and won 8-1 over an Auckland Invitation side, but the goodwill they left behind them lingered for a long time after.

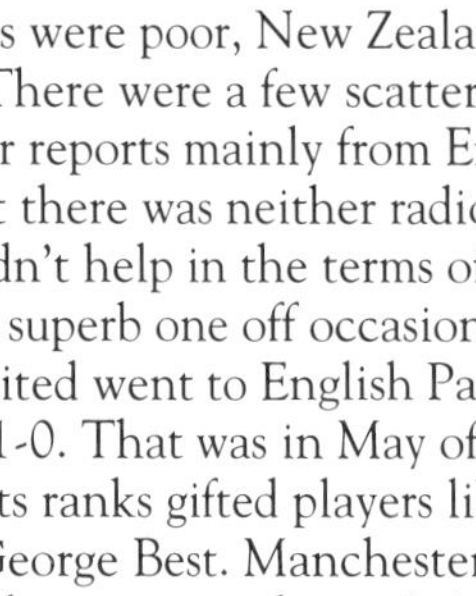

JIM WARRENDER

NEW ZEALAND 1, ENGLAND 6
Epsom Showgrounds, Auckland, 10/6/61.

Barbra Streisand summed it up in one word, "memories". Of all the teams that have visited this country post-war none has made a greater impact. From May 31 to June 14 a team from the mother country played six matches. The skill of these players had to be seen to be believed. In the process they gave a young and very green football writer called Hilton not only the chance to mix with them but, when they hammered Canterbury 11-1 at English Park, it was also his first taste of live reporting this for the old Wellington weekender the *Sports Post*. Like I said: Memories! The team was a mix of professional and amateurs and memories of the kindness of the side remain yet. The team was led by its player-manager, a giant in English professional ranks Tom Finney, who played no fewer then 76 times in full internationals for his country. The side also included a half back, then a current youth international who went on to play 108 games for his country. Bobby Moore's greatest moment as England's victorious World Cup captain in 1966 was still in the future when he arrived in New Zealand as part of the Finney entourage. Jim Warrender was the captain in the New Zealand side, coached by Ken Armstrong, who also played. He was a solid right half who led his Wellington province. He turned out for New Zealand against Tahiti and Costa Rica. A Scot, he played for a leading Aberdeen amateur team "Banks O'Dee." He won a Scottish junior cup winners medal with Banks O'Dee and achieved Scottish junior representative honours. England won the first test at Wellington 8-0 and at Epsom in Auckland 16,500 were present as England went on to score it's 6-1 success. England led 3-0 at half time and as the second half drew to a close that lead had been doubled. Finney, the master, had scored twice while other goals came from Ray

Tom Finney was one of England's finest players. He led the 1961 FA team to New Zealand and with Ken Armstrong makes a presentation to then Kiwi skipper Jim Warrender. Jim Warrender collection

Charnley, John Fantham, the personable Alan A'Court and the amateur Jim Lewis. The big crowd though had something to cheer about late in the game when Fred Else could not hold onto a fierce shot from winger Garry Eccles and the talented Duncan McVey touched the loose ball home. Dave Andrews, in the Auckland 8 O'*Clock* called it the "biggest step forward the code has taken here in several years". Warrender recalls. "It was a pity we missed a couple of good chances. If we had got a goal in the first half we might have played even better. However the game was more attacking and enjoyable for both players and spectators."

GRAHAME BILBY

NEW ZEALAND 0, ISRAEL 4
Ramat-Gan Stadium, Tel Aviv 28/8/1969
NEW ZEALAND 0, ISRAEL 2
Ramat-Gan Stadium, Tel Aviv, 1/9/1969

The Middle East was hardly the place for a New Zealand team to make its initial flurry into the hectic scene of World Cup football, but in 1969 they were there in order to progress further in the competition. The party was led by the then NZFA Chairman Jack Cowie and the team was coached by a talented Yugoslavian Ljubisa Brocic who had previous connections with both Juventas and Barcelona. In hindsight Brocic may have been just too soon for New Zealand football. He never did succeed here as he should have, though his talent was never in question. New Zealand's captain on that campaign was Grahame Bilby, a hugely gifted sportsman whose performances for Seatoun and then Wellington City in the early days of the National League kept him to the forefront until he hung up his boots. He also, I recall, caused one A. Hilton huge embarrassment in a charity fixture on the old Basin Reserve when he chipped the former goalkeeper from near halfway. I still though get on with "Bilbs" who was also an excellent cricketer, making a century in his very first first class innings and went on to play a couple of test matches against the 1965-66 England tourists. When he retired from active participation Bilby rendered service as a council member of the New Zealand Football Association before turning to a successful business career.

Englishmen coming out the woodwork at the Basin Reserve during an English tour but the New Zealand goalkeeper Derek Phillips has a safe pair of hands. Barry Smith collection

Bilby played 27 times for New Zealand, his debut coming with the ill-fated 1964 team. He was for a long time the most capped New Zealand player which tends to show these days how much international activity there is in New Zealand football. But to play these games against Israel was a new venture. Who can imagine today us Kiwis agreeing to play two World Cup matches away from home? But 22 years ago times were different and costs all important. New Zealand won two and lost one of its lead up games in the Far East on its way to Israel. The skipper of the day clearly recalls both games.-

"The bus picked us up from our hotel two hours before the kickoff for the first match. Although it was only a short drive to the stadium it was felt that traffic problems from the crowd attending could cause delays. In having the kick off at 4.30pm we were still able to play in daylight and although the temperature had a opportunity to drop we still played in 27 degree heat. That was always going to be a problem. There was a large crowd, in excess of 40,000 all supporting Israel with the lone rather odd Kiwi voice. The spectators were all set back from the pitch itself with an empty moat surrounding the football areas and inside of this a twelve foot wire netting fence topped by barbed wire. Armed soldiers patrolled inside the fence. It was no secret that the authorities were apprehensive of crowd disruption by bombings. They weren't the only ones! It was a most unusual setting for New Zealand to play its first World Cup game.

"From the start Israel attacked repeatedly without effect. The game was played at a fast pace with Israel's

The 1967 New Zealand touring party to New Caledonia. Back row: I. Kiss, J. Beck, D.R. Wallace, G.W. Lamont. Second row: M.R. Carter (coach), B. Kennedy, D. Strom, J. Habets, C. Martin, G.B. Smith, G.E. Petersen. Front row: P. Breslin, G.L. Whyte (manager), G.P. Bilby (captain), I. Gillies (vice-captain), J.K. Smith (assistant manager), J.K. Ironside. Absent: A. Williams (referee).

tactics based on the premise that they were the fitter side and they would run us off our feet. They mounted attacks through the centre with their two Belgium professionals Feigenbaum and Spiegel both at inside forward, being players of real class. We found it difficult to put together consistent attacks against opponents who possessed greater skills. We struggled both in skill and pace, yet it was 0-0 at half time thanks to Derek Phillips who played brilliantly in goal. Our defence was strong and we were able to drop back and cover each other. We did create a couple of chances but all were from well out and were covered by the Israel keeper.

"Israel ran away with the game straight after half time. Spiegel took advantage of a counter attack to head home after three minutes. He scored again in the 63rd minute and then Feigenbaum had a third in the 72nd and the last with his head three minutes from time. Our hero was Phillips who was brilliant up to the time he received a heavy knock. We should have lost by three but it seemed to me to be an error of judgment by the coach who did not realise the extent of the injury. It was not the keeper's fault that he stayed on the park".

New Zealand returned much wiser for its second match three days later. Phillips was cleared to play. It was at the same venue and the crowd was 20,000 and there is little doubt many lessons had been absorbed from the first fixture. The defence, Bilby said, was better organised and they were helped by the fact that Israel played with an amount of over-confidence. Even so, the touch of the first match was not there from the locals. Feigenbaum, who had been one of the stars of the first match, had an off day and before that was being hooted by his own fans. New Zealand, with good showings from Matt Guildea, Earl Thomas and Malcolm Bland, created openings and the skipper himself just missed from 35 metres. But Spiegel was playing and his touch was good. It was left to their skipper Spiegler to score after 23 minutes. Minutes later Bland tripped after breaking clear of the defence and within seconds Israel had swept back to score a second and clinch the match. Still there was much to admire in the tenacity of the Kiwi effort. Phillips had another fine game. In the second spell Mick Jones was introduced and with the defence getting on top of the Israel attack there was a greater opportunity for New Zealand to press forward. Jones was absolutely outstanding and the extra New Zealand pressure was unfortunate not to bring with it the reward of at least one goal.

Bilby reflects: "It could have been a huge advantage to New Zealand if we had played one World Cup match at home, but finance precluded this. In addition more games together would have helped. Considering the limited build-up and the professionalism of the Israelis, New Zealand did extremely well. Determination, guts and refusal to give up in the end could not match highly skilled professional opposition."

BOB ALMOND

NEW ZEALAND 1, ENGLAND B 3
Basin Reserve, Wellington 11/6/78

No touring teams have ever proved to be more popular then those of an English representative or club side. The visit by the England team of 1978 was no different. The boss of this party was Bobby Robson, soon to begin a long stint as England's manager which ended only after the 1990 World Cup in Italy. This was quite an efficient squad. They may have been held to a 2-2 draw by National League side Trans Tours United first up, but they had hardly stepped off the plane. England won all three test matches by dint of 4-0, 3-1 and 4-0 scores. Of those games the second test was easily the best. It was 0-0 at half time but 10 minutes after the break England was ahead. Within seconds Brian Turner had chipped goalkeeper Joe Corrigan for a superb leveller. The English heat went on and they were able to convert the extra pressure into two further goals. The game saw the national debut of Bobby Almond, a super defender who went on to serve New Zealand soccer quite splendidly and also national league sides of both Christchurch and Invercargill. On that June day though Almond played his very first game for New Zealand. He recalls:

"I made my international debut as sweeper in this game. The first held in Christchurch had ended in a 4-0 win for England. I was substitute that night and disappointed that I couldn't debut in front of my home ground. That low feeling turned to absolute excitement the night before the second match when Wally Hughes, then the national coach, took us to a local cinema in Wellington for a relaxing evening as part of the game preparation. While we were waiting to go into the theatre Wally asked me if I was looking forward to the game. I replied that I would be if I was playing. He literally made my night by telling me very quietly that I was. I don't think I slept a wink that night.

"The game, played in front of a large partisan Wellington crowd was the best on the tour as far as both performance and score was concerned. Although losing 3-1 we played with more purpose and enjoyed a good share of possession with the highlight being the Turner chip. I recall that the goal started from deep in defence and only three players other than Brian touched the ball. As well as being involved in my first game for New Zealand I was also named Man of the Match and awarded $50 for my efforts - I guess the NZFA had some money in the bank in those days. Not that the cash lasted long. It went straight on to the bar as we celebrated a moral victory. I went on to play another 48 games for New Zealand but that first outing remains the most memorable."

RON ARMSTRONG

NEW ZEALAND 4, MEXICO 0
Bill McKinley Park , Auckland 20/8/80

It was a result that rocked not only New Zealand but the whole of the football world. To the average kiwi a win over Mexico may not seem like much but the often troubled South American country has inherited the continent's passion for football. It was, at the same, the biggest and best win ever recorded by the national side. The game was played under lights at Auckland's Bill McKinlay Park, the home of Mount Wellington and the result came like a bolt out of the blue. It was the early period of the John Adshead reign and if you didn't live in Auckland it was hard to know what was happening. There was no national radio commentary of the game. Anyway, who would have wanted to listen? Adshead had taken his troops on an internal tour some three months earlier. They had drawn at Christchurch's English Park 1-1 with a South Region side and two days later lost at Wellington's Newtown Park 2-1 to a Central Region Side, a team that included Grant Turner and a college kid called Wynton Rufer. For the Mexico game Adshead rang a few changes. He brought debutantes like Turner, John Hill, Keith Mackay and Ricki Herbert. I can recall hearing a progress score on the radio that made me rush to try and pick up 1ZB in Auckland. They carried no commentaries but did have regular progress reports. The game was telecast live, but only back to Mexico. New Zealand received its highlights a little time after. Brian Turner thumped in a third minute penalty and then Steve Wooddin had a second in 25 minutes. When Brian Turner had a third before half time it was fairyland stuff. GT got the fourth in the second spell and a football world was stunned. So what if the season didn't quite end on the same high after a short but unsuccessful tour of Canada? But by now the march to the 1982 World Cup finals was only a few months away.

It was fitting that left back or sweeper Ron Armstrong should have been in the New Zealand side that day. In 1990 he was still a vital cog in the Bill McKinlay Park based outfit which saw the Mount win the Chatham Cup and only just stumble at the last fence in quest of the National League. Armstrong is a son of Ken Armstrong, the biggest influence in New Zealand football in the 60s and 70s and he, along with a brother Brian, was able to follow his father's footsteps and wear the silver fern. Ron Armstrong

Being a member of the 1982 World Cup squad is no place for the faint-hearted. Just ask Grant Turner. Grant Turner collection

was born in England in 1951 and came to New Zealand in 1957 when the family went to Gisborne. He made his Northern League debut with North Shore in 1968, played for Auckland the following year. In 1970 he went to Mount Wellington and played in the final three games of the first National League season.

Ken Armstrong would have been proud of his son at the end of 1990. When all was done in mid November 1990 Armstrong had made 351 national League appearances, 322 for Mount Wellington and 29 for Eastern Suburbs. In 1975 and 1976 Ron Armstrong tried his hand in England playing in the Combination League for his father's club Chelsea and in the Central League for Aston Villa. When the 1990 season ended Armstrong had won five National League winners medals and five Chatham Cup golds, those to go with three silvers. Armstrong won two Air NZ tournament winners medals and three Adidas Challenge Trophy winners medals.

But for business and family there seems little doubt that he would have secured more than the 33 international caps he was awarded, though he still ended up with 18 more than Ken which shows how the New Zealand international fixture list has grown in recent years. Ron Armstrong's first game for New Zealand was in 1971, his last in 1983. 1971 was a big year for him. He was elected the New Zealand Soccer Writers' Player of the Year, won the *Dominion-Sunday Times* awarded Arcus Trophy for the country's best and fairest. It says much for the Armstrong durability that in 1990 despite the ever-present conquering feats of the Auckland rugby team he was elected Auckland Sportsman of The Year.

GRANT TURNER

AUSTRALIA 0, NEW ZEALAND 2
Sydney Cricket Ground, Sydney 16/5/81

In the whole history of New Zealand soccer there has never been a moment like it. There were just six minutes left to play. The All Whites were a goal to the good. In Sydney they had produced a performance that had buried forever the World Cup hopes not only of Australia but also its coach Rudi Gutendorf. On this day more than most the impossible dream - a trip to Spain - became a reality. The New Zealand side had led through the left foot of Steve Wooddin when a suspect goalkeeper Greg Woodhouse had been very late to get down as the striker's left-foot shot went in. But six minutes from the end a very special second goal set the seal on the triumph. It was a superb headed goal from Grant Turner, a memorable moment that still finds its way on to New Zealand television. Of the many goals the All Whites scored on the way to and in Spain there was never one quite like it.

New Zealand was playing the fifth of its eight

That really is Grant Turner, the 1981 model during the World Cup match against Australia at Mount Smart. "GT" is watching the okkers get in each other's way. Picture: Eric Jelly

games in the elimination group. The first against Australia had been at Mount Smart and three times the Kiwis had been behind. The half-time score was 3-2 and a second half goal turned the match into a 3-3 draw. It was a game the All Whites should have won. After that New Zealand went on tour to beat Fiji 4-0, draw 0-0 at Taiwan and then score a splendid 2-0 triumph over Indonesia in Jakarta. Following the Australian triumph New Zealand scored five to beat Indonesia at home, twice to beat the durable Taiwanese and then demolished the hapless Fijians to win the group.

That THE GOAL appears in the name of Grant Turner is perhaps fitting. Few players in the 80s attracted more attention than this determined young man. A product of the Hutt Valley, Turner's time with the Central League Club Petone foreshadowed a lengthy spell that brought him to Gisborne City and under the wing of Kevin Fallon. The two may not always have seen eye-to-eye but Turner's respect for the coach has never dimmed. There followed a short stint in Australia and more recently time with two of the Wellington clubs Miramar and Wellington United though injury has curtailed his appearances. In the midst there was a further passionate season of Central League football with Petone. Turner, as a player, has always aroused emotion, but he always gave his best and asked the same of others. I enjoyed watching him play in the 80s and even as he slows a little the manner in which he reads a game remains an object lesson to all.

It will come as no surprise to find that GT has a video of the goal and also the fact that he has been quizzed many times about it.

"I must say that even though I managed to get the last touch on to the ball, a lot of the credit must go to a couple of people. They are Ian Gillies, my former manager at Gisborne and Kevin Fallon who gave me the confidence in the technique of correct heading.

"Even today I do not know how I got the power behind the strike. The move started in our own half as Australia was attacking, seeking an equaliser. One of them, Ken Bowden, had tried to play a ball through the middle from about 30 yards out. Bobby Almond cut it out and fed Steve Wooddin on around halfway on the left hand flank. I was outside him. Woody dribbled the ball and I made a run screaming for the ball, but Woody spotted Keith Mackay on the other touch line and fed him instead. I said 'oh, dash' - or words to that effect to Woody as I had wanted the ball and though I was knackered from the run I continued on towards the Australian penalty box. Meanwhile Buzzer had knocked the ball to Duncan Cole who took one touch and crossed. I gave myself a chance of getting to the ball and heading it closer to the Australian goal, so when I got in front of the Australian sweeper Eisendown I gave it all I had.

"I didn't know I had scored. After making contact I fell and didn't see the ball hit the net, but first the noise and the fact that Brian Turner wouldn't let go of me soon confirmed the end result. The rest of the lads came over. It was one hell of a feeling. I was ecstatic. I remember nothing about the last few minutes.

"My feelings are now mixed as the video has been played many times over the years and it will surprise many to know that I still get quite embarrassed when people mention the goal in front of me. However, when I feel down or injured I fetch out the Road To Spain video, especially that goal, and it gives me the incentive and inspiration to carry on playing. I know I could probably never do it again but just being part of the day we socked it to the Australians still brings a smile to my face and, dare I say it, even a little pride."

STEVE SUMNER

NEW ZEALAND 13, FIJI 0
Mount Smart Stadium, Auckland 16/8/81

When Russell Gray penned his report for Wellington's morning newspaper the *Dominion*, he had plenty of subject material. It was all about records. New Zealand's win was the biggest ever to that date in World Cup competition. In 1969 West Germany had beaten Cyprus 12-0 while in other internationals the Germans and the Spanish had also recorded international wins by such margins. New

Zealand could look back to Bernard Joy's team of 1937 and a couple of hefty test losses 12-0 and 12-1 and to balance that after, a home 12-0 win over Western Samoa in Auckland in November 1987. But this day it was New Zealand's turn for glory and didn't they do it well! It was the All White's last match in the Oceania qualifying division. They were the first side to finish its series of matches and a win would make a group win certain. Earlier New Zealand had recorded two draws and while Australia had only one draw, the loss in Sydney was clearly to the advantage of the Kiwis. Just a few days earlier Australia had thumped Fiji 10-0. Before 10 minutes of the first spell was done New Zealand led by three. At half time the score was 7-0 and it is to the credit of the home side that they knocked another six in. Steve Sumner scored six that day. Nine years later he was able to recall that whatever he touched that day turned to gold. Steve Sumner typified the drive of the 1982 World Cup cause. His attitude was then as it is now - totally professional in every respect. He still thinks fondly not only of the Fiji game but also the entire campaign. As the All Whites' assistant coach he has high hopes that it may not be too long before another Kiwi team graces the world stage. In 1990 the captain of New Zealand soccer's greatest campaign took time not only to reflect on the Fiji match but also the series in general.

Steve Sumner was born on April 2, 1955 in the English town of Preston. He is a Lancastrian and proud of it. After playing for a local YMCA he was picked up by Blackpool. He signed professional forms with them. He moved to the local Preston club for a short period of about three months. While there he met up with Peter Doherty, the assistant manager, who Sumner recalls had some faith in him. Things were going well enough at the time but at that stage Preston were off-loading players and Sumner was one who went. He spent three enjoyable months at Grimsby but managed to to get himself off-side mainly within the laws of the game and went back to Preston. Sumner recalled that some clubs in the North of England were interested in him. There was also queries from the United States, South Africa, Australia and one from France. But there was a Preston connection with New Zealand. Two players had been here and there was another showing interest. Sumner was told to go home and check it out with his parents. Within 24 hours arrangements were under way and Sumner was off to begin what was a long association with Christchurch City.

"I had eight football seasons with Christchurch and possibly two of them were a bit too long. Then I went on and played two seasons in Australia (with West Adelaide and Newcastle). I had four seasons in Auckland with Manurewa and one as player coach with Gisborne City. I actually came back to New Zealand to get closer to international football. The Olympics were on, but after I came back I broke my foot and that kept me out."

Sumner finished his playing career in 1989 with Christchurch and he had his sixth winner's Chatham Cup medal to show from seven finals. Steve Sumner has a silver medal "by default" as well but as he points out the "loss" wasn't a real one. In 1988 Waikato and Christchurch were level after two legs, both finals ending in draws. Waikato won on the most away goals rule, a system that the forthright Sumner feels is hardly the way to determine the outcome of a Chatham Cup final.

As the New Zealand quota of international matches grew Sumner's skill and determination were constantly in demand for New Zealand. He played over 100 games for his country and was proud every time he put on the shirt. It didn't matter if he led his country in a World Cup match against Brazil in Spain or a fixture against a Central League side on Wellington's Newtown Park. A match for New Zealand was an event to be treasured. For Sumner there was nothing to equal the Spain campaign of 1982.

"It's only now when you look back and you think what a fantastic time it was. When you are still playing you hope that something like it is going to come again. So you don't like to say it was the best, but now looking back, yes, it was the best time - there was nothing like it.

"The Fijians had played Australia about four days earlier and had been beaten 10-0 and we had heard that they were not altogether happy - something was happening within their own camp. But that didn't matter a damn to us. As soon as the Aussies got 10, we wanted more. And that was it - finish! The game itself was quite ridiculous really. If you can ever say you were almost embarrassed to shoot because you're going to score it was that day. Once six had gone it felt ridiculous. Everything I hit went in."

Steve Sumner played midfield that day. In the earlier six games he had scored only once. That was the last of six in the 3-3 draw with Australia. On one other occasion in a national league fixture for Christchurch Sumner scored five in an 8-0 demolition of Miramar Rangers. Sumner's recollection of the aftermath is one of satisfaction rather than elation. "We'd done the job, got the two points and scored more goals than the Australians. And at the end of the day that was all that counted."

Sumner scored only two other goals in the campaign. The first was in the 2-2 draw in Kuwait and the other was the first of the two in Spain against Scotland. His lasting memory of first the final Asia - Oceania round and then the actual World Cup finals was the enormity of the task.

"It was really hard," he said. "Sometimes you were just hanging on. It was like hanging on the edge of a cliff with your nails. In some games we were really on our backs. They were difficult teams to play against, China and Kuwait. They were very good sides. When we played Kuwait over there (after the controversial loss at Auckland and the aftermath) the players went on to test the pitch and they were confronted with rocks and stones. It was absolute hell out there just because of the way their players had been treated in New Zealand. If they could have buried us that night they would have done so."

As it happened Kuwait certainly went close to doing it on the park. On December 14, 1981 in the Qadsia Stadium, Kuwait led 1-0 at half time. But in the 65th and 66th minutes the All Whites struck a double blow. As the home side dallied over a free kick Steve Wooddin touched the ball to Sumner who cracked home a beauty from 25 metres. And while Kuwait was reeling Wooddin and Brian Turner set up a chance for Wynton Rufer. It might have been the 18-year-old's first international but his finish was spot on. The game was in its last minute when a right wing corner was turned in for a final scoreline of 2-2.

"That moment turned the night into a disaster," Sumner said. "We were less than a minute away from winning. I can remember saying to the guys that it was not finished yet. I was exhorting them saying we've got five minutes left that's enough time to get a winner. I asked the referee how much time was left, and he said 30 seconds. I remember thinking that's wrong, this is not written in our script but it was and it a was right sickener."

That draw meant that New Zealand had six days to recover, and to beat Saudi Arabia in Saudi on Astroturf by six goals to qualify for Spain. A 5-0 win would put them into a playoff with China.

RICKI HERBERT

NEW ZEALAND 1, CHINA 0
Mount Smart Stadium, Auckland, 3/10/81

It was the second game in the final group to determine the two Spanish spots which were still up for grabs and as it happens it turned out to be just a pipe opener for the Singapore showdown against the same opponents. New Zealand went into the game with a fair degree of confidence. After just a couple of weeks New Zealand had gone to Beijing earlier and fought hard for a 0-0 draw. Ricki Herbert remembers that first game well.

"It was hard," he said. "We played in front of some 80,000 people all willing a win for China. But we defended well, had a bit of luck and came away with a valuable point."

The name Herbert has served New Zealand soccer well. Ricki's dad Clive has been a most admirable patron of football in the north. Ricki himself spent most of his time with Mount Wellington and for just on 18 months was on the books of the famous old English club Wolverhampton Wanderers. He represented New Zealand soccer with distinction not only as a last line of defence but from time to time would pop up to score the odd vital goal. It was one of those rare sorties which won New Zealand a most satisfying triumph this day at Mount Smart just a minute before the interval.

"We had been working on those set pieces and for once it worked just as it should have. We won a corner on the left hand side. Billy McClure took it, Brian Turner flicked it on with his head and all I had to do was head it in. It was perfect. I was almost on my own. It was one of the easiest goals I ever scored."

Herbert scored one other goal on the campaign. Again it was a vital strike. Fresh from the trauma of the Kuwait loss, New Zealand was looking down the barrel of a 2-1 home loss against Saudi Arabia when Herbert stole in for an 86th minute header and the All Whites had escaped with a draw, a vital result when it came to the final count down.

The crowd for the China Home game was 27,000.

Full house. Ricki Herbert in action against the Australians in the 1981 3-3 opener. **Picture: Eric Jelly**

"It was a terrific buzz playing in front of a crowd like that," Herbert recalled.

New Zealand played 18 matches in that campaign. Herbert started in 17 of them and came on as a substitute against Scotland so he played in all the cup matches.

Herbert has now given away National League football. In 1990 he was included as player-coach for the Papakura team and when not involved in football he is involved in the training of standardbred horses with his father and it is a combination that has had its share of success.

JOHN HILL

NEW ZEALAND 1, KUWAIT 2
Mount Smart Stadium, Auckland, 11/10/81

I guess that if there is one match that New Zealand football would like to forget about then this is it. For 45 minutes all had gone according to script. New Zealand had control. The now customary Steve Wooddin strike had them a goal in front and the 30,000 or so Auckland crowd had few doubts about a final outcome. But in the second spell the control and the composure vanished from the All Whites. Seven minutes into the second spell an Indonesian referee, Hardiowasito Sudarso, awarded a penalty against Steve Sumner for a dubious handball. The crisis seemed passed when goalkeeper Richard Wilson saved splendidly from Jassem Yacoub. Yet 11 minutes later Sudarso penalised John Hill. This time Kuwait scored through Faisal Al'Dekheel and with the All Whites clearly shaken it was a battle to hang on which fell in a heap four minutes from time when Waleed Al Jassem's excellent diving header found it's way home. Would it be that the final whistle ended it all. Sadly far from it. A 17-year-old college sixth former was so enraged he found his way onto the park and threw a soft drink can at the referee. Matters became decidedly dodgy. The referee headed for the sideline. There was a real fear that the match would be called off. In his book *"The Dempsey Years"* (by Peter Devlin, published by Seto) the then New Zealand soccer supremo recalls that he and Malaysian Peter Velappan walked onto the pitch with Sudarso bemoaning the lack of security. He was going to call the game off. Dempsey, a forthright character bluffed his way into discussions and after some 10 minutes Sudarso continued. If the game had been called off the scoreline would have been a 2-0 credit to Kuwait. New Zealand would not have made it into the finals. As it was it took police an hour to clear an angry crowd. The end result was New Zealand fined $6675 by FIFA, but at least it was able to continue with it's next home match against the Saudis. For New Zealand it was a first World Cup loss in 10 outings but as it turned out the only one on the road to Spain.

When John Hill was asked to recall the match against Kuwait his first reactions were "Oh no, not that game again. Why didn't you ask me about the first Australian match when I helped set up two goals?"

Even so, Hill, the former Gisborne City player and now journalist with the *Gisborne Herald* agreed to recall what was a low point in his World Cup campaign. Hill was adjudged to have handled the ball for the second of the Kuwait penalties.

"It was definitely one of the low points in what otherwise was a great time in my career," said Hill, a born-again Christian. "But even though I will never forget the incident it is not something I have dwelt on. There are other more important things in life. I had been left out of the previous match against China but had come on as a second half substitute as we held on to win. And while it was great just being part of a smashing squad I was delighted to back in for the starting line-up. The weather was perfect, the ground packed and the atmosphere tremendous. And I was really looking forward to a good game. Kuwait used the 4-2-4 system and this really suited the over lapping fullback and they weren't too worried about defending in our half, preferring to close us down once we crossed halfway.

"I always liked to get forward and everything was going well and when Woody scored the day was going to plan. In the second spell though Kuwait brought on a midfielder with skill and experience and this made us defend considerably more than we had in the first spell. We began to lose shape at the back. The first penalty was against Steve Sumner who later

A goal by the All Whites raises "a little enthusiasm" especially when a trip to Spain is the end result! Grant Turner collection

claimed it hit his elbow. Wilson saved the first spot kick and became a national hero.

"I can't remember the exact time when the second penalty was given. I was on the left side with Adrian Elrick now in my place on the right. I remember their rightback coming towards me and looking as though he wanted to go outside, but at the last moment he cut in and bent the ball with the outside of his right foot for a cross and I turned away. The ball hit me on the back of the arm and I knew then that if the referee blew his whistle he would give a penalty. He blew and I felt terrible. They scored and of course went on to win. There was never any intention on my part to handle the ball so from that aspect it clearly wasn't a penalty though I must say the ball did strike my arm. So that was it."

The rumblings continued long after. It was not one of New Zealand football's finest hours. Hill continued to play to have a good campaign and played very well in the opening match of the final round against Scotland. The player admitted to being "quite chuffed" in 1990 when World Cup coach John Adshead named him in his best All White team in a poll organised by New Zealand soccer's own national weekly *Soccer Express*.

BRIAN TURNER

SAUDI ARABIA 0, NEW ZEALAND 5
Riyahd, 19/12/81

Christmas came a week early for New Zealand soccer. The present was a lifeline to Spain and it came in the most unexpected manner - five goals in 45 minutes of football in the Middle East. It came after two nerve tinglers against Kuwait. The first ended in a can-throwing controversy and defeat and the other in plain heartbreak. A week before the Riyahd fixture New Zealand had gone to Kuwait and had turned a half-time 1-0 deficit into a 2-1 lead until Kuwait equalised with seconds to go. Now five days later New Zealand had not only to win but prosper by five clear goals. Barely three weeks earlier New Zealand could only scrape a 2-2 home draw with the Saudis. Fat chance of winning here, let alone by five clear. So the game was barely 15 minutes old when New Zealand and its apprentice striker Wynton Rufer made it 1-0. Within two minutes that most faithful servant Brian Turner had hit home a superb volley. The Saudis were in turmoil and in the 38th minute Steve Wooddin took advantage of Rufer's skill and his left footed drive left the keeper Marwan embarrassed. Within a minute Wooddin had hammered in a drive which poor Marwan could only parry. Rufer said thanks: 4-0! There was still a minute to run to half time when Richard Wilson's long clearance out from the Kiwi penalty area ended up in the Saudi box. Marwan clattered Wooddin as he attempted to gain control. Penalty!

Enter Brian Turner! Already he had made his mark on the game. As soon as Wooddin went down Turner knew he was going to have to take a kick. He was the deputed penalty taker. He had scored seven goals in the group matches including a hat trick against Fiji.

"I knew I couldn't miss. If I did it would cost us a trip to Spain. I was nervous all right. We were playing on astroturf and for the life of me I could not get the ball to sit still on the spot."

In terms of matches for New Zealand, Turner was the most experienced in the side. It was his 92nd match. Early in his career he left New Zealand for Britain and had spells with Brentford, Chelsea and Portsmouth. When he played for the All Whites in the World Cup finals build-up against Watford he posted his 100th for his country - the first to do so. His very last New Zealand match, his 102nd, was the game against Brazil. Ian Garner and Ian Walter recall in "*The Impossible Dream*" (Hodder and Stoughton) that the excellent Dutch referee Charles Corver told Turner to steady down. "You only have to kick it once," he said.

"I really wanted to put the ball into a corner," Turner said. "But I was scared of missing it, but the keeper went the wrong way and we had five. I recall we returned to the dressing room and there was a high state of confusion. John (Adshead) said to us, 'OK, it's 5-0, you still need one more to get to Spain'. Then we all sat down. For a few minutes it was deathly quiet. Then John continued, 'you don't know what you've done, you've woken up a nation back home. Now you've got to go back and give it another 150 per cent.'

"We never had any doubts at half time that we would get another goal but of course we didn't in spite of a stack of chances. I got booked and then I asked to come off. I had backtracked but I was absolutely done and I worried that if I had to defend again I might make a mistake and we would lose that five goal advantage. It was the first and only time in my career that I bailed out."

That booking though meant that Brian Turner missed the next match which happened to be the third Chinese game, this one in Singapore. If the New Zealand veteran did have some disappointment it was that he and five of his colleagues who had gone almost all the way had to miss the trip to Singapore. He feels that with the money that had been raised it would have been a nice gesture for the NZFA to keep the squad together. The night of the Singapore game Turner and his wife Elizabeth watched the game from their flat in Sandringham in Auckland. When the Chinese pulled back to 2-1 with minutes to run, Turner got up and left the house.

"I told Elizabeth I couldn't watch. I worked it out that I could walk to Eden Park (Auckland's major rugby and cricket venue) and by the time I got back the game would be over. I walked. I could see the lights on in all the houses. I guessed they were probably watching the game. By the time I got back Elizabeth was at the front door. It's over, she told me but I still didn't know who had won. When I found out I just dropped to the ground, kissed the grass and shed a few tears and then felt sad that I wasn't there to enjoy the triumph."

Brian Turner went to Spain and could not have had a finer end to his international career than playing against Brazil. He still lives in Auckland and in 1991 was coaching the Auckland Bluebird League side Mount Roskill.

STEVE SUMNER

NEW ZEALAND 2, CHINA 1
Singapore National Stadium, 10/1/82

Steve Sumner summed up quite simply. "We have never played a more important game." After months of playing football New Zealand had won its own World Cup final. No one ever dreamed of a New Zealand soccer team winning the World Cup. But getting to the finals? That was a different story altogether. After two qualifying competitions the New Zealanders were just 90 minutes away from reaching that objective. It was, in effect, our own World Cup final. It was also that for China, the area with a massive population whose skill was not in question. New Zealand had at least drawn there and won at home, but this was different. There could be no losing.

"We were either in or out on that night. You couldn't blame anyone else. If you hadn't done the preparation it was your fault, there was no one else to blame. That evening was the night. It was that important."

It was a time that stretched kiwi nerves to the fullest. For the first 45 minutes the Kiwis did well despite the pro-China feeling among the 60,000 crowd. Steve Wooddin's trusty left foot put New Zealand 1-0 up and that was the score at half-time. It looked comfortable and with the second spell barely two minutes old Wynton Rufer hit home a glorious goal from just outside the penalty area. 2-0 but from then the traffic was one way, all at the New Zealand goal. Rufer, with a muscle and eye injury had to be replaced. The Chinese made the most of the pressure 14 minutes from time with a goal but with keeper Richard Wilson in excellent form New Zealand hung on for a famous win.

"It was here we are again, with 15 minutes to go, by the finger nails, hanging onto the cliff. The tension was enormous. The lads had worked hard and trained hard, but I can remember having cramp running down the back of my leg for the last 20 minutes. And I wasn't by myself with that. If we hadn't won that we would never have played the next three in Spain. And we weren't expected to do much in the next three anyway apart from going there and coming out with our pride intact which everyone said we did and I believe we did as well. The players learnt a lot by going to the World Cup. I certainly did."

STEVE WOODDIN

NEW ZEALAND 2, SCOTLAND 5
Estadio La Roselada Stadium, Malaga, Spain, 15/6/82

For the first and only time so far New Zealand was playing with the big boys. Yes, it really was Jock Stein in charge on the Scottish bench and was that Kenny Dalglish out on the park? It certainly was. How it must have felt not only for Charlie Dempsey in the stand but those other Scottish born heros Sam Malcolmson, Adrian Elrick and Alan Boath as they ran out. And what about the others? Maybe that first half was altogether too much. Scotland's history in World Cup finals hardly flatters, but this time they were switched on and it was the poor old Kiwis who copped a fired-up Gordon Strachan and his colleagues. Not that it started badly, indeed in the first five minutes Kenny Cresswell might even have scored. Yet Dalglish netted with barely 20 minutes gone and then John Wark had two in the space of a minute. At half time New Zealand were three down. Within 10 minutes of the second half a touch of class and a raking cross by Wynton Rufer had the Scottish defence in trouble. As Danny McGrain and keeper Alan Rough bumbled and fumbled Steve Sumner was able to hustle the ball over the line. Scotland were struggling. Ten minutes later John Hill floated over a long cross which Steve Wooddin controlled and hammered past Rough. 2-3 . The tension rises but Scotland are made of sterner stuff as a John Roberston free kick and a Steve Archibald header restore the three goal margin. The second half at least had ended even and while they did not know it at the time New Zealand's impressive campaign goal tally would not move beyond 46.

Maybe it was appropriate that Steve Wooddin should score the very last World Cup goal. Wooddin had netted the second goal in the first game against Australia. He gathered nine goals in the whole campaign with four in the second phase. He was a gifted striker and his sweet left foot brought joy to New Zealand many times. Playing against the Scots was a time that Wooddin enjoyed.

"It started about an hour and a half before the game when we arrived and went out to look at the pitch. Graeme Souness and John Roberston were there at the same time and for a time we had a most cordial chat mainly about New Zealand and the state of the game here. That soon changed once we got onto the park. They were determined. It's not that we

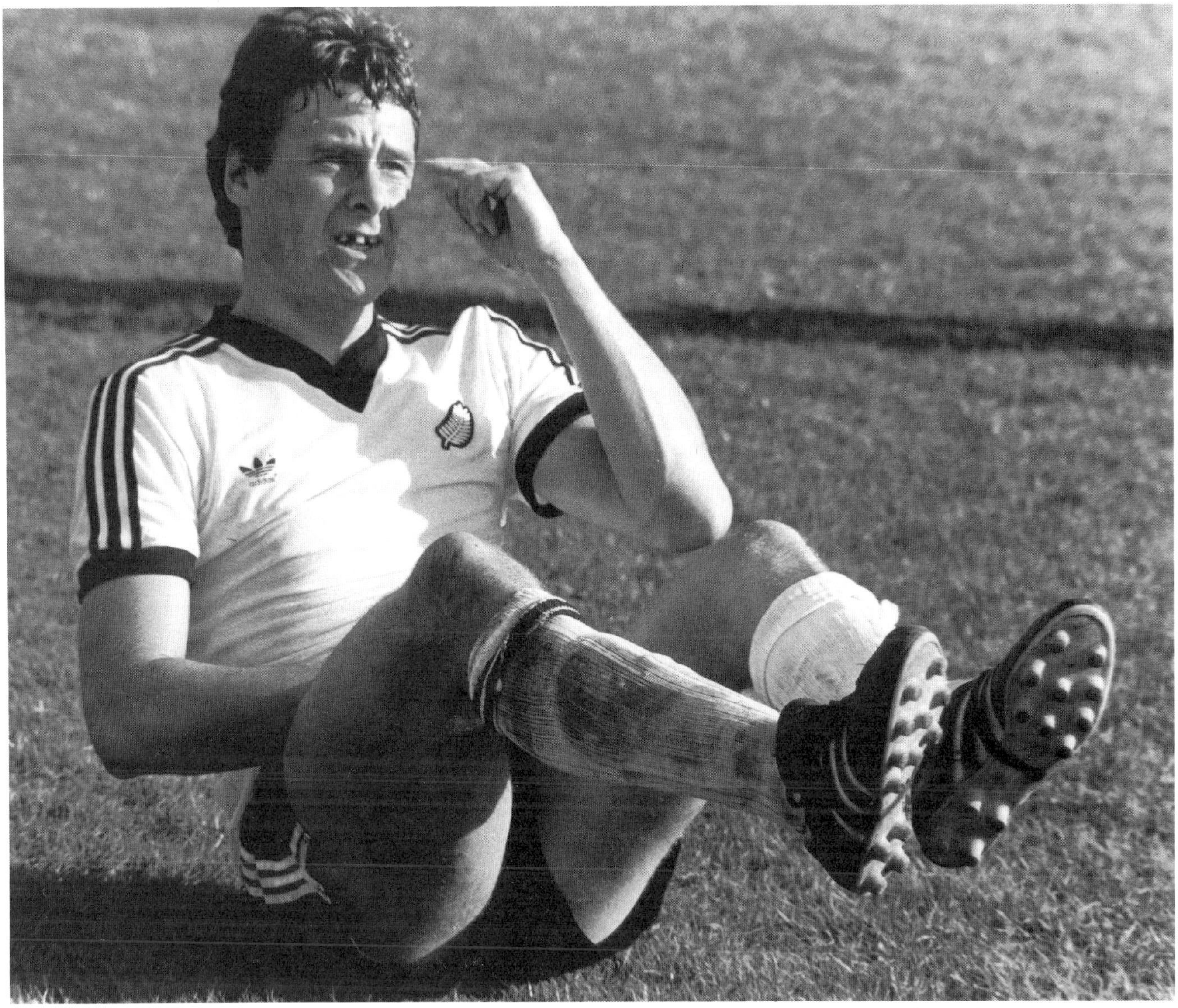

Steve Wooddin isn't singing "It's only just begun" but it would have been appropriate. The venue is Mount Smart Stadium and New Zealand and Australia are about to draw 3-3. And some of the Aussie tackling was fair dinkum. Vic Deverill collection

played badly but they were too good in the first half. We certainly were as fit as we could be. That changed after John (Adshead) talked to us at half time. The first goal was a bit messy but after the second they were really rattled. Out on the pitch we could tell that they were under pressure because the game suddenly was very competitive. We certainly were as good as they were in that second half."

The 5-2 scoreline proved to be a blow for Scotland. If they had won by one more goal they would have moved into the second phase of the competition. That they didn't was due to a draw with the Russians, Brazilian magic and Wooddin's strike.

Wooddin was born in Birkenhead but not the Auckland version. His accent is the big giveaway. He hails from Merseyside and played for a time with Tranmere Rovers before he came to New Zealand. One Saturday night back home he was reading the local sports paper when he came upon an advertisement.

"It was from Dunedin City looking for players. I had no idea where New Zealand was. I went to find an atlas and I remember thinking that it was pretty close to the Antarctic."

Wooddin arrived in New Zealand in 1977 just in time for Dunedin City to be relegated from the National League, but he remained in the south until after the World Cup campaign. He spent two years in Australia and then moved to Christchurch, still his home town. A couple of ankle operations more or less ended his international and National League career but in 1991 he still had an attachment to the Technical Club. He played in 1990 and in 1991 was heavily involved in a coaching role as his playing career draws to an end.

Of all the matches in the World Cup Wooddin remembers two very fondly. They were the 2-0 away wins over Indonesia and Australia.

"We played as well then as any other time during the campaign. The goal I scored that gave me the greatest pleasure was against Australia in Sydney. We played them off the park that day and the win was most satisfying. None of the media in Australia gave us the ghost of a chance. They wrote us off and yet after the game not one member of the Australian media came near our dressing room."

ADRIAN ELRICK

NEW ZEALAND 0, USSR 3
Estadio La Rosaleda, Malaga, Spain 19/6/82

This was probably the best performance by the New Zealand side in the World Cup finals, not that the scoreline showed it. In terms of class the Russians were clearly better but for a long time in the match the All Whites chased and fought. They might even have scored first. And most importantly luck was clearly on the side of the Russians. The first two goals had huge elements of luck about them as Gavrilov in the 24th minute and then Blokhin in the 48th minute netted. By the time Baltacha had a third in the 68th minute the game was done. New Zealand this day, as it was for over 100 occasions, were well served by Adrian Elrick. In the year of the finals, Elrick played in 13 of the 15 matches. These days he still hacks a ball about and has bloomed in a career as a television comments man. Elrick recalls the Russians.

"I remember sitting in the changing rooms contemplating the awesome task of having to play against the might of Russia. We had just made it to Spain. They were European finalists and seeded number two in Europe. Talk about class players, they had plenty. Dasaev was arguably the best goalkeeper in the world and what about Blokhin and Bal, Daraselia and Baltacha? We had done well against Scotland in spite of the 2-5 scoreline. The result had not truly reflected the closeness of the game. If the American referee David Socha had had more experience at that level we might have even managed a draw.

"So we were in a positive mood going into the USSR game. We felt confident we could compete at top level against a team of quality and not be embarrassed by the outcome. John Adshead had done his homework well. We had seen videos of the game between Brazil and Russia and felt that our opponents lacked individual flair, but then again any team playing against Brazil tends at times to look ordinary. Adshead had been around each member of the team reinforcing their commitments to their teammates, instilling pride and confidence in their own ability to compete and to come out with the creditability that each of the All Whites deserved.

"So it was up to the eleven players on the park. I can tell you that standing in the players' tunnel waiting to go out onto the park certainly gets the adrenalin pumping. Moving onto the park into the intense and humid area of battle carries with it a feeling that is hard to explain. You stand there in front of 20,000 people for the official introductions and handshakes feeling really proud to be out there representing your country and the emotional lift from hearing the national anthem is unbelievable. You just can't wait for the game to begin. Once the official business is done your concentration switches to the game itself although in the background the babble of noise is never far away.

"The game itself was very intense with both sides seeking early scoring opportunities. If anything, the All Whites played their best football in the first 20 minutes of the match. We looked sound and confident in our defensive zone and up front were creative and relaxed, making trouble for the Russians. Only a world class save from Dasaev prevented us from taking the lead midway through the first spell.

"But luck was not with us. A long range shot at our goal was clearly covered by keeper Frank Van Hattum but it struck an attacker in the back and gave Gavrilov a simple tap in. While the Russians went on to score two more goals we continued to chase and tackle, backtrack and overlap and compete in every sense of the word. At the final whistle we came off the field with our heads high. We had proved we could compete at top level not only to the rest of the world but to ourselves as well."

FRANK VAN HATTUM

NEW ZEALAND 0, BRAZIL 4
Estadio Benito Villamarin, Seville, Spain 23/6/82

There were Oscar and Junior, Zico and Falcao, Socrates and Eder, footballing greats. They were the stars of the show. Brazil in 1982 were the favourites to win the World Cup. They didn't, of course. History shows that Italy beat them a couple of matches later on, but on this balmy Seville night, the might of football's most famous nation was playing us, the All Whites. This match was the last of this country's most famous campaign. Maybe it was fitting. Whatever the result New Zealand would go no further, but even so it was a full international. A moment to remember for the rest of your life - particularly if you happened to be on the field. Goalkeeper Frank Van Huttum was. Along with Barry Pickering he had been sitting on the bench in every one of the lead up matches. But coach John Adshead had caused a stir by picking him for the game against Scotland. Van Hattum played well and now here he was about to play against the Brazilians. Van Hattum, a Kiwi, had to the end of 1990 played for his share of clubs. Christchurch, Hamilton, University, Papatoetoe, Mt Maunganui and lately Manurewa all benefited from his services. Apart from New Zealand there were also representative games; one remembers with pleasure the 1989 National

League fixture between Hutt Valley and Manurewa when both Van Hattum and Pickering were on show. The class of the two was self- evident and a 1-1 scoreline showed that both were human after all. But even at that stage Brazil was still a quite splendid memory. Like most of the Adshead squad, Van Hattum felt that the big game was the play off with China for that final spot in Spain but in terms of prestige, glamour and pure excitement playing Brazil Van Hattum recalls was the absolute ultimate. He takes up the story.

"After gaining selection for the first two games in Spain amid some controversy given that Richard Wilson had played all of the qualifying games, I was mentally preparing myself for the coaches to give Richard the last game. I felt I had earned the position to play in Spain. In all the lead up matches against Hungary, Watford and the League of Ireland I had performed well and felt that I had proved myself in the first two games in Spain. I would have been disappointed but would have accepted if they had named Richard for Brazil. So I was absolutely chuffed when the team for the Brazil game was named. It confirmed the view that there is no room for sentiment in international football and is a tribute to John (Adshead) and Kevin (Fallon) who maintained the same professional approach throughout the campaign. The temptation must have been there to give everyone a game.

"Words can hardly describe the feeling of playing against the best team in the world. When I was young, I would attend football evenings and watch early World Cup films which would feature Pele and the other greats of Brazil. The whole feeling then was unreal and now suddenly we were going up against the skills of Socrates, Junior and Zico. Yet the entire squad was quite relaxed about what was waiting for us. In the build-up Kevin emphasised that we had earned the right to play and to go out and enjoy it. There was no talk of stacking the defence and holding on for a respectable result, rather the reverse. The directions were positive - to go out and play and if we were to lose to go down in the Kiwi manner battling all the way. It was a tribute to New Zealand that Brazil named their first choice side. They could easily have rested players for crucial second phase matches.

"The dressing room was quite subdued before the game in stark contrast to the media build-up which saw television crews and journalists flocking to our hotel and the game, confident of the hiding that Brazil was about to dish out. Just before the game I was interviewed by several British television channels and they included big names, like Denis Law. All the questions followed similar lines - you must be scared they will knock in heaps of goals, don't you wish it was all over and aren't you worried you will be made to look stupid and so on.

"I recall I was pretty blunt with most of them. Listen! There are probably hundreds of goalkeepers in your country who wish they were me. Many top keepers will never play against Brazil, let alone in a World Cup, and here I am with a chance to play the world's best. I can't wait for it to start and what's more we are very confident of giving a good account of ourselves and what's more we won't be getting thrashed! Bravado? Maybe! But at that point I didn't care.

"Just before the game John mentioned that there was someone who wanted to meet us. Imagine our shock when the great Pele poked his head through our dressing room. Quite a few of the players grabbed his autograph and had pictures taken with him. It certainly was exciting. For all that, it was quite unnerving to hit the stadium tunnel. We had our first glimpse of the Brazil side and for all the bravado I'm sure the butterflies started then and there though that soon ended as we entered the arena. What a buzz that was. There is nothing to compete with the atmosphere of a Brazilian crowd. It's like a never ending carnival with drums beating, dancing and the continuous crowd hum.

"The game started well for us and for 28 minutes we looked composed, playing well and mounting a couple of attacks. From one such attack Brazil exploded and in one fluent move swept upfield with Socrates taking the ball to the byline then cutting it back for Zico to score with an amazing scissors kick. I felt it was one of the best goals scored during the entire football competition. It certainly oozed class and I had a better look at it than most. Three minutes later they had another gem, again through Zico. The rest of the half returned to a degree of normality if continuing drum drones could ever be called normal. At half time John and Kevin just kept telling us to play and to try and score. The temptation to shut up shop must have been great but no one in the camp ever saw it that way. The second half started just like the first with New Zealand giving as good as it got. Obviously Brazil were far superior in class and skill but we still managed to perform. Two further goals from Falcao (64m) and Serginho (70m) completed the scoring. The crowd was amazing during the game as the singing and chanting continued. The Brazil crowd had what appeared to be a remote controlled kite which buzzed the crowd and in the second half our goal. It would have been easy to lose concentration in the hubbub but to the lads' credit they hung in.

"A final thrill for the players was the swapping of jerseys with players making beelines for the jersey they wanted. Adrian Elrick had his eye on Zico's and we felt he spent the last five minutes man-to-man on the great Brazilian to make sure he would get it. Straight after the game those men of the media who had grilled me before the match were the first to offer congratulations and give us the credit we deserved. Yet my day wasn't quite over as I was selected to provide a drug sample which is not easy after playing for 90 minutes in Spanish heat. It took time and a vast quantity of liquid although as a bonus I did swap my shorts with Zico who had taken a fancy to them. The bus trip back to the hotel was reflective mainly through fatigue and a sense of disappointment that the World Cup adventure was now at an end. In hindsight I'm sure we could have done even better. At times luck deserted us and at other times over-eagerness or lack of confidence prevented us from scoring against Russia and Brazil.

"One thing is certain though. No matter what

happens to New Zealand football in the future the class of '82 captured the imagination of the New Zealand public and those memories will remain with them and with us forever. It was one hell of an adventure right out of Boys Own, one which I will always treasure."

CERI EVANS

NEW ZEALAND 3, ISRAEL 1
Mount Smart Stadium, Auckland, 26/10/85

Never has a New Zealand side had such a busy domestic year. In all, the All Whites played 22 matches, some against local sides, but there were matches against the English club Newcastle United, with a World Cup campaign the highlight right at the end of the season. And like the lead-in to Spain it looked for a time as though the dizzy heights of four years earlier may be repeated. What might have happened if English referee Keith Hackett had allowed what seemed a perfectly legitimate Wynton Rufer goal against Australia in the first game. That might have made the score 1-0 instead of a 0-0 final. But there was one campaign match that it produced one of the best international results of modern times. It was a game rich in drama and quality. Israel were no slugs. In keeper Bonni Ginsburg, defender Avi Cohen and striker Ronnie Rosenthal they had players who, then and now, are good enough to play first division English football. This day at Auckland, though, Rufer goaled after three minutes and while Ameli levelled, Mal Dunford had the Kiwis back in front before half-time. There was only one goal in the second half. It was a superb, teasing, swirling effort from the sideline delivered by Colin Walker. "It was," wrote *Soccer Annual* Editor Vic Deverill, "a goal that would have been talked about for weeks had it been scored at either Anfield or Old Trafford."

One of the lynchpins in the New Zealand side that day was Ceri Evans, a young man whose career has been paralleled to that of All Black captain David Kirk. Evans has quite a football pedigree. His father Gwyn, a Welshman, arrived in New Zealand in 1963 after having a long and distinguished playing career which included some 10 years with Crystal Palace. Evans senior was the rock around which a very successful Christchurch United side was founded. After years of playing, Evans turned to administration and became the Secretary General of the New Zealand Football Association. Ceri Evans played much of his junior football in Nelson and served that club, Wellington Diamond United, Dunedin City and Christchurch United. Like Kirk, he pursued a medical career, attained the honour of becoming a Rhodes Scholar to Oxford University and while there

Distinguished guests! All White Garry Lund contemplates the aura of the Israel international Ronnie Rosenthal. Picture: Eric Jelly

won a soccer blue. But that was not his only reward. The Oxford United club saw fit to make him a regular in its side and in 1990 he was very much on the club's books. Evans has been a New Zealand regular since 1984 and in 1987 was Player of the Year. His ability as a defender has never been questioned.

Australia won that World Cup qualifying competition by three points from Israel and New Zealand but it could have been so different especially if that goal had been allowed.

"I remember the incident well," Evans said. "It was a fast break and a free kick was awarded against the keeper. We took it quickly, Colin Walker slipped the ball to Wynton who scored. The goal was disallowed because the ball was not stationary when the kick was taken but we got the video of the game and it shows quite clearly the hand on the ball. It was quite frustrating."

From there New Zealand scored a brace of easy wins against the Chinese-Taipei side before the first game with Israel, who by then had lost, then drawn with Australia. The loss had come at home, but then they had a good draw in Australia.

"The game was important for us. It was our last home game and we had to win.

"I remember Walker's goal. There was a bit of indecision between Ginzburg and Cohen. It wasn't just a chip, it was a fair way out. We were playing formation with Alan Boath sweeping while behind Mal and I were marking the two strikers which included Rosenthal. They went out, played wide on the wing and made life very difficult for us. I remember it rained very hard in the second half, typical Auckland showers, but there was a good crowd there (10,600) and they produced some of the most vocal support we have ever had. It was even better than it had been for the Australian game."

From the high of the Israel win, the All Whites went to Sydney and were outplayed 2-0. By the time they got to Israel a week later it mattered not that the locals, with Messrs Ginsburg, Cohen and Rosenthal, won 3-0, even if, as Evans recalled New Zealand did play some of its best football of the series. It could easily have gone the other way.

MALCOLM DUNFORD

NEW ZEALAND 1, AUSTRALIA 0
Hutt Recreation Ground, Lower Hutt, 9/9/87
NEW ZEALAND 2, AUSTRALIA 0
Mount Smart Stadium, Auckland, 2/4/89

As New Zealand soccer ended the 80s and stepped into the 90s its captain was the personable Wellingtonian Malcolm Dunford. Dunford is one of the very few capital city players who has regularly kept his place in the side under a number of national coaches. He took part in both the 1985 and the 1989 World Cup campaigns and he has been a long time disciple of former National and now respected club coach Barrie Truman. Dunford played most of his club football with Wellington United, but when Truman moved to Miramar Rangers in 1990, Dunford followed. At times the critics have not been convinced about his club performances, but when it comes to national team efforts very few had given more than Mal Dunford. His headed goals for New Zealand have proved to be gems, none more so than the first in the 1989 match against Australia which set the All Whites on the road to an unexpected win and sent the Australians out of the 1990 World Cup finals. That win, maybe more than most in the last two years, strengthened New Zealand football's belief in itself and in 1990 that success was branded as the stepping stone for the excellent home international record.

The win at Hutt Recreation Ground followed a 1-1 draw in Melbourne. The ground that night was under water. There had been some debate about playing the game in the Hutt, but 5000 attended that match and not since the heady days of 1982 had a New Zealand team been subject to such support. There was just one goal and it came via Fred de Jong when Aussie keeper Jeff Olver failed to control the heavy ball.

Dunford recalls that wet win and the one splendid match in the 1989 World Cup campaign.

"There is always that little bit extra that comes out from our players and for that matter spectators when up against our friends from across the Tas! I remember the All Whites match at Hutt Recreation Ground against the Socceroos for a number of reasons; the result, the atrocious ground conditions and the vocal support and encouragement we received from the crowd.

"We had returned from Australia having snatched a 1-1 draw, a late goal from Robert 'Tyro' Ironside keeping alive our hopes of winning the Trans Tasman Cup for the first time. The day prior to the match we had trained on a rock hard Hutt Rec. and we were all ready to play in moulded stud boots. Nobody had banked on the skies opening up that night which resulted in the pitch being more like a swimming pool than a football field. We quickly adapted to the conditions and recorded that 1-0 win thanks to Fred de Jong's goal. Near the end of the match we came under a lot of pressure but thanks to the vocal crowd and a little luck we were able to hold out.

"Another of the All Whites victories over Australia came at Mount Smart and it was played as a curtain raiser to a rugby union match between Auckland and a New Zealand Barbarians team. This was part of the 1990 World Cup campaign but we had come back from a tour which had seen a brave 1-0 loss in Israel but a poor 4-1 loss in Australia, which hadn't done much for our hopes but had clearly bolstered the Australian hopes. After that Sydney showing not much was expected from us. We were clearly the underdogs. What the spectators and Socceroos did not expect was an All White squad fired up, prepared to battle, fight and run for each other. At no time did we give them a chance to settle. The All Whites were splendid this day, none more so than 'Tyro' Ironside and when Billy Wright curled a super shot to give us a second goal it was the end for Australia and, in effect, its chances of making it to the 1990 World Cup Finals."

It may have been modesty, but Dunford's own part in the win was comprehensive. He had been the only goal scorer in the 4-1 loss in Sydney and it was his header from a Noel Barkley chip that set the pattern for the match that was to follow. To score he had to brave a number of flying boots. It was during the campaign that Mal Dunford became a father for the first time but even with that natural concern hanging over him his leadership from the front was of the highest order.

Captain Courageous. Malcolm Dunford in action during the 1989 home international against Australia. Picture: Eric Jelly

REFLECTIONS

JIM KERSHAW

Being a football administrator in this country has never been an easy task. It matters not whether it is at national, provincial or club level. The work is hard and generally unrewarding. Thousands of hours have been spent by hundreds of administrators in the quest to improve the great sport. Yet even today they win little credit from those for whom they administer. New Zealand football has known literally hundreds of these men and women whose dedication to the greatest of all the games is without question. From the time that C C Dacre, J S Hill and their cronies kicked the ball around the Devonport Domain football has known a host of quite splendid administrators. Jim Kershaw is one of those. A tall, quietly spoken man, he served football diligently first as a player whose talent won international recognition and then as an administrator during the turbulent early 60s - a time when the code in this country was looking to find its international feet. Kershaw served his employers, the AMP Insurance, faithfully for 43 years and at the same time became the first NZFA chairman to attract what could only be described as more than his share of media attention. At that time the NZFA was based in Wellington and served by a part-time secretary Steuart Goodman, a most capable man. There was never ever enough time, Kershaw recalled in June of 1990, to put in the time and effort the game deserved. In 1964 matters came to a head when Kershaw had to chose between his job and soccer. He retired from administration in 1964. Twenty six years later at the age of 83 Jim Kershaw, the winner of a Chatham Cup medal in 1932 and then a New Zealand international took time out to reflect on the game.

"I began playing my football for the Marist school in Newtown in 1917 and I played soccer in those days because I was so cross with rugby administration which would not allow soccer to be played in the Marist schools. This seems strange in this day and age but is quite true and a priest from St Patricks College who did play rugby as well as soccer was acting chairman of the Rugby Union in Wellington. I went to Wellington College and they had no soccer so obviously I looked for something else and went to Marist Old Boys."

Jim Kershaw soon had another taste of football politics. He found that he was not really required for Marist but it was an internal matter. "You could say that I crept away with my tail between my legs," he said. "From there I went to St Thomas, a non entity of a club really. A friend of mine Snow Smyth was playing with them at the time. At the end of one year Smyth's father took an interest in Seatoun and we left St Thomas and went out there and I played for them until I was 26. I was captain of the Seatoun club which was playing senior B only for quite some years. At this time I heard from one of my friends that one person, a prominent referee who had two sons playing in this grade, had said that Kershaw would not be captain of Seatoun when he took charge. However, I continued to be loyal and turned out for Seatoun. Lo and behold came the first day of the new season and I wasn't even in the team. I thought that was rather strange and thought to myself what happens now? The person concerned said that he didn't think I was loyal enough to stick with the club. I said I wanted to play for the second team but I was told I

New Zealand Football Association Council members, 1969-70. Back row: T.J. Killalea, T. Rigby, R.A. Kelly, J. Hipkins, G. Jackson, W.G. Johnston, R.A. Kavanagh, P.E. Killick, G.H. Moore (secretary). Front row: L. O'Rorke, G.L. Thomas, C.J. Dempsey, R.V. Hullena, J. Cowie (chairman), P.W. Graham, D. McDonald, A.R. White, T. Gottermeyer. Absent: H. De Krey. NZFA collection

could not do that. After three weeks I was really tired of the whole thing and I sought from the Wellington Football Association a transfer and incredibly it was turned down. I heard from another friend - I had a few in football then - that it was on the casting vote of my refereeing friend at Seatoun that I was turned down. Immediately I put in an application to the New Zealand Football Association for a transfer, detailing the problems I had had up until this point and within a week had a transfer back to Marist, mainly I believe because of the help of a very dear friend of mine Bill Hicks, the secretary of the New Zealand Football Association.

"When I got there the club captain said I could not play for the first team straight away. I would have to play three games at least in the lower grades before coming into the first team. They had a good team in those days. I said I would like to be considered after that. I played three games in the second team and we won them all handsomely and I was getting to the stage where the football wasn't at all interesting though. I don't want it to sound like I'm skiting.

"At the end of the three weeks I asked what about it now? One of the Marist officials said that they could not possibly keep me out so I went into the team at the expense of Bill Cudby who retired from football. So that's what happened. Instead of playing centre half, a position I played in for many years, I went to inside left. I had played at inside right for the Marist second team. I played my first game in a Chatham Cup elimination game on the Basin Reserve against Manawatu and we thumped them - 6-1 I think. I scored at least one goal, maybe even two and we went on to win the Chatham Cup."

Kershaw at that point had been a Wellington under-18 representative and was also a Wellington senior regular. That 1932 season of turmoil culminated in Marist's 5-0 win over the Millerton All Blacks of Buller in the Chatham Cup. The name

A great New Zealand talent. Iain Ormond (left) with the Australian George Harris. Picture: Eric Jelly

Kershaw appears among the list of final goal scorers. The Chatham Cup was one of two playing highlights for Jim Kershaw. The very next year he was selected for the New Zealand team which toured Australia in 1933. It was just the third New Zealand team which toured abroad and in all 13 matches including three internationals were played. Kershaw not only competed in the three tests but in 12 of the 13 games on tour. Australia won all three test matches 4-2, 6-4, 4-2, its first ever series win over New Zealand. The former international recalls:

"Right at the beginning of the year I was selected as an international player. That was a terrific thrill. I didn't think I was up there but the selectors thought so. I recall at the final trial a Diamond player Johnny McLeod broke his leg. That really upset me. He was a nice guy and in my eyes a certainty to be selected. As happens to most teams that visit Australia we were beaten but only just. We were nearly up with the Australians. After that I came back to Marist and played a couple more seasons before giving up reluctantly. But I was getting to an age when I felt I did not want to be knocked about. I was most fortunate to have suffered practically no injuries at any moment throughout my career."

Jim Kershaw recalls playing his last game in 1935. He married Kit in 1936 and as young marrieds there was a family of four to be raised although a stint in administration that was to last close on 20 years was in the offering. Kershaw was elected to the council in 1948. In 1959 he was elected chairman and two years later became the fourth life member of the NZFA. He managed the 1954 team to Australia and the 1964 world tour. He resigned from all football in 1964.

"I'm pretty sure it was Bill Hicks (the then NZFA secretary) who had helped me early and was still such a great guy in my eye who asked me if I would go onto the New Zealand council. I was keen to accept. Bert Conner (Kit Kershaw's uncle) was the chairman and soon after he joined the council, Bill Arcus succeeded Bill Hicks as the secretary. During my time in administration the thing that sticks in my mind most was that we were not making any progress administratively, financially or in football. It was quite a concern. I couldn't work out why but I had a strong feeling that it was because, myself included, the councillors were not putting nearly enough effort into the administration side of football. It worried me

Welsh-born but 1964 World tourist Trefor Pugh in full cry. Tony Hilton collection

Back in the 1960s Keith de Maus (right) was the NZFA's representative on the Football Association in London. His work brought him life membership and his badge is presented by the then New Zealand High Commissioner, Sir Thomas McDonald.
Barry Smith collection

that this was happening because there were so many avid footballing fans on the council, people like John Shankie and Jack Cowie and others yet we were not getting any place."

Kershaw does subscribe to the opinion that, unlike today, the council office was a part not full-time institution. All the footballing administrators had to earn a living. There were only so many hours in the day to devote to football. New Zealand had to wait until 1970 for its first full-time office.

"It was all honorary then. Bill Arcus did it for many years as public accountant and if he got about 100 quid a year that would be about all it was. This opinion of not putting in more time made me feel what's the word - 'hamstrung' - that's as good as any."

Kershaw was the manager of the 1954 tour of Australia and the world tour in 1964. The first venture produced one test win in three and that was, in the 50s, New Zealand's most successful single result, even if the other two tests were lost. The world tour brought one win in 15 games. Kershaw recalls. "It was such a disappointment. Actually I would rather forget it, but coming back from that showed me how little we had progressed in the way of football skills over the many years that we had been playing and it made me think where on earth we were going. There was something radically wrong with administration in this country. We were not giving players the proper opportunity to achieve a higher standard. I must admit I had no real brainwave."

Kershaw does himself an injustice. On his return to New Zealand he said the NZFA council would have to introduce professionalism by degrees to lift the standard of soccer. Within a few months though Kershaw would be through with the administration of football. His workload became so heavy that football queries could not be attended to during business hours. Following on the failure of the world venture and other administrative matters, the public image of the NZFA had reached rock bottom. He resigned at a council meeting without any personal complaints. Kershaw believed in an open administration. Council meetings in those days were always open to and were attended by members of the media.

Jim Kershaw has faith in the future administration of New Zealand football. "I only hope that they continue on as well as they seem to have done in the last few years and I feel that the succession of Warwick Gendall to the chair will have started them on a new trend."

JOHN ADSHEAD

No one identity has quite dominated the modern day game in New Zealand as John Adshead has done. While his background was low key, the impact he has made since taking on a second-rate international side has made him arguably the best known face in New Zealand soccer, even now some eight years after he guided the All Whites to Spain and a place in the final 16. His disappointment that New Zealand did not take advantage of its then high profile when it was rivalling all other sports for media headlines is obvious still. "I knew the hours the players and the officials had put in and the cost, which included marriage breakups. But the playing decline in 1983 and through 1984 was very difficult for me to accept. I'm sure it was the same for the players as well," he says.

Adshead since 1982 had his differences with the New Zealand Football Association. Sadly many of them have been public but it's nice to see that much of the coldness between Adshead and soccer officialdom has now thawed. John Adshead is heavily involved in media work. He was, in 1990, the major television commentator for matches against Lokomotiv of Russia and the National team of China. John Adshead is a Lancastrian who spent time with Exeter City both in a playing and administrative role before coming to New Zealand via Western Australia. He reflects here on not only the Spanish campaign, but also on the media and his seemingly outrageous selection of Wellingtonian Wynton Rufer for the national team for Spain.

The Media

"The media is so important. I look for honesty from players. If you don't like what I am saying at least give me the chance to justify it. I don't like people gathering and saying that the boss is talking rubbish. If you have a problem with me then let us sort it out. By those methods I get honesty from players and that's what I expect from the media. I will give the news people everything they need. Only once during the 1982 World Cup campaign was I very angry with a newspaper report. It concerned a falling out between two players at training, which when you consider the amount of time we spent together was a very minor incident.

"I now know what it is like to work on both sides of the fence. I know when to approach coaches and when not to. There are times when we have to deal with requests even when we don't want to. The media is so vital. They are the people who are going to tell your story. You've got something to talk to this public about and that is to sell the team which means selling the individual players and once you get off side with the media and don't give them what they want it becomes frustrating, especially when it is 3.30am in the morning and you've only got to bed a couple of hours beforehand and you are woken from a deep sleep by a Scottish journalist who has just flopped into his office at 3pm and is looking for a fresh story.

"The intensity of the world media arrived after New Zealand had beaten China in Singapore to qualify for the final 16. The next day I had a call from a BBC crew who were filming a programme and wanted it wrapped up as quickly as possible. They said 'Look mate, we know it's a nightmare for you but could you front up tomorrow and do the programme?' I still remember clearly the opening remark of the interview. 'You've won your way to the World Cup finals. That was a tremendous challenge. You've achieved that. What is left for you?'

"I said if we win it three times we can keep the World Cup. That set a standard. They thought I was a bit of a card yet from that point on we were very open to the international media".

Sunday Showdown in Singapore

There seems little doubt that the most important international ever played by a New Zealand soccer team was the 2-1 success over China in Singapore. That fixture is recalled elsewhere by skipper Steve Sumner. But it wasn't all plain sailing. New Zealand landed on Friday January 8, 1982, barely 48 hours before the scheduled kick off. On arrival Adshead found that a planned training session at the National Stadium could not take place because of a religious festival. FIFA World Cup regulations allow for at least one training session at the match venue. Adshead was determined to have his!

"I left it very late to go there. Whether this was the right or wrong decision is open to debate though the result suggests it was the right one. I didn't want to take the players up to Singapore and keep them there for five days. I just didn't feel that Singapore was the right place to prepare for such a vital international fixture. They were a media hungry country and while it's nice to feel your product is going to be talked about the result was still all important. There is a lot of cheap shopping enticement and the players needed to have only one thing on their mind. We arrived about six or seven on the Friday night and in just a quiet discussion about training facilities I told them I wanted to go on the ground tomorrow (on Saturday). They said I couldn't because of a festival. I replied that no one had told me about the festival and that I had every right to go onto the ground as long as it was not within 12 hours of the match taking place. I told the locals that it was not for them to tell me I couldn't train. It was up to FIFA. And if I didn't get the session that could jolly well put the match back until Monday.

"It was a major story which blew up very quickly. The festival was already a 40,000 sell out. Mind you, there was no way FIFA were going to say don't play the game. If you don't play the game you forfeit. I knew that from day one. But we were a small country and we were not going to be pushed around. The next morning the press conference was very heavily attended. We knew the religious situation and because we were trying to attract good feeling said we would respect the religious aspect. The players were a little concerned because I hadn't had time to sit down and talk to them but once the game was closer and we got into the stadium it all settled down."

WYNTON RUFER

One of the Adshead legacies to New Zealand football is Wynton Rufer. When the chips were down in the World Cup campaign Adshead called in the then 18-year-old Norwich City professional into the side. Rufer played in the last three qualifying matches. He scored in the 2-2 draw in Kuwait; bagged two in the 5-0 Saudi Arabia thumping and scored the second of New Zealand's goals in the 2-1 showdown with China. Rufer, in 1990, is a proven performer in his own right. He had a spell with Grasshoppers but with the German division one side Werder Bremen he has reached heights never before scaled by a New Zealand player. Late in 1990 he was the subject of $3m debate between the Swiss and German clubs.

"I had problems with senior players, particularly Steve Sumner over the inclusion of Wynton Rufer. I had been monitoring Rufer since I brought him into the squad. I had left him training with Norwich because he was a prolific goal scorer and I always had it in the back of my mind that if ever goals were ultra necessary for us to be successful then he would be the man to do the job for us. At Norwich he was training every day and I was getting good reports from his manager Ken Brown. As soon as we drew at home with the Saudis instead of winning I made the decision to call him on. Not only did we have to start winning but goal difference might also play an important part. I had to leave two of the squad members back home and I remember Steve Sumner, who was the captain, speaking on behalf of his team.

"Steve was fairly blunt in his approach to me: 'Never mind his game; never mind his need to become a professional footballer in England; can the bugger play?' I told Steve the 'bugger' could in fact play. Sumner was still apprehensive; so were some of the players and you could hardly blame them. By this time the team had nurtured a close bond. This was one family and when you start leaving not one but two family members back home they want to know why. I put Rufer with Sam Malcolmson because Sam was not only one of the elder statesmen of the team he was a member of the squad who had entry into all the little households within the family. It was important that Wynton should be accepted into the squad and as quickly as possible.

"I remember telling Wynton on the morning of his first training session with the squad that it would be the most important session he would ever have for the national squad for by the time he came off the park he would have to be accepted not only for his ability but also as a person who would improve the context of the side. He was not there to sit on the bench. He was absolutely superb in that session and I remember Sumner's look as he walked off from the session. The skipper was never outspoken but he would give credit by just the nod of his head. He looked at me, nodded and said yes, the boy could play. Rufer was superb that morning as he was in everything he did after that."

Statesmen in Spain

As far as John Adshead is concerned the most important members of any touring party are the players.

"It's nice to be accepted by the world of football and the players sensed the air of difference once we arrived in Spain. They were the VIPs and always will be. We don't treat them as such or give them the credit they deserve. It's the same with all sports in this country. But when we did get to Spain I just took a step back, leant against the wall and had a look at the media reception to the side. With the cameras on them all the time you could sense them grow six inches. They were being treated like professionals and responded in kind. It made me feel that maybe we wouldn't do badly here. We certainly wouldn't get a tanning.

"Only once did I get a bit annoyed with them. In our first match we came in 3-0 down against Scotland at half-time. We had talked about it so long, but were still tentative. I said that if we were going to be beaten by 10 goals that would be my responsibility. I told them they had the licence to go forward, to get in advance of the ball. If Scotland were going to score 10 let's at least be a side that can knock in three against them. Let's at least get goals on the board in this tournament. Fourteen minutes later it's 3-2 and maybe it was only for four or five minutes but we frightened the life out of Scotland. You know the next four goals that were scored against us (the last two by Scotland and the first two by USSR in the next match) all had massive elements of luck about them.

"I recall looking at the faces of the squad as I was about to name the team for the game against Brazil - the last match of this super campaign. We had a family now for almost two years, we were out of the World Cup and you could feel some of them saying, come on boss, give us at least one game in Spain. There was anxiety on many faces, it was certainly there on the face of Richard Wilson. I was more disappointed than he was that he didn't play in that last game. He certainly deserved a chance to play in Spain. I could have changed the side completely and those on the park would have done a fine job. But we were getting paid by the NZFA to be professional and the side that went out was the best one possible.

"That was the worst moment of the campaign naming this particular team."

Gole

Gole was the official film of the 1982 World Cup finals. It was produced by a London firm and is readily available throughout the world on video. The feature, insofar as this country is concerned is a segment that revolves around the New Zealand camp and its match against the USSR. It also has, what was at the time, a rare insight into an international dressing room before, at half-time and then after the match in question was won by Russia 3-0. The narrator of the film is none other than superstar Sean Connery.

"I received a phone call from a London based firm asking if they could come to our hotel. They very tentatively asked if they could travel with a team on the bus to a game. We had already opened the door for Television New Zealand many months before that. I said of course they could travel with us and would they like to come with us into the dressing room. Their faces absolutely lit up. You mean you would let us in. Of course, we are used to it. The only ruling is that if I ask you to leave you just leave without question. That night I had a call from one of the crew who had a check of the security passes and they did not include entry to the changing room area. I told them not to worry about that, just to be at the hotel half an hour before we left for the game. When they arrived we put all the camera gear into our kitbag. There were cameras wrapped in New Zealand tracksuit tops. When you arrived at these grounds you have to be there at least two hours before the kickoff and the security was so intense that they ship you into the dressing room so fast that they wouldn't know if the squad was 20 strong let along 30. So the crew all arrived in as New Zealand international footballers. The end result was one of a kind. How often do cameras portray what goes on in an international dressing room in the middle of a World Cup finals match?"

TOM DELAHUNTY

It was a mistake to get on the wrong side of Tom Delahunty during a football match. He was an Englishman and without doubt one of New Zealand's leading referees. He went all the way from refereeing lower grade games in Wellington to gaining a FIFA badge and controlling 19 full internationals. The players of his era agree that Delahunty in his prime had no peers as a referee. Those he controlled soon knew not to have him on. When his dander is up the Delahunty eyes blaze - it can be a fearful experience. These days he has just quit a successful family book and toyship business in the northern suburbs of Wellington, yet his passion for football remains unchecked. Now that his refereeing days are done, he fights for the respect and the rights he believes referees deserve. Those men in black have never had a better ally.

Tom Delahunty was 21 when he arrived in 1956 from Manchester. Three years earlier he had started to referee back home. He landed with a Manchester County badge, controlling mainly "pub league fixtures". When he had the time away from his job as a linotype operator he was at Maine Road watching Manchester City.

Through a kiwi friend he became aware of New Zealand's presence and the prospects of the wide open spaces and total control of his own destiny made him determined to reach New Zealand. It took three years and two jobs before he was able to secure a passage on board the 'Captain Cook'. The trip took five weeks. Cynics will, I guess, say this country is still getting over the shock but that refereeing standards in this country have improved to gain world wide recognition is due to the determination of Tom Delahunty and his contemporaries who have set about their task with the same single-minded determination. Delahunty joined the Wellington Referees' Association in 1957.

"Football and refereeing have gone ahead tremendously," he believes. "As football in any country improves, it follows that the standard of refereeing will run in tandem. That has been the case here. Just look at all the referees who have gone overseas on FIFA appointments from New Zealand. To a man they have all come back having performed creditably. This is verified by the reports that follow the officials back.

"I don't think that referees here get the public credit they deserve for the job that they do overseas or here."

Tom Delahunty never kept a record of anything except his full internationals. Even so the medals collected for his 19 games remain in a bottom drawer at his Wellington home.

Delahunty firmly believes that first the regional leagues and then the expansion in the National League are the best things that happened to New Zealand football.

"These leagues started people thinking football in terms of coaching and standards.

"In the late 1950s and 1960s New Zealand had some marvellous men to guide the sport through its growing phase. I think of people like Ken Armstrong, Bert Ormond and Terry McCavana. They were professionals. They never made money in New Zealand. They seemed to me to be treated with a degree of suspicion by those who ran the game. We were an amateur country. These men were specialists. It was a gap which took years to bridge. They were tremendous fellows who deserve much more credit than they received."

Palmerston North in 1964 and referees gather for a National course. Tony Hilton collection

Delahunty recalls the 1961 Tom Finney side, a team of tourists who were not by any stretch of the imagination a full A side. They beat New Zealand twice and handsomely. Today he believes a full strength New Zealand side with the services of Wynton Rufer and Ceri Evans would be more than a match for a team like that.

"New Zealand born players were not given the credit they deserve. On this score I am quite critical of the local news media."

"One of the best things that happened to New Zealand refereeing was the arrival of the referee coaches, the Englishmen Ken Aston and Stan Lover and the Hungarian Dr Gyorgy Szilagyi. All made a big impact on not only the referees but also the coaches and assessors of referees."

Delahunty recalls failing a badge test because for the first 10 minutes of a match he didn't blow his whistle.

"What did I miss?" I asked. "I didn't see anything but you must have missed something," was the staggering reply.

Once that attitude changed the improvement in refereeing here went ahead in leaps and bounds. Delahunty refereed at top level until he was 49. In 1990 he was still actively involved as the chairman of the New Zealand Referees Association, chairman of the NZRA Appointment Board - which means he presides over all the major appointments in the country and he is on the coaching panel of the Referees' Association. He is well qualified to look ahead.

"Referees will go ahead as the standard grows and with the number of talented young players around the future looks good. We need though a little more of the continental flair in the game, not only on the pitch but also in the coaching field. We have to be careful not to become too British orientated in our approach.

"I would like to see the NZFA go back to a coaching for coaches system. It's only through good quality coaches and administrators that the game will prosper - the Centres of Excellence is a tremendous scheme but at some point the graduates have to be picked up from the schools and the education continue at a more senior level."

Of all the matches that Delahunty has refereed none made a bigger impression than a local 1960s Wellington derby between Miramar Rangers and Hungaria. It was a replay. The first, played at Petone's Memorial Park, had been called off as a riot threatened. The referee that day was one of New Zealand's best, Maurie Swain, a man who did an enormous amount for the code in the country. Young Delahunty was given the replay a week later.

In Wellington they are still regarded with awe. The 1967 Hungaria Venus Shield winning team whose football was a joy to watch.
Barry Smith collection

"I felt like a cork that had bobbed to the top. I was handed the appointment on a Monday night. I had nothing else to think about for the rest of the week. The people turned out in their thousands for the replay. They all expected a bloodbath. The two captains weren't speaking when they arrived at the centre circle for the toss of the coin. They stood still and silent waiting for me to say something - maybe warn that a repeat of the week's previous shenanigans would not be tolerated. I said nothing. They looked up and when they realised that I wasn't going to say anything they wished each other a good game. 'Let's show these bastards (the crowd). They've only come here to see a grudge match'.

"The game was a cracker, hard and fair. They were out to play football". Delahunty got the credit but it wasn't due to him. It was the players.

Since his retirement Tom Delahunty misses the contact with those on the park. "They are still the most important people. Without them we don't have a game. But you have to gain their respect. Then you can enjoy the job."

Each referee has embarrassing moments. Tom Delahunty has had his share, none more so than when he gave Mount Wellington a penalty in their own area and then ran slap bang into two club stalwarts Bill de Graaf and Brian Turner who were, to put it mildly, highly amused.

"We teach the referees that teams change round at half-time and they must remember to follow suit. This day it was Mount Wellington and Christchurch United, a top game with top players. The Mount had Warren Fleet and Christchurch Steve Sumner. They were on a man-to-man marking. Not dirty, but hard. Soon after half time Fleet was brought down from behind in the penalty area. I went in, blew the whistle and pointed at the spot. I looked up and saw the Mount's keeper Sandy Davie. I could hear Fleet and Sumner laughing. I swore and raced out of the area, straight into de Graaf and Turner. Both were laughing. 'You gave a penalty there Tom, didn't you?' The game continued. Only one of the linesmen picked up on it but the assessor didn't twig at all until we told him but by then he had given me a copy of my marks. I went into the dressing room to get the team cards signed. Turner and de Graaf continued to give me a hard time but by this time it was over a beer. They had after all won the game."

But when Tom Delahunty tells a story against himself it's the one involving son Sean which gets the biggest laugh. Tom and his wife Jessie have three adult married sons but when he was around nine young Sean didn't mind going to the football.

"He liked the after-match functions with the lemonade and chippies. This day I was at Te Whiti Park for a home Stop Out match. At some stage I looked over and saw Sean was on the roof of the dressing sheds with a mate. Today there is a ladder up to the roof and a press box and I assess referees from there, but Sean this day should not have been there.

He was lying on the roof to escape the attention of Hugh Stapleton the groundsman. Just before half time I had to give a decision against Stop Out. It didn't quite bring the stand down, but the crowd gave me some real stick. It had only just subsided when I heard a voice: 'Delahunty, you're a bum.' "The game kicked off again and I knew the voice - it belonged to a "lodger" of mine. The game finished. I was in the dressing room relaxing when the door opened and a fresh-faced nine year-old toddled in with a big smile. I stood up grabbed the lapel of his coat and lifted him out. "Delahunty, you're a bum," I said.

"You heard me alright then!"

BARRIE TRUMAN

"This one man, in my opinion, has done more for New Zealand soccer than any other person in the 25 years I have been coaching. This one man is, and always has been, the neatest coach this country has ever been fortunate enough to have working here. Far from preaching from the text books written by the academics, he has developed his own proven and successful coaching techniques that have helped countless New Zealand players and coaches reach their potential."

That tribute to Barrie Truman came in the mid-1980s from the then Petone soccer coach and now full time club manager Grant Williams at a time when his side was beating all before it in the Central Regional League. Williams was, and still is, one of Truman's biggest fans. The fact that club teams coached by Truman have continued to win Petone's own pre-season Hilton Cup tournament may have some influence but this tribute certainly recognised the worth of the pleasantly-spoken Englishman who arrived as New Zealand's director of coaching but who has since done more than his bit to break the northern stranglehold on the National League. In 1985, with a team of home-grown players, Truman's Wellington Diamond United won the League playing a brand of sparkling football rarely bettered in the 1980s. In the 1986 New Zealand Soccer Annual editor and National League guru Vic Deverill noted that the title was collected by a team of New Zealand born boys who, with an average age of 23, was the youngest ever squad to collect the title. Wrote Deverill: "No longer can soccer in New Zealand be labelled a game for imports."

Truman has taken time to reflect on the impact of the league, its players and, of course, its coaches.

"The New Zealand National Soccer league began in the autumn of 1970. It was a brave venture putting in place a league similar in concept to the National League structures of the United Kingdom, which was part of the heritage of so many players in the new league. No other sport in New Zealand had a national league and the arrival of a club team from the other end of the country to play a game against the locals created lively interest.

"I arrived in the country to take up the position of national director of coaching in May of 1970 and watched my first game in the National League between Stop Out and Eastern Suburbs at Te Whiti Park. The local supporters completely surrounded the pitch - two deep in places. The atmosphere was alive and vibrant which such close proximity to the action engendered. Alex Milne was the playmaker for Stop Out - a typical little Scottish player with the ability to control the ball closely and turn quickly. He was continually searching for the opportunity to deliver a long, high pass to Geoff Brand, the central striker, who looked like a figure out of a Western film with his bow legs and ambling gait. Geoff was a leading goalscorer who caused defences lots of problems with his ability to get on the end of crosses and power the ball into the net with his head. He later represented New Zealand in 1973 World Cup playoffs in Australia and gained national publicity in his career as the "sherrif of Taumarunui". In the Eastern Suburbs team Colin Latimour and John Staines were the central defensive pairing - as competent a duo as any combination through the 1970s with Mal Bland on the flank, one of the many English imported players who were to excite the league with their talents through its early years. Eastern Suburbs won the game 4-0 but missed out on the title to Blockhouse Bay on goal difference alone. The game was fast and exciting and good entertainment.

"After 20 years of existence the overall quality of the teams in the league has not changed greatly. In the early 1970s Mount Wellington, Christchurch United, Eastern Suburbs and Blockhouse Bay were the teams to beat, with others making up the numbers. Some teams remain in the memory not so much for their success but because of their type of play and the individuals that made them spark. Hungaria from Wellington were a fine example with the Polyanszky brothers, Andy and Lotsy, giving the game some light-hearted moments and real class. Steve Nemet and Julius Beck were other talented Hungarians to grace the league and provide it with some cosmopolitan flavour. The Otago side Caversham, under the control of player- coach Derek Daniels, was always good value and particularly hard to beat at home.

"Some of the National League players of the 70s have now entered into the folklore of the game. Wild Bill Fleming, from Dunedin, moving his portly frame at the back of the defence on a pair of twinkling feet was a sight to savour - as was Alan Marley of Christchurch United and New Brighton, twisting and turning like a leaping salmon to get a strike on goal. Dave Taylor, now the coach of Mount Wellington, together with Graham Storer, were a couple of buccaneering kiwis who played hard both on and off the pitch and never failed to give 110 per cent effort. Eric Lesbirel, David Farron and Grant McCulloch were a trio of poms who made Diamond of Wellington sparkle enough in 1976 to win a National League. Terry Conley, Ken France and Brian Hardman were Englishmen who helped give

Christchurch some of its memorable league titles.

"Mount Wellington have made the greatest impact on the league since 1970. Ken Armstrong, the old England international and Chelsea player was the coach in the first few years league. He was a great coach who had given much to the development of the New Zealand game. His Mount Wellington teams were full of international players - mainly from Auckland and mainly NZ born. Two of his sons, Brian and Ron, were in the side together with such notables as Brian Turner, Dave Taylor and Bill de Graaf. Ron Armstrong has been a fine example to young Kiwi players. He has always played hard but fairly with his very educated left foot being aided by his ability to read play. The Mount probably reached the zenith of their National League performances when John Houghton was the coach. John was a former international and Mount Wellington player and while he had limited experience when he took over he was blessed with a squad dripping with experience. He got the best out of it, creating an educated style of play which always pleased. Under John's tenure the Mount was always in the running for either a title or a Cup.

"The whole of New Zealand soccer owes a major debt to Gisborne City over the years. They had led the charge in the importation of good players as well as promoting and creating interest in the game. Alan Vest was the coach in the early 1970s and he brought in Maurice Tillotson and Kevin Fallon who later went on to make their mark in the game through their ability as coaches. Fallon brought to Gisborne its golden years developing in the process a number of youthful Kiwi players and importing a number of talented performers, notably Colin Walker. Together with John Adshead, Fallon shared in the fairytale adventure which culminated in New Zealand's participation in the 1982 World Cup finals.The National League had been the breeding ground for the successful NZ squad together with a topping of experience in the Australian National League for a number of the players. A strong group played a critical role in the national team's passage into the finals. Steve Wooddin, an import who had experience with Dunedin City and Christchurch, scored goals with a lethal left foot. Brian Turner, Steve Sumner and Ricki Herbert all found the net on vital occasions but the goals of the campaign came from Grant Turner and Wynton Rufer. Grant Turner was a Hutt Valley product who was groomed for stardom by Fallon at Gisborne and Rufer came through Wellington Diamond United via Rongotai College. Turner was devastating around the goal with both head and feet. He was willing to intimidate opponents with his aggression and bravery. Rufer was and is the ultimate individual talent. Apart from his mentor and aid Jim McMillan, few coaches have tried to influence his play. Rufer is a beautiful athlete possessing power, speed and amazing skills. He is without doubt the most successful player to come out of New Zealand, yet he only spent two seasons in the National League helping Wellington United to win the 1981 National League and then moving to Miramar Rangers the following season. Since then Rufer has been a major player on the world soccer stage first with Grasshoppers in the Swiss League and lately with Werder Bremen in the Bundesliga.

"Of great satisfaction was the winning of the 1985 National League with a squad of Kiwi-born players proving that the era of imported players was moving on. The DB Wellington Diamond United team was made up of players from the area apart from the captain Ross Durant who learned his football in Christchurch and keeper Don Finlayson, who came to Wellington from Auckland via Gisborne City. There will always be room in the National League for the top class imports like Trevor Brooking, the former Auckland and West Ham player, Peter Mendham and John Fashanu, who spent a season at Miramar and in 1990 was scoring goals for the English first division club Wimbledon. It has been evident in recent years that players from the lower divisions of the English league cease to make any real impact on our game and that maybe we should look to other countries to provide players who can give another dimension to our play.

"The late 1980s has seen the emergence of new names in the upper echelon of the National League. Napier City Rovers, Mount Maunganui and Waitakere from West Auckland have arrived to challenge the established Mount Wellington and Christchurch United who continue to be consistent challengers for national honours.

"As we move into the 1990s our own National League is now competing with other national competitions which are well promoted and very keen to compete for the spectator's dollar. Under the austere economic climate which prevailed in the early 1990s it was proving to be very difficult to secure enough sponsorship to cover the travel costs of clubs that were competing. The national trend of lowering match receipts was hardly helping. Soccer's National League has served its sport well and given the enthusiastic supporter a feat of happy memories. The concept of the best players from around the country playing each other through the season is a good one and it provides the national squad with a ready made selection system, not to mention its value as a testing ground of the ability of each player. However, there is the need for a change. Maybe we should try playing our National League on summer evenings, just as they do in Australia? Maybe we should make our teams provincial rather than club based in order to meet costs and make sure the best players are selected? Whatever is done it is appropriate at this time to celebrate the successful existence of a National League for 20 years and give thanks for the many happy memories and experiences that have taken place.

"As a suitable tailpiece I would suggest a panel of coaches who would, if they were able, provide a fabulous evening of soccer entertainment. How about this lot: - Ken Armstrong (Mount Wellington), Tom McNab (Eastern Suburbs), Bert Ormond (Blockhouse Bay), Don Jones (North Shore), Derek Daniels (Dunedin City), Ian Johnston (Diamond), Kevin Fallon (Gisborne City), John Adshead (Manurewa), Roger Wilkinson (Napier City) and Terry Conley (Christchurch United)."

One should also add Barrie Truman.

RUSSELL GRAY

Russell Gray has turned the field of New Zealand soccer writing into his own in recent years. He was born in Manchester and his devotion to Man United can best be gauged by the amount of early morning Sunday phone calls that head back home. Gray arrived here in 1970 as a computer operator at Wellington's *Dominion* newspaper. He coached at junior and senior level at Lower Hutt and gained a New Zealand Coaching Badge. He joined the *Dominion* sports department in 1979 and it can now be revealed that he really was Rhetorical Russ, the mystery writer who kept New Zealand referees entertained through the pages of their own official organ. Gray covered the 1982 World Cup finals and in 1989 and then 1990 he was named the Soccer Writer of the Year by that organisation's own body. With his close contacts in the game, Gray has been the "unofficial agent" for many a player and coach seeking a change. Gray, never appeared afraid to rock the boat, has his own thoughts on the media in football.

"New Zealand soccer and the media enjoy a unique relationship. Nowhere in the world is there easier access to the people who administer the game for those who pass on information to that most important group of all ... the supporter or potential supporter.

"It is the same with the players. The New Zealand media have no trouble communicating with those who play the game, unlike many countries overseas where cheque book journalism is the norm."

The special relationship, possible only in such a small country, was perhaps demonstrated best at the 1982 World Cup finals in Spain.

"Overseas reporters couldn't believe their eyes when the New Zealand press contingent were given the use of a mini bus supplied by FIFA to ferry officials around.

"That NZFA chairman Charlie Dempsey gave the media accompanying the team unlimited access to transport, including a driver, even rated a paragraph or two in the English newspapers.

"Such co-operation makes it all the more surprising that the media are still treated with suspicion by many administrators once they become national councillors.

"A decade ago media representatives were allowed into council meetings. Dempsey stopped that because he felt too many councillors were playing to the gallery. Perhaps he had a point, but football has suffered through the press being excluded from meetings over the past few years.

"Those who pay at the gate on a Saturday and Sunday, or coach the kids' teams who will provide the players of the future, are entitled to know what is going on. Those at the grass roots of football are the ones who pay the expenses for the ones at the top.

"New Zealand officials don't have the same problems as their overseas counterparts. On the whole the media representatives they deal with are honest and ethical.

"It isn't the Kiwi way of reporting to distort the facts. As far as I know quotes are reported accurately, though sometimes things that are said do look different in print next morning!

"There have been few sensation seekers among those given the task of reporting on the New Zealand soccer scene. Certainly at times views expressed may have annoyed officials but there is rarely malice involved.

"In a small country like New Zealand a reporter who deliberately misquotes would soon become an outcast and unable to do his or her job properly.

"New Zealand media have made a favourable impression on overseas visitors. Former England and Liverpool great Kevin Keegan, West Ham favourite Trevor Brooking, Wimbledon hard man John Fashanu and former England manager Sir Alf Ramsey have all expressed pleasant surprise at the way the Kiwi media operates."

England manager Graham Taylor visited with Watford in 1982 and made as favourable an impression on the New Zealand press as it did on him. Building on that foundation Taylor always co-operated with Kiwis in the following years.

This isn't an attempt to paint a lily-white picture of the media. They are human and mistakes have been made, but current chairman Warwick Gendall, his predecessor Dempsey and those before them would dread getting up in a morning and reading the papers, or listening to the radio, much more were they living elsewhere.

Probably the one thing a reporter hates hearing more than anything else is a coach or administrator saying "You should be writing for the good of the game". Journalists are hired by their employers to report the facts. If soccer gets itself in a mess that is their problem.

Overall though those who report the game invariably look on the bright side. There are few full time soccer reporters in New Zealand. Most are enthusiastic part-timers who really do have the code's welfare at heart.

It isn't a bad life though when a reporter is assigned to the soccer round, especially if he likes the game anyway.

I was fortunate in taking up full-time soccer reporting at a time when the game in this country was about to enter its most exciting era.

The first international match I reported on was New Zealand's 4-0 win over Mexico at Auckland's Bill McKinlay Park in 1980.

The result took everyone by surprise and at the after-match function it seemed everyone was trying to find excuses for the New Zealand win. The Mexicans may not have travelled well. It probably wasn't their top team. Maybe it was just a fluke.

That was the problem with New Zealand soccer. It didn't believe in itself. Dempsey and coaches John

Adshead and Kevin Fallon changed all that.

It would be fair to say that every media representative covering soccer in New Zealand has had a scrap with Dempsey at one time or another, but no one could ever doubt that he was the one who lit the touch paper to launch New Zealand soccer to its highest point.

Adshead was a reporter's dream, always ready with a quote, and Fallon would talk soccer all night long, though he didn't suffer fools gladly.

The exciting months which followed are well-documented elsewhere in this publication and it was exciting to be, in a small way, part of it.

Sharing the celebrations after a fine win, or discussing - almost till dawn in the bar of the Vacation Hotel - where things went wrong was an experience never to be forgotten.

It was the same in Spain and getting the chance to watch and talk to some of the best players in the world was, to a reporter, almost the same as a player being on the same pitch as these legendary names.

At the All Whites opening game against Scotland the legendary Portuguese striker Eusebio, who had one of the hardest shots in soccer, was seated alongside some of the New Zealand media and was full of admiration for Steve Wooddin's left foot!

One of the most satisfying things in life is to sit back and let the mind wander over what has gone before. Everyone involved with soccer will have their own memories. Some good, some disappointing.

From a personal point of view there are two moments which stand out above all else. Grant Turner's header which made sure of the World Cup win over Australia in Sydney is one. The other is Wynton Rufer's superb strike that made sure the All Whites would break new ground and go to the World Cup finals.

Much has been written and spoken about Turner's powerful header, a goal which ended Australia's World Cup hopes, cost Socceroo coach Rudi Gutendorf his job, took the Kiwis out of the shadow of their at times arrogant neighbours, and left the Australian media shell-shocked.

It was a magnificent goal celebrated wildly not only by New Zealanders at the Sydney Cricket Ground, but also by thousands of others gathered round television sets at home.

It was the same with Rufer's goal in Singapore which set the All Whites on the road to a 2-1 win over China and finally into the finals after 15 matches.

It was 2am in New Zealand when the match finished but few people had thought about bed as they sat transfixed in front of television screens as the final drama unfolded.

After Rufer had put the All Whites 2-0 up China stormed back, scored once, and put the New Zealanders under intense pressure. In households throughout New Zealand people - normally used to watching All Black victories - were on the edge of their seats. Surely the All Whites couldn't be denied after what they had been through.

They weren't, and while those at home went to bed the players celebrated in Singapore.

New Zealand soccer isn't just about the campaign however. There are other things which immediately come to mind.

The dignified manner in which Mount Wellington coach John Houghton accepted his team's shock cup final loss to North Shore at Papakura in 1979 is something I'll never forget. Some coaches today could learn from the way Houghton fronted up within minutes of his world crashing around him.

Too often coaches - glad of publicity when things are going well - duck for cover when the tide turns.

The picture of dejected Miramar stalwart Peter Chote leaving the Newtown Park pitch, accompanied by his young son, after his team had drawn 0-0 with Christchurch and consequently missed out on the 1986 National League title, is also etched into the memory.

Chote typified the perfect team player. Never missing a game, always giving 100 per cent, Chote looked likely to at least pick up a medal for all his efforts untill Miramar failed to score against Christchurch.

Football is emotional and it was never more apparent than that day.

Fortunes can change quickly too, typified by the elation on the faces of the Napier City Rovers players in the euphoria of their 1985 Chatham Cup final win over hot favourites North Shore, and then the look of disbelief on those same faces just days later when they were relegated from the National League after a playoff series in Palmerston North.

The enthusiasm of coaches like Fallon, Roger Wilkinson and Eddie Edge, the coolness of Barrie Truman as he guided unfashionable Wellington Diamond United to league titles, the gentlemanly manner of Ian Marshall ... the list could go on and on.

There are other things which come to mind which don't throw such a good light on a code which struggles against rugby and rugby league for column inches in newspapers and air time on radio.

The endless debate when John Adshead departed from the All Whites coaching position soon after the World Cup kept soccer in the headlines for the wrong reason. Did he jump or was he pushed was the question on everyone's lips. Only Adshead and Dempsey knew the real story and their versions differed.

The seemingly endless tinkering over the years with the National League did soccer no favours. One minute it was three up three down, then there were playoffs, and finally came the sad day when the administrators decided that the competition should be by invitation only with participants decided by councillors rather than on the playing pitch.

Eventually they saw the error of their ways but again those on the outside looking in were bewildered.

It was the same when someone had the brainwave that the Chatham Cup final should be played over two legs. Thank goodness things are now back to normal, but for three years New Zealand was the only country in the world where the early rounds of a cup competition were sudden death and the final played home and away.

CHARLIE DEMPSEY

Of all the modern day football officials no one person has created more debate than Charles John Dempsey CBE. He excited passion among followers up and down the country. Charlie Dempsey didn't tread the middle of the road. Once he took over at the NZFA he was clearly the boss. He gave his task 100 per cent and thought less of those who did not hold the same attitude. Clashes, some of them public, followed but for all that Dempsey was for the majority of New Zealanders one of soccer's most public figures. His devotion to the sport here has rarely been bettered. Dempsey came to New Zealand from Glasgow. In 1988 he was awarded life membership of the New Zealand Football Association and became the code's president. He served 24 years as an NZFA councillor, six as chairman. He had 18 years on the Auckland Football Association, 11 as chairman. He was joint tours director from the mid 60s up to and beyond the Spanish World Cup. He was in 1990 the head of Oceania, the organisation which is recognised by FIFA as looking after the interests of football in our part of the world. As 1991 approaches the Dempsey's enthusiasm for football has hardly dimmed as he regularly jets around the world. Here he reminisces not only about Oceania but some of his contemporaries around the administrative table.

"My 30 years of association with the NZFA go back to the days when Jim Kershaw was chairman.

At that particular time there was a councillor by the name of Otto Hilton who was obviously the inspirational "go-getter" behind him. Many schemes were put forward by Hilton to generate not only interest in football but also to improve standards. These were early days and communication was not as good as it is today, so everything was by letter. Many of the ideas from Otto Hilton were a bit mind-boggling. For example he had visions of a stadium for soccer where everyone supporting the game either bought a brick for the building of the stands or a square foot or so many square-inches of the football field. This was, in my opinion, the beginning of sponsorship thinking and the entrepreneurial approach to our game. I believe that at that particular time New Zealand was not ready, everything was on a strictly amateur basis.

"Jim Kershaw retired from the chair and unfortunately Otto Hilton died and that was the end of the great thrust that Messrs Kershaw and Hilton visualised for the game.

"After this Bob Smith became chairman and his vision was to promote youth football. He played a youth team against Sing Tao of Hong Kong which lost 8-6. The team had young players such as Mark Burgess (who was a great cricketer) and George Lamont. Many boys in that particular team played for New Zealand in the years to come. Bob Smith died and so was not chairman for any great length of time, but he did sow the seeds of youth football. A year after Smith died, the under-23s did well in a match against a Scotland XI at Wellington despite losing 7-2.

Otto Hilton . . . Charlie Dempsey called him New Zealand's first entrepreneur of soccer. Tony Hilton collection

"Next came Jack Cowie and Auckland at this particular period was bringing in many international teams. Jack's vision was of a Joint Tours Committee of New Zealand and Auckland and I became Director of this Committee for close on 20 years. It was during Jack's era we entered the first World Cup. I recall that when I proposed we enter the World Cup everyone was concerned about the great cost but we still entered in 1969. We decided to play both games in Israel, with all expenses paid, and played a game in Western Australia on the way back for $US2000. I can remember Jack Cowie handing me a large sum of American dollars and I didn't know whether the money eventually went to Auckland or New Zealand! I believe it was divided equally.

"I think this was an exciting era of entering World Cups. I took charge of the 1974 World Cup with Barrie Truman as coach, and I was still Director of Tours for the 1978 World Cup with Wally Hughes as coach and also the 1982 World Cup under John Adshead and Kevin Fallon. I believe it was through World Cups that New Zealand emerged into international football. The arguments that I put forward at the time were that we had to show ourselves internationally. So the emergence of New Zealand into the international scene owed much to the joint tours planning by Auckland and New Zealand.

"Oceania has had a very chequered career, but New Zealand has played a major part in its survival. It was started off by an Australian called Jim Bayutti who engineered an agreement in Tokyo at the 1964 FIFA Congress that a Confederation was required for the South Pacific countries. In 1964 I met with Bayutti who discussed Oceania. It was formed in 1966 by FIFA and at the inaugural meeting for the election of officers in February, 1967 Jack Cowie and a fellow called Dempsey represented New Zealand. First we had Sir William Walkley as President and he was succeeded by Vic Tuting of Australia. Little of importance occurred early though we had a few Oceania tournaments in which the Sir William Walkley Cup was up for competition.

"Unfortunately in 1974 Australia decided to join Asia. At this time it was left to three countries in Oceania - Papua New Guinea, Fiji and New Zealand to carry the can. It was felt that if Australia did get into Asia it would be the demise of Oceania, but Ahmed Hussain, Sashi Singh and I met at the Chevron Hilton after a meeting with the Australian Soccer Federation when we had released them and demanded and got US$1000 from them which would allow us to pay our fares and expenses for going to such a meeting. We elected Jack Cowie president and I became Secretary and Sashi Singh Treasurer.

"At my next meeting at FIFA I had a discussion with Sir Stanley Rous, the then President of FIFA, and asked his advice on what to do. Do we disband Oceania and also endeavour to join Asia? His advice was that Australia would not get into Asia as they were not looked upon as an Asian nation, and that there were enough problems in Asia at that time. He said 'Never give away your Confederation, it is something to hold on to. If you do relinquish it you may never get another opportunity of having a Confederation.'

Jack Cowie ensured that we retained Oceania. He attended a FIFA meeting with all the presidents when Dr Havelange became World President and he spoke on Oceania with all the other Confederation Presidents. Australia was rejected by Asia, and the President of Australia, who had gone to Teheran to the Asian Congress, was not allowed to stay and was in fact escorted from the meeting. Australia were then in limbo. Oceania had three countries and when we went to the FIFA Congress as a Confederation and met with the President of FIFA, the Australian contingent would be standing outside and they would request permission to attend. It was pretty much stalemate.

"Australia agreed to come back in in 1978 provided that their President, Sir Arthur George, got the presidency of Oceania. This was agreed to as they were the most important nation in the South Pacific. It wasn't the greatest relationship at the early stages as there appeared to be a situation of 'them and us'. When I say 'them and us' I mean Australia and the other Oceania countries.

"The presidency changed in 1982. I moved from secretary to become President, and we had what I consider an adjusting period where we gradually started to grow from three nations to four, from four to five, and today we have eight full nations with two at the present moment hoping to become full members in 1992, these being Tonga and New Caledonia.

"Today Oceania has a committee structure - which includes coaching, refereeing, administration and development. New Zealand has been playing a major part in Oceania including a very, very major part in its growth. I believe that New Zealand Football has something to be very proud of in its dedication to the Confederation and to the island countries of the Pacific. New Zealand must be given credit for the part it has played in the Oceania Confederation. It has remained steadfast in its direction, and the New Zealand Executive and Council have been very supportive over the 25 years of its existence."

NEW ZEALAND WOMEN'S FA

New Zealand Women's Soccer was actually born of necessity in 1975, originating when the Northern Women's F.A. (later to be called Auckland Women's F.A.) received a letter in early 1975, inviting a New Zealand women's team to enter a tournament to contest the Asian Cup to take place later in that year.

This letter set in motion the birth of the New Zealand Women's Football Association, because under the tournament rules, the New Zealand team could only enter if women had their own national association to administer the sport.

For quite some time there had been discussions between a number of provincial associations aimed at forming such a body, but even as late as eight weeks before the Asian Cup was to start, a fair amount of debate was still going on as to how it could be organised.

The Northern and Wellington associations were not seeing eye to eye at the time, so the New Zealand WFA was formed between Canterbury and Northern and Wellington was given a provisional affiliation which satisfied the needs of the Asian competition rules.

Nevertheless, the seeds of a national body had been sown and it was decided at the inaugural Annual General Meeting held on the 11th of October 1975 that a national tournament would be contested each year between affiliated provincial associations, the initial one to take place in July 1976 in Christchurch.

As time went by the New Zealand WFA was accepted as a bona fide affiliate of the New Zealand Football Association and in July 1979 became an Incorporated Society.

During that initial AGM the first Executive Committee was elected and is only right that they should be named for posterity. In the chair was Dudley Vosser of Wellington, his deputy, from Canterbury, was Ron Griffiths. Auckland's Jan Innes became secretary-treasurer while other members were Mrs P. Mack (Auckland), Mrs P. Webster (Southland) and Mrs J. Hobbs (Auckland).

The history books will record that New Zealand, coached by Dave Farrington, took its international debut by storm, winning the Asian Cup undefeated, beating Hong Kong, Malaysia and Australia before meeting Thailand in the final which they won, 3-1 goals scored by Marilyn Marshall (2) and Nora Heatherington.

However when it came to reporting the fact that the Kiwis had won such a prestigious international competition, the media of the day generally dwelt on the story of the final's aftermath when local gamblers, who having lost thousands of dollars by betting on Thailand, vented their spleens on the New Zealanders by pelting them with rubbish and assorted fruits as they did their lap of honour.

Not that it stopped there, as they left the Happy Valley Stadium their bus was the target of stones and beer cans, causing the players to lie flat on the floor of the vehicle until they reached their hotel.

Four years were to lapse before New Zealand entered again the international arena, this time it was for a three test tournament against Australia in Sydney and Brisbane with Dave Farrington again in control of the national side.

The first test in Sydney ended in a 2-2 draw but with many of the large contingent of NSW-based Kiwis, who actually outnumbered the hosts, questioning the neutrality of the local officials.

A referee was hardly needed in the second test as New Zealand kayoed their opponents with comparative ease 1-0, it should have been 2-0 as they had a goal disallowed although it was patently obvious that the Aussie goalie had carried the ball well over her goalline when attempting a save, a decision which again infuriated the many Kiwi fans at the match. The third test in Brisbane was a different story, injuries were gradually taking their toll and playing their third game in eight days and this time in a temperature of 33 degrees caused manifold problems for the Kiwis who had left their country still in the final throes of winter.

The final result was 1-0 to Australia, but New Zealand was not disgraced and came home knowing that with just the slightest piece of luck and they would have been the only name on the new Air New Zealand Trans-Tasman Cup.

1980 saw the Australians return the compliment by playing three tests in Auckland, Wellington and Christchurch. In the first test at Auckland University, New Zealand, now coached by Ken Armstrong who had taken on the job at very short notice, started off with a hiss and a roar by leading 3-0 at halftime. Whether it was over-confidence or lack

The 1979 New Zealand Women's Tasman Cup team. Back row: Ingrid Hall, Rosie Ah Wong, Debbie Leonidas, Tina Faichnie, Debbie Pullen, Julie Jerram, Maria Te Huia. Middle row: Julie Hogg, Nora Watkins, Jo Nicholson, Maureen Jacobson, Zay Cooper, Kathy Hall. Front row: Eric-Pritchard, Marilyn Marshall, Jenny Parkin, Dave Farrington.

of concentration New Zealand blew a wonderful chance of putting their opponents behind the eight ball when they gave away their handsome lead and tied the game at 3-3.

Wellington was the next venue and here again neither side was able to assert their authority, this time the result was 1-1. The Aussies had all their own way in Christchurch for the final game. The result was 3-2 for the visitors but New Zealand was flattered as the Australians, but for poor finishing in front of goal, should have scored more.

The Green and Golds again crossed the Tasman in 1981 for a one-off test which was played at Gallagher Park in Manurewa and again went home as winners, this time by 2 goals to 1.

However this result gave New Zealand the perfect motivation for their first ever World Women's Invitational Tournament to be played in Chinese-Taipei. Now coached by Dave Boardman, the girls did New Zealand proud winning six out of eight games, drawing one and losing to West Germany in the final. This second placing giving New Zealand a good standing in the world ranking of women's soccer.

1982 saw China-Taipei visit us for two tests, one each in New Plymouth and Hamilton. In this series New Zealand more than met their match and the Taiwanese went home joyfully after winning both games.

About this time the Oceania Women's Football Confederation was formed with representatives from Australia, Papua-New Guinea, Fiji, the New ZealandFA and the New Zealand WFA joining the steering committee.

The inaugural Oceania cup took place in New Caledonia during 1983, but only four teams, Australia, Fiji, New Caledonia and New Zealand took part in the tournament and it was not much of a surprise when New Zealand, who were selected and managed by Roy Cox and coached by Albert Evans, proved yet again that they play better off-shore, seeing off the Australians 3-2 in the final.

New ground was broken when an under-21 New Zealand side, managed and coached by Roy Cox and Jeff Coulshed respectively, went to New Caledonia in 1984 for a series of three tests winning all three games and scoring 14 times without reply.

Later that year New Zealand travelled again to China-Taipei for another World women's' Invitational Tournament but this time could not match their 1981 effort and ended up in fourth place as opposed to their runner-up position three years earlier.

1985 was a blank year for New Zealand as far as international games were concerned and it was at Easter 1986 before they played again, this time in Christchurch for the second Oceania Cup. Chinese-Taipei was now regarded as part of Oceania so it was obvious that it was going to be a difficult task to retain the trophy.

Because Papua-New Guinea had withdrawn from the tournament, New Zealand was able to field two teams, Roy Cox and Sandy Davie being in control of the national side with Fred Simpson and Jeff Coulshed taking charge of the B team.

The New Zealand performances were well below par and indeed in the third and fourth place final the senior home side could only beat their B team subordinates on penalties after extra time in a year that can best be forgotten. Chinese-Taipei went on to win the cup after beating Australia 4-1, so New Zealand still had not won a test against overseas opposition on their own soil.

A team from Western Samoa visited New Zealand in early December 1987 and played three games against a New Zealand side who were in preparation for their third trip to Chinese-Taipei for the World women's Invitational Tournament. Quite rightly, the New Zealand WFA did not regard the Western Samoans, who were in their embryonic stages as a team in the international theatre, as serious enough competition, and didn't give full representative recognition to the games which New Zealand won 10-0, 15-0 and 11-0.

For the Taiwan tournament selector-manager Roy Cox was assisted by John Adshead of Spain 1982 fame, but after losing three out of seven games New Zealand could only manage fourth place yet again. The failure of New Zealand in this tournament caused much heated debate around the country, the general feeling being that the national selection for Chinese-Taipei was not the strongest available. The upshot of all this furore was that in early 1988 the New Zealand WFA advertised for a new coach which eventually saw the return of the popular Dave Boardman who had not long since returned from a coaching and playing contract in the United Arab Emirates.

Like 1985, 1988 was also a barren year as far as the international scene went, so it was Easter 1989 before New Zealand went into battle again. Boardman had selected his squad after a week long coaching clinic in Hamilton aided by his recently appointed assistant, former New Zealand player Nora Watkins, the first woman appointed to such a position.

New Zealand left these shores for the third Oceania Cup in Brisbane in very high spirits, prepared to take on all and sundry the instant they met on the park. And so it proved to be, the leading Australian side The Greens were given a comprehensive soccer lesson before going down 2-0.

Chinese-Taipei were next and they too were treated in similar fashion, New Zealand winning this game 1-0, then it was Papua New Guinea's turn as they were walloped 5-0. The other Australian team The Golds, showing far more guts and determination than their seniors, still could not stem the Kiwi tide and succumbed 2-0.

In the final against Chinese-Taipei, mother nature dealt the New Zealanders a mean blow, sending rain in monsoon proportions for an entire 24 hours before the kick-off. Playing in water to a depth of five to eight centimetres, the match became, what was variously labelled as an aquatic farce, a lottery and quite a few stronger epithets. Despite showing the better performance, indeed most of the play took place in the Taiwanese half, New Zealand could not manage to find the net and when the odd goal did come, sadly it went to Chinese-Taipei on one of their very rare sorties into the Kiwi half.

Try as they might, New Zealand could not equalise despite peppering the Taiwanese goal with shot after shot which were somehow kept out of the net by the most desperate defending which eventually saw Taiwan take the Oceania Cup for the second time.

September and October saw the emergence of a New Zealand under-19 team, coached by Jeff Coulshed and former national player Kathy Hall, which played two tests in Wellington and Hamilton respectively, against a similar age selection from Australia. The New Zealand babes served their country well, winning both matches 2-0 and 1-0, at long last the hoodoo on New Zealand home performances had been well and truly laid to rest.

Many of the New Zealand's women soccer players have pulled a New Zealand shirt over their heads in other sports. On the softball scene Kathy Hall, Raewyn Hall, Debbie Leonidas, Leslie King, Cinnamon Chaney and Marilyn Marshall are all double internationals and in the case of Marilyn Marshall, she is arguably the only person in New Zealand to have captained New Zealand in two different sports. Other doubles have been won by Lorraine Taylor and Wendy Sharpe who have played touch rugby while Anne Smith has represented her country at volleyball. While mentioning Wendy Sharpe, she, along with Maureen Jacobson holds the record for the most games played for New Zealand, both having earned 37 caps in 1990.

Maureen Jacobson is the most celebrated of the New Zealand players as she is the only soccer player from these shores who has played soccer full-time. She spent a season with Helsinki's HJK in Finland and these days she is playing for top English team Millwall Lionesses. If New Zealand put up some very good performances in the World Cup it is likely that Jacobson will not be the only person to play for monetary reward, as the Italian and French club sides are always on the lookout for new talent and are quite prepared to put up the money to attract players into their domestic programmes.

Brisbane 1989 and Amanda Crawford scores her first goal for New Zealand against Chinese Taipei. Eric Pritchard collection

Wendy Sharpe

Maureen Jacobson

THE CHATHAM CUP

It all stemmed from the kindness that New Zealanders showed to a bunch of English naval types. The vessel was the HMS Chatham. The entire crew was of a mind to give New Zealand a football cup in return for all the goodwill that had been shown to them during the period of the ship's sojourn in New Zealand. So on December 14, 1922, Council members of the New Zealand Football Association received an invitation to visit HMS Chatham for the purpose of receiving a cup. Valued at 150 pounds the trophy was in immediate evidence on the arrival of the members of the Association and the entire ship's company paraded for the presentation. The Cup was handed over by Captain Pickett to Sir Charles Skerret. Rules were drafted on similar lines to England's own FA Cup competition and New Zealand football had its own blue riband.

Since that time the Chatham Cup has been the most sought after trophy in New Zealand football. It has been a worthy competition - one that has stood the test of time and a host of attempted changes that have at times tended to demean, or if you prefer cheapen, a quite excellent competition. The Cup has had its series of high points. Some finals have been stirring to say the least. Maybe three stand out more than others. The 1972 struggle between Mt Wellington and Christchurch United which began with a 4 -4 draw and was eventually won by Christchurch after no fewer than three matches. Earlier in 1962 there had been the success of the Hamilton Club Technical over the doughty Cup fighters Northern of Otago, the first time that the Cup had been away from the four main centres, and then there was the romance of 1949 when the Petone Settlers, a Wellington-based third division side, won the Cup – this triumph before a crowd reported to be in excess of 12,000. In the '60s and '70s no one person dominated the Cup more than Ken Armstrong, a former English professional who was involved with no fewer than nine Cup final sides as player and player-coach. Half a dozen times he came away with the goods. This then is the Chatham Cup and with the help of ageing newspaper files, club histories, vintage programmes and that most worthy of football publications, the *New Zealand Soccer Annual*, all those stirring Chatham Cup finals are recalled.

1923: Seacliff (Otago) 4
YMCA (Wellington) 0

There could be no doubt as to the superiority of the men from Dunedin over the Wellington based team. For Seacliff the final was its only match in the competition. One other team had entered from the South Island but in the end had not taken part. YMCA, on the other hand, had travelled to Nelson to beat the local Wanderers and the week before YMCA had beaten easily a team from Huntly. The match was played on a Monday, in Wellington and on the hallowed turf of not the Basin Reserve, soon to be the regular final venue, but Athletic Park. For much of the early spell YMCA had its share of possession and a match report notes that a number of good chances went begging. YMCA "made matters merry for a time keeping up a prolonged attack" but the honour of the first Cup final goal scored just before halftime went to the Seacliff centre forward Hooper. Right wing McDougall had a second goal for the Otago side early enough from a tight angle in the second spell. Seacliff now kept the pressure on and were rewarded late in the game through a second McDougall goal and within a minute of the third goal Seacliff had a fourth through the efforts of first half scorer Hooper. Seacliff had its moment of history. The side were to make another three Cup finals. They would lose in the next two and another in 1929. But on this Monday at Athletic Park they were clearly the best team on the field.

The 1923 Chatham Cup victor, Seacliff. Back row: Walters, Taylor, Howie Kerr (trainer). Second row: Dr Lee, G. Anderson, McKechie, Rivers, McDougall, Ellwood. Front row: Rogers, Hooper, J. Anderson, Burns, Murray. In front: Baxter, Hanlin. NZFA collection

1924: Harbour Board (Auckland) 3
Seacliff (Otago) 1

The second final was played in wet but good conditions at Athletic Park. The game was a severe test for both teams with the better staying powers of the Auckland side coming out on top after the match had gone to an extra half hour of play. The only goal in the first spell came the way of the Cup holders after intense pressure towards the end of the first half and was scored by Simmons. Harbour Board levelled in the second spell when Palmer scored with his head. In extra time Margison scored from a corner and after ends had been changed he put the issue beyond doubt with his second strike.

1925: YMCA (Wellington) 3
Seacliff (Otago) 2

Revenge is sweet. YMCA may have missed out in the first final but they gained success in the third which was now played at Newtown Park. Again the match went to extra time after 90 minutes had ended with the score at 2-2. The game was described by the *Dominion* as entertaining with a number of chances. Dempster put the home side ahead. Hanlin levelled and it was 1-1 at halftime. Seacliff led for the first time through Hooper but YMCA were on level terms before the finish, again through Dempster. Hanley grabbed the winner in the first quarter of extra time.

1926: Sunnyside (Canterbury) 4
North Shore (Auckland) 2

A match of some difference if only for the fact that a Canterbury side was in the final for the first time and North Shore, so far the most successful side in Cup history, made its first final appearance albeit a losing one. The game was notable if only for the fact that it was the first final to be played on the Basin Reserve. Six goals were scored but the *Dominion* noted that both teams missed opportunities through poor shooting. Sunnyside were in front after seven minutes via Pickering. Trotter scored a second before North Shore pulled one back when Hipkins goaled. That was the halftime score. In the second spell Trotter scored his second for a 3-1 Sunnyside lead and then ran through the Shore defence for an "exciting" goal which gave the South Islanders a

YMCA - 1925 Chatham Cup winner: Back row: H.J. Steptoe, H. Prince, W. Pearson, C. Trott, L.W. McGirr, W. Hodge (selector). Second row: A. Ward (secretary), W. Nicolle, C.S. Dempster, G. Campbell (captain), C. Ballard, D. Halley, B. Cohen. In front: F. Eaton, N. McArthur.

three goal cushion and Trotter the first Cup final hat-trick. Woolley pulled one back for Shore but by then it was too late.

1927: Ponsonby (Auckland) 3
Northern (Otago) 2

The area Ponsonby is best known as one of Auckland's leading rugby clubs. This day at Wellington's Newtown Park, on a good ground with a strong wind blowing, the *Dominion* described the game as the poorest Chatham Cup final so far played. Hunter opened the scoring for Ponsonby. They were soon two up via Innes. Adshead, with the help of the wind, made it 3-0 at halftime. Northern had the advantage of the elements in the second spell and first McDowell and then McTavish scored. Northern made solid attempts to try and secure an equalising goal but the Ponsonby defence held firm.

1928: Petone (Wellington) 1
Northern (Otago) 0

It was the first season of senior football for Petone in the Wellington A division and they did reasonably well in that grade but it was in the Chatham Cup the team made its mark. Marist was beaten in the local final 3-2. Petone beat Hastings United 3-1 at Palmerston North in the provincial final before going to Auckland and overcoming YMCA 2-1 in the North Island final. Petone were to complain to the Wellington Football Association. It cost 96 pounds to head north. From the gate receipts Petone were to receive just one pound. A crowd of 6000 was at the Basin Reserve to endure a strong southerly. The only goal of the game came from Farquhar, from as far out as 30 metres, halfway through the first half, though there is a suggestion in some match reports that a deflection by Northern's Scoular helped the ball through his own goal. Goalkeeper Peter McVean, centre half Jim Campbell and centre forward Andy Leslie were to the fore in a game which the *New Zealand Referee* described Petone as being a shade fortunate to take the win.

1929: Tramways (Auckland) 4
Seacliff (Otago) 0

Seacliff made its fourth appearance in a final but sadly it was to be a losing one. The game was at the Basin Reserve and on this occasion there was only one team in the picture. Dell opened the scoring with a volley. Seacliff almost levelled and it was 1-0 at halftime. The second half belonged to the Aucklanders. After five minutes of the second half a shot by Lewis took a deflection from the Seacliff keeper. Spencer got the third and also the fourth and Seacliff's misery was completed when the ref failed to spot a Tramways hand ball in the penalty area.

1930: Petone (Wellington) 2
Western (Canterbury) 1

The *Dominion* called it something like the real game. Petone had a solid core of the 1928 side, Leslie, Campbell and McVean, and with the wind at their backs they led by a first half goal to Craig. As the rain fell and conditions became more difficult Western were able to level through Falloon, then the South Islanders had a goal disallowed before Dodd grabbed the winner in the last few minutes to make his side the first dual winner of the trophy. The *New Zealand Referee* noted that Petone had the worst of the conditions when playing into the wind in the second spell. A year later Petone missed out on the Chatham Cup but won the Wellington championship.

1931: Tramurewa (Auckland) 5
Nomads (Canterbury) 2

Tramurewa were a combination of the old Tramways club and the newer Manurewa side. The game was again at the Basin Reserve and after a moderate scoreless first half the thrills followed in the second. Wilson scored first for Nomads and within two minutes the South Islanders were two up when Goode netted. Bell scored for the Auckland team and then the same player levelled. Nomads were under severe pressure but held out until fulltime was called. Tramurewa turned the screws, as first Donaldson and then Spong scored in the first period of extra time and Bell was able to complete a hat-trick in the second before time was called.

1932: Marist (Wellington) 5
Millerton All Blacks (Buller) 0

A soccer team described as All Blacks, hailing from Buller, made two Cup final appearances in successive years but both times went home empty handed. Before a crowd of 5000 at the Basin Reserve the *Dominion* called it the best exhibition of football seen in Wellington during the course of the season. Marist played into the wind in the first spell. After 25 minutes Marshment bundled the keeper and ball into the net for the first goal. Barton had a second before halftime. Jim Kershaw, later to be the NZFA chairman, scored the third direct from a corner and after Millerton had missed a penalty Barton scored twice more to complete his hat-trick.

1933: Ponsonby (Auckland) 2
Millerton All Blacks (Buller) 1

At least this time it was closer. Back at the Basin Reserve the *Dominion* called it another good match and labelled the team from the West Coast as unlucky. They dominated the first half but could not score. Jepson put the Aucklanders 1-0 in front after 20 minutes and it came after the northerners' first serious attack. Innes had a second before halftime after a defensive blunder. Pollock scored from a corner in the second half. Late in the game Millerton had a chance from an indirect free-kick in the box for steps but the Ponsonby defence held on .

1934: Thistle (Auckland) 2
Thistle (Canterbury) 1

In the presence of a large gathering at the Basin Reserve two teams with the same name met to celebrate a Celtic Occasion. The highland dancers and the pipe bands were ever present in the "Scottish" Cup final which the *Dominion* rated the "best since the first final in 1923". Christchurch scored first from an Adam header and then had a goal disallowed for offside but still led 1-0 at the break. G. Sutherland put the ball into his own net when attempting to clear under pressure in the second and the winner came five minutes from time through Wood.

1935: Hospital (Wellington) 3
Western (Canterbury) 1

More than 5000 people were present at the Basin Reserve to see a local team win. From the football point of view, Western were regarded by the *Dominion*'s correspondent as the more polished side but it had no answer to the "more robust methods" of the Hospital side. After just nine minutes McGrory scored from a rebound to put Hospital one up. A minute before half time Woods made it 2-0. In the second spell Gibb put the Wellington side three up from the penalty spot after 15 minutes and the game was now gone from Western who did gather some crumbs when Gordon scored close to time.

1936:Western (Canterbury) 3
Thistle (Auckland) 2

Western has a proud history in the Chatham Cup. They made no fewer than nine final appearances and won three times, sharing the trophy once. This time at the Basin Reserve they played grand football in greasy conditions and still had enough mettle to stall off a late bid by the northern side who had won two years earlier. White scored first for Western from the penalty spot after 12 minutes. He had a second after 27 minutes. Thistle had its share of misfortune. They had a goal scored through Angus after a free kick and then had another disallowed in the first half. With the score still 2-1 at the interval mark, they were down to 10 men through injury in the opening minute of the second half. Still Angus was able to equalise but Ellis put the South Islanders back in front. The injured player Williamson came back in the last few hectic minutes but Western held on for its first Cup success.

1937: NO COMPETITION

Why? The visit of the English amateur team was given as the main reason, but it seems that in a busy season the NZFA deemed that the final would be played in the South Island for the first time. When entries closed only 12 teams were in and there was not one from Auckland. Could it be that first the England tour, no Auckland entries and then a heavy domestic programme were too much?
Let the debate continue.

1938: Waterside (Wellington) 4
Mosgiel (Otago) 0

In front of a good crowd and in wet conditions Waterside adapted much better to the conditions than Mosgiel. The Otago team had the wind in the first half but were behind after six minutes when

Ward netted. That was the halftime score and Mosgiel were always going to be in some trouble facing the elements in the second stanza. Walker had goaled again soon after the break. Ward had set up the second and he laid on a pass for Janes who had the third in the 17th minute. Walker's tap in completed the scoring.

1939: Waterside (Wellington) 4
Western (Canterbury) 2

The match was described as a willing fixture. Waterside, adequate at both front and back, took full advantage of its goal scoring chances. They led 1-0, 2-1 and 3-1 at halftime. Western pulled one goal back and halfway through the second half Waterside regained its two goal advantage. McCarthy (2), Longbottom and Ward scored for the winners and Galbraith and Smith for the Christchurch-based side.

1940: Waterside (Wellington) 6
Mosgiel (Otago) 2

Waterside became the first team to complete a hat-trick of Chatham Cup wins when it scored at the Basin Reserve in front of 8000 people. The final was described as the most one-sided in the history of the competition. Yet Mosgiel led after two minutes through Sharpe. After 25 minutes Ward levelled. Walker put the Wharfies in front and within two minutes McCarthy's effort had established a two goal lead. McCarthy soon had a second and at 4-1 at halftime the game was safe. In the second spell McCarthy completed his hat-trick and then sent over the corner which Longbottom headed home for a sixth goal. Just on fulltime Rogers scored a second for Mosgiel.

1941-1944: NO COMPETITION

War years.

1945: Western (Canterbury) 4
Marist (Wellington) 3

In a most exciting Basin Reserve final Western came out on top. The first goal came after 17 minutes and went to Irvine for Marist. That was the only goal of the first spell. After 20 minutes of the second spell Marist were two up. Western fought back, scored and then levelled a minute before the end. In extra time Gordon of Western was credited with an own goal before his side fought back to level at 3-3. The winning goal came to Western via the penalty spot. Scorers for Western were Smith, whose hat-tick included the penalty, and Dowker. Price was the other scorer for Marist.

1946: Marist (Wellington) 2
Technical (Canterbury) 1

In front of 8000 spectators Marist held control for much of the game. Earlier its young team had won the Junior National Cup 3-1, also against Technical. Thomas scored in the first half for Technical but Hatchard levelled after 35 minutes. It was 1-1 at halftime and the winner came from Bell a few minutes after the resumption and Marist generally held command from that point.

1947: Waterside (Wellington) 2
Technical (Canterbury) 1

Technical were back again but they could not prevent Waterside from making its Cup final record four from four. The South Islanders held balance for the first 20 minutes. It was 0-0 at halftime. In the second spell, Bell scored first for Waterside, Bailey levelled for Technical before the game went into extra time. Janes scored the winner in extra time.

1948: Technical (Canterbury) 2
Waterside (Wellington) 0

This year it was third time lucky for the Christchurch side. Waterside were beaten for the first time in a Cup final and deservedly so the *Dominion* recorded. In front of a crowd of 3000 at the Basin Reserve there was no score at halftime and in the second spell the disappointing Waterside team went under to goals from first O'Malley and then Thomas. The Canterbury side has made it to seven Cup finals but this day in 1948 was the only time they won.

1949: Petone (Wellington) 1
Northern (Otago) 0

Of all the Chatham Cup finals ever played this one ranks among the more memorable ones. Not for the quality of the football on the day but for the utter magic of the occasion. There was never a collection of Cup winners quite like the Petone Settlers. Earlier in the year Andy Leslie, Peter McVean and Jim Campbell, all veterans of the 1928-30 Cup winning sides, had headed to the immigrants hostel at Fort Dorset in Wellington to hunt possible Petone players. The Wellington FA looked at the new outfit and deemed that it would play for the second A championship, in effect the capital's third division. Leslie, assisted by Campbell, coached the side and McVean was the manager. Petone's first Cup game against a first A side brought a 7-1 win over Marist. Railways and Institute followed as victims and then Petone went on to meet Waterside, the beaten national finalists the previous year, in the local final. It took two games and two 1-1 draws before a lone corner took the Settlers to Ohakea and a 2-0 provincial final success. Still the battle for Petone was not done. Eden hosted them at Blandford Park and after 90 minutes normal time and 40 minutes of extra time bad light stopped play with the scoreline locked at 2-2. The replay was held in Wellington and Petone won 4-0. The crowd at that Basin Reserve final was estimated to be 12,000. The first half may have been sluggish but in the second Petone were on top and according to match reports had the visitors on the backfoot. When David McKissock's shot was blocked by the excellent keeper Jim Stephenson, Wally Hewitt tucked the rebound away. There was one anxious moment when Petone keeper Ben Savage saved a penalty. McKissock, Hewitt, Leslie and Campbell all became life members of the club which these days is a feeder for the Hutt Valley United National League side.

1950: Eden (Auckland) 3
Technical (Canterbury) 2

Petone AFC - 1949 Chatham Cup winner. Back row: A. Leslie (coach), C. Jackson (committee), H. Pryor (secretary), P. McVean (manager), F. Body (committee), J. Robertson (committee). Second row: R. Williamson, J. Russell, W. Hewitt, J. Blundell, A. Sage, D. Parker. Front row: R. Walker, B. Savage, R. Reid, D. McKissock (captain), F. Peters, J. Jakens, F. Naylor. In front: M. Jackson (mascot), J. Gale.

In front of a crowd of 11,000 Eden brought the Cup north to Auckland for the first time in 16 years, however the game did go to extra time. Thomas scored first for Technical, but Eden were level when Goddard's shot struck a defender on the way into the net. After a torrid second half Jakens put Eden ahead but before the end Technical were level via Smith. Technical missed a penalty in the first period of extra time and the winner came to the northerners when Brewer turned Goddard's high cross into the net.

1951: Eastern Suburbs (Auckland) 5
Northern (Otago) 1

Eastern Suburbs have a proud record in the Chatham Cup with five wins. The first of them came in a most emphatic manner against those gallant men from Dunedin. The score was 1-1 at halftime. Northern, doing well, led through McFarlane but winger Frogley was able to level before the break. Frogley had to leave the field injured in the second spell but Suburbs went ahead for the first time through King and this advantage was further increased through Anderson. King, a solid centre forward, scored the last two to complete a hat-trick. In the Eastern Suburbs team that day was a blonde wing-half named John Jakens. It was his third winning medal in three successive finals for three different teams. He had played for Petone in 1949 and then for Eden in 1950.

1952: Cup Shared
North Shore (Auckland) 1
Western (Canterbury) 1

A strange result this, to say the least, between two grand cup final teams. This was before the days of penalty shootouts and replays. In extra time both goals and corners counted and with the very last kick of the game a defender's miskick screwed over the North Shore line and Western had won a corner. There wasn't even time for the kick to be taken. Western had saved its bacon and the trophy, for the only time in its history, was shared - six months in each port. It was a deserved result.

Joseph had scored for Western in the first half and though Western were in complete control the Shore keeper Gordon kept the Auckland team in the game. With 10 minutes to run Moyle was able to level. Shore had its corner in the first period of extra time and for a very long time they looked likely to hang on.

1953: Eastern Suburbs (Auckland) 4
Northern (Otago) 3

A thrilling fixture in every sense. Old-timers agreed that few finals carried such tension with it . Northern had led in after a few moments when a keeping error let a soft shot roll into the net. The game was end to end but the *Dominion* in its summary agreed that Eastern Suburbs were worthy winners with the decider coming late in the game. Injuries to two key players, Gibsy and Fleet, had not helped the cause of Eastern Suburbs. King (2), Fleet and Anderson scored for the winners while McFarlane (2) and Boardman netted for Northern.

1954: Onehunga (Auckland) 1
Western (Canterbury) 0

Displaying a defence that bordered on the ferocious Onehunga collected the Cup for the first time with a win over final veterans Western. Western had 70 per cent of the play but sadly for them McCullough scored the only goal 16 minutes from time. The northern side had plenty to thank its splendid keeper Holt for after the game.

1955: Western (Canterbury) 6
Eastern Suburbs (Auckland) 2

If Western felt aggrieved after their two previous final appearances they certainly made Eastern Suburbs suffer. Wellington's Basin Reserve was at its worst this day and Suburbs, after winning the toss, gave Western first use of the gale. By halftime the game was a good as over with Western ahead 4-0. After 11 minutes Western were two up through White and Davis. Saunderson, a capable and tricky winger, netted his first of three and Ralph got the fourth from a corner. Anderson scored from Suburbs in the second half and King pulled the deficit back to two before Saunderson grabbed the last two into the wind and gave Western what was at that stage a South Island winning record.

NZFA representative team to Australia, 1954. Back row: D.H. Charlton, W.A. Smith, W. Westerveld, A.H. Preston, F.J. Benge. Second row: K. Olley, M.B. Best, R.A. King, R.F. Morrison, G.W. Barker. Front row: T.M. Cooper, J. Kershaw (manager), J.C. Hunter (captain), W.W. Carruthers (assistant manager), P.P. Traynor. In front: K.C. Gibson, R.G. Hiddlestone, C. Steele.

1956: Stop Out (Wellington) 4
Shamrock (Canterbury) 1

Stop Out climaxed its silver jubilee year with a good win in the Chatham Cup. The Hutt side had been area champions for two years and they were worthy holders. Sharp had the first goal from a header and then Sergeant scored a splendid second before Schryvers and then Benge completed the scoring for the winners. Fields earned a consolation goal for the South Islanders.

1957: Seatoun (Wellington) 3
Technical (Christchurch) 1

Seatoun in the late '50s were a most competent side who left nothing to chance and in this case they were able to score a solid win over the Canterbury-based side. They were faster on the ball and with an on average age of 24 were hailed as one of the youngest teams to win the Chatham Cup. They scored after 13 minutes when Goddard netted a rebound. Two minutes later Logan put them two ahead. McAnulty pulled one back for the South Islanders before the halftime break, but Logan had a second just after and Seatoun were comfortably home.

1958: Seatoun (Wellington) 7
Christchurch City (Canterbury) 1

Seatoun won the Chatham Cup for the second year in succession and set a record it would hold outright until Christchurch United hit Rotorua City for seven in the 1989 final. This triumph was very much a one man show. Seatoun had a team loaded with talent. Bert Hiddlestone in goal, Gordon McClelland, Ron Kearns and the wingers Neil Kerr, who came on as a replacement for injured international skipper Keith Gibson, and Bill Logan. But on this August day at the Basin Reserve it was very much the John Donovan show. The tidy centre forward scored six goals, taking full advantage of great service from the wings. Seatoun played into a Wellington northerly and were in front through Donovan after 37 minutes and then in the last three minutes of the half three goals were scored. Donovan had a second and Wright put Seatoun three up before Giblet stole in for the South Islanders with the last kick of the first half. In the second Donovan scored four goals, three with his head, and the club - and Donovan - were in the record books.

1959: Northern (Otago) 3
North Shore (Auckland) 2

It took the Northern Club of Dunedin six attempts before they finally got their hands on the Chatham Cup. The win was a triumph for club stalwarts goalkeeper Jim Stephenson, who had his first winning medal after four attempts, and winger Bill Berry. The North Shore challenge was the first New Zealand Cup final experience for Ken Armstrong but on this occasion his class was not enough to see Shore through. The game had a sensational opening and after four minutes the scoreline was 1-1. Two minutes from the start Shore's replacement fullback Schmidt put through his own goal. Middleton's header levelled matters. Berry put Northern in front just before the break and five minutes after Little stretched the lead to two. Armstrong's skill set Foulkes up shortly before the finish but Northern had the will and the strength to hold on.

1960: North Shore (Auckland) 5
Technical (Canterbury) 3

A year later and Shore were back again, this time coming out on top. Nothing could have been more appropriate. The club was in the midst of its 75th Jubilee year and much of the triumph was due to the skill of Ken Armstrong who this time made sure of his Cup medal. It was 1-1 at halftime, but Shore quickly moved to a 3-1 lead. Technical pulled one back but Shore scored twice which only left Technical the last of the six second half goals. Lowndes (2), Ryan, Paterson and Armstrong scored for the winners, Charlton, Campbell and Vermen netted for the Christchurch side.

1961: Northern (Otago) 2
North Shore (Auckland) 0

North Shore made it to the final for the third year in succession but the history of 1959 repeated itself when Northern won for a second time. The South Island team's centre forward, Little, opened the scoring after 34 minutes of the first spell. Two minutes from the end he set up the chance for Campbell to net a second and a game full of excitement and spectacle was done. With Ken Armstrong subdued this time Northern were able to exert more control, but it must be said that North Shore were not favoured with the best of luck.

1962: Technical (Hamilton) 4
Northern (Otago) 1

The best final of the '60s. One of the very best Chatham Cup finals of all time. The win by a

Technical Hamilton 4, Northern Otago 1. A Chatham Cup final that is regarded as one of the very best with Hamilton keeper Mel Clarke in action here one of the many heroes. Tony Hilton collection

Hamilton team was the first scored by what was then regarded in football circles as a minor province. Northern were the Cup holders. They had won two years before that and were the holders as well of the Rothmans Trophy. But this time they came up against a side full of determination and a goalkeeper of rare courage in Mel Clarke. That man Little was on hand to head an opening goal after four minutes but the cheering had barely died when Nevison levelled. Jones put Technical in front seven minutes later and halftime was still nine minutes away when Jones scored his second and created a 3-1 halftime scoreline. Seven minutes after halftime Nevison scored his second, an act which may have taken much of the fire from the game but it never dampened the Technical spirit and the enthusiastic support from a Wellington crowd.

1963: North Shore (Auckland) 3
Nomads (Canterbury) 1

North Shore completed a treble for the season when they comfortably beat the team from Christchurch. The club team had won the Auckland first division and the Rothmans tournament. Only in the final 10 minutes of the first spell did Nomads look like causing any real bother. Winger Oden had the first half goal and a Maynard header 10 minutes into the second spell extended the lead. When Oden had a second goal Shore were able to ease down a cog and inside the last five minutes the hard-toiling Muirson was able to put the Christchurch team on the scoreboard. In the success of North Shore the continuing influence of Ken Armstrong was ever present. Muirson aside, no player did more for the Nomads cause than Derek Chapman, a quite gallant goalkeeper.

1964: Mt Roskill (Auckland) 3
Technical (Otago) 1

More understanding in defence and more determination on attack were the major qualities that won the Chatham Cup for Mt Roskill for the first time. They also made the ideal start when Cozens netted within 90 seconds. After 24 minutes the scorer lobbed a ball into the goalmouth which the keeper misjudged and Darby netted to give Roskill a 2-0 halftime lead. The game was put beyond Technical's reach in the 73rd minute when Darby scored, though 10 minutes from the end Porteous pulled a goal back.

1965: Eastern Suburbs (Auckland) 4
St Kilda (Otago) 1

Ten years earlier Eastern Suburbs had come to the Basin Reserve and faced a howling southerly. They gave Christchurch opponents Western first use of the wind and after being four goals behind at the break they never had a chance. Skipper Tom McNab was never faced with the same decision. St Kilda's Alec Caldwell opted to use the wind. Suburbs was a class act. With Ken Armstrong now the player-coach, Paul Rennell, Trevor Pugh, Ray Mears and local hero John Wrathall in the side, St Kilda were always going to find the going tough. Suburbs soaked up the pressure in the first 25 minutes before Pugh put the Aucklanders in front. St Kilda squared through Slinn but 1-1 at halftime was never going to be enough for St Kilda. Legg's header had Suburbs in front 12 minutes after the break. St Kilda threatened for a few moments but when Barnes topped a goalkick straight at Pugh, the centre forward hit it straight back into the net. A couple of minutes later the scoring was done when Wrathall's shot was blocked and Legg scored his second.

1966: Miramar Rangers (Wellington) 1
Western (Canterbury) 0

The Auckland connection was missing this time. Eastern Suburbs went out to Ponsonby who in turn were eliminated in the semis to the Wellington club Miramar Rangers. St Kilda made it to the semifinals but after drawing 1-1 with the grand Christchurch club Western went under 3-1 in the semi-final. As a National League club these days Miramar Rangers have a grand history and they were a proud close-knit unit whose results were built on true grit. With the country's leading goalkeeper Peter Whiting and the talented Taylor brothers Les and Barry, Miramar Rangers were always hard to beat. The final was hardly vintage and match reports suggest that Western played most of the football. Whiting had a nightmare first few minutes. Headed by the talented Terry Haydon Western pushed forward. Whiting saw a shot cleared off the line, was bundled into the net only to see referee Les Coffman rule out the goal and then a header struck an upright. Whiting and Rangers recovered and with centre half Jack Barton in fine form the first 45 minutes had nothing to show. The only goal came soon after halftime. Goalkeeper David Smith could not hold on to Stef Billing's header and Les Taylor's shot went in via an upright. Both sides had further chances but Rangers had enough left to hold on for what was regarded as a streaky win.

1967: North Shore United (Auckland) 2
Christchurch United (Canterbury) 1

The Ken Armstrong connection was to the fore yet again. He was the coach as North Shore won the Cup for the fifth time in its history. But it was a tight run thing. North Shore had anything but an easy path to the final with close wins that included a 2-1 win over holders Miramar Rangers. In the final they met Christchurch United, a team primarily established for the National League which was getting closer to reality. Christchurch was led by Gwyn Evans and it had the best of the Christchurch players like Terry Haydon, who did so well in the final the previous year, Tony Gowans and the highly talented Franco Madrussen. There seems little doubt that City should have won. They had the ball in the net, hit the post and missed open goals but with keeper Dennis Mack having the game of his life it was 0-0 at halftime. Shortly after halftime the deadlock was broken when Billy Rimmer netted for Shore but soon after Haydon levelled. Christchurch seemed to have the winning of the game when club stalwart Don Jones dumped Haydon in the penalty area. Tony Gowans shot wide. Time was up when Les Taylor, the scorer of the winning goal 12 months earlier and now

If only the ball had stayed on the line, but it didn't much to the delight of number nine, Les Taylor of Miramar Rangers. The only goal of the final. Barry Smith collection

based in Auckland, set up a chance which Shore skipper Ian Campbell cracked home. By all accounts few Chatham Cup finals have been so rich in entertainment.

1968: Eastern Suburbs (Auckland) 2
Technical (Canterbury) 0

Eastern Suburbs were back to win the Chatham Cup for the fourth time. Ken Armstrong wasn't there but headed by the astute McNab they were always too good for a brave South Island side and this time John Wrathall scored both the goals as for once a Cup final went to script amidst the cry for an open draw. Eastern Suburbs beat the Palmerston North side Thistle 6-2 in the semi-final. In previous rounds Thistle had dumped the best Wellington sides Western Suburbs and Miramar Rangers from the competition. Technical included none other than current national coach Ian Marshall in goal.

1969: Eastern Suburbs (Auckland) 2
New Brighton (Canterbury) 0

The 1969 Chatham Cup final was probably overshadowed by a couple of factors. Graham Moore became the first full time secretary of the New Zealand Football Association and just as important was the decision to kick off the National League in 1970. One of those teams was Eastern Suburbs who won the Cup for the second time in succession. New Brighton were a brave side who had a very capable goalkeeper in Derek Phillips and never at any stage did they give the contest away. Yet another Cup final goal by John Wrathall and a second by the talented Bill de Graaf gave Suburbs a decisive win. It was the fifth win for Suburbs all in the space of 18 years. The 1969 final saw the end of an era. Gillette, it was announced, would sponsor the 1970 Cup and for the first time since 1923 the zone inter-island plan would be scrapped. National League teams were given exemption from the early rounds. The last 16 would be drawn on a zonal basis and, at last, the final eight went into an open draw.

1970: Western Suburbs (Wellington) 2
Blockhouse Bay (Auckland) 2

Drama. Sheer stark, drama. Western Suburbs will still be wondering how the Chatham Cup escaped them. From the 14 games that the very first National

League produced they managed just one win and one draw. They were clearly bottom and grateful that no relegation clause existed; in fact the size of the league was increased from eight to 10 teams for 1971. Blockhouse Bay were the first National League champions, yet with seven minutes to play at the Basin Reserve, Wayne Huntley's brace of goals looked like causing a major boil-over. Then in the space of three minutes Colin Shaw scored twice for the Bay, the second from a retaken penalty. Into extra time first Bay dominated and then Suburbs, urged on by the home crowd at the Basin Reserve, hit the woodwork twice. After 120 minutes no further goals had been scored. The antiquated rule that the number of corners gained would win the Cup had been scrapped and a replay ordered. The players drew breath and headed to Auckland for the first ever replay and to play the first final outside Wellington.

Blockhouse Bay 3
Western Suburbs 2

Still the action goes on. Blockhouse Bay score first. Suburbs level. Bay in front 2-1, it goes back to 2-2. Time is running out when Suburbs find the net only to be called back for offside. Extra time is looking likely when the Bay grab the winner. Clive Campbell, Iain Ormond and Shaw score for the winners with Bruce Baker and Barry Humphrieys scoring for Suburbs. For excitement the final has everything.

1971: Western Suburbs (Wellington) 3
Wellington City (Wellington) 2

No one would have begrudged Western Suburbs success and again there followed in 1971 much of the drama that had followed the fortunes of the club in 1970. Suburbs had finished bottom of the National League again and this time were relegated on goal difference from Wellington City who were an amalgamation of Miramar Rangers and the colourful Hungaria. In time Miramar Rangers would come back again in their own right. Wellington City, who were lost from the National League at the end of the 1975 season, has since become part of the Wellington United setup. But on this day the wind howled as two teams from the same centre met in a final which went to prove that an open draw was here at last. Suburbs veterans Dave Wallace and Alan Jeffrey scored in normal time and those efforts were countered by goals from Paul Cameron and Julius Beck. Extra time was up on the clock when Barry Humphreys lobbed a centre downfield. The ball bounced and the wind hurled it into the net. There was not even time for the game to be restarted.

1972: Mt Wellington (Auckland) 4
Christchurch United (Canterbury) 4

It took three matches before Christchurch United won its first major trophy, the 1972 Chatham Cup. They were coached by Terry Conley and Mt Wellington by Ken Armstrong. First at the Basin Reserve, then at English Park in Christchurch and finally at Newmarket Park in Auckland no quarter was given as the marathon final tie went on. Playing with the wind United should have been given the lead early when keeper Kevin Curtin appeared to carry the ball back across his line from a Vic Pollard cross. United appealed for a goal. The referee gave a free kick to the northerners. United that day had Graham Dacombe and he scored all of United's goals. He goaled first. Ron Armstrong netted twice from the spot before Dacombe levelled. That was before halftime. Brian Turner put Mt Wellington ahead in the second half but it was 3-3 at fulltime. Dacombe scored in extra time but striker Earle Thomas confirmed a replay with a late goal. The Basin fixture is regarded as one of the best, a classic final, rich in sensation and a continuing high standard of football.

Christchurch United 1
Mt Wellington 1

This was the first time that a final had been played outside the North Island but sadly the football tended to suffer after the pulsating first tie. Dennis Tindall scored for the Mount who had the better of the second game. Ian Park squared the match which was still deadlocked after 120 minutes.

Mt Wellington 1
Christchurch United 2

The second replay was held at Newmarket Park and after three matches in the space of three weeks United made sure that Alan Park's first half goal was supplemented by Alan Marley's strike in the second. Ron Armstrong scored from penalty spot and there was some real feeling three minutes from the end when David Taylor, who had come on as a substitute, had a goal ruled out. At least Mt Wellington had a first National League success to celebrate.

1973: Mt Wellington (Auckland) 3
North Shore United (Auckland) 0

In the 1960s and early 70s no one person dominated the Chatham Cup quite like Ken Armstrong. The former Chelsea professional and England international arrived in 1957. He went for a time to Gisborne before going to Auckland and spells with North Shore, Eastern Suburbs and Mt Wellington. In 1973 Mt Wellington made up for the loss in the previous year's marathon by scoring an emphatic win over their Auckland City rivals in the first all Northern final played at Newmarket Park. Armstrong had led North Shore to three wins, Eastern Suburbs to two and this was the sixth success. As well, three other Armstrong-inspired sides had made the finals. Mt Wellington had been tipped to win the National League for a second time but mixed results allowed Christchurch United to win that in a canter. As Cup holder, Christchurch had gone out in the third round with its first ever loss to Blockhouse Bay since the start of the National League. North Shore's goalkeeper David Turner had to be subbed early and Shore were always under pressure in the final. Dave Taylor scored twice and John Houghton once. Shore missed a penalty as well as hitting the woodwork twice.

1974: Christchurch United (Canterbury) 2
Wellington Diamond United (Wellington) 0

Mt Wellington won both the Air New Zealand

Western Suburbs AFC - 1971 Chatham Cup winner. Back row: K. Barton, A. Polyanszky, J.P. Young, T. Heptinstall, W.D. Huntley, B.G. Humphreys. Second row: T.A. Davie, G.L. Paddison, N.R.S. Palmer, B.P. Baker, N.R.P. Cattle. Front row: I. Kiss (coach), D.J. McBride (manager), A.F. Jeffery (vice-captain), D.R. Wallace (captain), G.E. Smith (president). Absent: B. Nicoll, J. Conner. Barry Smith collection

pre-season tournament and the National League quite easily in the end. Yet in the Cup they went out to Eastern Suburbs 8-7 on a penalty shootout after the scores had been level 1-1 after extra time. Wellington Diamond United had to go to a replay in the semi-finals to beat Gisborne City 2-1, while Christchurch United beat North Shore 2-1, also after extra time. Wellington Diamond United, in its current state, has only played in one final and it had to go to Christchurch and the first final at Queen Elizabeth II Park, the venue earlier in the year of the Commonwealth Games. Rain didn't help. One thousand gallons of water had to be drained from the surface to make the pitch playable. Ian Park scored the first goal and the industrious Brian Hardman put the issue beyond doubt some four minutes before the finish. Given the wet surface the game was of good value.

1975: Christchurch United (Canterbury) 4 Blockhouse Bay (Auckland) 2

Success in the National League for Christchurch was backed up by another excellent win in the Lion Chatham Cup. Despite the success of the Christchurch final 12 months earlier, this one went back to Auckland. With Iain Ormond in grand touch, Blockhouse were so much on top early that Mike Farac and Colin Shaw were able to score in the first 10 minutes. Norman Moran pulled one back for the Cup holders soon after and while the Bay had its chance to clinch the Cup, the South Islanders became dominant and 10 minutes from time Gary Lake turned a cross into his own net. In extra time Christchurch turned its superiority into goals, first from Kevin Mulgrew and then from sub Mark McNaughton. One of the features of the competition was the first round exit of a number of teams and the gallant bid by Lower Hutt City who, helped by a favourable draw, made it to the last eight before going under 3-2 to the eventual Cup winners.

1976: Christchurch United (Canterbury) 4 Eastern Suburbs (Auckland) 0

Christchurch had a miserable year in the League. It finished third from bottom but for all that it equalled a record set by Waterside, winning three

Cups in succession. Three players, Graham Griffiths, Brian Hardman and Ian Park, played in all the games and Terry Conley was the guiding light. For Eastern Suburbs it was the team's seventh Cup final and the second loss, ironically by four goals and at the feet of a Christchurch-based team. The game was played at Queen Elizabeth II Park. After an early own goal from Tom Bell, Norman Moran added two and Mark McNaughton one as the home side scored easily. Christchurch had a much tougher time in the semi-final against old foes and 1975 finalists Blockhouse Bay, getting home 1-0 in a replay following a 2-2 draw.

1977: Nelson United (Nelson) 1
Mt Wellington (Auckland) 0

At the start of the season Gisborne City had been replaced in the National League by Nelson United. Nelson were determined to make a good fist of things. At some stage of the final Ken Cresswell, Peter Simonsen and Keith Mackay all made the field. So did Kevin Fallon. The 1977 Chatham Cup was his first major New Zealand title and it was the first time since Hamilton in 1962 that the Chatham Cup had gone away from a main centre. Mt Wellington had the home advantage. The only goal came via the penalty spot 15 minutes into the second half. Referee John Perkins adjudged that the Mount's Stewart Carruthers had fouled David Powdrell and John Enoka happily converted the spot kick for the game's only goal.

1978: Manurewa (Auckland) 1
Nelson United (Nelson) 0

Kevin Fallon had gone from Nelson 12 months later but Nelson just about went all the way in the defence of their title. For the first time the now Adidas Chatham Cup went to the provinces and the final was contested at Nelson's Trafalgar Park. Nelson had done well to finish mid-table. But they were beaten by a team that completed a double. Manurewa had won Northern League and promotion into the National League for the following season. Manurewa had Frank Van Hattum, David Bright and Mark Armstrong in the side and the coach was none other than John Adshead who was later, along with Fallon, to go on the long and rewarding road to Spain with the national team. The only goal came after 12 minutes when Nelson Keeper Owen Nuttridge failed to hold a David Bright cross and Bruce Foster headed the home winner. Back in 1931 Manurewa had been part of an Auckland amalgamation Tramurewa (Manurewa and Tramways) which won the 1931 Cup and then went out of existence. In winning the Cup Manurewa beat Blockhouse Bay and Mt Wellington and then beat National League winners Christchurch United 2-0 in the Adidas Challenge Trophy fixture.

1979: North Shore United (Auckland) 2
Mt Wellington (Wellington) 1

The 1980 issue of the *New Zealand Soccer Annual* called it "The Cup that Slipped Away". A landslide removed much of the area at Newmarket Park. After a number of offers had been made the final was played at Papakura's McLennan Park. As comfortable winners of the National League, Mt Wellington were the favourites but prior to the final Brian Turner's slip of the tongue resulted in a sending off, a suspension and the lost chance of playing in a fourth Cup final. Then, five minutes into the second half, Stewart Carruthers was sent from the field and though the Mount tried to hang on Iain Ormond was brought down in the box and scored from the spot. Earlier John Leijh (Mt Wellington) and Keith Hobbs had been successful. Don Jones coached North Shore to a fifth Chatham Cup win which equalled the record of Eastern Suburbs as the most successful side in the history of the competition.

1980: Mt Wellington (Auckland) 2
Dunedin City (Dunedin) 0

For the first time since St Kilda in 1965, a Dunedin team was in the Cup final. The occasion returned to an old home, Wellington's Basin Reserve, but the match sadly was not one of the better ones. At least Stewart Carruthers had a welcome change of fortune. He headed home from a Clive Campbell corner after 11 minutes and then skillful Billy McClure added the second. In earlier rounds Northern League title winners Takapuna City had beaten both Hamilton and Blockhouse Bay participants in the National League before going out to Dunedin 2-0 in the semi-final.

1981: Dunedin City (Dunedin) 3
Mt Wellington (Auckland) 1

It took 20 years and Northern's win over North Shore but this time the Chatham Cup went back South to Dunedin. For just the second time in the history of the competition the same finalists met and as had happened in 1947 and 1948 the final result was reversed. When Billy McClure beat Jimmy Taylor from the penalty spot Mount looked on the way to a further Cup win. However two excellent goals from the very talented Mike Glubb and a third from Terry Wilson were fine rewards for a committed Dunedin effort. Stop Out, now back in the Central League, caused the upsets by beating Nelson, Miramar and Wellington Diamond United before losing 3-1 at Dunedin in the semi-finals.

1982: Mt Wellington (Auckland) 1
Miramar Rangers (Wellington) 0

Mt Wellington made its seventh final appearance in 11 years and won for the fourth time, courtesy of a Keith Nelson goal after 107 minutes of play. The win completed a double for the Aucklanders. Miramar, in its first Cup final since 1966, fought hard for a home-town success. They were well served in goal by Barry Pickering and also sent to England to bring back from Norwich City John Fashanu who earlier had played half a dozen games for Miramar. The move went very close to coming off as they contained Mt Wellington for much of the time and then looked very sharp on the breaks. It wasn't a bad final.

1983: Gisborne City (Gisborne) 2
Mt Wellington (Auckland) 2

For the fifth time in succession Mt Wellington were in a Chatham Cup final. But this time they had

Keith Nelson (Mt Wellington) scores the goal that sank Miramar in the 1982 Chatham Cup final. Mt Wellington won the match 1-0.

to travel to Gisborne's home ground at Childers Road. There was plenty of pre-match fun in the build-up and the final was as tough as it could have been . Fred de Jong put the Mount ahead after 14 minutes only for Colin Walker to square seven minutes later. Spurred on by a partisan crowd, Walker scored after 64 minutes and there were barely two minutes left when Keith Nelson made it 2-2. The Mount had the better of the extra time period but Gisborne held on and it was up to Bill McKinlay Park to give the Mount the home town advantage.

Mt Wellington 2
Gisborne City 0

The match was always going the Mount's way. At home and under lights they led after 29 minutes when John Price scored from the penalty spot. And just as it had happened in the first final a Keith Nelson special two minutes before the end gave the Mount a comfortable margin and the Chatham Cup for the fourth time.

1984: Manurewa (Auckland) 2
Gisborne City (Gisborne) 1

Gisborne City made it into the Chatham Cup final for a second time. It had been a fine season for the club which had won the National League. With Colin Walker, Grant Turner and Ken Cresswell in the side Gisborne were the favourites at Mt Smart Stadium but they were foiled first by Steve Sumner and then by Rudi Feitsma. Injury had kept Sumner down to just four National League appearances and coach Maurice Tillotson took a gamble by playing him. His faith was not misplaced. First in the 11th minute and then in the 28th Sumner scored to take Manurewa to a 2-0 lead. Gisborne City came back. A Walker goal was disallowed and Feitsma made two exceptional saves - first from Walker and then Turner. Cresswell gave Gisborne hope with a goal 11 minutes before the finish but Manurewa held on to record a third Chatham Cup win.

1985: Napier City Rovers (Napier) 3
North Shore United (Auckland) 1

A mismatch? Far from it. North Shore battling for top honours, Napier clearly rooted at the bottom of the National League, and soon to lose for a short time only its National League status. Yet for the seventh time in something like nine years the final favourites went out the back door. This day at Mt Smart Napier made all the running. By halftime Harry Clarke and the talented Paul Halford had sent the underdogs out to a 2-0 advantage. Barry Weymouth pulled one back for North Shore but striker Greg Brown's 84th

A flashback. North Shore United wins the Air New Zealand Cup and Adrian Elrick (with cup) and Keith Hobbs are ecstatic.
Picture: Eric Jelly

minute goal gave Napier something to smile about. Napier had paralleled the unenviable 1971 record of Western Suburbs, winning the Cup and losing National League status in the same season. Napier, though, were back in the elite class after barely 12 months while those in the Western Suburbs of Wellington still seek that recognition.

1986: North Shore United (Auckland) 0
Mt Maunganui (Mt Maunganui) 1

The mid-table National League side North Shore were matched against the Swiss Maid winners in the first of a two leg final. The first final was played at North Shore's Fuji Stadium and the second went to the Mount's Links Avenue home base. North Shore were able though to make some history by winning the Chatham Cup for a record sixth time. In the first leg Tony Ferris scored in the 22nd minute and Shore missed from the penalty spot.

Mt Maunganui 1
North Shore United 4

Even without captain Allan Boath, Don Jones ended 13 years at the club with a big win. Kevin Hagan had them in front after five minutes and while Grant Proudman levelled after 22 minutes, Darren McLennan had Shore ahead at halftime and even on goal aggregate. In the second half Kim Wright (65 minutes) and late in the piece Brian McKeown (87) brought Shore a good win on the day and a comfortable aggregate success.

1987: Gisborne City (Gisborne) 5
Christchurch United (Canterbury) 1

Yet another two leg affair, with the first at Childers Road and the second at Queen Elizabeth Park, and it was a first for both clubs. Gisborne City, in its third successive final, were able to win the Cup for the first time, while for the South Islanders it was a first loss in a final after four previous winning attempts. It was one of those occasions where the teams involved were first and second in the National League in the same season, with Christchurch winning by seven points. Ironically Steve Sumner, who had done so much first with Christchurch and then grabbed a medal with Manurewa, was with Gisborne. The first final was an excellent affair and while Christchurch went under in a big way, the football was always of high quality. Fijian Stan Morrell, followed by Paul Nixon, scored before the break. Morrell had another in the first 10 minutes of the second half before Johan Verweij pulled it back to 3-1. In the last eight minutes Kevin Birch and then Sumner gave Gisborne an enormous advantage going into the second leg.

Christchurch United 2
Gisborne City 2

The outcome may have looked cut and dried but the fixture in Christchurch was still entertaining. Paul Nicholls for Christchurch and Sean Byrne were on target in the first half and the teams turned round at 1-1. Allan Carville had the home side back in front with 15 minutes to run but Brian Strutt's penalty seven minutes from the time meant that honours were shared. The two legs of the final produced no fewer than nine different scorers.

1988: Christchurch United (Canterbury) 2
Waikato United (Hamilton) 2

Shades of 1962. With 18 minutes left to play at home Christchurch United were trailing 2-0. Tate and Bauerfiend had done the damage in the first half. Waikato's second goal came with 18 minutes to play but the National League winners fought back as strikers Hansen and Verweij levelled the tie. Christchurch, it was said, were at their best when the odds were stacked against them.

Waikato United 1
Christchurch United 1

Taking full advantage of playing at home, Waikato clinched the Chatham Cup on a dubious away goal ruling - if the scores are level the team playing away from home who scores the most goals wins. Having won the National League by no fewer than 26 points, Christchurch made a brave effort to complete the double but just failed. Tate scored after 17 minutes of the first half which meant that Christchurch had to goal twice. A penalty by Braithwaite 15 minutes from the end offered some hope but Waikato held on to win.

1989: Christchurch United (Canterbury) 7
Rotorua City (Rotorua) 1

It was a Cup for records. After two defeats Christchurch not only beat the regional league club Rotorua City but also equalled the record score of 1958 set by Seatoun. John Donovan scored six goals that day and six was the magic number as well for Steve Sumner who collected his sixth winner's medal. Rotorua had Dave Harris in goal. In the first four minutes he made two good saves but after eight minutes he was beaten for the first time as Keith Braithwaite scored. It was 5-0 by halftime as Michael McGarry, Johan Verweij and Laurence Fitzpatrick netted. In the second half Sumner fittingly got on the sheet and McGarry completed his hat-trick. Eleven minutes from the end Shane Zohs (Rotorua) scored from the penalty spot. Few Cup finals have been won more easily.

1990: Mount Wellington 3
Christchurch United 3
(Mount Wellington won 4-2 on penalties)

Not since the three epic matches of 1972 had these footballing giants met in a Chatham Cup final. This time one fact was for certain - in 1990 the game would be decided then and there, in this case Wellington's Basin Reserve. If the scores were level at full time, the game would go to extra time and if still level then be decided by a penalty shoot-out which would be the first in the history of finals.

The class of '90 didn't let the fans down. The final scoreline of 3-3 certainly compares with the 4-4 of the first 1972 fixture and it was a game that had everything. Christchurch needed one more success to equal the most number of wins - held by North Shore. It was the club's eighth final. In the first of the losses they went under in the two-leg final, in the second lost on the away goal rule and now it was the penalty shoot out. The fates were not kind. Then there was Armstrong factor. The former Chelsea professional Ken Armstrong as coach and player had a marvellous record in the competition. He led North Shore to win three times, Eastern Suburbs twice and Mount Wellington once. He had been with losing teams three times as well. Playing in the 1990 was the final was a 38-year-old son Ron Armstrong. Armstrong had played in the 1972 game. This final was his eight and after he had five winner's medals and three losers - that to go with four National League titles. Steve Sumner, the previous year had played in his seventh final and collected his sixth winner's title.

But while the Sumner success of 1989 had been clear-cut, there were times in 1990 when Ron Armstrong must have wondered what fate had in store. The Mount had gone one behind to an Allan Carville goal, only to lead at halftime when a lofted passback from a pressured Johan Verweij held up in the wind long enough to beat his keeper Alan Stroud and float in under the crossbar. The 1990 Player of the Year Noel Barkley then curled home a beauty to put the Mount 2-1 in front. From that point until half time and for just about all the second half Christchurch and in particular the gifted Michael McGarry tormented the Mount but as a result of some fine keeping from Grant Schofield, a second goal for Carville was its only reward. It was 2-2 and in extra time Christchurch skipper Keith Braithwaite missed a penalty. There was real drama with minutes from time when Franklin referee Roger Woolmer ran half the field to determine that Stroud had taken too many steps. When Stroud failed to hold a fierce shot it was Armstrong, a defender, who thumped the ball into the net. McGarry was not done and with two minutes to run he superbly glanced a Julyan Falloon cross home and when Woolmer called time it was 3-3. During the last few hectic minutes of normal time the Mount's Dave Witteveen was sent from the field for a second bookable offence.

Armstrong was one of the five designated penalty takers and his shot was saved by Stroud, but teammates Terry Torrens, Barkley, Grant Lightbown and finally Steve O'Donoghue scored. McGarry missed and so did Braithwaite as Schofield saved, but Woolmer ruled the keeper had moved and Braithwaite scored. The unhappy Verweij had three attempts and Schofield saved each time and though Michael Boomer took the best Christchurch penalty the early damage had been done and Mount Wellington had a fifth cup win. It was always going to be Mount Wellington's Cup year. They were less than two minutes from losing at home to the gritty Hutt Valley United in the semi final when a goal in injury time levelled the score at 2-2. Mount won 4-2 in extra time after having been 2-0 behind and that doesn't include another Schofield saved penalty. Hutt Valley United were the year's cup heroes. After beating the Central League side Raumati Hearts, it disposed of fellow National League opponents Napier City Rovers, Miramar Rangers and league champions Waitakere City before going out to the Mount. Each of the Hutt Valley games were played away.

THE NATIONAL LEAGUE

Background

The National League competition began life in 1970. That the New Zealand Football Association will celebrate its centenary and the league its first 22 years at the same time is a happy coincidence. It is a fact that National League has achieved a consistent standard of football. It certainly put paid to the old form of interprovincial football as the country knew it. The main problem today is clearly apathy. The public reaction has been moderate to say the least which is a pity for the League has produced some of New Zealand soccer's best moments. Perhaps some of the decisions made in regard to the running of and the criteria for entry to the League have hardly been judicious but the fact remains that the League has stood the test of time. The future and vision of football in this country remain vital. Not to have a National League is unthinkable.

If the League became a fact in 1970 the call for a national competition began in the late 50s probably around 1958 and 1959. Jock Houston was a Scot who spent much of his life serving football as author of the Jubilee Yearbook and also by dint of his time on the NZFA. It is he who is generally regarded as the initial crusader in quest of a league. The first concrete steps came in 1959 when at the annual meeting of the Association the general thought of operating a state league was suggested. The meeting asked the propounders Houston and Otto Hilton to prepare reports. Two were returned to the then secretary Bill Arcus and later circulated. Houston noted that any scheme or plan which brings with it a different vision can not be expected to meet with approval without opposition, particularly when individual identity with an older system could be affected. Houston noted the prevailing transport difficulties and inner conflict with three forms of loyalty - to club parochialism and with the game itself. Houston delved into costs which he based on average crowds of 2000 at two shillings. He suggested eight teams for a first league - two from Auckland and one each from Poverty Bay, Waikato, Wellington, Hutt Valley and two South Islanders. Hilton, a post-war refugee from Europe, had a short but exciting career as an administrator. He was barely 50 when he died in 1965 but his enthusiasm for football and its administration was something of a revelation for his more conservative NZFA colleagues, a fact noted in these pages by Charlie Dempsey. In his report to the NZFA he differed from Houston in that while he felt the league should also have eight clubs he suggested it should be confined first to North Island clubs, these to be replaced or the league enlarged by the inclusion of South Island teams. Auckland and Wellington were to be given two teams and Poverty Bay and Waikato one each. Hilton suggested that the other two teams should come from the Manawatu, Taranaki and Wanganui areas.

These early skirmishes showed that the country was interested in a form of state league and plans went a stage further when in August 1963 the NZFA circulated a blueprint of an outline of National League football in New Zealand. The plan had been prepared by NZFA council member Gordon Whyte in association with two of his colleagues Charles Wilkins and Ernie Harris. The actual arrival of a National League still took time but with the NZFA and its affiliates obviously willing, the direction of "domestic" football took a fresh twist. In late 1963 and early 1964 the NZFA had a world tour on its plate. But after that Northern, Central and Southern Leagues were established in 1968 and these proved at the time to be most successful forerunners to the league itself. Today the regional league remains an integral part of the New Zealand football scene but in 1969 the final standings in the leagues could not have been more important. Western Suburbs, Stop Out,

Gordon Whyte, a former NZFA councillor and the architect of the 1960s National League blueprint. Tony Hilton collection

Gisborne City and Hungaria were the first four in the Central League. They were joined by Mount Wellington, Eastern Suburbs and Blockhouse Bay, the top trio in their northern league and a new club Christchurch United, a team backed by four Christchurch establishments Christchurch City, Shamrock, Rangers and Technical. That season Technical were clear winners of the Southern League. The National League was only a few months away.

History - By Vic Deverill

While the course of New Zealand soccer has taken numerous twists and turns during its lifetime the one event that set the game in this country on a direct path to success was the creating of a National League in 1970.

The concept of a National League had been years in the melting pot and its introduction was reported by one scribe as 'the greatest soccer adventure ever on the New Zealand scene'.

It resulted in the immediate raising of playing, coaching and refereeing standards which led to New Zealand's finest hour - the qualification for the 1982 World Cup finals in Spain.

Eight clubs comprised the inaugural league, this being extended to ten the following season, with subsequent increases in 1977 (to twelve) and a further two a decade later brought the league to its present strength of fourteen.

Entry into the league is an issue that has demanded the attention of New Zealand Football Association Councillors more than any other aspect. An end-of-season playoff series involving the three regional league winners and the bottom placed National League club was later replaced by an automatic three-up-three-down system. This meant one quarter of the league was relegated each year and soon lost favour to be supplanted by a controversial 'entry by invitation' method of admission which favoured clubs formed by amalgamation.

Three such composite sides, Hutt Valley United, Waikato United and Waitakere City, have both performed with distinction and established themselves as worthy members of the league. Now the cycle has come full turn as the league reverts back to a playoff series involving the top three regional league qualifying teams.

The league has been sponsored throughout its existence first by Rothmans (NZ) Ltd from 1970-1986 and through to 1990 by Air New Zealand. In 1991 Winfield (a subsidiary of Rothmans) picked up the tab. Rothmans played a vital role in the promotion of the league in its formative years and established a close rapport with the New Zealand Soccer Media Association. Rothmans also produced a well presented Media Kit containing vital information on the league and participating clubs.

Two clubs have dominated the league since its inception. Mount Wellington (six) and Christchurch United (five) have won 11 of the 21 titles at stake between them. Wellington United with three wins is the only other club with more than one success of the ten clubs who have earned the title "League Champions."

It is a widely held view that there exists less individual skill at National League level these days compared to the 1970's. Certainly there is increased emphasis on team play and physical fitness and 'work rate' has become a trendy term. With more time being spent developing those two aspects it follows that less time is devoted nowadays to individual techniques.

National League coaches enjoy a high profile in New Zealand soccer highlighted by the fact that of 14 Personality of the Year awards announced by the New Zealand Soccer Media eleven had gone to a coach.

Men like Eddie Edge, Kevin Fallon, Don Jones and Tom Heptinstall with strong opinions about the game have not always been top of the popularity parade but there is no doubt that they have added much needed colour to a sport which has to fight for every column inch of press coverage.

The National League exists primarily to provide top competitive soccer in as many geographical centres as possible and to maintain the best playing standards. Every top playing country in the world has a highly competitive, efficiently structured domestic league to feed off.

The league's format will need adjusting from time to time (fine tuning, to coin a popular political phrase) to meet the needs of the day. Our top teams and players should be exposed to the highest level of organised competition week in week out if progress is to be sustained.

Entrusted with running the league the New Zealand Football Association faces the task of knowing its decisions are always more likely to produce a steady hail of brickbats rather than a gentle flutter of bouquets. Its decisions must not be based on appeasing the majority but on assisting New Zealand soccer through what should continue to be a most progressive and exciting period of its history.

1970

The Rothmans Soccer League kicked off on 11 April amid widespread interest and speculation. As the first sport in New Zealand to launch a National League, soccer provided the blueprint for other sports to follow, which a number did with varying degrees of success.

Auckland and Wellington dominated the league's composition with three teams apiece and along with sole representation from Christchurch and Gisborne made up the eight founding members.

One could not have written a better script to mark the league's opening chapter. It had all the ingredients of a best seller - drama, controversy, suspense and a great cast with the title in doubt until the curtain fell at the final whistle on the last round.

Having won the Northern League the previous year, Blockhouse Bay justified its pre-season favouritism by taking on the role of pacesetter throughout. With both Christchurch United and Mount Wellington getting off to poor starts Eastern Suburbs provided the main title threat.

Bay and Suburbs indulged in a titanic battle as Christchurch and The Mount gradually struck form. Christchurch went through the second half of the season undefeated, dropping just one point in the final eight games and the Mount put together a nine match unbeaten run, the season's best, which ended in the final game against Christchurch - the only match to be played under floodlights that season. Played before 3000 it decided third place and the large crowd was rewarded when Christchurch won through in an eight goal thriller in the season's equal top scoring match.

Wellington teams never ventured above the halfway point finishing in 5th, 7th and 8th positions. Their collective wins (8) were exceeded by all three top teams individually and, along with Gisborne, they struggled throughout against the better performed top four.

The 1952 NZFA representative team for the Pacific Islands tour. Standing: C. Banham, D.F. Kendrick, I. Upchurch, J. White, F.H. Albrechtsen, E.J. Stephenson, R.E. Coxon, L.D. Hope-Ede. Sitting: G. McAnulty, R. Quickenden, J.W. Newall (captain), W.P. Smith (manager), D. Smith (vice-captain), A. Davis, R.F. Morrison.

New Zealand hit the front against Australia in Auckland in 1989 via Malcolm Dunford and the neighbours are going out of the World Cup. **Picture: Eric Jelly**

Wellington teams held the key to the championship with Blockhouse entertaining Stop Out and Western Suburbs hosting Eastern Suburbs as both contenders went into the final round of matches level pegging. With just three matches to go, Eastern Suburbs had looked set to take the title leading Blockhouse by three points and then stumbled to a home draw against Mount Wellington where Ken Armstrong had his the first game in charge as coach while his son Ron was making his debut after transferring from Northern League club North Shore. This was followed by a home defeat against fast improving Christchurch which allowed Blockhouse to sneak into the lead on goal average.

Colin Shaw played a true captain's role in the final match and his hat-trick made Bert Ormond the league's first successful coach. Eastern Suburbs, aided by a Bill de Graaf brace, won also but paid the price for a recent lapse in form.

Despite the gap in standard between the top and bottom four the league was an unqualified success. The average match attendance reached 1140 with champions Blockhouse Bay attracting an average 1840 to its seven home games.

1971

The success of the inaugural season prompted the NZFA to increase the league by two. By virtue of finishing first and second in the qualifying playoffs Mount Albert-Ponsonby and Dunedin Suburbs filled the vacant berths.

The two extra teams increased the number of matches from 56 to 90 but this didn't affect the dominance of last year's top four who were again the leading contenders for the title.

Gisborne City managed to close the gap between the top and bottom groups finishing one point behind Blockhouse Bay in fifth place. Wellington teams again struggled, occupying the bottom three spots and this time there was no reprieve for last placed Western Suburbs. It finished a distant last the previous year but preserved its league status on account of the league being extended.

Suburbs actually headed the table after four matches with three wins and a draw but a failure to win any of the remaining 14 greased its downward slide. The club could rue the fact that goal average was the deciding factor in those days and not goal difference which wasn't introduced until 1978. Under goal difference Suburbs would have finished above Wellington City instead of below on the strength of a .002 inferior goal average.

Beaten into second place the previous year on goal average Eastern Suburbs dispensed of the need to indulge in mathematics, winning the league by a three point margin over Mount Wellington even though its goal average was marginally inferior.

The dominance Auckland teams enjoyed over their Wellington counterparts is reflected in the 42 meetings to date between the clubs of those two cities. Auckland teams won thirty-four of those encounters with Wellington claiming just five successes. Eastern Suburbs could boast a 100 per cent record winning all 12 meetings against Wellington opposition for a 37-7 goal tally. Christchurch also enjoyed a degree of supremacy over capital-based clubs, suffering just one reversal in two seasons.

Mount Wellington had lost the opening game of the season to Eastern Suburbs 2-5 then went on an unbeaten 12 match run and seemingly on course for the title. Just one point adrift of Suburbs and with a game in hand and a significantly superior goal average, The Mount suffered a shock 1-3 away loss to second bottom Stop Out on the same day as Suburbs lost 1-2 at home to Dunedin Suburbs. Eastern Suburbs learnt from that let-off and scraped home in a thrilling nine goal away encounter to Gisborne, beating third-placed Blockhouse in front of an estimated 10,000 at Newmarket Park and drew 2-2 with The Mount in what was a virtual title decider. Rated as one of the best National League games of all time referee Les Coffman hardly endeared himself to The Mount or its supporters disallowing three of its goals for offside.

This completed Suburbs' league programme and with an unassailable lead the Mount's final match, lost 0-1 away to Gisborne, was of academic interest only.

The season's personal highlight was Johnny Wrathall's 1000th goal in twenty-six years of competitive soccer. This milestone was reached when he scored the final goal of his hat-trick in Eastern Suburbs' 3-1 win against Mount Albert - Ponsonby.

Attendances increased with Mount Wellington pulling the largest support, attracting 17,690 through the turnstiles (average: 1965). The Mount's home form warranted such support with one draw, that vital penultimate 2-2 clash with Suburbs, spoiling an otherwise perfect nine match home record (30-6).

1972

For the second time in three years mathematics were brought into play to decide the league title. While Blockhouse Bay benefited from the system in 1970, this time it had to bow to a fast finishing Mount Wellington.

In the closest finish so far one point separated the top three as Christchurch filled third place in as many years. Mount Wellington's impressive home form tilted the scales in its favour, a defeat against Blockhouse spoiling an otherwise perfect record. The Bay was no doubt aggrieved at losing the title to The Mount after having won both league encounters 2-1 and 3-2.

Mount Wellington's success was a personal triumph for coach Ken Armstrong who, as a player and coach, had now won every honour the game has to offer. His cause was assisted greatly by gaining the services of Dave Taylor, following a stint with Sydney-Croatia, Brian Turner, after playing

Eastern Surburbs hero John Wrathall nets one of many, this goal from the penalty spot. Tony Hilton collection

Early days of the National League. Wellington City host Caversham at the Basin Reserve. Both teams have long since departed the scene. Barry Smith collection

professionally for Chelsea, Portsmouth and international Dennis Tindall from Dunedin Suburbs.

The Mount dropped one point in the second half of the season, a draw with Christchurch, overcoming a backlog of fixtures to win the last six matches (21-3). An extended cup run resulted in the playing of five games in 21 days. Blockhouse attracted the most fans through the turnstiles in 1972, pulling in 20,540.

Iain Ormond netted 22 of the Bays' thirty-five goals scoring in all but three matches - Blockhouse scoreless in all three. Christchurch was the only team undefeated at home and started the season in fine style by defeating Blockhouse 3-0. The South Island side showed it was clearly closing the gap on its northern rivals.

Eastern Suburbs shared the lead with Blockhouse and Christchurch with five matches remaining, the Mount in fourth place three points adrift but with a game in hand. Three straight losses followed killing stone dead Suburbs' title hopes. The first was a shock 1-5 away loss to Wellington City followed by odd goal defeats against close rivals Blockhouse and the Mount.

Blockhouse Bay finished its league programme with a scoreless away draw at Gisborne, a result that was to ultimately cost it the title. The draw left the Bay at the head of the table and it suffered the trauma of an agonising two week wait as Mount Wellington, four points behind and with two games still to play, completed its programme. The Mount secured the two required victories (3-0 v Wellington City and 2-1 v Stop Out) to depose the Bay on goal average.

Never out of the first three, Christchurch United led the table at the halfway point and even at the advanced stage of round 15. Gisborne then did to United what it later achieved against Blockhouse - it ruined its title chances winning by the only goal. Two final match wins left Christchurch embracing third place for the third successive year. Eastern Suburbs, Mount Wellington, Blockhouse Bay and Christchurch United have occupied all four top places in the three seasons to date.

Poor away form blighted Gisborne City's chances as it secured just one victory but it destroyed the title hopes of both Blockhouse and Christchurch with crucial wins. The season heralded the arrival of Kevin Fallon from the UK. He missed most of the first half of the season through injury but still gained selection to the NZ squad. Six of seven losses were by the odd goal.

Wellington, reduced to two teams, made little impact on the league, Stop Out and Wellington City again failed to break into the top half of the table. Both teams provided harder opposition than in the past securing five victories and three draws against Auckland opposition, Wellington City's 5-1 win over Eastern Suburbs gave the capital's soccer a great fillip.

Michael Groom was a gifted New Zealander whose international career was altogether too short. Here he is in action against Malaysia. Picture: Eric Jelly

Caversham (previously Dunedin Suburbs) failed to capitalise on a good start to the season, prevailing in five of its opening seven matches which included a victory over Mount Wellington but did not win a further game picking up just three points in the remaining eleven matches. Despite its lowly position it was never seriously threatened by relegation. The team was one goal short of an average identical to last year's.

Only two clubs were under the relegation cloud. Promoted at the expense of Western Suburbs, New Brighton was the only team that failed to win away.

It recorded only one success during the eighteen match campaign, 4-1 v Caversham. Despite this dismal effort The Seasiders were saved by an even worse performance from Auckland City (previously Mount Albert-Ponsonby). Despite winning an extra match City finished level on points and with a far inferior goal average. Ironically its best results were against New Brighton winning 4-3 and drawing 1-1 away, the only team it avoided defeat against. Auckland City fared little better in the playoffs and was replaced by Wellington Diamond United.

1973

Christchurch United became the fourth team in as many years to take the title and in so doing broke the Auckland stranglehold. The eight point winning margin was the most impressive to date and was based on near invincibility at home where just a single point was surrendered.

Despite the winning margin the league was full of interest throughout with the five following teams being separated by a single point. A far superior goal average carried Mount Wellington into the runner-up spot ahead of Blockhouse Bay.

Gisborne City at last thrust its nose into the top four displacing ever present Eastern Suburbs - goal average again being the major factor. Further back on goal average was league newcomer Wellington Diamond United - a commendable effort first up to get so close to the prize-money.

Stop Out and Wellington City dropped a place each and New Brighton finished one place off relegation for the second successive year but this time was in no danger of relegation as Caversham had a nightmare season netting just six goals during the eighteen match campaign. Christchurch set a league record of only 11 conceded which still stands and while thirty-eight goals was the lowest scored by a title winner and its own lowest to date its success was never in doubt, remaining at the top from round three onwards.

United broke the succession of three third placings, equalled the record number of wins, amassed the highest total of points and the only disappointing feature was being been beaten by nearest challenger Gisborne City away, to virtually win the league, but failed to go out in style in the final four games which involved the bottom three sides.

Despite its pre-season favouritism and 14 past or present internationals Mount Wellington failed to match the South Islanders pace. The supply of nine members of the World Cup squad placed extra demands on the team and Dennis Tindall breaking his leg in World Cup training after only two league appearances certainly added to the pressure.

Blockhouse Bay recovered well after the loss of both opening matches and suffered a mid-season run of defeats. Third place was achieved despite scoring only three more goals than it conceded with prolific scorer Iain Ormond netting over half his team's total. Ormond, Clive Campbell, Gary Lake and John Morris had been ever present during the Bay's 68-match campaign.

Gisborne City at last gained a share of the prize-money which had been shared exclusively among Auckland and Christchurch teams. City scraped into fourth place following the awarding of a controversial penalty in the last minute of its final match (v Wellington City). Usually a poor away performer, City's four successes this season equalled its total wins of the previous three campaigns. To nullify that improvement five matches were lost on home soil - only Caversham fared worse.

The solitary away loss to champions Christchurch 1-2 was the league's best and had it not been for a disappointing final run-in that produced just one win in the last five including three successive home defeats City would have easily secured runner-up spot.

Eastern Suburbs failed to make the top four for the first time. Its final fifth placing was a commendable effort after its early form which produced just six points at the halfway stage. A decision to increase player payments following financial problems coincided with a reversal of form which resulted in only four points being dropped from the halfway stage to leave Suburbs one point adrift of runner-up position.

1973 signalled the end of Tom McNab and Ray Mears' association with the club. As players, and in McNab's case latterly as coach, they had both made significant contributions to Suburbs' success in recent years.

To finish one point away from the runner-up spot in its first season was not adequately reflected in a final sixth position. Yet Wellington Diamond United could still extract a degree of satisfaction from its initial showing in the National League.

United achieved more wins and points than had any other Wellington team at that stage and held out the hope that it may at last provide a real threat from the capital. WDU became only the third club to achieve the 'double' over Mount Wellington.

Stop Out had the rare experience of sharing the lead with Christchurch after it won the opening three matches. Then followed a run of nine games without victory including six straight losses with the season to end the way it began - with three straight wins. Despite the modest seventh placing Stop Out created seven new club records and scored, for the first time, more goals than it conceded.

With seven games to go Wellington City trailed leader Christchurch by two points and then created a new club record by losing seven matches consecutively. It set a club record for goalscoring in a season when the main highlight was a 1-0 win over Christchurch.

New Brighton finished one place above relegation for the second straight year. It was reputed to offer the highest match payments in the league but it did not produce results or stability with Alan Vest's appointment for the following season making him the eighth coach in as many years. Eleven goals conceded in the final two games contributed toward a club record of forty-three against - a flow even new import Bobby Almond could not stem.

Six goals in 1620 minutes of soccer is a record no team is ever likely to prise from Caversham's unwilling grasp. Vince Alcock netted fifty percent but it remains the lowest total of goals by a club top scorer. Caversham's scoring statistic apart, the most notable aspect of the season were its only wins were achieved against such notables as Mount Wellington and Blockhouse Bay.

1974

Spurred on by Christchurch United's runaway title win last season Mount Wellington set out to emulate its South Island rival winning the championship in almost as convincing fashion.

With last year's top positions reversed the Mount became the first club to win the league twice. The Mount also was the first team to go through a season undefeated away and to lose just one match overall. That loss was recorded against city rival Eastern Suburbs which ended one place above relegation.

The Mount hit a mid-season slump of three draws and a loss. But that mini disaster still left the team

The big K. Kevin Fallon at Hutt Park making life difficult for Stop Out during a National League match. Vic Deverill collection

striding the top while the remainder of the league clearly had problems. The Mount finished with the best winning sequence of the season - five straight wins - to equal Christchurch's record points tally of the previous year. It did not suffer its first setback until match eleven when old foes Eastern Suburbs snatched an only goal win - a setback the champions took retribution for in the season's final fixture winning 5-1.

Competition for minor places was almost as intense as last season with two points separating the next four positions. Christchurch United amassed its lowest points total for an 18 match season yet it still managed to squeeze into second place. It recovered well from its worst start to a season which produced a mere nine points at the halfway stage. A club record unbeaten 10-match run enabled the South Islanders to become, along with the Mount, the only teams to quality for prize-money every year since the league's inception. United's runner-up spot was somewhat fortuitous as it was achieved through higher placed New Brighton and Stop Out losing their final matches - both at home.

After finishing one place off relegation in its previous two seasons New Brighton, under new coach Alan Vest, improved six places creating a number of club records in the process. Needing a home win over lowly Gisborne in its final match to secure runner-up berth New Brighton inexplicably lost 0-2 to virtually hand second place to city rival United on a plate. The team won seven at home, the best in the league, and two more than its previous two seasons combined.

The Seasiders' poor away form continued, at season's end it had won three of 27 since entering the league and was still without a victory in Wellington. It set a new club record of six successive matches without defeat and the four goals scored against the Mount was more than any other club had achieved.

Stop Out got into the top half of the table at its fifth attempt throwing away a gilt-edged opportunity to finish in runner-up spot by losing the final match at home to Wellington City. It was the fourth straight home loss to its close rival in as many seasons. No team bettered Stop Out's away defensive record while nine victories were the highest posted by a Wellington region team to date, making it the first Wellington club to qualify for prize-money.

A Gisborne City National league goal. Sandy Davie is the North Shore keeper and in just a few seconds a crouching John Warrington is going to get on the scoresheet in this 1974 fixture. Barry Smith collection

Blockhouse Bay's fifth placing meant it had filled all top five positions in the league's five seasons of operation. It finished two places lower than last year despite a superior goal average. All six losses were by the odd goal and its supremacy against Wellington teams continued, losing just four of 28 encounters to date.

North Shore United marked its first season in the league with an average performance. Shore scored almost twice as many goals away as at home. It scored more than one at base on only one occasion and in defeating Eastern Suburbs 5-2 recorded the most goals by a side making its National League debut.

Wellington City recorded its lowest number of losses in a season and most goals for, yet failed to translate this improvement into a higher league placing. It was the third time it had reached seventh position and became the first club to concede 100 away goals.

Gisborne City slipped to its lowest league position and suffered its heaviest league defeat in losing 1-6 at home to the Mount. A coaching upheaval after nine matches resulted in the departure of newly appointed coach Kevin Fallon. At that stage the team had one win and four points to its credit and four victories achieved in the second half of the season were sufficient to keep City above bottom spot.

Eastern Suburbs achieved what no other team managed in inflicting defeat on Mount Wellington and securing two draws against runner-up Christchurch. These results belied Suburbs' close brush with relegation and a 23-45 goal average was easily the league's worst. Five consecutive losses constituted a club record in Suburbs' worst season to date.

It is difficult to reconcile a record league victory with a team finishing bottom of the heap yet that was the unlikely event that stole the headlines in 1974. Wellington Diamond United turned on a display of soccer befitting title aspirants rather than relegation candidates in demolishing Eastern Suburbs 8-0 to set a new league record victory. That win was registered the week after Suburbs had inflicted the only defeat of the year on table topping Mount Wellington.

It was not enough to save the Wellingtonians whose failure to win away proved too big an obstacle. Seven of twelve defeats were by the odd goal - another league record - and for the first time the team finishing bottom did not have the worst goal average - Gisborne and Eastern Suburbs were both inferior. It scored more goals when finishing in a healthy sixth place the previous year, while conceding only seven more but never succeeded in overcoming a disastrous start that produced six successive defeats.

1975

The private battle between Christchurch United and Mount Wellington continued with United this time upstaging its close rival who slipped to fifth place - the first time prize-money had eluded its grasp.

Increased sponsorship by Rothmans coincided with the tightest league on record. Just fifteen points separated top and bottom, the smallest margin in the league's history.

Christchurch United hit the lead at the halfway stage although at no time did it manage to establish a comfortable lead. It accumulated enough points to survive two defeats and a draw in the final seven matches. United's points tally and 11 victories were the lowest for an 18 match programme by a title winner. Despite this its success was well merited having overcome an average start of two wins in its opening six games, both by the odd goal, yet they had secured the championship with two games still to play.

For the first time United won more matches away than at home and the overall total of thirty-five goals was the lowest netted by a title winner.

In only its second year North Shore United eased into second place on the strength of a far superior goal average. Don Jones thus became the first New Zealand born coach to end up winning prize-money. A distinction which brought him the axe five days later!

Shore never fell below third place and actually led the table for five weeks. An eight match spell that produced just one win caused enough damage to its title hopes which an end-of-season six match undefeated run could not repair. It never lost out of Auckland and conceded more than one in only four matches and top scored away with fifteen.

For the third time goal average cost Blockhouse Bay prize-money. To be in contention for a pay-out would have been a distant thought when the Bay occupied second from bottom spot after eight matches. The final 10 games produced eight wins and two draws - a league best for the season - this gave the team the highest number of victories behind the champions.

To finish fourth after winning just four matches out of 18 raises a few questions about the strength of the league in general. However, Caversham's position was bolstered by a record number of draws for an eighteen match competition. Ten times points were shared with the opposition and on eight occasions the referee's final whistle produced a 1-1 scoreline.

Back in the league after a season's absence, Caversham's greatest contribution to the season was importing the elongated Alf Stamp. The 6 ft 4 striker from Partick Thistle had the skills to display with his physical presence and he proved himself a favourite with the fans.

Never before had it been so necessary to look so far down the table to find Mount Wellington's name. The Mount's 7-4-7 record had aeronautical connotations and its performance was certainly airy-fairy for a playing through champion.

Despite 11 internationals in the squad the Mount struggled in the goalscoring department and the 19 goals netted were way below the club's previous thirty-five low achieved in a fourteen match season. Only Ron Armstrong (in England) and Vivian Hope-Ede were missing from last year's title line up and the lack of goalscoring power was reflected in the fact that no player succeeded in scoring more than one goal in one match throughout the season. Despite the drop in form The Mount raised its game against arch rival Christchurch inflicting the only home defeat on the champions.

In second spot with four games to play Stop Out was on target for its highest ever final placing. One

The 1975 NZFA representative team for the tour of the Peoples Republic of China. Back row: I. Park, G. Griffiths, B. Turner. Second row: G. Te Au (manager), T. Sibley, W. Fleet, A. Elrick, P. Jerram, O. Nutteridge, G. Storer, K. Weymouth, W. Hughes (coach). Front row: J. Legg, K. Mulgrew, B. Armstrong, B. Truman (coach), E. Thomas, D. Taylor, K. Barton. NZFA collection.

point from those remaining games squashed its hopes and the Hutt Valley side settled for a now familiar bottom half table position. After conceding just 13 goals in the opening 14 matches the remaining four boosted the goals against tally by a further 11.

Eastern Suburbs improved marginally over the previous season, never threatened by relegation and far from being title aspirants. Seventy-eight goals conceded in the past two seasons is without equal and despite the record high of thirty-three for the year, goalkeeper Pravan Jeram was the NZFA's choice of Player-of-the-Year.

Gisborne City finished in the same position three points clear of relegation for the second successive year. After eight matches Gisborne sat in third place but the remaining 10 games reaped a modest four points. All five victories were achieved by a 1-0 scoreline and the thirteen goals netted were the second lowest in the league to date. City operated most of the season with a thirteen man squad.

New Brighton dropped six places from the previous year finishing one place above relegation for the third time in four years. It did not post a win until the 11th match then won three in succession. The side went into the final match needing two points to avoid relegation - after filling bottom spot for 12 weeks - and got them courtesy of Gisborne. A mid-season change of coach brought New Brighton's count to ten coaches in nine years.

After six years of continual struggle Wellington City finally lost the battle. It was the fourth time in six years that a Wellington team had filled bottom berth. City's 18-29 goal average was the best of any relegated team while no other lowly placed side had amassed more points or suffered fewer defeats.

1976

It took seven seasons for the Auckland-Christchurch monopoly to be broken and it was well worth the wait as Wellington Diamond United added a new dimension to title winning - the bizarre. It is difficult to reconcile a 31-29 goal aggregate with a championship performance yet Diamonds achieved both - an exploit that received scant recognition.

Certainly some of the statistics that arose from Diamond's season were not of what championships are made. The twenty-nine goals conceded were easily the most by a title winner for an eighteen match season while the thirty-one scored were an all time low. The 0-5 away loss to then league leader Caversham remains the heaviest defeat suffered in a championship winning year.

However, other statistics better reflect Diamond's emergence as the best team in the league. No club has exceeded Diamond's 13 victories or the eight won away. The four point winning margin has been bettered only twice before and all told the team set eleven club and fifteen league records.

An incredibly stable line-up resulted in all but two of the 198 league positions during the season being accounted for by 12 players, 10 of whom were with the club during its relegation from the league two years earlier: a fine reward for their loyalty. Of 13 victories 12 were by the odd goal and several were won coming from behind. It showed the character of the side which had no stars unlike every title winner before and since.

After five matches Mount Wellington was in the unaccustomed position of being the only team without a win. Only two defeats (both at home) in the remaining matches enabled the Mount to fill runner-up spot for the third time. It conceded only five goals away to equal Christchurch's 1973 feat and its overall defensive record was easily the league's best while only Caversham scored more goals.

Caversham looked likely title winners in late June after defeating WDU at home 5-0 to establish a five point lead at the top. Inexplicably it was all downhill from then on with only one win in the eight remaining matches. Four points came from the final seven games just enough for the Dunedin side to hang on to third spot but it still had the league's best home record.

One point from relegation last year to within two points of a runner-up spot sums up New Brighton's up and down form of recent years. Its success was based on a vastly improved away form. After having won four away games in four seasons the Seasiders won six on their travels this year and had its home form matched this it would have reached runner-up position. Michael Glubb top scored with 11 goals - the only player in the league to get into double figures. For the first, and only, time New Brighton finished ahead of city rival United.

Blockhouse Bay maintained its record of having finished in the top half of the table every season - but only just. It required goal average to hoist it above city rival Eastern Suburbs and enable coach Bert Ormond to bow out on a high note as the league's longest serving coach to date.

Eastern Suburbs, struggled to regain its former league glory and finished in a safe middle-of-the-table position despite winning only two home games. Striker Gary Jenkins was back in action after a full season sidelined following a transfer wrangle with Gisborne.

With the league's only goalkeeper player-coach (Sandy Davie) at the helm, North Shore United slipped from runner-up spot to seventh place in a season when the dumping of former coach Don Jones was seen as a grave error. More points were gained away than at home although the home goal tally was exceeded only by Caversham. Shore reached the halfway mark with a six match winless spell to hover just above the relegation area but recovered well in the second half. Only Stop Out lost more at home in a season that marked the start of 17-year-old Peter Henry's colourful league career.

What a difference a name makes. As Christchurch United, the club had a record to match any other but a sponsor led to a change of name. Trans Tours United altered the team's luck as well. Before the name change part way through the season Christchurch had won five of its six matches but after it could win only two of the remaining 12. It was the club's second lowest ever league placing and the first to carry a sponsor's name in its title.

United's eighth position was five lower than it had finished before and the lowest ever by a playing

New Zealand's 1981 Merdeka tournament representatives. Standing: S. Davie, M. Oram (physio), G. Fleet, M. Simenoff, B. McClure, A. Brown, A. Sibley, B. Pickering, J.W. Gendall (tour leader), C. Evans, A. Metzger, D. Taylor, B. De Graaf, J Houghton (assistant manager), T. Scheirlinck, A. Jones (manager), G. Evans (secretary general, NZFA). Kneeling: K. Cresswell, J. Leijh, K. Nelson, I. Marshall, I. Masson. NZFA collection.

through champion (a record later shared by Mount Wellington 87-88). Nine losses were five more than its previous worst and its position was not assisted by a fixture backlog that resulted in five matches being played in fourteen days.

Despite acquisition of six new players including Derek Gibson-Smith (Sydney-Croatia) and Grant Turner (Hungaria) Stop Out struggled for most of the season to stave off the threat of relegation in the final match. It conceded the most goals in the league and suffered its heaviest defeat in a televised 0-6 away loss to North Shore. Fullback Maurice Tillotson had been ever present for the past six seasons and took over as coach midway through the season.

Gisborne City never recovered from a run of eight straight losses. It won only one fixture at home and three overall and dropped to the bottom after six matches and apart from easing ahead of Stop Out on two occasions on goal difference the threat of relegation was ominous. Gisborne became the third founder member to lose its league status. The season was not totally without reward with the side finishing runner-up ($500) in the Fair Play Award.

1977

A new name appeared on the Rothmans Soccer League trophy for the second successive year when North Shore United became the fourth Auckland club to reign supreme. It was a personal triumph for coach Don Jones. Axed by the club after taking the team into the league in his first season as coach and then into runner-up spot Jones stayed with the club in an administrative position when many coaches would have departed.

Two extra teams were brought into the league for the second time for a total of 12 and prize-money was simultaneously doubled by Rothmans.

In a season when there was no outstanding team in the league North Shore proved itself the most consistent even if its form at times was anything but championship related. Reinstated as coach after one season's absence Jones guided Shore to the title following a battle with a rejuvenated Stop Out.

North Shore became the first team to lose its opening match and go on to win the title. The opening loss was it heaviest defeat to date (0-4) and was to a team eventually relegated. That defeat underlined the paradoxical nature of Shore's season.

That loss was followed by six straight wins then only one win in the next six games included its heaviest home defeat to date (1-4). Next came a club record, undefeated nine match run that included seven wins to seal the title. It won five of the six local derbies drawing the other while seven away successes was the league's best. Shore won three more fixtures than runner-up Stop Out despite finishing just one point ahead.

From second to bottom one year to second from top the next traces the marked improvement of Stop Out. The club took a leaf out of previous title winner WDU's book and used a small squad. Of 242 league positions eleven players accounted for all but 10.

Stop Out owed much to the contributing skills of newly signed Iain Ormond acquired from Blockhouse Bay after a job transfer, and from the effective strike force of Derek Gibson-Smith and Sam Malcolmson. They netted 31 of Stop Out's 40 goals between them.

A lean mid-season spell of one win in six matches was a costly sequence for the Moera side. An 11 match undefeated run was six better than its previous best and one short of the league record. Three points were taken off North Shore and only three defeats was the league's best as was its undefeated home record.

Christchurch United returned to its known form as it recovered from third from bottom the previous year to fill third place. United's cause was not assisted by a six week gap between fixtures in mid-season which resulted in six successive away matches. The season was marked by a high proportion of draws and United set a league record at that stage of four in succession. Highlight of the year was undoubtedly the 4-0 away win over long time rival Mount Wellington - the biggest winning margin between the two in league and cup outings.

League newcomer Hamilton had a good year first time up ending with the best goal average (41-22) despite a fourth placing. Had goal difference applied - it was introduced the following year - Hamilton would have edged into third place by four clear goals.

The Waikato side led the eventual champions by three points at the 15 match stage but the final seven games produced a solitary win. Hamilton was the only team to score in every away match and also to escape defeat in Auckland.

Wellington Diamond United ended equal top scorer with Hamilton but a generous defence left the playing-through champions in a safe mid-table position. Diamond began impressively enough netting 15 in the opening three games. The 5-0 defeat of Blockhouse was the team's first ever away win by more than a single goal (total of 28 games). A 7-3 success at New Brighton immediately followed to produce a league record goal aggregate. Two wins in the last 10 matches effectively destroyed any hope of prize-money.

Mount Wellington maintained its record of always finishing in the top half - just. As pre-season favourite the Mount was again affected by players involved in World Cup qualifying play. At the halfway stage the Mount trailed leader Hamilton by one point with two games in hand but only seven points were gleaned from the remaining half including a spell of four consecutive matches without scoring.

Newly promoted Nelson United led the table with North Shore after five matches and suffered just one reversal in the last eight games. However, a mid-season spell of 10 matches without a win and a penchant for draws restricted the South Islanders to a safe final mid-table placing. It drew against every team except Christchurch and managed more than one goal at home on just one occasion. Blockhouse Bay finished out of the top half of the table for the first time. The Bay was not the same force without striker Mike Farac and the Ormond brothers. Duncan collected a title winners' medal with North Shore and Iain helped Stop Out into second place. They were the only team to beat Christchurch away.

Eastern Suburbs avoided relegation on goal average due largely to 5-1 and 6-2 defeats of New

Brighton who finished on the same points total. Those two wins plus a 4-1 win over Caversham resulted in half Suburbs' goals for the season in just three games. They lost a number of players to Courier Rangers but signed the mercurial Peter Henry from North Shore.

New Brighton continued its up and down form to finish 9th, 3rd, 9th, 4th and now 10th and relegated. Of thirty-six goals conceded, Eastern Suburbs, Hamilton and WDU accounted for 25. Graham Dacombe top scored with ten but failed to score in the second half of the season.

Dunedin City just avoided relegation following a marvellous second half season recovery. City made the worst start to a season of any club to date with just a solitary draw to show for the opening nine games. City's form over the remaining 13 matches befitted a championship rather than relegation contender.

The 16 points accrued from those matches were exceeded only by title winner North Shore. Needing a solitary point from its final away match to Stop Out (who required a win to keep its title hopes alive) to avoid relegation, it was a heart rending moment when City conceded a disputed goal in the 90th minute to lose 1-2.

Import Steve Wooddin arrived for the final two games. City scored against every team except city rival Caversham, both encounters ending 0-0. It was ironic that those two goalless matches between Dunedin's two representatives effectively contributed to the elimination of the Rothmans Soccer League in Otago.

Caversham filled bottom spot for the second time although its performance was an improvement on its 1973 showing. Last year Caversham finished as the league's top scorer and at one stage was title favourite. This time the Dunedin club produced the lowest total of goals (14) and failed to find the net in the final eight matches - a league record for a scoreless spell. Finishing seven points adrift of the next team was the largest margin after the eight points league record set by Caversham in 1973.

1978

Another intriguing year with the top two teams finishing level on points for the third time, the last occasion being six years ago. It was another Christchurch-Auckland monopoly, Christchurch United securing its third title and the five Auckland clubs occupying the immediate positions below.

For the first time the team winning the most matches was not the title winner. Second placed Mount Wellington had that distinction managing one more victory than Christchurch but an extra defeat was also registered and United triumphed with a superior 15 goal difference.

Usually points on the board are better than games in hand but Christchurch United again found itself with a fixture backlog and gradually eroded a five-match, nine-point deficit to take the title for a record third time. Once again a championship was won with a small, settled squad with virtually thirteen players seeing United through the 22 match programme.

For the only time in the league's history a team won the title after surviving a change of coach - Terry Conley replaced after 13 matches by Brian Hardman. The leeway of matches, caused by adverse weather and the visit of the England 'B' side, meant Christchurch United was well off the pace for most of the season. The opening two weeks apart United did not hit the front until a final match draw away to Blockhouse gave it the point needed to unseat Mount Wellington. It had just one loss in the final 17 games which laid the foundation for United's success along with the best home record and best away defence - just six conceded a record for a 22 match campaign.

Mount Wellington finished runner-up for the fourth time in nine seasons and on this occasion threw away an excellent chance of lifting the title. Needing a win in its final match the Mount could only draw at home to Nelson, a result that cost the club $10,000 in prize-money. Not only did Nelson deny the Mount a valuable point it also ended its unbeaten nine-match run at the start of the season. This result followed on from Nelson's upset Chatham Cup final win over hot favourite the Mount the previous year to establish the South Islanders as the Aucklanders' undisputed bogey team.

The Mount could feel justifiably aggrieved at not securing the title having led the table for 17 weeks and also beating Christchurch at home and away.

Following its lowest ever league placing last year Blockhouse Bay recovered to a creditable third position. It won only four at home, drawing a record equalling six and suffered a single loss to relegated Hamilton. The team scored 15 more than the previous season's record low and an eight match undefeated mid-season spell ended with a record 0-5 away loss to Christchurch.

After avoiding relegation last year by goal average, Eastern Suburbs took the innovative step of importing two professionals from Nottingham Forest for a three month period. The immense influence Steve Elliot and Bryn Gunn had can be gauged by the results. Suburbs won nine of 12 matches (34-13) during the professionals stay but could manage only two victories in 10 (12-11) during their absence.

Elliot in particular made a notable impact netting 17 goals including four hat-tricks in those dozen outings. Nelson United lamented Elliot's presence, the professional netting three and four goals respectively in Suburbs' 8-1 and 5-0 victories.

With five matches to play, Suburbs led the table and were title favourites. At that stage Christchurch was in sixth place nine points adrift of Suburbs although having five games in hand. Suburbs' final five produced two points - both draws - losing the other three to title contenders Mount Wellington, Christchurch and Blockhouse.

Newly promoted Courier Rangers attracted a number of players with generous signing-on fees. Consolidation was achieved and finishing only nine points adrift of the title was a far better performance than most people foresaw. Just seven goals conceded at home was easily the league's best while eight netted away was as easily the league's worst. Only the champions had a better defensive record. Seven of eight defeats were by the odd goal

North Shore United failed to produce the previous year's form winning half the number of

New Zealand's 1986 Winfield Trans-Tasman Cup team. Back row: Eddie Edge (assistant coach), John Hannah (masseur), Duncan Cole, Darren McLennan, Malcolm Dunford, Allan Gilgrist, Frank van Hattum, Kevin Hagan, Dave Witteveen, Michael McGarry, Grant Turner, Richard Mulligan, Kevin Fallon (coach). Front row: Kenny Cresswell, Noel Barkley, Allan Boath, Gwyn Evans (secretary, NZFA), Charlie Dempsey (chairman, NZFA), Ricki Herbert, Andy Deeley, Billy McClure. NZFA collection.

matches although scoring two more goals than when winning the title. It lost four players from last year's winning squad to Mount Wellington (Dave Snedden, Graham Edwards, Sandy Davie and Eddie Donnelly) which markedly affected Shore's performance. The team occupied a mid-table position for most of the year except when a mid-season 0-5 away loss to Christchurch pushed the team into relegation contention.

Nelson United finished in the same position for the second year, both times exactly 10 points from the top. Only bottom placed Woolston scored less, a problem highlighted by the fact that United's three strikers did not find the net from 11 June to 17 September. It suffered heavily at the feet of import-strengthened Eastern Suburbs losing 1-8 and 0-5. United's squad, with an average age of 20, contained 13 New Zealand-born players, easily the largest representation of home-bred talent in the league at that stage.

Stop Out, with a youthful squad containing nine players under 20, dropped six places and 11 points. It won only one away fixture easily the league's worst performer and only once exceeded two goals in a match. Despite its drop down the table Stop Out conceded only three more than when finishing second in 1977.

Two years after winning the league Wellington Diamond United missed relegation by one point losing all five encounters in Auckland and the 31 goals conceded away set a new league record. WDU plunged into relegation contention after winning just two of its final twelve games.

Hamilton lasted but two seasons in the league dropping six places from its debut year. Keith Nelson missed a last minute penalty, the team going down at home to bottom placed Woolston 2-3. The extra point would have saved the Waikato team.

Even going into its last match it had control of its own destiny. Playing at home against North Shore which was weakened by the absence of three players (with the New Zealand team in South Korea), Hamilton went down 1-4. With Steve Elliot claiming a 'visitors' goalscoring record Keith Nelson became the first player to end as leading goalscorer and be relegated in the same year.

Wellington Waterside was the chief architect of its own downfall. Dismissals, missed penalties and own goals cost the team six points in all. Add to that six matches in which Waterside led at various stages yet ultimately lost. Of twenty available points against Auckland teams Wharfies surrendered seventeen.

Newly promoted Woolston Working Mens' Club struggled throughout, its cause not helped by a dismal

1991 NZFA Council. Back row: W. Munro, R. Pelosi, T. Mann, A. Kennedy, T.N. Robinson (executive director), D. Fenton, Mrs L. Story. Front row: J. Denley, H. Dods, B. Cunningham (deputy chairman), J.W. Gendall (chairman), B. Clement, T.J. Killalea. Photography by Woolf

The 1991 New Zealand (All White) squad for the Winfield Trans Tasman series with Australia. Back (from left): Allan Carville, Thomas Edge, Danny Halligan, Rodger Gray, Ceri Evans, Michael Ridenton, Noel Barkley. Centre: Keith Pritchett (assistant coach), Bryce Hastings (physiotherapist), Grant Schofield, Ian Marshall (manager), Clint Gosling, Bryan Cunningham (NZFA council), Steve Sumner (assistant coach), Noel Robinson (NZFA Chief Executive). Front: Tony Ferris, Declan Edge, Robert Ironside, Malcolm Dunford (captain), Michael McGarry, Carl Jorgensen, Brian Roberts. NZ Photocorp picture

No better way to celebrate a goal. Grant Lightbown (9) and Steve O'Donoghue of Mt Wellington enraptured after a Chatham Cup final goal at the Basin Reserve in the 1990 final. Good news, the Mount won. Picture: John O'Brien

It all seemed lost for Christchurch United when defender Ron Armstrong (red) scored in extra time to put Mount Wellington 3-2 in front in the 1990 Chatham Cup final. But there was more to come. Christchurch levelled, only to lose the final after a penalty shoot-out. Picture: John O'Brien

A day off for the Russian club side Moscow Lokomotiv at the Lower Ashford Park stud farm of Wellington Soccer Association president Arthur Williams. Picture: John O'Brien

Action in the Lokomotiv goalmouth in the 1990 Basin Reserve fixture between New Zealand and Lokomotiv. Robert Ironside (first in white from left) missed out here but he scored twice as the All Whites won 2-1. Picture: John O'Brien

The heroes - 1982 World Cup tourists. Back, from left: Kevin Fallon (assistant manager), Dave Bright, Ken Cresswell, Duncan Cole, Grant Turner, Brian Turner, Frank van Hattum, Richard Wilson, Barry Pickering, Glen Adam, Sam Malcolmson, Ricki Herbert, Wynton Rufer, Peter Simonsen, John Adshead (manager). Front, from left: Glen Dodds, John Hill, Billy McClure, Steve Wooddin, Steve Sumner (captain), Allan Boath, Bobby Almond, Adrian Elrick, Keith Mackay. Picture: Eric Jelly

The meeting of the codes. Earle Kirton (left) and Alex "Grizz" Wyllie (second from right) mix with NZFA chairman Warwick Gendall (second left) and Russian Yuri Semen who is here to assist with the development of the game. Warwick Gendall collection

A rare picture for more than one reason. The All Blacks and the All Whites are about to take part in a social game not long after the end of the Spanish campaign. And then a close look at the silver ferns suggest that the technician who printed the negative had a reverse day. The "competitors" are: Back (from left): John Hill, Gary Whetton, Richard Wilson, Andy Haden, Peter Simonsen, Tim Twigden, Ricki Herbert, Richard Dunn, Adrian Elrick. Centre: Bruce Robertson, Kenny Cresswell, Gary Cunningham, Dave Bright, Allan Hewson, Duncan Cole, Lin Colling, Fran van Hattum, Bernie Fraser, Brian Turner, Stu Wilson, Keith Mackay. Front: Bill McClure, Dave Loveridge, Bobby Almond, Graham Mourie, John Adshead, Bryan Williams, Kevin Fallon, Greg Burgess, Steve Sumner, Alan Whetton. Picture: Eric Jelly

International duty. 1989-90 All White skipper Malcolm Dunford introduces the then Minister of Sport Noel Scott to Ceri Evans, Oxford United professional and a doctor to boot. Picture: John O'Brien

Keith Mackay ponders what others have done before and still do - the skill of John Barnes, this time in the yellow shirt of Watford as the English club tours New Zealand in 1981. Picture: Eric Jelly

Football Association head Bert Millichip and New Zealand FA chairman Warwick Gendall at the centenary dinner at Wellington in 1991. Photography by Woolf

A relaxed group, but the fortunes of the game rest in their hands. From left Keith Pritchett (assistant coach), Warwick Gendall (NZFA chairman), Yuri Semen (USSR coach on loan to NZ), Steve Sumner (NZ assistant coach) and Ian Marshall (NZ National coach). Warwick Gendall collection

home record. Just one win in eleven home fixtures plus five goals scored tell the sorry tale. It failed to score in the six matches and gained just two points from the last possible twenty-two.

1979

Never in the history of the league has the title been won in so commanding a fashion. Mount Wellington's 14 point winning margin was easily a record and the magnitude of its triumph was reflected in the fact that it was greater than the eleven points that separated the runner-up and bottom-placed Eastern Suburbs.

The Mount became the first team to end with a perfect home record winning all eleven fixtures for a 34-4 goal difference. It was the fourth time in the past seven years that Christchurch United and Mount Wellington had occupied the top two positions with the Mount's latest success levelling the record at three wins apiece.

The ease of the Mount's success did not make for a very exciting league season with most interest centering around the relegation battle and the jostling for minor placings. In only two matches did the Mount surrender points, Dunedin City winning 3-2 and bogey team Nelson registering an emphatic 3-0 scoreline.

The Mount equalled the league record of eight successive wins and created a record away victory in defeating WDU 7-0 in a season when it operated with a virtual 12 man squad. Just four goals conceded at home and nine away victories, both records for a 22 match season, further emphasised the near total monopoly of the Mount.

Christchurch United headed a pack of six separated by a mere five points. That Christchurch finished runner-up despite winning just 10 of 22 matches underlines the mediocrity of the league, the Mount apart whose 20 victories was double that of the next best.

United scored a record 47 goals but underlined its inconsistency by failing to win more than two in succession. It occupied second spot from the halfway mark onwards, held jointly with North Shore for most of that time.

North Shore gained just two extra points from the previous year yet jumped three places. The season marked a change of name to Hanimex North Shore - the start of the longest and most successful sponsorship in the league. It surrendered runner-up spot by losing its final two matches, conceding nine goals without reply, possibly still affected by the euphoria following its Chatham Cup Final win over red-hot favourite Mount Wellington. Duncan Cole won the inaugural Young Player of the Year award presented by the New Zealand Soccer Media Association.

Despite a record 5-0 win over North Shore, Manurewa could not displace its neighbour, ending with an inferior goal difference to the Shore and just missing out on the prize-money. It made a strong second half season surge accumulating 15 points from a maximum 22, a total exceeded only by the champions. Handicapped by poor away form, Manurewa never scored more than one win away and only the three relegated clubs won less than Rewa's two.

Back in the league after a season's absence Dunedin City finished a creditable fifth, its 10

Old hyphen himself. Prolific goal scorer Derek Gibson-Smith scores for WDU in a National League game against Wellington city rivals Miramar Rangers. Gibson-Smith was, in 1991, coaching and still giving all and sundry a "hard time." Vic Deverill collection

victories being exceeded only by the Mount. While only the top two netted more than City's 39 all but the bottom two had a tighter defence, conceding fourteen more than when relegated in 1977.

Nelson United finished in its highest league position assisted by the second best home record but handicapped by one of the worst travelling ones. The season marked the debut of Ceri Evans while the highlight was undoubtedly the 3-0 hammering of the Mount. Only the champions won more and conceded less at home while the three relegated sides fared worse on their travels.

After starting the season in emphatic fashion securing 14 points from a possible eighteen and occupying second spot Wellington Diamond United crashed with just a solitary win in the remaining 13 games. Only relegated Manawatu scored less and the 0-7 home defeat to the champions helped make it a less than memorable year.

Blockhouse Bay dropped five places but after being bottom with just two games to go did well to jump four spots and clear the relegation hurdle with a last gasp effort. In so doing it achieved something it had not managed all season - two wins in succession. Those wins over fellow relegation contenders Stop Out and Eastern Suburbs halted a run of 18 consecutive weeks anchored to a relegation berth. Stop Out survived its closest brush with relegation. A superior three goal difference was all that separated the team from regional league play as it survived a spirited late run from Manawatu. Three wins was the league's joint low while only the bottom three won less away. It was the fourth occasion mathematics had been used to decide relegation.

After a collection four points from the opening 11 matches Manawatu United looked relegation certainties. However a much improved second half performance where just nine points were dropped saw United almost claw its way to safety. Had three points a win applied (it was introduced in 1983) Manawatu would have reversed positions with Stop Out.

Courier Rangers lasted only two terms in the top flight dropping six places from its inaugural season. Rangers' fate was far from evident in the opening stages with three of the first five matches won. Then followed a dismal spell that produced a solitary win in the final 17 games. It was not until the 20th match that Courier finally slipped into the relegation area and its place was finally surrendered with two further defeats. Of ten losses eight were by a two goal margin or more.

Eastern Suburbs' steady decline from the heady days of the early seventies was complete when it finished bottom of a very ordinary league (Mount Wellington excepted). The loss of captain Warren Fleet to the Mount had a marked effect although Suburbs still possessed sufficient players of quality to do the job.

1980

Mount Wellington became the first club to win the title four times and the first to achieve two on the trot. While the margin was less convincing than the previous year it was no less emphatic with only Gisborne City providing the possibility of the title ending up elsewhere.

More league milestones fell to the Aucklanders with a record 9-1 away victory over Stop Out also equalling the league match aggregate. Thirteen matches undefeated eclipsed the previous record held jointly by the Mount (1971) and Christchurch (1978) by one. Such had been the dominance of the Mount over the past two seasons that the club considered applying to join the Australian Philips Soccer League.

Newly promoted Gisborne City, relegated in 1976, made a successful return to the top flight securing second place by a comfortable five point margin. A high proportion of nine draws hampered City's title chances while its scoring and defensive records were superior to all but the champions. It was the only team to remain undefeated at home where it attracted attendances almost double to that of the next best supported club. The season saw the return to National League of controversial Grant Turner when he moved to Gisborne from the Hutt.

In only its second season Manurewa maintained its good form on the strength of solid away performances. At home only the bottom two won less. 'Rewa owed its third placing to an impressive start of six straight wins while the remaining 16 matches produced a meagre 14 points. Irregular displays of form saw the Franklin side lose by the narrowest possible margin, twice to the champions, but it was unable to match it with relegated Blockhouse Bay and Nelson United and succumbed 1-4 and 1-5 respectively. At home !

Wellington Diamond United recovered well from a poor start when it took five matches to achieve a win - the last team in the league to do so. It lost both fixtures to relegated Stop Out and set two club records with a low of 26 conceded and an eight match undefeated run. Fourth placing was Diamond's second best performance in seven seasons.

North Shore United dropped two places over the previous year despite securing the same number of points and winning an extra match. Shore recovered well after it had lost four of its opening five fixtures and its home record of eight wins was exceeded only by the champions. It set a new league record by keeping a clean sheet in six consecutive home matches and in losing 1-3 away to Stop Out conceded the most goals in 15 visits to the capital.

Dunedin City did well to finish in the top half after winning only six of 22 matches - only relegated Blockhouse scored less. City suffered from an inexplicable mid-season slump of just three points (all draws) from seven games. That spell was sandwiched between 6-0 and 5-1 home successes over Blockhouse and Nelson and a 4-0 away spanking of Christchurch United.

No team scored more at home than City's 26 and five of its six wins were by a three goal margin or more. Its scoreline registered the highest number of home draws, all six ending in the same result, 1-1.

For only the second time in 11 seasons Christchurch United failed to make the top three. The season began in promising enough fashion with five successive wins and an undefeated eight match run. But then things started to go wrong and the final 14 games produced a solitary success. A 10 match

New Zealand's World Cup team of 1973 (Oceania Cup winners). Back row: D.W. Tindall, M.J. Davis, M. Tillotson, A. Sibley, R.W. Armstrong, A. Marley, B.D. Armstrong. Second row: G.T. Lake, D.H. Taylor, M.R. Ferguson, B.A. Turner, G. C. Brand, C.W. Latimour, T. Randles, M. Bland. Front row: R.A. Kelly (assistant manager), B. Hardman, J.B. Truman (coach), J. Morris, J.A. Staines (captain), A. Vest (vice-captain), C.J. Dempsey (manager), K. Curtin, P. Heim (physiotherapist). NZFA collection.

spell without a win was its worst ever and for the first time United failed to record a 'double'. United's misery was complete when losing at home to Dunedin City 0-4, a team with the second worst away record in the league.

Newly promoted Hamilton soon came to grips with the reality of National League soccer. In winning the Northern Regional League the year previous Hamilton conceded four goals in the 18 match season. That number of goals was conceded in Hamilton's first league match v Manurewa. The Waikato club travelled badly losing eight fixtures - the season's high - but the team did string together four consecutive wins for a new club record.

Christchurch Rangers fought a season long battle against relegation securing a 1-1 away result against Hamilton in the final match to preserve its league status. A 1-5 opening day loss was the heaviest inflicted on a newly promoted club and began a spell of five defeats in the first seven games. A slight recovery was made mid-season but leading up to the final fixture only two points were gained from a six match spell.

Stop Out was one of two founder members to lose what had on occasions been a tenuous hold on National League membership. Only twice in 11 seasons had Stop Out managed to finish in the top half of the table with its best performance being three years previously when it finished one point short of the title.

One point was the crucial margin on this occasion also but it eluded the Hutt Valley side in its final match at home to Manurewa going down 0-2. Stop Out need look no further than to its two clashes with Rangers, who survived on the strength of a superior goal difference. Stop Out led Rangers 2-0 away to finally lose 3-4 while at home surrendered a 2-0 halftime lead to lose 2-3. Just one point from either fixture would have seen the two final positions reversed. The season marked the league debut of Wynton Rufer for them.

Blockhouse Bay was the other founder member to lose league status. For Bay it was a higher fall from grace having finished eight of the 11 seasons in the top half including six in the top four. An opening run of 10 defeats in 12 games put the Bay on the back foot and despite a spirited revival of only two defeats in the remaining 11 fixtures the deficit proved too great.

Those two defeats, both by the odd goal, came in the final three matches and the overall seven losses by the odd goal equalled the league record. Problems with its home pitch resulted in six consecutive 'away' matches being played for a solitary point return.

With just one win in the opening 10 fixtures Nelson United was always going to struggle to extend its four season tenure in the top flight. A spirited recovery of just one defeat in the next eight only flattered to deceive as United lost the final four and along with it league status. The season was not without its highlights and included a double over Christchurch and a record 5-1 away win over Manurewa. Three successive wins were recorded for the first time in a season.

1981

For the first time in the league's history an Auckland team failed to finish in the top two in what was the tightest championship race to date. In five out of eight seasons Wellington Diamond United scored more away goals than at home and it was an impressive away record that carried the club to its second title success.

United's win was not dissimilar to its 1976 championship. Its players were utilised better than in any other team in the league, its victories were achieved generally in workmanlike rather than spectacular fashion and there was a marked reluctance within certain sectors to extend to Diamond and coach Barrie Truman the credit that was due. Six new clubs records were set and Jeff Strom became only the second New Zealander to captain a title winner.

After finishing three points from relegation the previous year Dunedin City improved all round to not only miss out on the title on goal difference but come within a whisker of achieving the double beating Mount Wellington in the final of the Chatham Cup. A 13 match unbeaten run at the start of the season put City right on course but a 0-2 home loss to the eventual champions saw City slip to third spot and despite three wins in the final four matches it failed in a last gasp effort to unseat Diamond.

A vintage Mount Wellington performance of seven consecutive wins (24-1) placed the playing-through champions into the lead and on course to achieve a hat-trick of title successes. However, a slender 0-1 away defeat in its penultimate match to North Shore finally cost the Mount its title chance. Six defeats exceeded the combined total of the previous two seasons.

No club had more to ponder over what might have been than Gisborne City. After seven matches City sat at the top unbeaten having just thumped third placed Manurewa away by five goals. With four players and coach Kevin Fallon in the World Cup qualifying matches Gisborne sought, and was granted, a seven-match dispensation. When City resumed its league programme it was well placed in third position but with a leeway of as many as seven matches.

A 4-0 victory over Woolston suggested City was still the team to beat but five successive defeats put Gisborne 12 points adrift of leader Mount Wellington. A 3-0 home win over Christchurch arrested the slide and then followed a 23 day spell in which the remaining eight matches were played including a demanding five games in nine days. Such a level of commitment is not asked, nor expected of professional players in England.

That City won six of those eight in three weekends of double headers says much for the commitment of the players and coaching staff. Unfortunately, those two defeats during that period were against the eventual title winner and runner-up, going down 1-2 both times. A draw in either match would have given City second place at least. Leading scorer Grant Turner was voted Player of the Year by the Soccer Media.

After beating league leader Mount Wellington with just three matches to play North Shore United suddenly came into title contention. Two successive home defeats saw those hopes fizzle out and despite a final match win over champions WDU, North Shore would have been disappointed with its fifth placing after having led the table part way through the season. Only Diamonds could match its away record.

Christchurch United's start to the season was a first for the league - three consecutive scoreless draws - and the six United featured in by the season's end was a league record. It won only one away match as United compiled its worst record in 12 seasons although seven draws helped boost the points tally. It took maximum points only once in eight meetings with Auckland opposition.

Manurewa was also granted dispensation and went into the break in third place. On the resumption 'Rewa had slipped to third from bottom although with Rangers firmly entrenched in bottom spot relegation held no imminent fear. Two successive losses destroyed any realistic hope of finishing among the prize-money and with half the fixture list still not complete the remainder of the season offered very little prospect for the Manurewa players.

Not surprisingly the climate produced a hotch-potch of scores with one four match sequence, all played away, resulting in a 1-6 loss followed by a 5-0 success and a 1-4 defeat then another 5-0 victory. Goals scored and conceded were both club records in what was Manurewa's lowest position to date.

League newcomer Miramar Rangers performed creditably although a lowly eighth placing could indicate otherwise. The club secured a lucrative sponsorship and then brought out Norwich professional Peter Mendham for a brief yet productive six match stay. He left Rangers in the top half of the table after featuring in three wins and three draws and his contribution to Miramar's cause, both on and off the field, was invaluable. Arthur Brown and Shane Rufer netted 15 of Rangers' 23 goals. Miramar was the league's third best supported club and in 12 matches fielded an all New Zealand- born line up.

With only one win to its credit at the halfway stage Hamilton improved sufficiently in the second stanza to escape the relegation net for the second straight year. It's win, draw, loss and points record were identical to that at the previous season while dropping one place. Only bottom of the table Rangers scored less and of the 18 goals netted five came from penalties.

Newcomer Takapuna City was the chief architect of its own downfall. In five defeats and two draws City scored first and the most glaring reversal, when home side Woolston turned a 0-3 halftime deficit into a 5-3 winning scoreline, must still give coach Ray Hill nightmares.

With the youngest squad in the league - average age 22 - City found the twin handicaps of inexperience and injuries telling factors. Only one player started and finished all 22 games while three were available for every match. Seven penalties were conceded and none awarded, another daunting statistic. A home record produced just one victory and a failure to score in seven games underlines Takapuna's chief problem.

Gisborne City under pressure. Keeper Dave Reynolds and defender John Gillies foil a scoring bid by Fred de Jong, one of this country's most exciting strikers. Vic Deverill collection

Woolston Working Mens' Club's second season in the league ended the same as the first - in relegation. Woolston suffered some very heavy defeats along the way including 1-7 home loss to Gisborne and a 0-8 reversal away to Mount Wellington. The 53 goals conceded had been exceeded only once in the league before while the thirty-one lost away is an all time high shared with WDU (1978).

Travelling was a problem for all three Christchurch clubs. Of 27 away trips by Christchurch United, Woolston and Rangers only United returned with a win, 4-0 in Hamilton.

Rangers completed a non-too-happy season for Christchurch proving beyond doubt that the City cannot support three clubs and remain competitive. Five points was the worst return of any club in the history of the league and the first time a team had gone through a season without achieving a win. The only highlight in a year of continual despondency was to hold the eventual champions to a goalless home draw and recovering from 1-3 down away to Takapuna to snatch a draw.

1982

With the fixture list severely disrupted for the second year by the All Whites' World Cup exploits Mount Wellington comfortably took out its third title in four seasons.

The final league table resembled a map of New Zealand. Auckland at the top, Invercargill at the bottom and Wellington sandwiched mid-table between Gisborne and Christchurch. Unfortunately Dunedin, Napier, Manurewa and East Coast Bays ignored AA signs and spoiled what would otherwise have been a perfect story.

Referee Lennox Sharp keeps a close eye on proceedings. Dunedin City's Pat Berry has the ball and Miramar's Mike Simenoff isn't giving him an inch. Vic Deverill collection

The same five clubs filled the top five positions for the second year and prior to that (1980) the same five finished in the top six. The season was marked by a high percentage of draws. Almost one in three ended all square with teams mindful that a quarter of the league would be relegated.

Undefeated in its last 17 matches Mount Wellington, unhindered by World Cup dispensation, cruised to a comfortable seven point championship win. Just one equalled its own record set in 1974. Keith Nelson was league top scorer with 15 goals, the fourth time he netted 15 in a season - a feat as yet unmatched.

The most amazing statistic to accompany North Shore United's runner-up performance was that of its only one away victory. The previous year Shore won seven away games and finished fifth! By contrast Shore's home form was the best in the league with only the Mount spoiling what would have been a perfect record. Shore has now finished in the top half every year but one in its nine year league history.

Smitten by a plethora of 1-1 scorelines, all seven draws ended that way, plus a further six matches finishing with a 1-0 margin, Dunedin City's season produced the lowest aggregate of goals in the league. City held off Gisborne's late run to secure third spot with a one goal superior difference to end up in the prize-money for another year.

For the second year running World Cup dispensation left Gisborne City with a daunting leeway of matches. Both times City chipped away at a sizeable points deficit to end in fourth place. One can only surmise what World Cup dispensation - and the subsequent need to play two games on several weekends cost Gisborne during 1981 and 1982 in terms of lost points and lost prize-money.

The almost three month gap between league matches left City as many as nine matches in arrears of some teams and 15 points away from the league leader. After having won five of eight fixtures before dispensation City could only manage the same total of wins from 14 games on resumption. Gisborne managed to string together a 10 match unbeaten run during that leeway of matches but a high proportion of draws - six - dispelled all chances of a share of prize-money.

Playing-through champions Wellington Diamond United could not recapture last year's away form when seven successes laid the foundation for its title win. In 1982 Diamond could manage just one win on foreign soil, a narrow 2-1 victory over bottom placed Thistle. Five successive draws put the club into the record books and its overall eight were exceeded only by Christchurch. Six players were ever present in a season when several young players were blooded. Lack of a recognised striker was evident when central defender Malcolm Dunford ended up joint top scorer with four goals.

Miramar Rangers showed a gradual improvement over its debut year, reflected in a higher placing, more wins and goals scored and less conceded. Rangers suffered four consecutive losses in the first half of the season and managed only three wins but doubled its percentage of wins in the second spell. It avenged the previous year's 0-7 loss at the hands of Diamond with

One of the first English professionals and one of the best. Peter Mendham came to Miramar Rangers from Norwich City and had a most stabilising influence. He is on the ball here against Takapuna City. Vic Deverill collection

a celebrated 'double' its only such success of the season.

Christchurch United emerged as the undisputed draw experts. Over the past two seasons 20 of its matches ended all square - nine scoreless and eight at 1-1. At almost a draw every other match as well as a mid-season spell of nine matches without a favourable result, this placed United three points above the bottom team but its programme ended with an unbeaten nine match run which included an inevitable six draws.

Newcomer Napier City Rovers learned the harsh realities of top flight soccer in the first match when it was alleged to have fielded an unregistered player. Its opponent in its opening match 1-1 draw, Manurewa, lodged the complaint which the NZFA upheld and resulted in Napier losing the point it had gained and the scoreline altered to 1-0 in Manurewa's favour.

It was the first occasion in the league's 13 year history that points had been won off the field and not on it. Hopefully it would be the last but history proved otherwise. The deducted point cost Napier two league placings at the season's end but the year could still be looked upon with satisfaction. Napier suffered just one home loss (1-2 v the Mount) while the 29 goals conceded away was the league's high.

Despite its gifted point Manurewa had to bow to Napier in the final league standings. Like Gisborne, Manurewa was granted dispensation with players on World Cup duty but with half its programme completed, 'Rewa trailed the table end, even with as many as seven games in hand of some teams, survival was still top priority. That was achieved with four straight wins and despite only five points from the final six matches the side ended comfortably clear of the relegation zone.

After battling in the relegation basement for the past three seasons Hamilton City lost its league berth for the second time in five years. Having kept one place clear of the relegation zone for seven rounds City could only watch as Manurewa, with a leeway of matches, slowly eroded the points deficit to leapfrog the Waikato side.

It was a short and hardly sweet stay in the league

for debutante East Coast Bays. Five defeats in a row marked the start of its campaign (4-17) before three wins out of five games gave supporters some hope. Then followed an 11 match spell without victory which sealed Bays' fate. Despite its lowly position it suffered only one comprehensive defeat (1-6 v Gisborne at home) losing seven matches by the odd goal to equal the league record.

The season started well enough with a draw and a win and its best performance was saved for the final match - a 4-0 home win over Miramar. Alas for Invercargill Thistle. What transpired in between could produce but one result. The nineteen match spell generated just six points and included eight successive defeats.

On reflection the club may question the wisdom of having four first team regulars commute to matches from as far as Christchurch and Auckland. World Cup commitments cost the team the services of star defender Bobby Almond for half the season. The loss of his experience and stability was clearly a factor in Thistle's low placing.

1983

Auckland teams filled the top four positions to monopolise the league for the first time since the early seventies. The value of a win was increased from two to three points and created additional interest as teams were able to move at increased speed up and down the table.

The likes of WDU, Miramar and Gisborne would view the change with mixed feelings as they would have all finished higher in the league under the old system. But for every loser there has to be a winner and on this occasion it was Mount Wellington, Christchurch and Dunedin City.

For the first time in seven seasons there was no automatic relegation for the bottom three and the playoff system was re-introduced in its place. Bottom placed Dunedin Technical decided not to re-apply for admission which left the three regional league champions to contest the vacant position.

That a team can lose its opening two matches and draw the next to find itself propping up the league, yet go on to win the title by a comfortable eight point margin suggests one of two things. Either the team was exceptional or the league mediocre. Discussion would obviously extend to both sides of the argument. The feeling however is that the mediocrity of the league overall allowed the championship to be won in such a fashion.

That Manurewa deserved the title can not be disputed. Not only did it finish eight points clear but also registered three more victories, lost fewer, scored more and conceded less than any other team. The one ingredient that set it apart from the remainder of the league was consistency. After an average start of only 12 points from a possible 27 Manurewa lost just one of its remaining thirteen games which included ten victories.

At the halfway stage the league was the closest in its entire history. The difference between Christchurch United at the top and Dunedin City in ninth position was just two points. Manurewa in eighth place also trailed the leader by that margin and it was clear the title would be won by the team showing the greater consistency.

'Rewa was aided by the effective striking duo of Steve Sumner (signed from West Adelaide) and Mark Armstrong. Between them they accounted for 30 of the team's forty-six goals. Sumner, with 18, became the inaugural winner of the Rothmans Golden Boot. Two rounds after, occupying eighth place at the halfway stage, Manurewa hit the front after beating previous leader Christchurch - its first ever league success against the South Islanders in ten meetings.

North Shore United ended up as bridesmaid for the second consecutive year but how different it could have been? It is difficult to understand how a team could play so convincingly at home - a draw with Miramar spoiling an otherwise perfect record - yet produce such abject displays away. For the second year Shore won ten of its eleven home fixtures but whereas last season one victory was achieved on 'foreign' soil, this time Shore could not manage a single success. In two seasons twenty home wins have been offset by a solitary 'away' victory achieved in Auckland (v Manurewa). It was Shore's third runner-up placing, its 1975 effort also being affected by an average away record.

Newcomer Papatoetoe was the league's surprise packet. Third placing represents the highest position achieved by a team in its first season (the inaugural year excepted). Papatoetoe's performance was the antithesis of North Shore's. 'Toe rode to third place on the strength of its away record - the best in the league - whereas at home it could win just three and only bottom placed Dunedin Technical conceded more. It gave away only eight goals, half the total in one match.

A very ordinary season by Mount Wellington's standards and its lowest position since 1977. The Mount led the table for most of the period up to the halfway stage but then Manurewa took over and was never headed again. The Mount benefited from the newly introduced three points for a win. Under the previous system it would have finished two places lower. A feature of the Mount's play was a mid-season spell when the team went six weeks without scoring from free (open) play. Manurewa became the first team since Stop Out in 1977 to complete the double over the Mount.

Christchurch United had its best season since 1979 despite dropping points in seven of its last 11 games. After 12 matches United was a clear leader but five defeats in the following six games saw United plummet to second from bottom. It's best win of the season, 5-0 v Nelson, equalled its record score - a feat it has now achieved six times. Christchurch became the first team to score four goals against the Mount in 134 league matches the last to achieve the feat (in 1977).

Wellington Diamond United was another team to show early promise to take the title when an eight match undefeated run put the side at the top level pegging with Manurewa. Then followed a three week break and a 0-6 loss to North Shore on the resumption. From then on it was all downhill. Only the bottom four clubs netted less.

Never to be taken lightly, Diamond took more

points (18) from clubs that finished above its sixth placing than from those finishing below (14). With 29 drawn matches in the past four seasons WDU was starting to challenge Christchurch as the draw experts.

Miramar Rangers got off to the best start of all with an unbeaten eight match run to head the table. Even as far as the 15th round Rangers were up there in contention, following a 4-2 win over eventual champions Manurewa. Like the other title aspirants, Rangers lost its way after securing only two wins in the final seven matches. Two extra goals in the goals scored column would have lifted Miramar three places to fourth spot and an extra $1600 in prize-money.

A vastly improved second half season performance enabled Napier City Rovers to end with a record similar to its debut year in 1982. Only the champions accumulated more points and recorded more wins over the final eleven matches. Rovers' poor form in Auckland continued and after two seasons and eight visits had only a draw with East Coast Bays to add to its points tally. Poor discipline three players were dismissed - plus two crucially missed penalties cost Napier at least four league placings.

The tightness of the league was experienced by Dunedin City, poised in second place after 17 games. A disastrous run of four successive losses and a draw saw City plummet from runner-up to ninth. A spell during which City's struggling strike force really lost its way, failing to score in four of those final five. Bottom placed neighbour Technical netted less over the season.

After three successful seasons Gisborne City found itself encamped at the bottom of the league for virtually the entire season. Two victories had been recorded at the halfway stage as City sat one place above the relegation spot. Then followed a frustrating period for City and its supporters as the second half saw City almost double its points tally, suffer defeat only three times, yet improve its league placing by

If North Shore United did well is should not have come as a surprise. Manager Roy Cox (left) and coach Don Jones were in no mood to take prisoners. Picture: Eric Jelly

just one position although it placed considerable distance between itself and the prospect of relegation. It was the first time Gisborne had finished out of the top four since its promotion in 1979.

Nelson United was yet another team to enjoy a brief moment of glory - heading the table following a 3-0 opening round win at Gisborne. That was one of only two away successes by United both won by impressive three goal margins. No other leading teams won more matches at home while only bottom placed Technical conceded more goals. Nelson was always likely to surprise as evidenced by single goal victories over champions Manurewa and playing-through champs Mount Wellington.

Invercargill Thistle and East Coast Bays in 1982 and Dunedin Technical in 1983 proved that in an age of instant coffee, instant food and instant cash can now be added instant relegation. All three lasted just one term and once again it was confirmed that Otago can ably support just one National League club at a time.

Dunedin Technical trailed the rest of the league a very distant last and had the dubious honour of inscribing its name twice in the record books. Fifty-nine goals against was a league record as was the 34 conceded away while 17 defeats equalled the previous record set by Christchurch Rangers in 1981. Highlight of the season had to be Technical's solitary success, a 1-0 victory over second placed North Shore who, with Technical, shared the distinction of being the only teams unable to win away.

1984

In 15 years of National League play the 1984 competition produced in Gisborne City arguably the most popular and widely acclaimed title winner of that time. From the most far flung outpost of league soccer the provinces had thrown up a team that had risen from the ashes of relegation in 1976 to a title success of runaway proportions eight years later.

The turnaround was due in no small measure to the effort of one man, namely Kevin Fallon. There can be no argument, though credit may be grudgingly given in some quarters, but it is essentially the story of a whole community rather than a single individual which made Gisborne's success sweeter to savour.

Only one team managed to lower City's colours during the season and that came in the form of a narrow 1-2 away loss to bogey side Manurewa. Stung by that reversal which halted an unbeaten 10 match run Gisborne won its next six matches without conceding a goal (18-0) before stuttering with three successive draws, two at home.

With two matches to play and the title already secure it would not have reflected on the character of the team to simply go through the motions of playing out the season. The team chose to cement its championship success in the most emphatic manner. City's penultimate match was away to second placed Christchurch United and the final match at home to Mount Wellington, the league's most successful side and winner of the title three times in the past six seasons. Gisborne inflicted 5-0 defeats on both teams which remain Christchurch and Mount Wellington's heaviest league defeats in 21 seasons. It was the final act in what had been a memorable season for New Zealand's top provincial team.

Running a close second in the popularity stakes was Papatoetoe. In only its second year in the league the Franklin side was still within striking distance of a title after 15 matches, but an inexplicable loss of form resulted in four losses in a row and the chance of higher honours. The rot began with the defeat by close rival Manurewa and 'Toe avenged that loss in no uncertain manner winning its final match against the playing-through champions 5-0 to secure runner-up berth. In nine matches Papatoetoe came from behind to escape defeat.

Christchurch United enjoyed its best season since finishing second to Mount Wellington in 1979. A poor return of only five points from the final possible eighteen not only denied United a mathematical chance of lifting the title but also cost the side its second placing. United's 5-0 loss to Gisborne was its heaviest defeat in 297 league games and in going down 4-5 to Napier became the second club to score four goals and end up losing.

The playing-through champions started the season in the same manner as when winning the title - with two defeats and a draw - but that is where the similarity ended. Equal bottom after six games Manurewa did improve to move into second place before losing the final two and conceded nine goals in the process. Never before had a team finishing as high as fourth yielded more goals than it scored.

Miramar Rangers finished in its highest position two places above the previous year when it gained an extra point and had a superior nine goal difference. There was no shortage of goals where Rangers was concerned, averaging almost four a game and they were the only team in the league not involved in a 0-0 scoreline.

A mid-table position was the right place for a team that never lost more than one match at a time and which only once strung two consecutive victories together. It finished above city rival WDU for the first time although had two points a win applied the positions would have been reversed. It provided the league's second highest scorer in consecutive years and had Brian Field been the team's penalty taker, as leading scorer Colin Walker (Gisborne) was, he would almost certainly have collected the Rothmans Golden Boot, for Miramar was awarded seven penalties during the season.

Well poised to earn a share of prize-money with five games remaining Wellington Diamond United produced its worst sequence of results - three points (all draws) from a possible 15 - to finish on a disappointing note. It won only two of 11 home matches, the equal lowest in the league, while its defensive record was bettered only by the champions.

For the third year Diamond drew a high proportion of matches bringing its total to 38 in five seasons. A goal incorrectly awarded to Papatoetoe in a 2-2 draw at the Basin that denied Diamond an extra two points would have resulted in a higher placing. It used a nucleus of just 14 players with an average age of 22 and a half, with seven 21 or under, who, goalkeeping excepted, had all learned their skills in New Zealand.

What transforms a team virtually overnight from a

Life was never meant to be easy for a goalkeeper. In 1984 Bobby McDonald kept goal for East Coast Bays against Lyndale in a Swiss Maid League final and the goal by Steve Roberts is one of five that found its way in the net. Picture: Eric Jelly

struggling, hapless outfit into an effective, cohesive unit? In Dunedin City's case it took the unlikely remedy of a 0-6 thrashing from champions Gisborne. That defeat in the 12th match of the season left Dunedin six points adrift at the bottom with just a solitary win. It also brought the total of goals conceded in the previous four matches to 17.

What happened next cannot be logically explained. After having netted 10 goals in the previous 12 matches City then scored the same number in the next two winning seven of the remaining 10 fixtures and losing one narrowly away to Manurewa. The transformation was enough to wipe the points deficit and haul City into a safe and creditable seventh spot. Five wins and two draws in the final seven games was a record even Gisborne could not match. Andrew Deeley and Dave Bradley netted 21 of City's 34 goals.

Consistency is a word Napier City Rovers had taken to extremes having now finished eighth in all three seasons since promotion in 1982. On actual performance however the season was probably Rovers' worst, losing and conceding the highest total to date. While Napier may not have produced the results, its matches certainly produced the goals. Only three clubs scored more while 53 conceded was easily the league's worst.

No team matched Napier's ninety-one goals match aggregate brought about by such high scoring encounters as 4-4, 5-4, 7-3, 0-5, 3-4, 1-6, 0-6. It finally recorded a win in Auckland (2-1 v Varsity) and the 3-0 home defeat of Mount Wellington was the Mount's first three goal defeat in 114 games.

After two successive runner-up placings North Shore United plunged to its lowest ever league position. The past two seasons had been marked by Shore's almost invincible home form and an inability to win away. This year was almost a reversal with two home victories the league's joint worst, while only Gisborne won more away. After restricting the opposition to a goal or less in 17 matches Shore conceded almost a third of the season's total in the final two games - both played at home.

To have Mount Wellington finish so close to relegation almost justifies a commission of inquiry. How a team boasting nine past or present internationals could produce such an uninspiring sequence of results was mystifying. The Mount did not win one match out of Auckland and was able to record just one victory in the last 12 games - and that a narrow 1-0 win over North Shore.

In the match prior to that dismal run the Mount recorded what was to prove to be its most crucial win of the season. Down to 10 men the Mount trailed University three times before scraping home 4-3. Had the Mount not been let off the hook then it and not Varsity would have finished bottom and contested the playoffs. It was the first time the club had finished out of the top half of the table and its last match defeat to Gisborne 0-5 was its heaviest ever league loss. That fixture marked the final league appointment of highly respected referee Tom Delahunty.

Nelson United hovered around the relegation area all season finally hitting the bottom in round 17, when Dunedin City started its upward surge. Two defeats and a draw, even though it was a fine performance away to champions Gisborne, hardly improved Nelson's situation but then it achieved something it had not managed all season. United strung together successive wins - just when it mattered. It was enough to leapfrog Varsity and ensure the South Island's representation stayed three the following season. Nelson failed to score in seven home matches while the 10 scored was easily the league's low. It featured in two matches where four penalties were awarded while four of its five victories were against Auckland sides.

Auckland University occupied bottom place only two weeks during the season. Unfortunately for the club it was the final two weeks despite the fact the team made a valiant last match effort by beating North Shore 5-0 after surrendering home advantage.

For a team finishing last its goal difference was unreal conceding only five more than it scored - a record unmatched by a bottom placed club in the league's entire history. Its goal difference was superior to five higher placed teams including fifth placed Miramar and nine of 13 defeats were by the odd goal to equal the league record. The team's best result was a Trevor Brooking inspired 5-0 victory at Napier. It survived the end of season playoffs to retain its National League berth for 1985.

1985

For the first (and only) time in the league's history the composition of the league remained the same for two consecutive years. This followed Auckland University successfully winning the end of season playoffs after finishing bottom of the league. It was the first occasion an incumbent had survived a playoff series.

Despite featuring the same clubs as the previous year the final table barely resembled that of 1984. Only Gisborne, Miramar and Dunedin finished within four places of the previous seasons's final positions with the biggest reversal in form coming from Papatoetoe. From runner-up in 1984 to one place off relegation the next. North Shore and Mount Wellington improved six positions while Christchurch and Manurewa dropped a similar distance.

When all the movement up and down finally ceased, unfancied Wellington Diamond United topped the league to take its third title, a record bettered only by Mount Wellington. There was no early indication that United was championship material. Its first match ended in a resounding 1-4 away loss to Mount Wellington, followed soon after by a 1-6 thrashing from Gisborne. After only six matches WDU had conceded the league's top total of 16 goals - the same number as Gisborne when winning last year's title. From then on Diamond gradually picked up the points and when the pressure was on the top three teams over the final five matches, it was the only one to survive that period without defeat, collecting 13 out of a possible 15 points compared to Gisborne (10) and North Shore (4). WDU's win was a deserved if unspectacular achievement. It was the only team never to lose more than one match on the trot; it won more matches, lost less and scored more goals than any other side. It gained the title by playing attacking soccer not only netting the highest total of goals but in conceding 33 exceeded the previous highest number of goals by a title winner - the 29 when it first won the league in 1976. Many title successes have been based on a strong, defensive pattern - this was not one of them. Only once before has a team lost five matches yet still won the league - just reward for producing the season's highest aggregate of goals (83) in a 22 match programme.

The title was won by the youngest ever squad (average age 23), all New Zealand-born and Ross Durant became only the third New Zealander to captain a team to the Rothmans Soccer League championship. The other two occasions - when WDU won the title in 1976 (Mike Simeonoff) and again in 1981 (Jeff Strom). Only Malcolm Dunford was accorded international status during the year.

Gisborne City failed to make it two title wins in a row after leading the table at the halfway stage. A totally uncharacteristic mid-season run of three successive home defeats saw City's hopes take a dive but four wins in the next five matches left WDU, Gisborne and North Shore all going into the final round with title prospects open. Gisborne lost away

All White Kenny Creswell is in action for Gisborne City against Bruce McLachlan of DB Wellington. The match was played at Childers Road in Gisborne and the home side won 3-0. **Vic Deverill collection**

to Manurewa 1-2 when a 2-0 win would have been enough to pip Diamond on goal difference. While City's usually reliable home form was blemished its away record was the league's best with just two defeats and eleven goals conceded.

North Shore United, intent on making amends for last season's showing, was never out of the top three from the third round onwards and led the table for eight straight weeks into the final run in. Shore improved six places, 12 points and 20 goals over the previous year's showing - the best improvement in the league. Its record could have been more impressive had it not faltered in the final stage, gaining just one point from the last four games and failing to score in three of them after having netted in every prior match.

Mount Wellington slotted back into a final placing to which the club is more accustomed. While it was a vast improvement on last year's showing it was still far removed from the halcyon days of the late seventies and early eighties. Although only one home defeat was suffered, its record at Bill McKinlay Park was clouded by five consecutive matches without a win which included four 1-1 results. Miramar, 3-1 winners, were the only team to beat the Mount by more than a single goal.

After five seasons in the league Miramar Rangers had still to advance above a mid-table position. It had displayed rare consistency winning eight matches in each of the last three seasons and finishing with a comparable points tally and goal difference. A 10 match winless spell left Rangers one place off the bottom but six victories in the final ten games avoided any prospect of entering the playoffs. Auckland proved to be a graveyard with just two points gained from five visits.

They say it is the filling that makes the sandwich and Nelson United would subscribe to that. The season started with a four match winless spell and ended without victory in the final seven. Sandwiched between was a purple patch of nine wins in 11 games. That spell left United equal top with North Shore but the final return of two points from a possible 21 started Nelson on a downward spiral.

Having survived last year's playoffs, Auckland University started the year with only three survivors from the previous campaign. Despite improving six places and eleven points Varsity's record carried the anomaly of an inferior 10 goal difference. Never a team to be taken lightly, Varsity defeated Gisborne, Nelson and North Shore when all three occupied runner-up spot. The double defeat of North Shore within the space of four days effectively cost that club the league title.

Dunedin City's final record was very similar to the previous years' gaining an extra point but dropping one place. Inconsistency marked City's play. A home loss one week to lowly Manurewa was followed by an away victory over high flying Gisborne then after inflicting defeat on title chasing Diamond, a 5-2 beating was next on the agenda from Napier trailing the league by 10 points. With five matches to go City got within sight of second spot but one win only from the final five blocked that vision.

Christchurch United experienced one of its worst seasons brought about by a mid-season 10 match spell that produced eight defeats. Twenty-four goals scored was easily the league's low while in defence no other team conceded less. It follows therefore that United's 49 goal match aggregate was easily the lowest, 18 goals adrift of the next team and 32 short of the highest (WDU). No team finishing as low as ninth has ever boasted the best defensive record. Seven goals netted away was also a league low while United never scored more than one goal in a match.

Manurewa dropped six places and the performance was a far cry from its title success only two seasons earlier. Its lowest ever league placing was brought about by an opening spell of one win in eight and latterly six losses in an eight match run. A declining financial situation, from which the club would ultimately recover, was given wide press coverage and clearly would not have assisted the players' performance during that period.

Eleventh was quite a tumble down the table for Papatoetoe after third and second placings in its two previous seasons. The team certainly did not perform as poorly as its position suggests. At the halfway stage Papatoetoe was just four points off the lead but its form fell away immediately and only two victories were recorded in the final 11 matches. Eight of Papatoetoe's defeats were by the odd goal. Curiously, the 36 goals scored were more than when the club finished second and third in 1983 and 1984.

A disastrous opening spell of one point from nine matches virtually condemned Napier City Rovers to the end-of-season playoffs even at that early stage. A mini-recovery of three defeats, four draws and four wins in the final eleven games eliminated the slight prospect that Napier may end its season long tenure of bottom spot but the deficit finally proved too great.

Napier did not record its first victory until the 18th match, and it came against the eventual champions with the next victory six matches later achieved against second placed Gisborne. That Napier accounted for third placed North Shore in the final of the Chatham Cup proved it was not the usual bottom of the table performer. Even its goal difference was seven better than when finishing eighth the previous year. Following the fine form shown in defeating North Shore 3-1 in the Chatham Cup final Napier was expected to win the playoff series that commenced the following week but Manawatu upset the pundits to top the table and qualify for the 1986 National League.

1986

For only the second time in the league's history a season commenced without the threat of relegation following the decision to increase the league to 14 in 1987. With the fear of relegation lifted the climate was right for a season of attacking , entertaining play and all we got was a five goal increase over the previous year.

The 1986 season could be best described as 'unspectacular' and a golden opportunity to place more emphasis on entertainment rather than results was irretrievably lost. Three clubs which could claim exemption from criticism were Wellington United (former WDU), Miramar Rangers and Papatoetoe, widely acknowledged as the most entertaining teams

Two of the new teams in the National League do battle. Mark Wroe of Hutt Valley United wants the ball and Waitakare's Tony Laus is trying to make certain he doesn't get it. Picture: Eric Jelly

in the league. Gisborne City also, who featured in a number of high scoring encounters and produced the league's leading scorer.

It was very much a league of two halves. The top five clubs were separated by just six points while seven points covered the bottom seven clubs. The two groups were divided by a substantial twelve point margin.

Mount Wellington was the pre-season favourite to take out the title having made five significant signings, four of which were quality defenders. Mount's early season results fluctuated and the side alternated between third and fourth position. A run of five straight wins accelerated the side into the lead but a patchy six match spell put Miramar on top with one match remaining. Against second from bottom Manawatu at home the Mount had to come from behind and an own goal with virtually the final kick of the match gave the title to the Aucklanders in storybook fashion. In a season when no other team won 50 percent of its home fixtures the Mount's eight wins and no defeats was significant. No team had won less matches to win the title since a 22 match programme was introduced, or drawn as many games (8). It was the least impressive of the Mount's six title wins.

If any sympathy was to be extended during the season Miramar Rangers was an obvious recipient. It led the table for 16 weeks only to have the title snatched from its grasp in the last match. With two games to play Miramar led the Mount by two points and with both games home fixtures, the title looked headed for the capital for the second successive year. Playing-through champions Wellington United had other ideas, defeating Rangers by the only goal and despite monopolising possession against Christchurch, Miramar could not break the deadlock and the match ended scoreless. The Mount meanwhile, so often pipped at the post itself, got the last kick winner against Manawatu to leave Miramar one point short. Ironically, Miramar had scored in every match right up to those final two games.

Six home draws counted heavily in the long run although eight away successes and the twenty-six scored were both league bests. The decline of goalscorer Greg Brown was a decisive factor. He raced to 14 goals after only 12 matches but then added just one in the remaining 10.

For the second time no team scored more than Wellington United and no club boasted a younger squad. United need look no further than its home form when analysing why the Rothmans

National League action in Napier. Kevin Murray of Napier City Rovers won't get far if Tony Sibley of Mount Wellington has his way. Vic Deverill collection

All White Keith Nelson has a problem to chew over. Picture: Eric Jelly

championship trophy left the clubrooms. Four successive home defeats, three in consecutive matches, took Wellington from one point off the top to a snug mid-table berth. Curiously, those home defeats followed on from the 8-0 record home victory over North Shore.

Of 22 matches played in Wellington, Miramar Rangers and Wellington United won just eight between them yet had two of the best away records in the league winning 15 out of 22, losing just three.

Christchurch United bounced back from its lowest ever final placing in 1985 to move into title contention with three games to go. Its fate was in its own hands as two of those matches were against two teams barring its path to the title. With a loss and two draws not only did the title slip away but along with it third place.

Ian Marshall, who stepped into the coaching breach just prior to the commencement of the season, enjoyed the luxury of a stable line-up. His squad, the tallest in stature, was the smallest in number. Six players were ever present while four missed one match each. It was the second consecutive year United's final match had a bearing on the title. A scoreless draw with Wellington United last year was enough to give the latter the trophy. Its scoreless draw with Miramar this season denied Rangers its goal.

For the first time since its re-entry into the league in 1980 Gisborne City won more games away from, than at, Childers Road. After a disappointing start an unbeaten seven match run mid-season placed City into title contention but successive defeats against Miramar and Christchurch pushed City to its final fifth placing despite winning its final three games.

Gisborne reserved its biggest win for its final match (6-1 v University) a fitting farewell to coach Kevin Fallon. The 7-4 home win over North Shore set a new league aggregate record.

The 12 point gap between Papatoetoe and Gisborne can be placed in perspective when one remembers that just 15 points covered all 10 teams in 1975. At the halfway stage Papatoetoe was bottom on just six points (all draws) from a possible thirty-three. Then followed one of those inexplicable reversals of form as, Toe won six of the following seven with the other drawn. Papatoetoe fell off toward the end but still held sixth place - a fine achievement after that disastrous start. 28 goals were scored in the second half - the league's highest - while the seven match undefeated run and four successive wins were both club records.

North Shore United suffered the biggest drop over the previous year from third to seventh. In a year when coach Don Jones opted for youth following the loss of seven established players it was always going to be a struggle. Seven of the squad gained selection for the Auckland under-19s with six going on to represent New Zealand at that level. Shore conceded fifteen goals in two successive away matches (4-7 v Gisborne and 0-8 v Wellington United). Its heaviest defeat and record win of the season featured Wellington United. The season was marked by the debut of Robert Ironside.

Dunedin City finished in the same position as the last year despite totalling six fewer points. All City's six victories were crammed into a mid-season ten match spell. Both the start (five matches) and the finish (7) to the season were winless and ensured City would permanently occupy a lower half table berth. Of eleven defeats, non resulted in anything greater than a two goal deficit.

The ejection from the league of ninth placed Auckland University because it did not meet NZFA criteria remains one of the most controversial incidents in the history of the league. University's stay in the league was brief, just three years, and followed a rapid rise through the northern regional league gaining promotion in successive seasons under former international Dennis Tindall.

University finished two points adrift in its first season with the best goal difference ever (31-36) of a bottom placed club. A five place improvement followed in 1985 before a disappointing second half performance this year saw University tumble from a fifth place mid-season high to its final ninth position.

Nelson United started with a 10 match winless spell which, coupled with the seven matches without victory that marked the end of Nelson's 1985 season, meant when victory did finally come (3-2 v Manurewa) that ended an almost year long drought. While Nelson's season did not exactly take off after that enough points were accumulated to provide a platform from which a win and a draw in the final two games fired United away from a position it had held for 14 weeks. Nelson won just five matches all season, three in the final five fixtures.

Back in the league after a six year break Manawatu United started promisingly enough before it reverted to where it had left off - fighting relegation. A 10 match opening spell saw Manawatu nicely positioned mid-table but then the wheels fell off and only one win was registered in the final 13 games. United reserved its best performances for its opening and final match. It equalled its record league victory in its first match (4-1 v North Shore) and narrowly lost to a last minute goal away to the Mount in its final game.

No one envisaged after five matches that Manurewa would be the team propping up the league at season's end. It was third place 10 points clear of the bottom team following impressive results after meeting last year's top four teams for three wins and a draw. What followed were two wins from the remaining 17 matches and the inevitable downward spiral. Of 13 losses none were by a greater margin than two goals. No bottom placed team has ever achieved that.

1987

With seven rounds to go the newly sponsored Air New Zealand Soccer League was headed toward an exciting climax. Five points separated the leading six clubs while at the opposite end a three point difference covered the bottom four. At the conclusion however the championship race petered out as Christchurch United cruised to a seven point winning margin. The league was extended to fourteen teams with the re-appearance of Napier City Rovers after a one season break, Mount Maunganui and newly formed Hutt Valley United in place of the ejected Auckland University.

The season was marked by a number of individual achievements including Keith Braithwaite's six goals for Christchurch against Manawatu, Peter Chote's (Miramar) new league record for the most consecutive appearances and Wellington United's Billy Harris who was voted Winfield Players' Player of the Year for the second time in three seasons.

Christchurch United broke a nine year drought in winning its fourth league title. United earned its success on the strength of the final 20 matches which produced a single loss after having suffered three defeats in the opening six games. United took the title in true championship style winning 10 of the

A Papatoetoe-Gisborne City National League game in 1984 had some familiar faces. Not the least of which were Colin Walker (second from left), keeper Don Finlayson, Bill de Graaf (third from right) and Grant Turner in the seven shirt. **Picture: Eric Jelly**

final 12 matches including the last seven (23-4). The most impressive final run-in of any previous title winner. The 60-24 goal difference emphasises the degree of Christchurch's superiority with thirteen of the eighteen victories achieved by a two goal margin or more.

An attack of drawitis effectively killed off Gisborne City's hopes of a second championship. The team's opening 14 games were plagued by eight draws to leave City 10 points off the lead. An undefeated 13 match run - the season's best and a club record - overtook a flagging Wellington United and placed it into second place. One home loss and three defeats overall was the best in the league while only North Shore could match those title damaging nine draws.

Wellington United finished in the top half of the table for the eighth consecutive season - a record unequalled. 52 goals - a new club record - took United's total over the past three seasons to 148 another record unmatched. An undefeated nine match run took the team beyond halfway stage and into top place. For four rounds only goal differences separated Christchurch and Wellington United until four matches from the finish Wellington handed the title to Christchurch when it could manage just one win. Wellington had the consolation of being the only team to defeat the champions twice. It received its first double defeat in three seasons from newcomer Mount Maunganui.

Considering a lean mid-season spell of only two wins in 11 matches Mount Maunganui did exceptionally well to finish fourth in its first season. The 15 games played outside of that spell produced 12 victories including seven in succession, one short of the record. Eight away wins and the 11 goals conceded were without equal. During a six match spell the Mount met title aspirants Wellington United, Christchurch, Mount Wellington, Papatoetoe and Napier winning all but the Christchurch encounter. In five consecutive matches a clean sheet was kept in what was an impressive league debut.

Papatoetoe finished as the top Auckland club in its fifth season. It was one of five different clubs to head the table albeit for a brief two weeks right at the season's start. Seven of eight defeats were by the odd goal while the away goals total was boosted by 5-0 and 5-1 wins over Manurewa and Hutt Valley. For the second successive year the league's top Auckland club sacked its coach, this time serving notice after the penultimate match. Fred Goodwin's car-park dismissal receiving wide press coverage.

Napier City Rovers headed the table for three weeks prior to the halfway stage after starting with a 10 match unbeaten run but seven defeats in the second half including four consecutive losses left Rovers among the also rans. Despite its fall off it was Napier's best league season to date. All eight defeats were inflicted by teams placed below City at the time, three filling bottom spot. Napier enjoyed its first success over Manurewa in 10 attempts.

It is difficult to reconcile an opening run of just one defeat in 17 games with a final seventh placing. Yet that was the fate of North Shore United following a disastrous final nine match spell that produced only five points from a maximum 27. North Shore led the table for seven weeks during that opening period but a high proportion of draws prevented Shore from establishing a lead of any significance.

An 18th round defeat away to coach Kevin Fallon's old charges at Gisborne gave the lead to Christchurch which it never relinquished. Fallon shored up the United defence which conceded 23 less goals than the previous year despite playing four extra games. Shore's inability to get results against close rivals was decisive. Of 12 encounters against the six clubs finishing above only one victory was recorded with seven defeats.

For only the second time in eighteen seasons Mount Wellington finished out of the top half. Lack of consistency was the Mount's let-down. Of 11 victories none were consecutive and seven were immediately followed by defeat. Most of the Mount's seasons have been characterised by a lengthy run but on this occasion no impetus developed and that expected surge up the table never eventuated.

But the Mount was never short on entertainment, its matches producing over a century of goals - a total exceeded only by the defensively generous Miramar. The 48 conceded was a club record while the double defeat by newcomer Hutt Valley was a major surprise. A season rarely passes without the Mount entering the record books and a consecutive scoring sequence of 30 matches ensured the season was not all in vain.

Hutt Valley United made its National League entry in controversial circumstances replacing the ejected Auckland University. The team started with four straight losses confirming the predictions of those who doubted the fledgling team's ability to match it at this level. However, the tide slowly began to turn and five victories in six matches including four consecutively showed that lessons were being learned fast. The going in the second half was tougher with only three victories to count among 13 fixtures. Those wins included the completion of doubles over Mount Wellington and Napier City. Hutt Valley had arrived.

While Manurewa's performance was an improvement on last year's bottom placing it was a worrying time for the club as a repeat would have placed its league status in jeopardy. Three wins in the first half of the season that included seven straight losses suggested Manurewa had a one way ticket to the northern regional league. The second half resulted in a slight improvement sufficient to give the club a seven point breathing space away from last position. It netted 16 away goals, half that total coming in the final two fixtures: a 4-5 thriller against Mount Wellington and a 4-0 upset away to the other Mount, Maunganui.

Considering Nelson United did not move off the foot of the table till the 17th match, it did well to finish 11th - a flattering position as it was just two points above bottom place. Its start to the season of seven straight losses did the damage (4-22).

Nelson's abysmal away form continued. One away success brought its total since re-entry in 1983 to nine victories in 57 away matches (134 conceded). Mount Maunganui, in just one season, has already recorded eight away successes!

Dunedin City sat briefly at the top of the table after a shock opening 5-2 away win against last year's runner-up Miramar. After that there was only one place to go - and that is where Dunedin went, fast, not even stopping for long to view the scenery. City hit rock bottom in round 18, stayed transfixed for four weeks pointless and almost goalless before a final spurt of three victories in the last five games showed there was still some life left. The reprieve was temporary however as Dunedin later withdrew from the league for financial reasons.

Manawatu United continued its now accustomed battle against relegation. Well practised in the art, United eased clear of bottom place by a single point, the same margin as last year. Abysmal home form produced a solitary 2-1 success and the final home loss of 1-8 v Christchurch exemplified the difference between the two clubs' fortunes in 1987.

Few clubs if any would feel there was much Manawatu could teach them on the years' performance. However discipline was an area where the Palmerston North club set a perfect example. It was the only team in the league not to have a player sent off and an opposition player dismissed. Which goes to show you not only learn from those at the top but from those that finish one off bottom.

No team goes from runner-up position one year to bottom place the next without a very good reason and it has to do with more than fear of heights. Miramar Rangers did not have time to operate the parachute as it plunged to the bottom in the very first week. Rangers shared its disasters equally around the country - losing nine at home and nine away.

The league record of most goals conceded in a season just eluded its grasp. Eighteen defeats were a record given a great boost by 11 in succession - another record. That included the frustration of losing six consecutively by the odd goal.

1988

Despite the almost total monopoly of the leadership stakes by Mount Wellington and Christchurch United the season never lacked interest and the title was in the balance up to the penultimate match. So quickly did those two establish an ascendancy over the remainder of the league that it was not far into the season when most clubs had realised that third place was the highest they could

Clive Holmes of Napier City Rovers has been one of the most consistent National League goalkeepers in recent seasons. This save at Napier to deny Christchurch United is just one example. Vic Deverill collection

hope for.

Just past the halfway stage the difference between first and third had reached 17 points. A massive lead which, although reduced to 10 points by season's end, effectively made the championship a two horse race. An enforced two week break just past halfway, clearly affected the momentum of the league and spectator interest. Introduced to accommodate an anticipated tour by Brazil which did not eventuate, a halt to proceedings was the last thing wanted by teams injury free and on a winning run. In the round immediately prior to the break 27 goals were scored - one of the highest totals of the season. The first round on the resumption produced 11 goals - the lowest for the entire season. Of the seven teams that won prior to the break only Miramar managed a victory.

The season provided a personal highlight for two players. The one survivor from the league's inaugural year, Ron Armstrong, reached 300 league appearances in the final match of the season. While Mount Wellington made much of the milestone there was virtual silence from the Papatoetoe camp when Keith Hobbs reached his 300 mark earlier in the year.

For 20 weeks the league table showed Mount Wellington in first place followed by Christchurch United. It was a most absorbing struggle as Christchurch stuck to the Mount like a barnacle to a ship's hull. The Mount established a five point lead in round 11 and the two teams marched in tandem until round 21 when United at last managed to cut the deficit. Christchurch eventually got its nose in front in round 23 when the Mount stumbled away to Miramar, to deservedly hold onto its title.

Christchurch emulated the Mount's consecutive title successes of 1979 and 1980 and also leapfrogged its rival as the league's leading prize-money earner. It was the second club in 11 seasons to win the title without having a player sent off. An undefeated run of 16 matches (including 14 wins) would have been enough to burn off the opposition in most seasons but Mount Wellington, while enjoying a 15 point lead over third placed Mount Maunganui, still had Christchurch United to contend with. The Mount was the only team undefeated at home while ten away victories was the league's best. The team continued to enter the record books, its 9-0 home victory over Manurewa equalling the previous league record.

While it was apparent early in the season that the title would end up either in Christchurch or Auckland, it was equally obvious with one third of the season still to go that third place was destined for the Bay of Plenty.

Mount Maunganui sat on the tail of the top two for 23 weeks ending the season 15 points clear of fourth placed Napier. Mount Manganui had a very strong second half run accumulating 31 points equal to Christchurch and seven points superior to Mount Wellington.

That it was unable to improve on third place was due to the points deficit caused by an earlier disastrous eight match spell which produced a solitary victory and a meagre eight points. The dominance of Christchurch and the two Mounts can be reflected in the fact that the combined total number of matches lost by the trio (nine) was less than the next best loss record - Waikato with ten defeats.

Napier City Rovers achieved its highest ever league placing in six seasons heading an eight team mid-table coterie separated by a mere eight points. Rovers recovered well from a lowly 10th position after 19 rounds - the consequence of three successive defeats. The remaining seven games produced five victories including one over Mount Wellington to severely dent its title aspirations.

Having gained its league berth following Dunedin City's late withdrawal, Waikato United could be well pleased with its final fifth placing. At the halfway mark United temporarily displaced Mount Maunganui in third spot but three successive defeats put the Hamilton club back among the mid-table pack. The sequence ended with a home win over Mount Wellington, the league leader's first loss. Only the top two clubs had a better defensive record at home or overall.

No team experienced such fluctuating fortunes as North Shore United. An opening stanza of one point from six matches placed the team rock bottom of the league yet such was the recovery that had Shore not suffered a final match shock home defeat it would have finished a creditable fourth. The opening run of four consecutive defeats was the worst in the club's 15 year history. That the team went on to almost equal its own record for the most successive wins sums up Shore's season in a nutshell.

The turning point came following a demoralising 0-4 away defeat to a nine-man Waikato United. That sparked a run of five consecutive wins including a resounding 5-1 over third-placed Mount Maunganui. A 2-1 win over Christchurch was followed by 5-1 against Manurewa and suddenly North Shore was the team to beat. Unfortunately for Shore it was what most clubs tried to do and just nine points were gained from the last possible twenty-four.

The most disappointed band of supporters probably belonged to Wellington United. After having finished third last season the expectation was that United would at least maintain that position. A mid-season six match winless spell shattered the prospect and the priority became a top half table final placing. Despite United's failure to mount a serious title challenge it was, as usual, one of the more entertaining teams in the league. Its matches produced 109 goals (over four a game) easily the league's top aggregate. Fourteen fixtures produced four goals or more and six resulted in seven goals or more. Unfortunately for United, too, great a proportion went in at the wrong end. While the season fell short of expectation Wellington still managed to maintain its record of finishing in the top half and, just as important to some fans, finish ahead of close city rival Miramar.

After having risen to fourth place at the 18 match stage Miramar Rangers would have been disappointed that the momentum of the unbeaten six match run which put it there was not sustained. Just two wins were secured in the final eight games to undo much of the good achieved by that unbeaten run. Rangers set a new club goalscoring record of 47 and registered their highest league win (5-0 v Manurewa). On the

1990 coaching tactics. Doug Moore (left) and national coach Ian Marshall. Picture: Eric Jelly

debit side a rampaging Christchurch United inflicted a record 8-0 defeat. Eighth spot was a vast improvement over the previous year's bottom placing.

Gisborne City was another to disappoint its supporters. After finishing runner-up and Chatham Cup winner the previous year City fans were unprepared for a season of inconsistency. Only twice did Gisborne manage to string two victories together and after tasting defeat at Childers Road only once last season did it allow six clubs to take maximum points with them on their homeward flight.

Gisborne's form off the field declined. Its match programme, a leader in its field for a decade, fell in standard and relinquished its title as the country's best.

Goalscoring was Hutt Valley United's major problem during the season. Of Valley's first 16 matches it failed to find the net in 11. That included four consecutive at home and seven successive away. While things did improve Hutt failed to score in 50 per cent of its games that season. Just past the halfway stage Valley dropped to equal second to last following a 10 match run without a win. The final loss in that sequence was 0-5 away to Christchurch - Hutt's heaviest defeat of the year.

This loss could have set Hutt on a permanent downward move but the reverse occurred. It sparked a nine match undefeated run that produced 22 points from a possible 27. Almost one third of the season's goals came in two away matches: 5-1v Manurewa and 4-1 v Nelson.

Papatoetoe dropped six places over the previous year due mainly to a poor home record and an unproductive strike force. Forty-three goals conceded was a club high while the 27 netted was a club record low. Five successive defeats and 13 in total were also club records. The team also experienced its heaviest defeat in six league seasons. The South Auckland club failed to capitalise on a final run-in that had it playing five of its final eight matches at home. Only one of those home fixtures was won, a narrow 2-1 over bottom-placed Manawatu, and the team actually dropped three places.

Things did not fare too well off the field either. When the team sponsors of the previous three years, Landbase Securities, was placed in liquidation with nine matches to play, the fortunes plummeted in sympathy. Papatoetoe lost the next five games, picking up just seven points from a possible 27. A permanent fixture at the basement end of the league for the past four seasons, Manurewa again successfully drew on its powers of survival. There was a distinct pattern about Manurewa's results. It never won more than one game at a time, never lost more than two in succession and every victory was followed immediately by a defeat.

Its defence, allied to its away form, was the biggest problem. The 69 goals conceded easily set a new club - almost league - record while forty conceded away established a new mark. The away tally was boosted by a 0-9 loss to Mount Wellington. To 'Rewa's credit it shouldered the monumental defeat commendably' soon bouncing back to beat Wellington in a nine goal thriller and then complete its only double over fourth-placed Waikato.

Another club familiar with the lower regions is Nelson United. Six of its last seven league seasons have been battles of survival. The team had to call on all its experience to finally vacate the bottom spot it had occupied for nineteen straight weeks. A last minute escape achieved by virtue of a desperate final match 1-0 away win over North Shore.

The after-match celebrations in the changing rooms were more akin to a title success than a team in 13th position. Unlucky 13 it proved to be as the club soon after received notice that it did not match the NZFA's criteria and was expelled. United's abysmal away form continued losing eleven games - a league record. In 70 away matches, Nelson won 11. No club can survive long on that statistic.

Three seasons of struggle finally ended for Manawatu United. It filled bottom spot only twice during the season - rounds 5 and 26. Unfortunately for United the last one is the one that counts and for Manawatu it was too late for redemption. An appalling home record of just one victory laid the foundation for the season long struggle. A new league record was created with the 71 goals conceded while no team has ever before conceded seven goals in consecutive matches. Palmerston North is large enough to support a National League team. In the interests of New Zealand soccer it is hoped it will not be long before it will have the opportunity.

1989

Any season where the championship is not decided until the final whistle of the final match has to be deemed a success. 1989 was no exception. It did not always look that way as Mount Maunganui progressed through an unbeaten 17 match run to establish a healthy seven point lead over second-placed Christchurch United with a game in hand. Only a dramatic reversal of form, it appeared, could deny the Mount its first National League title.

Its defence had been the lynchpin of its success, at one stage maintaining eight consecutive clean sheets. Its attack, by comparison, had been effective without

Classy All White Robert Ironside is still in flying form against Australia. Picture: Eric Jelly

managing to have its dominance reflected in the goals for column, winning half its matches by the narrowest margin.

While Mount Maunganui set a brisk pace and led from the start Napier City Rovers stayed happily placed within the leading pack throughout. It saved its best run for the end finishing the season with a 16 match unbeaten spell.

Win your matches in Auckland and you will win the league title. It is an adage that has proved itself many times in the past and it held true for Napier. It was the only team in the league not to taste defeat in Auckland with a draw at Waitakere preventing a clean sweep. While Mount Maunganui built its success around a solid defence, Napier was more attack orientated. Its tally of goals was exceeded only by Mount Wellington and in only two games did it remain scoreless - a record no other team could match. Park Island fans were treated to 51 goals, a total matched only at Mount Wellington's Bill McKinlay Park.

A certain degree of sympathy has to be felt for Mount Maunganui. Having led the table, at times commandingly, for 12 consecutive weeks the Mount suffered from an injurious eight match spell that produced just two wins and nine points. Coupled with a lack of discipline (three players received their marching orders) and the leading pack, previously set to dispute runner-up spot, suddenly began to pull in the Bay of Plenty representatives.

A failure to translate dominance into goals during its early season form was to haunt the Mount. It clearly cost the team the title as at the final count the championship was lost by an inferior two goal difference and those six slender 1-0 victories in matches the Mount had dominated, was the telling factor. New league records were set when a clean sheet was kept for eight consecutive matches and twenty-three games were played without defeat.

Pre-season favourite Mount Wellington fell just one win short of taking the championship out. Despite the near miss the Club never seriously impressed as likely title winners. It failed to win the matches that counted against other leading contenders managing just two draws in six matches against Napier, Mount Maunganui and Waitakere.

As it has done so often in the past it headed the goalscoring charts aided and abetted by Noel Barkley's record 24 goals and its 32 goal difference was far superior to any other since. It lost two at base consecutively for the first time in 77 games (since 1983) while the 3-5 home loss to North Shore was the first occasion it had conceded five at Bill McKinlay Park.

Waitakere City was the season's surprise packet. An impressive showing in its first season of existence, enhanced by its style of play which won popular support around the country. It won seven of eight derbies with an impressive 17-2 goal difference. Only a surprise 2-3 home defeat by Papatoetoe prevented a 100 percent record. The team recovered from a moderate start when the first six games produced half the season's losses. It was undefeated against top three teams but dropped unexpected points against bottom four.

For a team that suffered the season's heaviest defeat, 0-8 v Mount Wellington away, Hutt Valley United's fifth placing was a commendable effort. It improved five places over the previous year - a league best - to finish as the top team in the Wellington region, a prediction that would not have been treated seriously at the start of the season.

Hutt's success had much to do with on-field organisation, hard work and determination and showed that a lack of star status need not necessarily be a handicap. Its best victory was a 4-1 triumph over eventual champion Napier which was followed immediately by that record loss against Mount Wellington.

An uncharacteristic end-of-season performance by reigning champions Christchurch United relegated the club from second to sixth place, 13 points adrift of Napier. The turning point came with a 0-3 away loss to then leader Mount Maunganui, United's heaviest defeat in 93 games. The final nine matches produced a solitary win, a narrow 2-1 success over struggling Gisborne, and six points from a possible 27. The loss of key defender Ceri Evans to Oxford and striker John Hanson to Burndale plus an injury ridden season that blunted the scoring skills of skipper Keith Braithwaite reduced United to a shadow of its former self.

In finishing in the same position as the previous year, the only team to do so, Wellington United, again failed to realise its true potential. It lost more games at home than it won while only the top four teams had better travelling records. It inflicted the first defeat of the season on runaway leader Mount Maunganui saving its most inept display for the local derby against Hutt Valley losing 0-4 at home.

Goalscoring was Waikato United's chief problem. In 18 matches United scored a single goal or failed to score, only twice managing more than two goals in an encounter. A record equalling 11 draws was a product of that lack of scoring power which ultimately anchored Waikato to eighth spot. United conceded the same number as it scored, restricting the opposition to one goal or less on 17 occasions. Only Mount Maunganui had a lower aggregate of goals (for and against).

For a club locked into the process of re-establishing itself after a testing period, Manurewa's eighth has to be seen as successful. Its points tally and matches won improved 50 percent over the previous year while 29 fewer goals were conceded. It never lost more than two in succession gaining maximum points from a 2-2 draw with Gisborne following an indiscretion by the Poverty Bay club. The personal highlight was club stalwart Mark Armstrong who became the first player to score 100 National League goals while the team's highlight was a dramatic scoreless final match draw away to Mount Maunganui that denied the latter the league title.

For a team that propped up the table for 17 weeks North Shore United's final 10th placing was no mean achievement. The season began with seven straight defeats and a goal difference of 3-18. The first 16 matches produced just seven points (from a maximum 48), stark contrast to what was to follow. Shore's final 10 games produced three more points than title

The multi-talented entertainer Alf Stamp. Picture: Eric Jelly

chasing Mount Maunganui could muster. Twenty-five goals were netted in that period a total unmatched by any other side. Shore made an art of losing by the odd goal - nine defeats coming in that manner to equal the league record. For a team so lowly placed its record as the leading scorer away from home (26 goals) says much for the attacking policy of coach Alan Parkin.

Five points from Miramar Ranger's opening 11 matches was the legacy of coach Tom Heptinstall's philosophy of playing entertaining soccer - whatever the cost. The National League was deprived of one of its colourful characters when Heptinstall succumbed to the pressure and was replaced by club faithful Dave Farrington. One feels that Heptinstall was the victim of his players' inability to translate their undoubted skills into results.

After 15 rounds Colin Tuaa had not netted a goal but his 11 goals in the final 11 matches contributed largely towards Miramar's best spell, losing just one of its last seven games. Mr fix-it-Farrington's influence was immediate, halting the run of 11 matches without a win with two instant successes (4-3 and 6-2). While that arrested the slide it hardly reversed the team's fortunes as only three additional wins were achieved in the remaining thirteen games.

Back in the league after a 10 year absence Waterside-Karori could not attune to travelling and failed to win a match out of Wellington. It had three lean spells of five, five and nine matches without victory interspersed with signs of recovery that never lasted beyond four matches. Highlight of the year was the 3-1 victory over Mount Wellington when the Aucklanders were still in the title race. Rather than trigger a revival it signalled instead a final nine match winless spell that produced just two points. It created a new club record in defeating Gisborne 7-0, then suffered its heaviest loss in going down 1-5 to North Shore.

If a 50th jubilee's is a time of celebration, Gisborne City had little to enthuse over. The loss of several key players made it clear from the outset that there would be a season of struggle. Two 0-7 defeats in the opening seven games underlined the gravity of the situation. That Gisborne survived with a mixture of veterans and novices speaks volumes for the spirit within the club and the determination of player-coach Richard Mulligan in his first season as coach and the first Maori to fill that position at league level. Financial problems had Gisborne axed from the league in December but magnificent community support enabled the NZFA to offer re-instatement, an offer gratefully accepted.

Fourteen defeats in 15 matches including eleven in succession would place most teams in dire straits and Papatoetoe proved no exception. It has been a long fall since the heady days of 1984 when Papatoetoe finished runner-up to Gisborne. It finished one place behind Gisborne this year and while 1984 cost it the title, this year it lost its league status. Just two points were gained in the second half of the season and eighteen defeats equalled the league record. A 2-1 win over struggling Gisborne was its sole home success. A change of coach after 10 matches had little effect on the teams' performance as just two points from the last 15 matches would indicate.

1990

Skill alone will never win a league. It must be allied to discipline, determination and resolution. Add perseverance to those attributes and it fully explains why Waitakere City overcame daunting odds to win the 1990 Air New Zealand Soccer League.

Not for the first time a team that has started the season with an impressive undefeated run (Mount Wellington did not lose until its 13th match) has succumbed to a side that has strung together a succession of wins at the latter end of the campaign.

Had Waitakere not stuck to its task of keeping Mount Wellington within its sights the league title race would have been a non-event from an early stage. They were the only two teams to regularly display the resolution and consistency necessary to stamp themselves as potential champions.

By comparison the relegation area was shaded in doubt for most of the season. New Plymouth seemed destined for a brief one term stay as it opened with six straight losses but as it found its National League legs it started to haul Waterside-Karori and Gisborne in.

There can be no valid argument against Waitakere City's deserved title success. Bottom of the league and pointless after two games City settled into second spot behind Mount Wellington in round eight and there it remained until round 23 when it finally hit the front. Thus ended 15 rounds of doggedly pursuing its quarry but the Mount had a game in hand and a superior goal difference so there was still much to be done.

Waitakere completed its programme three points ahead then endured a nine day wait until The Mount played its final match away to doomed Waterside. Needing a two goal winning margin to pip Waitakere, the task seemed a formality after Noel Barkley had put his side in front after just 82 seconds. But Waterside scored a fine equaliser and dogged defence prevented any further scoring.

A spell of 17 wins in 19 matches was the base for Waitakere's little push and with the most wins, the highest number of goals in the league, best home record and longest undefeated run, its claim as worthy title winner is difficult to refute.

For the second time in three seasons Mount Wellington failed to capitalise on an impressive start to the season to be run down in the home straight with the title looming. Victim of a late charge by Christchurch United in 1988 the Mount was unable to withstand the constant pressure applied by a determined Waitakere. Only one defeat after 23 games is an outstanding record (at that stage Waitakere had four losses) and it must have been demoralising to trail its rival by two points after producing that type of statistic.

Christchurch United failed to win any of eight encounters against Auckland opposition, losing five of the eight and conceding half its season's tally of goals in the process. This contributed largely toward the 14 point gap between itself and the title winner.

To underline the importance of downing Auckland opposition, Christchurch achieved it twice in winning the top five playoffs. United had no such

National League action in 1985 between Manurewa and North Shore, with Peter Henry to the forefront. Picture: Eric Jelly

problem against Wellington region teams, winning all eight encounters for a 22-4 goal difference. It never lost more than one game on the trot and the 0-2 v Mount Wellington was the only defeat by more than a single goal margin. It was the sixth occasion Christchurch had finished in third place.

Waikato United assumed fourth place in round 16 to spend the remainder of the season snapping at Christchurch United's heels. While managing to gnaw away at a seven point deficit, Waikato never got closer than two points to end up a creditable fourth - its best season to date - and a commanding nine points clear of fifth place Manurewa.

Any attempt to play a more prominent role in the title race was hampered by an inexplicable failure to win at home. After a first up success against New Plymouth, United then went seven consecutive games without a win on home turf. This was a follow-on from the previous year and produced a spell of just two victories in fifteen successive home fixtures. During that same period nine away wins were chalked up.

While Manurewa exceeded the expectations of many with its final fifth placing the team justified the confidence it held in itself all season. However, it could hardly have stage managed its final match away to Hutt Valley which it needed to win by six clear goals to leapfrog Napier and qualify for the top five series. 1-1 at halftime the required second half six goals seemed better suited to an Enid Blyton novel than to Te Whiti Park, particularly with the final and decisive seventh goal coming at the final whistle.

For the second successive year Manurewa had decided Napier's fate. The previous season it performed against the odds in its final match holding Mount Maunganui to a scoreless away draw to give Napier the title. Manurewa's 7-1 victory over Hutt Valley, not its record away score, was achieved in its 100th league match. What a difference a year makes. In Napier City Rovers' case it meant a drop of 17 points and five places caused mainly by an accumulation of draws - eleven - in which the 1-1 variety held particular attraction, there being eight in all. It could manage only one win against Auckland opposition, and by comparison losing just one of eight encounters against Wellington teams.

Despite its drop down the table Napier was never an easy team to beat and only the top two lost less. Last season's successful striking duo of Gary Parker and Martin Akers was reduced to a single muted act with Parker again ending as club top scorer but Akers failing to find the net in any league encounter.

Mount Maunganui plummeted to its lowest league placing. No doubt affected by its agonising last gasp title failure in the previous year the club had to endure the additional trauma of a coaching upheaval as long-time club identity Eddie Edge sought to sever his ties. It was another team to fare badly against Auckland opposition, winning just one of eight.

It also discovered, as other clubs did, commuting players from outside areas on match days rarely prove successful.

With its fifth coach in as many years 1990 was never going to be an easy season for North Shore United and so it proved to be, initially at least. At the halfway stage Shore had lost nine of 13 fixtures, had the league's worst goal difference and held bottom spot. Things could only get better - and they did. The second half produced an improvement in every department as Shore climbed six places. Only the top two leading teams lost less over that period as 22 points were gained. The team included a high proportion of players with limited National League experience and the input of stalwarts Duncan Cole and Keith Hobbs proved invaluable.

A disappointing year for Wellington soccer was reflected in Miramar Rangers' final placing. In ninth spot it finished top of the four Wellington region sides which among them recorded 27 wins against 54 losses. Six players along with coach and assistant-coach made the short journey across town from close rival Wellington United and one season was clearly not enough to knit together into an efficient unit players who for years have faced each other in opposition and indulged in keen personal rivalries. It was ironic that Miramar should have headed the Wellington contingent after having won only one of six local derbies.

Of eight victories - six won by the odd goal - all but one was followed immediately by a defeat. Miramar has only once strung together more than three successive wins in 10 seasons.

For the second consecutive season Hutt Valley United suffered a mid-season slump. Handily placed in fourth position at the halfway stage Hutt gleaned only eight points from a remaining maximum of 39. Goalscoring was United's biggest liability averaging less than a goal per match and managing to score in excess of one in only six games. Until that shock final match 1-7 defeat to Manurewa its home defensive record was fourth best in the league.

Having lost 10 experienced players from the previous season Wellington United was always going to be well off the pace. That only goal difference denied the club top placing among Wellington clubs says much for the coaching department and resolve of the chiefly young squad. It suffered a number of resounding losses: 0-4 (three times), 1-5, 0-5 and 2-6, keeping only four clean sheets. The 54 conceded was the league's highest, most of those picked up away as the home defence conceded a respectable 19. Only two of eight victories were back to back while the final 11th placing kept United out of the top half of the table for the first time since 1979.

Sentimental favourites Gisborne City delighted its horde of nationwide supporters by surviving another testing season in the top flight. Bottom spot was avoided all season although relegation was a close spectre up to the penultimate match. With the threat of relegation removed City won a nine goal thriller (5-4) in its final match away to Miramar coming back from 1-3 down. All six victories were by the odd goal including the opening home success against eventual champions Waitakere.

A mid-season nine match winless spell that included eight defeats had the alarm bells ringing out across Childers Road Reserve but one loss in the final six games underlined the determination of the City squad. Player-coach Richard Mulligan stepped down after ensuring City's survival, following two testing seasons with limited resources. The league needs Gisborne as much as Gisborne needs National League fare and it is to be hoped Mulligan's work has not been all in vain.

After six rounds New Plymouth looked a safe bet for relegation. It had gone into the league with a coaching and playing staff experienced at regional league level but comparatively untested in the National League. This inexperience had shown with six straight defeats. It was not until round 18 that the Taranaki side vacated bottom spot - never to return.

The team performed better on its travels than it did at home. Nine home defeats was the league's high while only three times did the home supporters have more than a single goal to cheer. Highlight was a 1-1 away draw against Mount Wellington, a result that saw the Mount displaced at the top for the first time, a position it never regained.

Never far from the relegation area, Waterside-Karori's fate was sealed by its dismal away form. Since its readmission to the league in 1989 it has failed to win a game out of Wellington. A mid-season spell of just two points from a possible 27 lubricated its downward slide and a solitary win in the last 15 games tells the story. It will be best remembered for its final match performance in holding title chasing Mount Wellington to a 1-1 draw. The previous year Mount Wellington lost one match out of Auckland, 1-3 away to Waterside, in a season when one extra win would have secured the championship.

NZFA Council, 1950-51. Back row: W.A. Chapman, E.C. Hall, J. Houston, J. Cowie, J.G. Shankie, G.L. Jackson, B.T. Martin, J.J. Kean. Sitting: W.L. Wilson (hon. treasurer), J. Kershaw (vice-chairman), B.S. Connor (chairman), M.H. Webley (junior council), W.B. Hicks (secretary). NZFA collection.

STATISTICS

COMPLETE UNTIL THE START OF THE 1991 SEASON

NEW ZEALAND REPRESENTATIVES 1904-1990

This is the complete list of players who represented New Zealand, at home and abroad, against overseas opposition.
The list includes appearances at home against local opposition where the match took place, either on departure or on return from overseas.
The list also includes other appearances at home against local opposition where the players were presented with some form of certification for representing New Zealand.
The listing is in alphabetic order and in the following form:
- Surname, initials, christian name (or name commonly used)
- Club(s) and year(s) of appearance
- Total number of appearances

The assistance of John Beazley in the gathering of these records is acknowledged.

ADAM GNJ (Glen)
Christchurch United 1978 (4)
Blockhouse Bay 1979-80 (14)
Mt Wellington 1981-83 (14)
Auckland University 1984 (1) **33**

AIRD JR (Jock)
Eastern Union 1957-58 **5**

ALBRECHTSEN FH (Frank)
New Plymouth Old Boys 1952 **8**

ALMOND RR (Bobby)
Christchurch United 1978-81 (38)
Invercargill Thistle 1982 (11) **49**

AMIES JT (James)
St Johns 1904 **1**

ANDERSON G (George)
Seacliff 1924, 1927 **6**

ANDERSON J (Jock)
Seacliff 1924 **2**

ANTON WC (Bill)
Waterside 1922 **1**

ARMSTRONG BD (Brian)
Mt Wellington 1973, 1975 **9**

ARMSTRONG K (Ken)
Eastern Union 1958 (7)
North Shore United 1959-64 (8) **15**

ARMSTRONG MJ (Mark)
Manurewa 1978, 1980 **9**

ARMSTRONG RW (Ron)
Mt Wellington 1971, 1973, 1977, 1980, 1983 (31)
Eastern Suburbs 1978 (2) **33**

ASHURST NC (Nigel)
Mt Wellington 1972 **5**

BAKER JP (Jack)
Diamond 1933 **4**

BALK HCR (Harold)
Maori Hill 1923, 1927 **17**

BALLARD WC (Charles)
YMCA 1922-24, 1927 **19**

BANHAM C (Cliff)
Thistle, Auckland 1952 **8**

BARKER GW (Gordon)
Mt Roskill 1954 **9**

BARKLEY NW (Noel)
Mt Maunganui 1986 (6)
Papatoetoe 1987-88 (15)
Mt Wellington 1988-90 (13) **34**

BARTON EJ (Eddie)
Marist 1933 **7**

BARTON K (Keith)
Stop Out 1975 **1**

BARWELL LJ (Len)
Rangers 1922 **1**

BAXTER SPM (Shaun)
Manurewa 1980 **7**

BEAVIS LA (Len)
Nomads 1947 **1**

BECK J (Julius)
Hungaria 1967 **1**

BELL J (Jim)
Northern, Wellington 1959 (1)
Onehunga 1960 (3) **4**

BENGE FJ (Fred)
Stop Out 1954-55, 1957 **14**

BERRY WJ (Bill)
Northern, Otago 1951 **1**

BEST MB (Murray)
North Shore United 1954 **4**

BILBY GP (Grahame)
Seatoun 1964, 1967, 1969-70 (25)
Wellington City 1971 (2) **27**

BILLOT KG (Ken)
Mt Wellington 1980 **2**

BIRCH KJ (Kevin)
Manurewa 1984 (13)
Gisborne City 1985 (2) 15
BISSETT A (Alex)
St Johns 1905 10
BLACKIE FS (Frank)
North Shore United 1933 (7)
Ponsonby 1937 (2) 9
BLAND M (Malcolm)
Gisborne City 1969-70 (9)
Eastern Suburbs 1971, 1973 (12) 21
BOATH AR (Allan)
Christchurch United 1980, 1983-84 (13)
Woolston Working Men's Club 1981 (7)
West Adelaide 1982 (9)
Auckland University 1984 (12)
North Shore United 1985-88 (24) 65
BOYES RV (Rex)
Seatoun 1948, 1951 8
BOYLAND SJ (Steve)
Stop Out 1973 1
BRAITHWAITE JRF (Rewi)
Huntly 1922 (3)
Ponsonby 1923 (14) 17
BRAITHWAITE K (Keith)
Christchurch United 1988 1
BRAND GC (Geoff)
Stop Out 1971-73 14
BRESLIN PJ (Paddy)
Kiwi United 1967-68 4
BRIDGE EJ (Ernie)
Rangers, Poverty Bay 1936 1
BRIGHT DJ (David)
Manurewa 1979-82 13
BROWN AG (Arthur)
Miramar Rangers 1981 1
BROWN G (Greg)
Miramar Rangers 1986 4
BROWN SN (Stephen)
Roslyn 1905 9
BROWNLEE W (Bill)
Thistle, Wellington 1922, 1923 14
BRUCE SA (Steven)
Miramar Rangers 1969 5
BRUNDELL WH (Walter)
Northern, Otago 1922 2
BRYDON PR (Paul)
Nelson United 1986-87 (5)
Papatoetoe 1988 (4) 9
BULLER D (Dave)
Northern, Wellington 1961 1
BURGESS DJ (David)
Miramar Rangers 1983-84 6
BURGESS MG (Mark)
Eden 1967 1
BURKE JM (Joe)
Marist 1927 1
BUTTS TMD (Mack)
Eden 1951 1
BYRNE S (Sean)
Gisborne City 1984-85 13
CALDWELL A (Alex)
St Kilda 1967 2
CALLAGHAN JP (Joe)
Shamrock 1959-1960 4
CAMERON CP (Paul)
Wellington City 1972 4
CAMERON FWJ (Frank)
North Shore United 1937 3
CAMERON G (Graeme)
Waitakere City 1990 2
CAMPBELL CW (Clive)
Blockhouse Bay 1970 (1)
Mt Wellington 1977, 1979-80 (19)
Wollongong City 1981 (7) 27
CAMPBELL GM (George)
Thistle, Wellington 1922-23 (18)
YMCA 1924 (2) 20
CAMPBELL JM (Jim)
Petone 1927 2
CARVILLE A (Allan)
Christchurch United 1988, 1990 6
CAWTHERAY S (Stan)
Western 1936-37 4
CHADWICK RJM (Monty)
Northern, Otago 1905 4
CHAPMAN HL (Harold)
Ponsonby 1936 1
CHAPMAN WA (Bill)
High School Old Boys 1933, 1936 12
CHARLTON DH (Dennis)
Christchurch City 1954-55 (13)
Technical Old Boys, Canterbury 1957 (4) 17
CHARLTON E (Ted)
Technical Old Boys, Canterbury 1960 3
CHOTE DA (David)
Miramar Rangers 1986, 1988, 1990 6
CHRISTIE J (Jim)
Tramways 1933 11
CLAPHAM A (Archibald)
Queens Park, Wellington 1904-05 13
CLARK RB (Bert)
Queens Park, Wellington 1904 1
CLEAL OC (Ossie)
Metro College 1936, 1947 3
COCHRAN RJ (Ron)
Mt Roskill 1964 1
COLE DE (Duncan)
North Shore 1978-79, 1982, 1984-88 (64)
Canberra City 1981, 1983 (28) 92
COOK E (Ted)
Corinthians, Southland 1922, 1924 5
COOPER MB (Tim)
Eastern Suburbs 1951, 1954-55 19
COOPER WR (Wattie)
Rangers, Southland 1924, 1927 3
CORBETT DO (Jock)
Philomel 1922 3
COSSEY M (Mark)
Waikato United 1988 2
COTTON P (Perry)
Scunthorpe United 1990 3
COWE J (Jim)
Runanga 1936 1
COXON RE (Roy)
Hospital 1951-52 14
CRABB DA (Don)
Hamilton United 1933 10
CRAGGS F (Fred)
Technical Old Boys, Canterbury 1936 1
CRAXTON RW (Reg)
Northcote 1922-24 19

CRESSWELL KG (Ken)
Nelson United 1978-79 (5)
Gisborne City 1981-88 (59) **64**
CURTIN KA (Kevin)
Courier Rangers 1970, 1977 (8)
Mt Wellington 1972-73, 1976 (17) **25**
CUTHILL GM (George)
Mosgiel 1958 **3**
CUTLER LR (Lyndsay)
Palmerston City 1969 **1**
DACRE CCR (Ces)
North Shore 1922-24 **17**
DANDO P (Phil)
Christchurch United 1973, 1975-77 **8**
DANIELS L (Lew)
Diamond 1924 **1**
DAVEY FR (Ray)
Technical Old Boys, Canterbury 1947 **4**
DAVIDSON BR (Brian)
Wellington Diamond United 1976 **2**
DAVIE AG (Sandy)
Mt Wellington 1978-81 **18**
DAVIS A (Alex)
Western 1952 **7**
DAVIS GK (Grahame)
Technical, Canterbury 1968-69 **2**
DAVIS MJ (Max)
Mt Wellington 1973 **1**
de GRAAF W (Bill)
Eastern Suburbs 1968-71 (13)
Mt Wellington 1980 (12)
Wollongong City 1981 (3) **28**
de JONG FSJ (Fred)
Mt Wellington 1984, 1986-87 (8)
Marconi 1988-90 (15) **23**
DEBENHAM NT (Nigel)
Dunedin City 1978, 1980 (4)
Mt Wellington 1988-89 (3) **7**
DEELEY AN (Andy)
Gisborne City 1986 (4)
Heidelberg Alexandra 1987 (2) **6**
DODS GL (Glenn)
Mt Wellington 1976-77 (9)
Blockhouse Bay 1978 (3)
Adelaide City 1980-82 (23) **35**
DONALDSON A (Adam)
Southern 1923 **6**
DRYDEN J (John)
Northern, Otago 1923-24 **11**
DRYLIE G (George)
Stop Out 1946-47 **2**
DUNCAN SF (Stuart)
High School Old Boys 1937 **1**
DUNFORD MP (Malcolm)
Stop Out 1980 (5)
Wellington Diamond United 1984-90 (49)
Miramar Rangers 1990 (5) **59**
DURANT RJ (Dick)
Western 1957 **1**
DURANT RW (Ross)
Christchurch United 1980 **6**
ECCLES GP (Gary)
Point Chevalier 1957 (1)
Onehunga 1961-62 (3) **4**
EDGE DJJ (Declan)
Mt Maunganui 1985, 1987-88 (22)
Gisborne City 1985 (8)
Notts County 1987 (4)
Waikato United 1990 (5) **39**
EDGE TA (Thomas)
Waitakere City 1990 **1**
ELDER AG (Alistair)
Manurewa 1980 **5**
ELIADIS PD (Peter)
Eastern Suburbs 1971 **1**
ELRICK AC (Adrian)
North Shore United 1975-79, 1981-84 **91**
EVANS CL (Ceri)
Nelson United 1980-81 (12)
Dunedin City 1983 (5)
Christchurch United 1984-88 (45)
Oxford United 1989-90 (5) **67**
EVANS JA (Tony)
Northern, Wellington 1962, 1964 (17)
Petone 1964 (1) **18**
EWING JS (Jimmy)
Thistle, Wellington 1924 **2**
FARNAN T (Tommy)
Mosgiel 1936 (1)
Ponsonby 1937 (1) **2**
FARQUHARSON RA (Robert)
Mornington 1904 **1**
FEITSMA RJ (Rudi)
Petone 1980*
FELTON MD (Martin)
Papatoetoe 1984 **6**
FERGUSON MR (Malcolm)
Northern, Otago 1968 (4)
Queens Park, Southland 1972-73 (9) **13**
FERGUSON RB (Bob)
Maori Hill 1946 **1**
FERRIER JM (Jim)
Northern, Otago 1967 **2**
FERRIS A (Tony)
Mt Maunganui 1988, 1990 **15**
FINLAYSON DC (Don)
Wellington Diamond United 1987-88, 1990 **4**
FITZGERALD M
Diamond 1905 **12**
FLEET WK (Ken)
Eastern Suburbs 1951, 1955 **12**
FLEET WL (Warren)
Eastern Suburbs 1972, 1975-77 **26**
FLOOD JP (Jim)
Nomads 1923 **5**
FLYNN PL (Peter)
Shamrock 1957 **4**
FORSHAW W (William)
Corinthians, Auckland 1904-05 **12**
FORREST T (Thomas)
Christchurch 1905 **10**
FRANCE K (Ken)
New Brighton 1967 (4)
Christchurch United 1971, 1973 (2) **6**
FRANCIS T (Terry)
Gisborne City 1969 **1**
GALLAGHER J (Jim)
Blockhouse Bay 1964 **1**
GARLAND K (Keith)
Manurewa 1984 **13**
GERRARD JP (Peter)
North Shore United 1933, 1937 **14**

GIBSON KC (Keith)
Seatoun 1954 **7**
GILGRIST AD (Allan)
North Shore United 1986 **1**
GILLIES J (Iain)
Eastern Union 1967 **2**
GLUBB M (Mike)
Dunedin City 1980 **2**
GORDON MA (Merv)
Western 1936-37, 1947 **5**
GOSLING CC (Clint)
Eastern Suburbs 1978 (1)
Newcastle KB United 1984-85 (6)
Sydney City Hakoah 1987 (3)
Melita Eagles 1987 (4)
Sydney Olympic 1988-90 (28) **42**
GOWANS AW (Tony)
Christchurch City 1967 **5**
GRAHAM A (Tony)
Millerton All Blacks 1933 **10**
GRAY RG (Rodger)
Mt Wellington 1989 (1)
Waitakere City 1990 (2) **3**
GRIFFIN EJ (Eric)
Ohakea 1957 **3**
GRIFFITHS GW (Graham)
Technical, Canterbury 1969 (9)
Christchurch Utd 1970-71, 1973, 1975, 1977 (8) **17**
GROOM M (Michael)
Hamilton 1980 (14)
Manurewa 1983-84 (8) **22**
GROOTELAAR HG (Henk)
Stop Out 1955 **3**
GROVES LJ (Les)
High School Old Boys 1933 **8**
GUILDEA MJ (Matt)
North Shore United 1969 **9**
GWILLIAM R
Corinthians, Southland 1924 **1**
HABETS JC (Joe)
Thistle, Manawatu 1967 **2**
HAGAN KJ (Kevin)
Manurewa 1984 (1)
North Shore United 1985-87 (20)
St George 1987-88 (7) **28**
HAGGETT RF (Reg)
Ponsonby 1936-37 **2**
HAINES NW (Neil)
North Shore United 1978 **2**
HAINES SV (Syd)
Petone 1936 **1**
HALFORD PG (Paul)
Napier City Rovers 1984-85, 1987-88 (6)
Brisbane Lions 1988 (7) **13**
HALL PD (Peter)
Ohakea 1948 **3**
HALLIGAN DR (Danny)
Christchurch United 1987-90 **35**
HANSON J (John)
Christchurch United 1987-88 **7**
HARDMAN B (Brian)
Christchurch United 1971, 1973 **9**
HARRIS AJ (Pat)
Waterside 1947-48 **5**
HARRIS RW (Bill)
Wellington Diamond United 1980, 1984-87 **18**

HARRISON J (Jim)
Northern, Otago 1905 **11**
HASTIE JB (Iain)
Mt Wellington 1971-72 **7**
HATCHARD JH (Jack)
Marist 1936 **1**
HAYDON TJF (Terry)
Rangers, Canterbury 1968 **3**
HENRY PR (Peter)
North Shore United 1983, 1985 (12)
Mt Wellington 1987 (1) **13**
HERBERT RL (Ricki)
Mt Wellington 1980-82, 1986-89 (55)
Sydney Olympic 1983 (12)
Auckland University 1984 (16)
Wolverhampton Wanderers 1985 (1) **84**
HIDDLESTONE RG (Bert)
Seatoun 1954 **12**
HIGGINS R (Ray)
King Edward Technical College Old Boys 1957 **1**
HILL JB (John)
Gisborne City 1980-82 **23**
HISLOP R (Dick)
Thistle, Auckland 1927 **2**
HOBBS KA (Keith)
North Shore United 1976, 1980, 1985 **15**
HODGSON RJA (Ray)
North Shore United 1948 **4**
HOOPER WG (Bill)
Seacliff 1927 **2**
HOPE-EDE LDM (Leo)
North Shore United 1951-52 **12**
HOUGH GK (Greg)
Manurewa 1977 **2**
HOUGH KW (Ken)
North Shore United 1958 **7**
HOUGHTON D (David)
Stop Out 1969 **1**
HOUGHTON JE (John)
Mt Wellington 1971, 1975-77 **28**
HOWARTH T (Tom)
Kaiapoi 1924 **1**
HUFF DA (David)
Papatoetoe 1980 *
HUME WM (Bill)
Hamilton Wanderers 1958 **7**
HUNTER JC (Jimmy)
Mangakino United 1954 **11**
HUNTER W (Bill)
Eden 1967-70 **12**
HUTCHINSON HD (Howard)
Mt Albert Grammar Old Boys 1946-48 **5**
INGLIS A (Arthur)
Northern, Wellington 1961-62, 1964 **17**
INNES RC (Bob)
Ponsonby 1923-24, 1927, 1936 **21**
IRONSIDE JK (Ken)
Hamilton 1967 **2**
IRONSIDE RW (Robert)
North Shore United 1987-88 (4)
Sydney Olympic 1988-90 (25) **29**
IVES CE (Charles)
Port Chalmers 1933 **6**
IVES W (Bill)
Western 1936 **2**
JACKSON C (Chris)

Napier City Rovers 1990 **2**
JACOBS SR (Stuart)
Miramar Rangers 1988 **2**
JEFFERY AF (Allan)
Western Suburbs 1969 **1**
JEFFERY EJ (Ernie)
Hospital 1937 **2**
JENKINS GS (Gary)
Eastern Suburbs 1979 **3**
JENNISON MJ (Martin)
Mt Wellington 1988 **2**
JEPSON JD (Jack)
Mt Albert Grammar Old Boys 1936 **1**
JERAM P (Praven)
Eastern Suburbs 1971, 1975-78 **18**
JOHNSON GH (Gordon)
Stop Out 1946 **1**
JONES DG (Dan)
Waterside 1922 (3)
Harbour Board 1924 (1)
North Shore 1927 (3) **7**
JONES GE (Ponty)
Hawera 1923 **1**
JONES MR (Michael)
Seatoun 1969 **5**
JONES RD (Robert)
Sydenham 1905 **10**
JUNER AW (Alex)
Miramar Rangers 1957 **1**
KAY GM (Murray)
Thistle, Auckland 1933, 1936 (13)
Abels 1937 (3) **16**
KEARNS RC (Ron)
Seatoun 1958-59 **7**
KEMP JG (John)
Mt Roskill 1960-62, 1964 **22**
KENDRICK DFB (Don)
Eastern Suburbs 1952 **10**
KENNEDY W (Bill)
St Kilda 1967 **2**
KERSHAW JI (Jim)
Marist 1933 **12**
KIDD JT (Jack)
Technical Old Boys, Wanganui 1946, 1948 **2**
KILGOUR WA (William)
Northern, Otago 1904 **2**
KING RA (Reg)
Eastern Suburbs 1954-55 **6**
KING RH (Bob)
Eden 1948 **3**
KIRK D (Derek)
Napier City Rovers 1990 **1**
KISS I (Imre)
Hungaria 1967 **2**
KISSOCK JG (Joe)
Hospital 1923 **15**
KNOTT W (William)
Northcote 1922 **1**
KUIPER PJ (Pieter)
Mt Wellington 1990 *
LAFFEY AJP (Tony)
Western 1955, 1957-59 **10**
LAING A (Alex)
Western 1948 **1**
LAKE GT (Gary)
Ponsonby 1967-68 (7)
Blockhouse Bay 1970-71, 1973 (8) **15**
LAMONT GW (George)
Mt Wellington 1967, 1970-71 **4**
LAPWOOD DJ (Doug)
Eastern Union 1958-59 **8**
LATIMOUR CW (Colin)
Ponsonby 1967-69 (17)
Eastern Suburbs 1973 (8) **25**
LAUS AM (Tony)
Waitakere City 1990 **1**
LAWSON JF (Jim)
Northern, Wellington 1964 **10**
LEGG JER (John)
Eastern Suburbs 1967-69, 1973, 1975 **21**
LEIJH JM (John)
Mt Wellington 1979-81, 1984-85 **24**
LEONG AW (Arthur)
Technical OB, Waikato 1959, 1961-62, 1964 **15**
LESBIREL E (Eric)
Wellington Diamond United 1977 **4**
LESLIE A (Andy)
Petone 1936-37 **4**
LEVY AS (Tony)
North Shore United 1988 (2)
Mt Wellington 1989 (4) **6**
LITTLE GDR (Greg)
Mt Maunganui 1985, 1988, **7**
LOTHIAN J (Jim)
Scottish Wanderers 1924 **3**
LUND GW (Garry)
Christchurch United 1986, 1988-89 **13**
McANULTY GGB (George)
Thistle, Canterbury 1952 **5**
McARTHUR N (Neil)
Thistle, Wellington 1922-24 **6**
McAULEY RT (Robert)
Kaitangata 1922-23 **15**
McBRIAR R (Bob)
Waterside 1964 **1**
McCABE TG (Tom)
Marist 1957-58 **8**
McCALLUM AG (Mac)
Abels 1937 **2**
McCLENNAN D (Darren)
North Shore United 1986 (4)
Lynndale 1988 (9)
Mt Wellington 1989-90 (5) **18**
McCLURE WJSM (Bill)
Mt Wellington 1981-82 (18)
Papatoetoe 1983-86 (27) **45**
McCORMACK T (Tom)
Northern, Otago 1927 **2**
McCREANOR H (Harry)
Nomads 1924 **2**
McDERMID JA (John)
Hamilton 1979 **4**
McDOUGALL JDC (Jim)
Mosgiel 1927 **4**
McELLIGOTT MJ (Maurice)
Marist 1924 **1**
McFARLANE PA (Paddy)
King Edward Technical COB 1957-58, 1960 **14**
McGARRY MD (Michael)
Dunedin City 1986-87 (12)
Mosgiel 1988 (16)
Christchurch United 1990 (8) **36**

McGIRR LW (Les)
YMCA 1924, 1927 7
McKINSTRY J
Piako United 1924 2
McKISSOCK D (Dave)
Railways 1948 (4)
Petone 1951 (8) 12
McLAREN GS (George)
Western 1958 5
McMILLAN DP (David)
Wakari 1904 1
McNAB T (Tom)
Eastern Suburbs 1967-69 8
McNICHOLL T (Tom)
Onehunga 1957 4
McQUARRIE A (Archie)
Mornington 1936 1
McRAE DAN (Don)
Nomads 1936 1
McVEY DJ (Duncan)
Northern, Otago 1960-62 3
MACDOUGALL M (Malcolm)
Seacliff 1924 2
MACKAY KG (Keith)
Gisborne City 1980-82 (25)
Manurewa 1983-84 (23) 48
MACKIE CW (Charles)
Rongotai 1936 1
MALCOLMSON SA (Sam)
Stop Out 1976-77 (6)
Eastern Suburbs 1979 (14)
Manurewa 1981 (5)
East Coast Bays 1982 (7) 32
MARLEY AD (Alan)
Christchurch United 1972-73 13
MARSHALL J (Iain)
Christchurch United 1981 4
MARTIN CFW (Chris)
Christchurch City 1967 1
MASON KJ (Ken)
Metro College 1947 4
MASON TJR (Tommy)
Papatoetoe 1986 (2)
Farnborough 1989 (4) 6
MASSON IA (Ian)
Mt Wellington 1980-81, 1983 4
MASTERS A (Arthur)
Comrades 1948 1
MAWSON W (Billy)
Queens Park, Wellington 1905 11
MEARS R (Ray)
Eastern Suburbs 1967-69 16
MEEHAN TW (Wally)
Northern, Otago 1951 7
METHVEN T (Tom)
Ohakea 1948 3
METZGER AJ (Alex)
Blockhouse Bay 1979 (2)
Manurewa 1981 (4)
Mt Wellington 1983 (4)
Papatoetoe 1984 (2) 12
MIDDLEMASS GM (George)
Kaitangata 1905 8
MIDDLETON CJ (Jim)
King Edward Technical COB 1960 (3)
Eastern Suburbs 1961 (2) 5
MILNE A (Alex)
Stop Out 1968 2
MOORE R (Ron)
Northern, Wellington 1964 14
MORRIS J (John)
Blockhouse Bay 1971-73 10
MORRISON H (Herbert)
Wakari 1904-05 5
MORRISON RF (Bob)
Brigadiers 1951-52, 1954 20
MORRISON W (Billy)
Northern, Otago 1904 2
MOUAT AL (Andy)
St Johns 1904 1
MOYES JG (Jim)
Huntly Thistle 1967, 1969 8
MOYNIHAN A (Tony)
Eastern Union 1959-60 4
MULGREW KP (Kevin)
Christchurch United 1975-76 24
MULLIGAN RT (Richard)
Gisborne City 1985-88 43
MURRAY WK (Bill)
Seacliff 1924 1
MUTIMER JR (Jim)
Masterton Athletic 1951 6
NAIDU P (Perumal)
Victoria University 1957 2
NEESHAM APF (Phil)
Ponsonby 1924 2
NELSON KR (Keith)
Hamilton 1977-78 (16)
Mt Wellington 1979, 1981, 1983 (23) 39
NEMET I (Istvan)
Hungaria 1967 5
NEWALL JW (Jock)
Petone 1951-52 17
NEWMAN E
Roslyn 1905 3
NEWMAN FE (Geordie)
Millerton Wanderers 1924, 1927 5
NICOLLE WJ (Billy)
YMCA 1927 1
NIXON P (Paul)
Gisborne City 1989 6
NUTTRIDGE OF (Owen)
Christchurch City 1967 (1)
New Brighton 1975 (1) 2
OLLEY K (Ken)
Western 1954 9
O'MALLEY PW (Peter)
Technical Old Boys, Canterbury 1946-48 3
O'NEILL B (Brent)
Wellington Diamond United 1986 1
ORMOND DT (Duncan)
North Shore United 1979-80 8
ORMOND JL (Iain)
Blockhouse Bay 1972, 1975-76 (22)
North Shore United 1978 (1) 23
ORMOND RD (Bert)
Eastern Union 1961 (2)
Thistle, Poverty Bay 1962 (2)
Blockhouse Bay 1964 (17) 21
OTTLEY DWC (Doug)
Brigadiers 1948, 1951 8
PADDISON GL (Gary)

Blockhouse Bay 1975 (3)
Wellington Diamond United 1979 (1) **4**
PARK I (Ian)
Christchurch United 1973, 1975-78, 1980 **37**
PETERSEN GE (Graeme)
Stop Out 1967 **2**
PHELAN FJ (Francis)
Petone 1980 **5**
PHILLIPS D (Derek)
New Brighton 1968-69 **9**
PICKERING BT (Barry)
Stop Out 1978 (4)
Christchurch United 1981 (2)
Miramar Rangers 1982-84, 1986 (14) **20**
POELMAN F (Frits)
Technical Old Boys, Waikato 1958 **4**
POELMAN KF (Klaas)
Technical Old Boys, Waikato 1957 **2**
POLLARD V (Vic)
Rangers, Canterbury 1968 (2)
Christchurch United 1970-72 (10) **12**
PRESTON AH (Alan)
Victoria University 1954 **9**
PROBERT PM (Paul)
Gisborne City 1986, 1988 **5**
PUGH TJL (Trefor)
Eastern Union 1962, 1964 **10**
QUICKENDEN R (Bob)
Petone 1951-52 **9**
RAAT JC (John)
Diamond 1960, 1964 **4**
RAE J (John)
Northern, Otago 1962 **1**
RANDLES T (Tom)
Christchurch United 1973 **4**
REID RE (Rodney)
Miramar Rangers 1958 (2)
Seatoun 1961 (2) **4**
REILLY R (Bob)
Northern, Otago 1904 **2**
RENNELL PL (Paul)
Eastern Suburbs 1967-68 **6**
RENNIE JC (Clive)
Western 1967 **1**
RIDENTON ME (Michael)
Mt Wellington 1988-90 **10**
RILEY CA (Chris)
North Shore United 1988 (4)
Miramar Rangers 1989 (3) **7**
RITCHIE D (Duncan)
Seatoun 1962 **2**
ROBINSON G (George)
North Shore United 1947 **1**
RODGER WJS (Bill)
Western 1960 **1**
ROMIJN RL (Richard)
Wellington United 1990 **2**
ROOTS PS (Phil)
Tarehuru 1924 **1**
RUFER SA (Shane)
Stop Out 1979 (11)
Zurich 1985 (3) **14**
RUFER WWA (Wynton)
Stop Out 1980 (4)
Wellington Diamond United 1981 (3)
Miramar Rangers 1982 (13)
Zurich 1985 (3)
Grasshopper 1988-89 (2) **25**
RUSSELL HB (Harold)
North Shore United 1964 **10**
RYAN JJ (John)
Petone 1964 **9**
RYAN P (Pat)
High School Old Boys 1946 **1**
SALE EV (Ned)
Corinthians, Auckland 1904 **1**
SAUNDERSON P (Peter)
Western 1957 **1**
SCHEIRLINCK AJ (Tony)
Mt Wellington 1981 **3**
SCHOFIELD GR (Grant)
Manurewa 1986, 1988 **4**
SCOTT R (Dick)
Runanga 1937 **2**
SCOTT SC (Syd)
Northern, Wellington 1964 **11**
SEFTON AJ (Alan)
Eastern Union 1964 **11**
SERGENT BW (Brian)
Institute Old Boys 1948 **1**
SHARP JH (Jack)
Stop Out 1947-48, 1955 **7**
SHAW CH (Colin)
Blockhouse Bay 1967-68 **6**
SIBLEY A (Tony)
Mt Wellington 1972-73, 1975-81 **85**
SIEBERT NJ (Neville)
Mt Wellington 1967-68 **9**
SIMEONOFF M (Michael)
Wellington Diamond United 1976, 1978, 1981 **11**
SIMONSEN PR (Peter)
Nelson United 1978 (5)
Gisborne City 1981-82, 1984-85 (20)
Manurewa 1982 (3) **28**
SIMPSON CD (Craig)
Nelson United 1986 **2**
SINGER RJ (Reg)
Stop Out 1948 **1**
SKINNER J (Jack)
Mosgiel 1936 **2**
SMALLBONE FJE (Frank)
Roslyn 1904 **2**
SMITH A (Alex)
New Brighton 1973 **1**
SMITH AL (Alf)
Ponsonby 1936 **2**
SMITH D (Dennis)
Thistle, Auckland 1952 **9**
SMITH GB (Brian)
St Kilda 1967 **1**
SMITH GWG (Gordon)
Western 1947-48 **6**
SMITH LD (Lankford)
High School Old Boys 1946, 1948 **3**
SMITH RN (Roger)
Western 1946, 1948, **2**
SMITH VR (Vic)
Technical Old Boys, Canterbury 1946-48 **7**
SMITH WAA (Allan)
Thistle, Nelson, 1954 **8**
SPEED RA (Ray)
Metro College 1936 (2)

Mt Albert Grammar Old Boys 1947 (4) **6**
SPENCER HG (Harry)
Tramways 1927 **2**
STAINES JA (John)
Eastern Suburbs 1968, 1971, 1973, **14**
STAMP AJ (Alf)
Eastern Suburbs 1978-79 **8**
STARK A (Alex)
Christchurch 1904 **1**
STEELE C (Sr) (Charlie)
Stockton Hearts 1927 **2**
STEELE C (Jr) (Charlie)
Thistle, Southland 1954-55, 1960 (15)
Western 1957-58 (8) **23**
STENHOUSE A (Alex)
Mosgiel 1933 **11**
STEPHENSON EJ (Jim)
Northern, Otago 1951-52, 1955, 1957 **24**
STICKLAND LM (Lee)
Manurewa 1980 **2**
STONE RH (Ron)
Glen Innes 1933 (10)
Thistle, Auckland, 1937 (2) **12**
STORER G (Graham)
New Brighton 1975 (12)
Christchurch United 1976 (1) **13**
STROM DG (David)
Seatoun 1967 *
STROM JW (Jeff)
Wellington Diamond United 1980-81, 1983 **16**
STROUD A (Arthur)
North Shore United 1964 (7)
Ponsonby 1967 (1) **8**
STROUD AJ (Alan)
Christchurch United 1986, 1988 **2**
SUDLOW K (Ken)
Blockhouse Bay 1964 **15**
SUMNER SP (Steve)
Christchurch United 1976-80, 1988 (47)
Newcastle KB United 1981 (17)
West Adelaide 1982 (7)
Manurewa 1983-86 (34) **105**
SUTHERLAND A (Alex)
Maori Hill 1936-37 **4**
TAYLOR BPF (Barry)
Miramar Rangers 1964 **1**
TAYLOR DH (Dave)
Blockhouse Bay 1967 (1)
Mt Wellington 1972-73, 1975-76, 1980-81 (54)
Courier Rangers 1977-78 (9) **64**
TAYLOR WJ (Joe)
Diamond 1904-05 **10**
TEN BROEKE RJ (Robert)
Stop Out 1978 **4**
THOMAS WE (Earle)
Mt Wellington 1967-71, 1973, 1975-76, 1976-77 (40)
Eden 1976 (1)
Eastern Suburbs 1978 (2) **43**
THOMAS WR (Bill)
Marist 1923-24 **13**
TILLOTSON M (Maurice)
Gisborne City 1972-73 (16)
Stop Out 1975 (4) **20**
TINDALL DW (Dennis)
Dunedin Suburbs 1971 (2)
Mt Wellington 1972-73 (17)
Hamilton 1976 (8) **27**
TINKLER J (Jack)
Tramways 1927 **2**
TODD G (Joe)
Hospital 1936-37 **3**
TORKINGTON D (Derek)
Western 1964 **11**
TRAYNOR PP (Phil)
Waterside 1948 (2)
Seatoun 1951 (8)
North Shore United 1954 (10) **20**
TURNER BA (Brian)
Eden 1967 (5)
Chelsea 1968 (1)
Mt Wellington 1972-73, 1975-80 (74)
Blacktown City 1981 (15)
Gisborne City 1982 (7) **102**
TURNER CM (Chris)
Manurewa 1979-80 **15**
TURNER GJ (Grant)
Gisborne City 1980-84 (51)
Petone 1985 (8)
Miramar Rangers 1986 (5)
Wellington United (7) **71**
TUAA CW (Colin)
Papatoetoe 1983-84, 1988 **10**
UPCHURCH IE (Ian)
Seatoun 1951-52 **9**
USSHER FP (Fred)
Roslyn 1905 **11**
VAN DEN BROEK TH (Theo)
Eastern Suburbs 1958 **7**
VAN HATTUM FM (Frank)
Manurewa 1980-82, 1990 (17)
Christchurch United 1983 (3)
Papatoetoe 1984 (7)
Auckland University 1985-86 (13)
Mt Maunganui 1987 (1) **41**
VAN HELDEN JC (John)
Gisborne City 1980 **1**
VAN ROOYEN A (Arie)
Nomads 1959 **1**
VERWEIJ J (Johan)
Christchurch United 1979, 1983 **13**
VEST A (Alan)
Gisborne City 1972-73 **19**
WALKER C (Colin)
Gisborne City 1984-85, 1988 **34**
WALKER KM (Max)
Kawerau Town 1955 **3**
WALLACE DR (David)
Western Suburbs 1962, 1967-68 **7**
WALSH IA (Ivan)
Northern, Otago 1951 **4**
WARMAN DT (Des)
Ohakea 1948 **2**
WARRENDER JM (Jim)
Railways 1959-61 **6**
WATSON D (Doug)
Christchurch United 1970 **1**
WELCH GW (Garry)
Wellington Diamond United 1980 **3**
WESTERVELD WJH (Bill)
Mornington 1954 **9**
WEYMOUTH KD (Kevin)
North Shore United 1975 (9)

Mt Wellington 1976-78 (14) **23**
WHITE J (John)
Western 1952 **9**
WHITE L (Len)
Swifts 1904 **1**
WHITING PL (Peter)
Miramar Rangers 1961-62, 1964 **14**
WHITTAKER D (Dick)
Onehunga 1957 **2**
WILKINSON A (Alan)
Mt Albert Grammar Old Boys 1946-47 **2**
WILLIAMS L (Dummy)
Thistle, Auckland 1924 **1**
WILSON R (Bob)
Wigram 1948 **1**
WILSON RH (Richard)
Nelson United 1979 (9)
Canberra City 1980 (3)
Preston Makedonia 1981-82, 1984-85 (28) **40**
WITTEVEEN D (Dave)
Mt Wellington 1986, 1989 **9**
WOOD RL (Les)
Thistle, Auckland 1936-37 (4)
Metro College 1947 (4) **8**
WOODDIN S (Steve)
Dunedin City 1980 (5)
Sth Melbourne 1981-83 (26)
Christchurch United 1984 (6) **37**
WOODS WS (Billy)
Hospital 1947 **3**
WRATHALL JD (John)
Eastern Suburbs 1959-61 **5**
WRIGHT G (George)
Thistle, Auckland, 1936 **1**
WRIGHT K (Kim)
North Shore United 1988 (3)
Waitakere City 1990 (3) **6**
WRIGHT W (Billy)
Mt Wellington 1988 (6)
Morwell Falcons 1989 (2) **8**
YORK GR (George)
Ponsonby 1967 **1**
YOUNG AR (Alex)
Hamilton 1977 **1**
ZORICICH CV (Chris)
Papatoetoe 1988 **3**
ZUILL WH (Bill)
Onehunga 1933 **11**

**Toured overseas but did not play*

BROTHERS WHO REPRESENTED NEW ZEALAND

Anderson G and J
Armstrong BD and RW
Ives CE and W
Ormond DT and JL
Poelman F and KF
Rufer SA and WWA
Smith GWG and RN and VR
Strom DG and JW (Strom DG toured but did not play)

FATHERS AND SONS WHO REPRESENTED NEW ZEALAND

Armstrong K and BD and RW
Durant RJ and RW
Fleet WK and WL
Jeffery EJ and AF
Ormond RD and DT and JL
Smith GWG and GB
Steele C Sr and Jr
Stroud A and AJ

APPEARED FOR AND AGAINST NEW ZEALAND

Byrne S	League of Ireland
Hough KW	Australia
Naidu P	Suva and Southern

DOUBLE INTERNATIONALS SOCCER AND CRICKET

Bilby GP
Burgess MG
Dacre CCR
Hough KW
McRae DAN
Sale EV

MOST APPEARANCES

105 Steve Sumner
102 Brian Turner
92 Duncan Cole
91 Adrian Elrick
84 Ricki Herbert

NEW ZEALAND REPRESENTATIVES 1904-1990 LISTING BY "ASSOCIATION" AND BY "CLUB"

AUCKLAND

Abels (2)
Kay
McCallum

Blockhouse Bay (13)
Adam
Campbell C
Dods
Gallagher
Lake
Metzger
Morris
Ormond I
Ormond R
Paddison
Shaw
Sudlow
Taylor D

Comrades
(Refer Western Springs)

Corinthians (2)
Forshaw
Sale

East Coast Bays (1)
Malcolmson

Eastern Suburbs (25)
Armstrong R
Bland
Cooper T
de Graaf
Eliadis
Fleet K
Fleet W
Gosling
Jenkins
Jeram
Kendrick
King RA
Latimour
Legg
McNab
Malcolmson
Mears
Middleton
Rennell
Staines
Stamp
Stone (Glen Innes)
Thomas E
Van den Broek
Wrathall

Eden (6)
Burgess M
Butts
Hunter W
King RH
Thomas E
Turner B

Glen Innes
(Refer Eastern Suburbs)

Harbour Board (1)
Jones D

Lynndale (1)
McClennan

Metro College (4)
Cleal
Mason K
Speed
Wood

Mt Albert Grammar OB
(Refer Mt Albert-Ponsonby)

Mt Albert-Ponsonby (16)
Blackie (Pons)
Braithwaite R (Pons)
Chapman H (Pons)
Farnan (Pons)
Haggett (Pons)
Hutchinson (Mt A)
Innes (Pons)
Jepson (Mt A)
Lake (Pons)
Latimour (Pons)
Neesham (Pons)
Smith AL (Pons)
Speed (Mt A)
Stroud A (Pons)
Wilkinson (Mt A)
York (Pons)

Mt Roskill (3)
Barker
Cochran
Kemp

Mt Wellington (40)
Adam
Armstrong B
Armstrong R
Ashurst
Barkley
Billot
Campbell C
Curtin
Davie
Davis M
de Graaf
de Jong
Debenham
Dods
Gray
Hastie
Henry
Herbert
Houghton J
Jennison
Kuiper
Lamont
Leijh
Levy
McClennan
McClure
Masson
Metzger
Nelson
Ridenton
Schierlinck
Sibley
Siebert
Taylor D
Thomas E
Tindall
Turner B
Weymouth
Witteveen
Wright W

Northcote (2)
Craxton
Knott

North Shore United (31)
Armstrong K
Best
Blackie
Boath
Cameron F
Cole
Dacre
Elrick
Gerrard

Gilgrist
Guildea
Hagan
Haines N
Henry
Hobbs
Hodgson
Hope-Ede
Hough K
Ironside R
Jones D
Levy
McClennan
Ormond D
Ormond I
Riley
Robinson
Russell
Stroud A
Traynor
Weymouth
Wright K

Onehunga-Mangere United (5)
Bell
Eccles
McNicholl
Whittaker
Zuill

Philomel (1)
Corbett

Point Chevalier
(Refer Western Springs)

Ponsonby
(Refer Mt Albert-Ponsonby)

Thistle (8)
Banham
Hislop
Kay
Smith D
Stone
Williams
Wood
Wright G

Tramways (3)
Christie
Spencer
Tinkler

University (4)
Adam
Boath
Herbert
Van Hattum

Waitakere City (5)
Cameron G
Edge T
Gray
Laus
Wright K

Western Springs (2)
Eccles (Point Chev)
Masters (Comrades)

BAY OF PLENTY

Kawerau Town (1)
Walker M

Mangakino United (1)
Hunter J

Mt Maunganui (5)
Barkley
Edge D
Ferris
Little
Van Hattum

BULLER

Millerton All Blacks (1)
Graham

Millerton Wanderers (1)
Newman G

Stockton Hearts (1)
Steele Sr

CANTERBURY

Christchurch (2)
Forrest
Stark

Christchurch City
(Refer Christchurch United)

Christchurch United (33)
Adam
Almond
Boath
Braithwaite K
Carville
Charlton D (City)
Dando
Durant RW
Evans C
France
Gowans (City)
Griffiths
Halligan
Hanson
Hardman
Lund
McGarry
Marley
Marshall
Martin (City)
Mulgrew
Nuttridge (City)
Park
Pickering
Pollard
Randles
Storer

Stroud AJ
Sumner
Van Hattum
Verweij
Watson
Wooddin

Kaiapoi (1)
Howarth

New Brighton (5)
France
Nuttridge
Phillips
Smith A
Storer

Nomads (5)
Beavis
Flood
McCreanor
McRae
Van Rooyen

Rangers (3)
Barwell
Haydon
Pollard

Shamrock (2)
Callaghan
Flynn

Sydenham (1)
Jones R

Technical OB (8)
Charlton D
Charlton E
Craggs
Davey
Davis G
Griffiths
O'Malley
Smith V

Thistle (1)
McAnulty

Western (17)
Cawtheray
Davis A
Durant RJ
Gordon
Ives W
Laffey
Laing
McLaren
Olley
Rennie
Rodger
Saunderson
Smith G
Smith R
Steele Jr
Torkington

White J

Wigram (1)
Wilson R

Woolston WMC (1)
Boath

FRANKLIN & DISTRICTS

Courier Rangers (2)
Curtin
Taylor D

Manurewa (18)
Armstrong M
Baxter
Birch
Bright
Elder
Garland
Groom
Hagan
Hough G
Mackay
Malcolmson
Metzger
Schofield
Simonsen
Stickland
Sumner
Turner C
Van Hattum

Papatoetoe (10)
Barkley
Brydon
Felton
Huff
McClure
Mason T
Metzger
Tuaa
Van Hattum
Zoricich

HAWKES BAY

Napier City Rovers (3)
Halford
Jackson C
Kirk

MANAWATU

Kiwi United
(Refer Manawatu)

Manawatu (3)
Breslin (Kiwi)
Cutler (Palm City)
Habets (Thistle)

Ohakea (4)
Griffin
Hall
Methven
Warman

Palmerston City
(Refer Manawatu)

Thistle
(Refer Manawatu)

NELSON

Nelson United (7)
Brydon
Cresswell
Evans C
Simonsen
Simpson
Smith WA (Thistle)
Wilson RH

Thistle
(Refer Nelson United)

OTAGO

Dunedin City (10)
Chapman W (HSOB)
Debenham
Duncan (HSOB)
Evans C
Glubb
Groves (HSOB)
McGarry
Ryan P (HSOB)
Smith L (HSOB)
Wooddin

Dunedin Suburbs (1)
Tindall

High School OB
(Refer Dunedin City)

Kaitangata (2)
McAuley
Middlemass

Maori Hill
(Refer Northern)

Mornington (3)
Farquharson
McQuarrie
Westerveld

Mosgiel (6)
Cuthill
Farnan
McDougall
McGarry
Skinner
Stenhouse

Northern (19)
Balk (Maori Hill)
Berry
Brundell
Chadwick
Dryden
Ferguson M
Ferguson R (Maori Hill)
Ferrier
Harrison
Kilgour
McCormack
McVey
Meehan
Morrison W
Rae
Reilly
Stephenson
Sutherland (Maori Hill)
Walsh

Port Chalmers (1)
Ives C

Roslyn (4)
Brown S
Newman E
Smallbone
Ussher

St Kilda (3)
Caldwell
Kennedy
Smith B

Seacliff (5)
Anderson G
Anderson J
Hooper
Macdougall
Murray

Southern (1)
Donaldson

Technical OB (3)
Higgins
McFarlane
Middleton

Wakari (2)
McMillan
Morrison H

POVERTY BAY

Eastern Union
(Refer Gisborne City)

Gisborne City (27)
Aird (Union)
Armstrong K (Union)
Birch
Bland
Byrne
Cresswell
Deeley
Edge D
Francis
Gillies (Union)
Hill
Lapwood (Union)
Mackay
Moynihan (Union)
Mulligan

Nixon
Ormond R (Union)
Probert
Pugh (Union)
Sefton (Union)
Simonsen
Tillotson
Turner B
Turner G
Van Helden
Vest
Walker C

Rangers (1)
Bridge

Tarehuru (1)
Roots

Thistle (1)
Ormond R

SOUTHLAND

Brigadiers (2)
Morrison R
Ottley

Corinthians (2)
Cook
Gwilliam

Queens Park (1)
Ferguson M

Rangers (1)
Cooper W

Thistle (2)
Almond
Steele Jr

TARANAKI

Hawera (1)
Jones G

New Plymouth OB (1)
Albrechtsen

WAIKATO

Hamilton (10)
Groom
Hume (Wanderers)
Ironside K
Leong (Technical)
McDermid
Nelson
Poelman F (Technical)
Poelman K (Technical)
Tindall
Young

Hamilton United (1)
Crabb

Hamilton Wanderers
(Refer Hamilton)

Huntly (1)
Braithwaite R

Huntly Thistle (1)
Moyes
Piako United (1)
McKinstry

Technical OB
(Refer Hamilton)

Waikato United (2)
Cossey
Edge D

WANGANUI

Rongotai (1)
Mackie

Technical OB
Kidd (1)

WAIRARAPA

Masterton Athletic (1)
Mutimer

WELLINGTON

Brooklyn-Northern United (8)
Bell (Northern)
Buller (Northern)
Evans A (Northern)
Inglis (Northern)
Lawson (Northern)
Moore (Northern)
Scott S (Northern)
Sergent (Institute)

Diamond
(Refer Wellington United)

Hospital
(Refer Porirua-Viard United)

Hungaria
(Refer Wellington United)

Institute Old Boys
(Refer Brooklyn-Northern United)

Lower Hutt City (2)
McKissock (Railways)
Warrender (Railways)

Marist Brothers' OB (7)
Barton E
Burke
Hatchard
Kershaw
McCabe
McElligott
Thomas W

Miramar Rangers (15)
Brown A
Brown G
Bruce

Burgess D
Chote
Dunford
Jacobs
Juner
Pickering
Reid
Riley
Rufer W
Taylor B
Turner G
Whiting

Petone (11)
Campbell J
Evans A
Feitsma
Haines S
Leslie
McKissock
Newall
Phelan
Quickenden
Ryan J
Turner G

Porirua-Viard United (7)
Coxon (Hospital)
Jeffery A (Western Subs)
Jeffery E (Hospital)
Kissock (Hospital)
Todd (Hospital)
Wallace (Western Subs)
Woods (Hospital)

Queens Park (3)
Clapham
Clark
Mawson

Railways
(Refer Lower Hutt City)

St Johns (3)
Amies
Bissett
Mouat

Scottish Wanderers (1)
Lothian

Seatoun (11)
Bilby
Boyes
Gibson
Hiddlestone
Jones M
Kearns
Reid
Ritchie
Strom D
Traynor
Upchurch

Stop Out (19)
Barton K
Benge
Boyland
Brand
Drylie
Dunford
Grootelaar
Houghton D
Johnson
Malcolmson
Milne
Petersen
Pickering
Rufer S
Rufer W
Sharp
Singer
Ten Broeke
Tillotson

Swifts
(Refer Waterside-Karori)

Thistle (4)
Brownlee
Campbell G
Ewing
McArthur

Waterside
(Refer Waterside-Karori)

Waterside-Karori (6)
Anton (Waterside)
Harris A (Waterside)
Jones D (Waterside)
McBriar (Waterside)
Traynor (Waterside)
White L (Swifts)

Wellington City
(Refer Wellington United)

Wellington Diamond United
(Refer Wellington United)

Wellington United (23)
Baker (Diamond)
Beck (Hungaria)
Bilby (City)
Cameron P (City)
Daniels (Diamond)
Davidson (WDU)
Dunford (WDU)
Finlayson (WDU)
Fitzgerald (Diamond)
Harris W (WDU)
Kiss (Hungaria)
Lesbirel (WDU)
Nemet (Hungaria)
O'Neill (WDU)
Paddison (WDU)
Raat (Diamond)
Romijn
Rufer W (WDU)
Simeonoff (WDU)
Strom J (WDU)

Taylor J (Diamond)
Turner G
Welch (WDU)

University (2)
Naidu
Preston

YMCA (4)
Ballard
Campbell G
McGirr
Nicolle

WEST COAST

Runanga (2)
Cowe
Scott R

AUSTRALIA

Adelaide City (1)
Dods

Blacktown City (1)
Turner B

Brisbane Lions (1)
Halford

Canberra City (2)
Cole
Wilson RH

Heidelberg Alexandra (1)
Deeley

Marconi (1)
de Jong

Melita Eagles (1)
Gosling

Morwell Falcons (1)
Wright W

Newcastle KB United (2)
Gosling
Sumner

Preston Makedonia (1)
Wilson RH

St George (1)
Hagan

South Melbourne Hellas (1)
Wooddin

Sydney City Hakoah (1)
Gosling

Sydney Olympic (3)
Gosling
Herbert
Ironside R

West Adelaide (2)
Boath
Sumner

Wollongong City (2)
Campbell C
de Graaf

ENGLAND

Chelsea (1)
Turner B

Farnborough (1)
Mason T

Notts County (1)
Edge D

Oxford United (1)
Evans C

Scunthorpe United (1)
Cotton

Wolverhampton Wanderers (1)
Herbert

SWITZERLAND

Grasshopper (1)
Rufer W

Zurich (2)
Rufer S
Rufer W

GOALSCORERS FOR NEW ZEALAND

28 Jock Newall
27 Steve Sumner
25 Brian Turner, Keith Nelson
20 Roy Coxon
19 Grant Turner
18 Earle Thomas, Colin Walker
15 George Campbell, Jim Kershaw
13 William Forshaw, Dave Taylor, Michael McGarry
12 Charlie Steele Jr, Steve Wooddin
11 Fred Ussher
10 Ces Dacre
9 Colin Shaw, Bill de Graaf, Iain Ormond, Malcolm Dunford, Robert Ironside
8 Ken Fleet, Reg King, Bill Hume, Ron Moore, Wynton Rufer
7 Gordon Smith, Don Kendrick, Allan Smith, Alan Vest, Bill McClure, Ricki Herbert
6 Alex Bissett, Ted Cook, Fred Benge, Ray Mears, Kevin Mulgrew, Clive Campbell, Allan Boath, Kevin Hagan, Andy Deeley, Noel Barkley
5 Stephen Brown, Murray Kay, Duncan McVey, Dennis Tindall, Sam Malcolmson, Mike Groom, Billy Wright
4 Herbert Morrison, Charlie Ballard, Jim Lothian, Ivan Walsh, Ken Armstrong, John Wrathall, Ted Charlton, Bert Ormond, Alan Marley, Mark Armstrong, Duncan Cole, Glen Adam, Paul Halford, Darren McClennan

3 Harold Balk, Alan Wilkinson, John White, Jim Mutimer, Alan Preston, John Raat, Jim Bell, John Legg, Malcolm Bland, Geoff Brand, John Houghton, Ian Park, Kevin Weymouth, Ken Cresswell, Alistair Elder, Fred de Jong, Danny Halligan

2 Monty Chadwick, Bill Mawson, Bob Innes, Adam Donaldson, Geordie Newman, Tony Graham, Bill Chapman, Les Groves, Doug Ottley, Bob Quickenden, Tom McNicholl, Eric Griffin, Trefor Pugh, Arthur Inglis, John Ryan, Istvan Nemet, Paddy Breslin, Grahame Bilby, Colin Latimour, Shane Rufer, Keith Mackay, Ceri Evans, Roger Gray

1 Ned Sale, Joe Taylor, Bill Knott, Joe Kissock, Bill Brownlee, Bill Thomas, Lew Daniels, Tom Howarth, Dick Hislop, Harry Spencer, Tom McCormack, Bill Hooper, Jack Baker, Charlie Ives, Alex Stenhouse, Jack Skinner, Reg Haggett, Dick Scott, Jack Kidd, Pat Ryan, Ken Mason, Les Wood, Arthur Masters, David McKissock, Leo Hope-Ede, George McAnulty, Ken Olley, Dennis Charlton, Gordon Barker, Bob Morrison, Jack Sharp, Klaas Poelman, Jock Aird, George McLaren, George Cuthill, Jim Warrender, Tony Moynihan, Harold Russell, Ken Sudlow, Tony Evans, Jim Ferrier, Tony Gowans, Paul Rennell, Terry Haydon, Matt Guildea, Iain Hastie, Maurice Tillotson, Brian Hardman, Greg Hough, Mike Simeonoff, Peter Simonsen, Robbie Ten Broeke, Duncan Ormond, Chris Turner, Johan Verweij, Bobby Almond, Nigel Debenham, Shaun Baxter, Adrian Elrick, Alex Metzger, Greg Little, Declan Edge, Dave Witteveen, Garry Lund, Colin Tuaa, Allan Carville.

Own Goals 7

NZ NATIONAL TEAM MATCHES 1904-1990

1904

1
July 23 v New South Wales at Caledonian Ground, Dunedin. Lost 0-1. Referee: W.G. Smith (Otago). NZ: Smallbone, L. White, Clapham, Kilgour, J. Taylor, Farquharson, Reilly, H. Morrison, McMillan (cpt), Stark, W. Morrison.

2
July 30 v New South Wales at Athletic Park, Wellington. Drew 3-3. Goals: Forshaw 2, Sale 1. Referee: A. Williams (Wellington). NZ: Smallbone, Amies (cpt), Clapham, Kilgour, J. Taylor, Clark, Reilly, Sale, Forshaw, Mouat, W. Morrison.

1905

3
June 10 v Wellington at Athletic Park, Wellington. Lost 3-5. Goals: Forshaw 2, Ussher 1.Referee: A. Williams (Wellington). NZ: Fitzgerald, Harrison, Clapham, Forrest, J. Taylor (cpt), R. Jones, H. Morrison, Bissett, Forshaw, Ussher, Mawson.

4
June 17 v Metropolitan Association at Epping Racecourse, Sydney. Lost 2-3. Goals: Brown 1, Chadwick 1. Referee: J. Thompson. NZ: Fitzgerald, E. Newman, Clapham, Forrest, J. Taylor (cpt), Middlemass (Harrison, sub), S. Brown, Bissett, Forshaw, Chadwick, Mawson.

5
June 21 v Wednesday Association at Epping Racecourse, Sydney. Won 8-3. Goals: Bissett 3, Forshaw 2, Brown 2, Mawson 1. Referee: E. Lyons. NZ: Fitzgerald, Harrison, Clapham, Forrest, J. Taylor (cpt), R. Jones, S. Brown, Bissett, Forshaw, Ussher, Mawson.

6
June 24 v New South Wales (1st Test) at Epping Racecourse, Sydney. Won 6-4. Goals: Ussher 3, Brown 1, Forshaw 1, Taylor 1. Referee: J. Thompson. NZ: Fitzgerald, Harrison, Clapham, Forrest, J. Taylor (cpt), Middlemass, S. Brown, Bissett, Forshaw, Ussher, Mawson.

7
June 28 v Navy at Epping Racecourse, Sydney. Lost 2-3. Goals: Ussher 1, Mawson 1. Referee: Ayre. NZ: Fitzgerald, Harrison, E. Newman, Middlemass, J. Taylor (cpt), R. Jones, H. Morrison, Chadwick, Forshaw, Ussher, Mawson.

8
July 1 v New South Wales (2nd Test) at Epping Racecourse, Sydney. Lost 0-2. Referee: C. Harvey. NZ: Fitzgerald, Harrison, Clapham, Forrest, J. Taylor (cpt), R. Jones, S. Brown, Bissett, Forshaw, Ussher, Mawson.

9
July 5 v Northern Districts at Rugby Ground, Newcastle. Won 5-4. Goals: Morrison 2, Ussher 1, Bissett 1, Chadwick 1. NZ: Fitzgerald, E. Newman, Clapham, Forrest, J. Taylor (cpt), R. Jones, S. Brown, H. Morrison, Bissett, Chadwick, Ussher.

10
July 8 v Northern Districts at Showgrounds, Newcastle. Won 1-0. Goals: Bissett 1. NZ: Fitzgerald, Harrison, Clapham, Forrest, Middlemass, R. Jones, S. Brown, Bissett, Forshaw (cpt), Ussher, Mawson.

11
July 12 v Granville at Parramatta Oval, Sydney. Won 6-2. Goals: Forshaw 3, Ussher 1, Morrison 1, Mawson 1. Referee: W. Leydecker. NZ: Fitzgerald, Harrison, Clapham, J. Taylor (cpt), Middlemass, R. Jones, H. Morrison, Bissett, Forshaw, Ussher, Mawson.

12
July 15 v South Coast at Centennial Ground, Wollongong. Drew 3-3. Goals: Forshaw 3. Referee: J. Thompson. NZ: Fitzgerald, Harrison, Clapham, Forrest, Middlemass, R. Jones, S. Brown, Chadwick, Forshaw (cpt), Ussher, Mawson.

13
July 19 v Metropolitan Association at Epping Racecourse, Sydney. Won 5-0. Goals: Ussher 4, Brown 1. Referee: W. Smith. NZ: Fitzgerald, Harrison, Clapham, Forrest, Middlemass, R. Jones. S. Brown, Bissett, Forshaw (cpt), Ussher, Mawson.

14
July 22 v New South Wales (3rd Test) at Epping Racecourse, Sydney. Drew 1-1. Goals: Bissett 1. Referee: J. Thompson. NZ: Fitzgerald, Harrison, Clapham, Forrest, Middlemass, R. Jones, S. Brown, Bissett, Forshaw (cpt), Ussher, Mawson.
H.G. Mayer (Wellington) managed New Zealand on the Australian tour.

1922

15
June 17 v Australia at Carisbrook, Dunedin. Won 3-1. Goals: Cook 2, Knott 1. Referee: M. Thornley (Canterbury). NZ: Craxton, R. Braithwaite, McAuley, Brownlee, Corbett, D. Jones, Brundell, Knott, Cook, G. Campbell (cpt), Ballard.

16
June 24 v Australia at Athletic Park, Wellington. Drew 1-1. Goals: Cook 1. Referee: R.S. Lithgow (Wellington). NZ: Craxton, R. Braithwaite, McAuley, Brownlee, Corbett, D. Jones, Brundell, Anton, Cook, G. Campbell (cpt), Ballard.

17
July 8 v Australia at Domain, Auckland. Won 3-1. Goals: Ballard 1, Cook 1, Dacre 1. Referee: L.C.H. Dawson (Taranaki). NZ: Craxton, R. Braithwaite, McAuley, McArthur, Corbett, D. Jones, Barwell, Dacre, Cook, G. Campbell (cpt), Ballard.
B.L. Salmon (Wellington) selected the New Zealand teams for this three 'test' series.

1923

18
May 24 v Granville at Clyde Oval, Granville. Lost 1-3. Goals: Kissock 1. Referee: W. Allerton. NZ: Craxton, R. Braithwaite, Flood, Brownlee, Kissock, Dryden, Innes, Donaldson, Balk, G. Campbell (cpt), Ballard.

19
May 26 v New South Wales at Wentworth Park, Sydney. Drew 2-2. Goals: Dacre 2. Referee: E. Lukeman. NZ: Craxton, R. Braithwaite, McAuley, W. Thomas, Kissock, Brownlee, Innes, Dacre, Balk. G. Campbell (cpt), Donaldson.

20
May 29 v Newcastle at Tramway Ground, Newcastle. Lost 0-2. Referee: C. Nix. NZ: Craxton, R. Braithwaite (Flood, sub), McAuley, Brownlee, W. Thomas, Dryden, Innes, Dacre, Donaldson, G. Campbell (cpt), Balk.

21
June 2 v Ipswich & West Moreton at North Ipswich Reserve, Ipswich. Won 4-2. Goals: Dacre 1, Ballard 1, Campbell 1, Balk 1. Referee: R. Kemp. NZ: Craxton, R. Braithwaite, McAuley, McArthur, Kissock, Brownlee, Innes, Dacre, Ballard, G. Campbell (cpt), Balk.

22
June 4 v Queensland at Cricket Ground, Brisbane. Won 3-1. Goals: Campbell 2, Innes 1. Referee: C. Lyst. NZ: Craxton, R. Braithwaite, McAuley, W. Thomas, Kissock, Brownlee, Innes, Dacre, Ballard, G. Campbell (cpt), Balk.

23
June 6 v North Coast at Nambour. Won 2-0. Goals: Dacre 1, Balk 1. Referee: W. Donnellan. NZ: Brownlee, Flood, G. Jones, McArthur, Kissock, Dryden, W. Thomas, Dacre, Donaldson, G. Campbell (cpt), Balk.

24
June 9 v Australia at Cricket Ground, Brisbane. Lost 1-2. Goals: Dacre 1. Referee: A. Jackson. NZ:Craxton, R. Braithwaite, McAuley, McArthur, Kissock, Brownlee, Innes, Dacre, Ballard, G. Campbell (cpt), Balk.

25
June 13 v South Maitland at Cessnock. Lost 1-2. Goals: Brownlee 1. Referee: J.W. Earp. NZ: Craxton, R. Braithwaite, McAuley, W. Thomas, Kissock, Dryden, Innes, Brownlee, Dacre, G. Campbell (cpt), Ballard.

26
June 16 v Australia at Cricket Ground, Sydney. Won 3-2. Goals: Campbell 3. Referee: W.A. Wright. NZ: Craxton, R. Braithwaite, McAuley, W. Thomas, Kissock, Brownlee, Innes, Dacre, G. Campbell (cpt), Ballard, Balk.

27
June 20 v Metropolis at Manly Oval, Sydney. Lost 3-4. Goals: Thomas 1, Campbell 1, Balk 1. Referee: R. Burns. NZ: Craxton, Kissock, Flood, McArthur, W. Thomas, Dryden, Innes, Brownlee, Donaldson, G. Campbell (cpt), Balk.

28
June 23 v Granville at Wentworth Park, Sydney. Won 3-1. Goals: Campbell 2, Dacre 1. Referee: J.H. Lester. NZ: Craxton, R. Braithwaite, McAuley, W. Thomas, Kissock, Dryden, Innes, Dacre, G. Campbell (cpt), Ballard, Balk.

29
June 25 v New South Wales at Wentworth Park, Sydney. Drew 1-1. Goals: C. Dacre 1. Referee: A.L. Peaty. NZ: Craxton, R. Braithwaite, McAuley, Brownlee, Kissock, Dryden, Innes, Dacre, G. Campbell (cpt), Ballard, Balk.

30
June 30 v Australia at Showgrounds, Newcastle. Won 4-1. Goals: G. Campbell 4. Referee: L. Tamlyn. NZ: Craxton, R. Braithwaite, McAuley, W. Thomas, Kissock, Dryden, Innes, Dacre, G. Campbell (cpt), Ballard, Balk.

31
July 3 v South Maitland at Weston. Lost 1-4. Goals: Ballard 1. Referee: T. Crawford. NZ: Craxton, R. Braithwaite, McAuley, W. Thomas, Kissock, Dryden, Innes, Dacre, G. Campbell (cpt), Ballard, Balk.

32
July 7 v South Coast at Wollongong. Lost 0-2. NZ: Craxton, R. Braithwaite, McAuley, W. Thomas, Kissock, Brownlee, Innes, Dacre, G. Campbell (cpt), Ballard, Balk.

33
July 11 v Western Districts at Glanmire Sportsground, Lithgow. Won 4-0. Goals: Donaldson 2, Dacre 1, Ballard 1. Referee: G. Donoghue. NZ: Craxton, Flood, R. Braithwaite, W. Thomas, Kissock, Dryden, Innes, Dacre, Donaldson, Ballard (cpt), Balk.

B.L. Salmon (Wellington) selected the New Zealand tourists. H.G. Mayer (Wellington) was the tour manager and H.I. Graves (Wellington) the assistant manager.

1924

34
August 16 v Chinese Universities at Domain, Auckland. Won 2-1. Goals: Campbell 2. Referee: S. Masters (Auckland). NZ: Craxton, J. Anderson, McKinstry, McCreanor, Neesham, McGirr, Innes, Dacre, Cook, G. Campbell (cpt), Ballard.

35
August 23 v Chinese Universities at Basin Reserve, Wellington. Drew 2-2. Goals: Dacre 1, Daniels 1. Referee: W.G. Bryce (Wellington). NZ: Ewing, J. Anderson, McKinstry, McCreanor, Roots (cpt), Neesham, Macdougall, Dacre, Lothian, Daniels, Williams.

36
September 6 v Chinese Universities at Carisbrook, Dunedin. Won 5-3. Goals: Cook 2, Lothian 2, Howarth 1. Referee: W.P. Smith (Otago). NZ: Gwilliam, G. Anderson, McGirr (cpt), McArthur, W. Cooper, Murray, Macdougall, McElligott, Cook, Lothian, Howarth.

37
September 13 v Chinese Universities at Lancaster Park, Christchurch. Won 4-2. Goals: Lothian 2, Newman 2. Referee: M. Thornley (Canterbury). NZ: Ewing, G. Anderson, McGirr, W. Thomas, D. Jones, Dryden, Innes, G. Newman, Lothian, G. Campbell (cpt), Ballard.
B.L. Salmon (Wellington) selected the New Zealand teams for this four 'test' series.

1927

38
June 25 v Canada at Carisbrook, Dunedin. Drew 2-2. Goals: Hislop 1, Innes 1. Referee: W.P. Smith (Otago). NZ: McDougall, G. Anderson, McGirr, Tinkler, Steele Sr, D. Jones (cpt), Innes, G. Newman, Spencer, Hislop, Balk.

39
July 2 v Canada at Lancaster Park, Christchurch. Lost 1-2. Goals: Spencer 1. Referee: J. Stout (Canterbury). NZ: McDougall, G. Anderson, McGirr, Tinkler, Steele Sr, D. Jones (cpt), Innes, G. Newman, Spencer, Hislop, Balk.

40
July 9 v Canada at Basin Reserve, Wellington. Won 1-0. Goals: McCormack 1. Referee: A.E. Caisley (Wellington). NZ: McDougall, G. Anderson, McGirr, W. Cooper, J. Campbell, Burke, Nicolle, G. Newman, Hooper, McCormack, Ballard (cpt).

41
July 23 v Canada at Carlaw Park, Auckland. Lost 1-4. Goals: Hooper 1. Referee: G. Cox (South Auckland). NZ: McDougall, G. Anderson, McGirr, W. Cooper, J. Campbell, D. Jones, Innes, G. Newman, Hooper, McCormack, Ballard (cpt).
B.L. Salmon (Wellington) selected the New Zealand teams for this four 'test' series.

1933

42
May 20 v New South Wales at Cricket Ground, Sydney. Lost 0-5. Referee: D. Quinn. NZ: Zuill, Stone, Gerrard, W. Chapman, Christie (cpt), Graham, E. Barton, Blackie, Baker, Kershaw, Kay.

43
May 24 v South Coast at Floyds Park, Bulli. Won 1-0. Goals: Baker 1. Referee: H. Reay. NZ: Zuill, Stone, Gerrard, W. Chapman, Christie (cpt), Crabb, C. Ives, Groves, Baker, Kershaw, Kay.

44
May 27 v Northern Districts at Sportsground, Newcastle. Lost 1-7. Goals: Kershaw 1. Referee: J. Harris. NZ: Zuill, Gerrard, Graham, Stenhouse, Christie (cpt), Crabb, E. Barton, Blackie, Baker, Kershaw, Kay.

45
June 1 v Ipswich & West Moreton at North Ipswich Reserve, Ipswich. Lost 4-5. Goals: Graham 2, Kershaw 1, Kay 1. NZ: Zuill, Stone, Gerrard, Stenhouse, Christie (cpt), Crabb, E. Barton, Blackie, Graham, Kershaw, Kay.

46
June 3 v Queensland at Exhibition Ground, Brisbane. Won 5-1. Goals: Kershaw 3, Kay 2. Referee: W. Donnellan. NZ: Zuill, Stone, Gerrard, Stenhouse, W. Chapman (cpt), Crabb, Blackie, Baker, Kershaw, Groves, Kay.

47
June 5 v Australia at Exhibition Ground, Brisbane. Lost 2-4. Goals: Chapman 1, Kershaw 1. Referee: Z. Korotcoff. NZ: Zuill, Gerrard, Graham, Stenhouse, Christie (cpt), Crabb, E. Barton, W. Chapman, Kershaw, Groves, Kay.

48
June 10 v Australian X1 at Hobart Park, Newcastle. Drew 2-2. Goals: Kershaw 2. Referee: H. Richardson. NZ: Zuill, Gerrard, Graham, Stenhouse, W. Chapman, Crabb, Blackie, E. Barton, Kershaw, Christie (cpt), Kay.

49
June 13 v South Maitland at Cessnock. Lost 0-1. NZ: Zuill, Stone, Gerrard, Stenhouse, Christie (cpt), Crabb, C. Ives, Blackie, Kershaw, W. Chapman, Groves.

50
June 17 v Australia at Cricket Ground, Sydney. Lost 4-6. Goals: Ives 1, W. Chapman 1, Kershaw 1, Kay 1. Referee: D. Quinn. NZ: Zuill, Stone, Gerrard, Stenhouse, Christie (cpt), Crabb, C. Ives, W. Chapman, Kershaw, Graham, Kay.

51
June 21 v Metropolis at Royal Agricultural Ground, Sydney. Lost 2-3. Goals: Groves 1, Kay 1. NZ: Zuill, Stone, Gerrard, Stenhouse, W. Chapman (cpt), Crabb, C. Ives, E. Barton, Graham, Groves, Kay.

52
June 24 v Australia at Cricket Ground, Sydney. Lost 2-4. Goals: Kershaw 2. Referee: J. Harris. NZ: Zuill, Stone, Gerrard, Stenhouse, Christie (cpt), Graham, C. Ives, W. Chapman, Kershaw, Groves, Kay.

53
June 26 v Granville at Clyde Oval, Granville. Won 4-2. Goals: Kershaw 3, Groves 1. Referee: H. Reay. NZ: Gerrard, Stone, Graham, Stenhouse, Christie (cpt), Crabb, C. Ives, W. Chapman, Kershaw, Groves, Kay.

54
June 28 v Gladesville-Ryde at Sportsground, Gladesville. Lost 2-7. Goals: Stenhouse 1, Kershaw 1. Referee: D. Quinn. NZ: Gerrard, Stone, Graham, Stenhouse, Christie (cpt), W. Chapman, E. Barton, Blackie, Kershaw, Groves, Kay.
Manager: H.L. Godber (Wellington). Assistant Manager: N. McArthur (Wellington). Trainer: T.A. Langridge (Sydney).

1936

55
July 4 v Australia at Logan Park, Dunedin. Lost 1-7. Goals: Skinner 1. Referee: W.P. Smith (Otago). NZ: McRae, Cawtheray, Speed, W. Chapman, Gordon (cpt), Cowe, Craggs, Hatchard, Leslie, Farnan, Skinner.

56
July 11 v Australia at Basin Reserve, Wellington. Lost 0-10. Referee: G. Jackson (Wellington). NZ: A.L. Smith, Cawtheray, S. Haines, Todd, Sutherland, McQuarrie, Mackie, Innes (cpt), Cleal, W. Ives, Skinner.

57
July 18 v Australia at Blandford Park, Auckland. Lost 1-4. Goals: Haggett 1. Referee: A. Firth (Auckland). NZ: A.L. Smith, Haggett, Speed, Todd, G. Wright, H. Chapman (cpt), Wood, Jepson, Bridge, W. Ives, Kay.

Selectors: F. Sanders (Wellington), J. Tinkler (Auckland) and J. Cawtheray (Canterbury).

1937

58
June 5 v England Amateurs at Carisbrook, Dunedin. Lost 0-12. Referee: W.P. Smith (Otago). NZ: F. Cameron, Haggett, Gerrard, Todd, Sutherland (cpt), Gordon, Wood, Duncan, Leslie, Farnan, Kay.

59
June 19 v England Amateurs at Carlaw Park, Auckland. Lost 0-6. Referee: A. Kyle (Auckland). NZ: F. Cameron, Cawtheray, Stone, Blackie, Sutherland (cpt), E. Jeffery, Wood, McCallum, Leslie, R. Scott, Kay.

60
June 26 v England Amateurs at Athletic Park, Wellington. Lost 1-12. Goals: Scott 1. Referee: G. Jackson (Wellington). NZ: F. Cameron, Cawtheray, Stone, Blackie, A. Sutherland (cpt), E. Jeffery, Wood, McCallum, Leslie, R. Scott, Kay.

Selector: A.P.F. Neesham, (Auckland).

1946

61
September 14 v Wellington at Basin Reserve, Wellington. Won 5-2. Goals: Wilkinson 3, Kidd 1, Ryan 1. Referee: R. Scott (Wellington). NZ: Johnson, O'Malley, R. Ferguson, Drylie, V. Smith, Hutchinson, L. Smith, P. Ryan, Wilkinson, Kidd, R. Smith.

Selector: W.B. Hicks (Wellington).

1947

62
June 28 v South Africa at Lancaster Park, Christchurch. Lost 5-6. Goals: G. Smith 3, Mason 1, Wood 1. Referee: C.G. Sweeney (Canterbury). NZ: Davey, A. Harris, Speed (cpt), Gordon, Cleal, Beavis, Sharp, Wood, G. Smith, Woods, K. Mason.

63
July 5 v South Africa at Carisbrook, Dunedin. Lost 0-6. Referee: P. George (Otago). NZ: Davey, A. Harris, Speed (cpt), Drylie, Cleal, V. Smith, Sharp, Wilkinson, G. Smith, Wood, K. Mason.

64
July 12 v South Africa at Athletic Park, Wellington. Lost 3-8. Goals: G. Smith 3. Referee: A. Aspen (Wellington). NZ: Davey, A. Harris, Speed (cpt), Gordon, V. Smith, Hutchinson, Sharp, Wood, G. Smith, Woods, K. Mason.

65
July 19 v South Africa at Eden Park, Auckland. Lost 1-4. Goals: G. Smith 1. Referee: F.O. Green (Auckland). NZ: Davey, O'Malley, Speed (cpt), V. Smith, Gordon, Hutchinson, Robinson, Wood, G. Smith, Woods, K. Mason.

Selector: W.A. Chapman (Wellington). Manager/ Coach: J.R. Sheffield.

1948

66
August 14 v Australia at Basin Reserve, Wellington. Lost 0-6. Referee: V. Wheeler (Wellington). NZ: R.H. King, A. Harris, Hodgson, McKissock, V. Smith, Hutchinson (cpt), Sharp, Sergent, G. Smith, Kidd, R. Smith.

67
August 28 v Australia at Lancaster Park, Christchurch. Lost 0-7. Referee: T.C. Gottermeyer (Canterbury). NZ: R.H. King, Hall, Hodgson, McKissock, V. Smith (cpt), Traynor, L. Smith, Methven, G. Smith, O'Malley, Ottley.

68
September 4 v Australia at Basin Reserve, Wellington. Lost 0-4. Referee: J. Sanderson (Wellington). NZ: Laing, Hodgson, Hall, McKissock, Boyes, V. Smith (cpt), L. Smith, Methven, Warman, R. Wilson, Ottley.

69
September 11 v Australia at Blandford Park, Auckland. Lost 1-8. Goals: Masters 1. Referee: C.G. Edwards (Auckland). NZ: R.H. King, A. Harris, Hodgson, Boyes, Traynor, Hutchinson (cpt), Hall, Methven, Warman, McKissock, Singer (Masters, sub). Selector: T.W. Dick (Wellington).

1951

70
August 11 v Victoria at Basin Reserve, Wellington. Won 3-1. Goals: Mutimer 2, Fleet 1. Referee: R. Scott (Wellington). NZ: Stephenson, T. Cooper, Upchurch, Butts (cpt), Meehan, McKissock, Mutimer, K. Fleet, Berry, Newall, Quickenden.

71
September 10 v Auckland at Blandford Park, Auckland. Won 2-0. Goals: Newall 1, Ottley 1. NZ: Stephenson, Boyes (cpt), R. Morrison, McKissock, Meehan, Traynor, Mutimer, K. Fleet, Coxon, Newall, Ottley.

72
September 15 v Suva at Albert Park, Suva. Won 6-1. Goals: Coxon 2, Newall 2, Fleet 1, Ottley 1. NZ: Stephenson, T. Cooper (Boyes, sub), R. Morrison, McKissock, Meehan, Traynor, Mutimer, K. Fleet, Coxon, Newall (cpt), Ottley.

73
September 19 v New Caledonia at Velodrome Georges Brunelet, Noumea. Lost 0-2. NZ: Stephenson, Boyes (cpt), R. Morrison, McKissock, Meehan, Traynor, Hope-Ede, K. Fleet, Coxon, Newall, Ottley.

74
September 22 v New Caledonia at Velodrome Georges Brunelet, Noumea. Won 6-4. Goals: Newall 4, Fleet 1, Walsh 1. NZ: Stephenson, T. Cooper, R. Morrison, McKissock, Meehan, Traynor, Mutimer, Walsh, Newall (cpt), K. Fleet, Ottley.

75
September 24 v New Caledonia at Velodrome Georges Brunelet, Noumea. Lost 0-2. NZ: Stephenson, T. Cooper, R. Morrison, McKissock, Meehan, Traynor, Mutimer, Walsh, Newall (cpt), K. Fleet, Ottley.

76
September 30 v New Caledonia at Velodrome Georges Brunelet, Noumea. Won 3-1. Goals: Coxon 2, Fleet 1. NZ: Stephenson, T. Cooper, R. Morrison, Boyes (cpt), Meehan, Traynor, Walsh, Hope-Ede, Newall, K. Fleet, Coxon.

77
October 4 v New Hebrides at Velodrome Georges Brunelet, Noumea. Won 9-0. Goals: Coxon 3, Walsh 3, Newall 2, Fleet 1. NZ: Stephenson, T. Cooper, R. Morrison, McKissock, Boyes (cpt), Traynor, Walsh, K. Fleet, Coxon, Newall, Ottley.

78
October 7 v Fiji at Albert Park, Suva. Won 6-4. Goals: Newall 3, Coxon 1, McKissock 1, Mutimer 1. Referee: M.S. Koya (Fiji). NZ: Stephenson, T. Cooper, R. Morrison, McKissock, Boyes (cpt), Traynor, Mutimer, Hope-Ede, Newall, K. Fleet, Coxon.

Selectors: J.G. Shankie (Wellington), J.I. Kershaw (Wellington) and W.P. Smith (Otago).

1952

79
August 31 v Suva at Albert Park, Suva. Won 1-0. Goals: Newall 1. Referee: R.S. Bansraj. NZ: Stephenson, D. Smith, Upchurch, R. Morrison, Albrechtsen, Banham, Kendrick, McAnulty, Coxon, Newall (cpt), Quickenden.

80
September 3 v Southern Districts at Albert Park, Suva. Won 8-3. Goals: Kendrick 3, Newall 3, Coxon 2. Referee: T. Ram Prasad. NZ: Stephenson, D. Smith, Upchurch, R. Morrison, Albrechtsen, J. White, Hope-Ede, A. Davis, Coxon (Kendrick, sub), Newall (cpt), McAnulty.

81
September 7 v Fiji at Albert Park, Suva. Won 2-0. Goals: Hope-Ede 1, White 1. Referee: M.S. Koya. NZ: Stephenson, D. Smith (cpt), Upchurch, R. Morrison, Albrechtsen, J. White, Kendrick, A. Davis, McAnulty, Hope-Ede, Quickenden.

82
September 9 v Lautoka at Churchill Park, Lautoka. Drew 0-0. Referee: Tamik Khan. NZ: Stephenson, D. Smith (cpt), Upchurch, Banham, Albrechtsen, J. White, Quickenden, A. Davis, Kendrick, Hope-Ede, McAnulty.

83
September 11 v Northern Districts at Churchill Park, Lautoka. Won 5-0. Goals: Newall 2, Coxon 2, McAnulty 1. Referee: S. Sharma. NZ: Stephenson, Banham, R. Morrison, Hope-Ede, Albrechtsen, J. White, Kendrick, A. Davis, Coxon, Newall (cpt), McAnulty.

84
September 14 v Fiji at Churchill Park, Lautoka. Won 9-0. Goals: Newall 3, Quickenden 2, Kendrick 2, White 1, own goal 1. Referee: J. McMillan. NZ: Stephenson, D. Smith, Upchurch (Albrechtsen, sub), Banham, R. Morrison, J. White, Kendrick, Hope-Ede, Coxon, Newall (cpt), Quickenden.

85
September 16 v Fiji at Albert Park, Suva. Won 5-2. Goals: Coxon 2, Kendrick 2, White 1. Referee: J. McMillan. NZ: Stephenson, D. Smith, R. Morrison, Banham, Albrechtsen, J. White, Kendrick, Hope-Ede, Coxon, Newall (cpt), Quickenden.

86
September 21 v Tahiti at Stade de la Fautaua, Papeete. Drew 2-2. Goals: Newall 1, Coxon 1. NZ: Stephenson, D. Smith, Upchurch, Hope-Ede, Banham, J. White, Kendrick, A. Davis, Coxon, Newall (cpt), Quickenden.

87
September 25 v Chinese Selection at Stade de la Fautaua, Papeete. Won 7-1. Goals: Coxon 4, Newall 2, own goal 1. NZ: Upchurch, D. Smith, R. Morrison, Hope-Ede, Albrechtsen, J. White, Kendrick, A. Davis, Coxon, Newall (cpt) (Banham, sub), Quickenden.

88
September 28 1952 v Tahiti at Stade de la Fautaua, Papeete. Won 5-3. Goals: Newall 4, Coxon 1. NZ: Upchurch, D. Smith, R. Morrison, Hope-Ede, Banham, J. White, Kendrick, A. Davis, Coxon, Newall (cpt), Quickenden.

Selectors: J.G. Shankie (Wellington), R.A. Speed (Auckland) and W.P. Smith (Otago).
Manager: W.P. Smith (Otago).

1954

89
July 31 v Wellington at Basin Reserve, Wellington. Won 6-0. Goals: Preston 3, Smith 2, Benge 1. Referee: R. Scott (Wellington). NZ: Hiddlestone, R. Morrison, Best, D. Charlton, J. Hunter (cpt), Traynor, Steele Jr, W.A. Smith, Preston, Benge, Barker.

90
August 3 v South Australia at Norwood Oval, Adelaide. Won 3-2. Goals: Smith 2, Steele 1. Referee: J. Harvey. NZ: Hiddlestone, T. Cooper, Westerveld, D. Charlton, J. Hunter (cpt), Traynor, Steele Jr, W.A. Smith, Preston, Olley, Barker.

91
August 7 v Australian X1 at Kensington Oval, Adelaide. Won 3-1. Goals: King 3. NZ: Hiddlestone, T. Cooper, Westeveld, D. Charlton, J. Hunter (cpt), Traynor, R.A. King, W.A. Smith, Preston, Olley, Barker.

92
August 11 v Victoria at Showgrounds, Melbourne. Lost 1-2. Goals: Benge 1. Referee: Nicholson. NZ: Hiddlestone, T. Cooper, Westerveld, Gibson, Traynor (cpt), D. Charlton, Steele Jr, W.A. Smith, R.A. King, Benge, Barker.

93
August 14 v Australia at Showgrounds, Melbourne. Won 2-1. Goals: King 1, Steele 1. Referee: G. Gatt. NZ: Hiddlestone, T. Cooper, Westerveld, D. Charlton, J. Hunter (cpt), Traynor, Steele Jr, Preston, R.A. King (Benge, sub), Olley, Barker.

94
August 18 v Granville at MacArthur Park, Granville. Lost 0-3. Referee: H. Evans. NZ: Hiddlestone, R. Morrison, Best, Gibson, J. Hunter (cpt), D. Charlton, Steele Jr, Benge, Olley, Preston, Barker.

95
August 21 v New South Wales at Sportsground, Sydney. Won 4-1. Goals: Benge 2, Olley 1, Charlton 1. Referee: K. Urwin. NZ: Hiddlestone, T. Cooper, Westerveld, Gibson, J. Hunter (cpt), Traynor, Steele Jr, Benge, Olley, D. Charlton, Barker.

96
August 25 v Queensland at Exhibition Ground, Brisbane. Drew 2-2. Goals: Smith 1, Steele 1. Referee: J. Perotte. NZ: Hiddlestone, T. Cooper, Best, Gibson, J. Hunter (cpt), Traynor, Steele Jr, W.A. Smith, Olley, Benge, Preston.

97
August 28 v Australia at Cricket Ground, Brisbane. Lost 1-4. Goals: Smith 1. Referee: V. Robertson. NZ: Hiddlestone, T. Cooper, Westerveld, D. Charlton, J. Hunter (cpt), Traynor, Steele Jr, W.A. Smith, Olley, Benge, Preston.

98
August 29 v Northern Districts at Cricket Ground, Newcastle. Drew 1-1. Goals: Smith 1. Referee: G. Muir. NZ: Hiddlestone, R. Morrison, Best, Gibson, J. Hunter (cpt), Westerveld, Steele Jr, W.A. Smith, Olley, Benge, Barker.

99
September 4 v Australia at Sportsground, Sydney. Lost 1-4. Goals: Steele 1. Referee: S.G. Thorpe. NZ: Hiddlestone, T. Cooper, Westerveld, Gibson, J. Hunter (cpt), Traynor, Steele Jr, Benge, Olley, D. Charlton, W.A. Smith (Preston, sub).

100
September 5 v South Coast at Slacky Flat, Bulli. Drew 4-4. Goals: Benge 2, Barker 1, Morrison 1. Referee: G. Richardson. NZ: Hiddlestone, T. Cooper, Westerveld, Gibson, J. Hunter (cpt), Traynor, Steele Jr, Benge, R. Morrison, D. Charlton (Preston, sub), Barker.
Selectors: J.G. Shankie (Wellington), R.A. Speed (Auckland) and W.P. Smith (Otago).
Manager: J.I. Kershaw (Wellington). Assistant Manager: W.W. Carruthers (Canterbury).

1955

101
June 18 v South China Athletic Assoc. (Hong Kong) at Lancaster Park, Christchurch. Drew 1-1. Goals: Steele 1. Referee: P. George (Otago). NZ: Stephenson, T. Cooper, M. Walker, D. Charlton (cpt), Laffey, Grootelaar, Sharp, Benge, R.A. King, K. Fleet, Steele Jr.

102
July 2 v South China Athletic Assoc. (Hong Kong) at Athletic Park, Wellington. Won 7-4. Goals: King 3, Steele 2, Fleet 2. Referee: C.G. Edwards (Auckland). NZ: Stephenson, T. Cooper, M. Walker, D. Charlton (cpt), Laffey, Grootelaar, Sharp, Benge, R.A. King, K. Fleet, Steele Jr.

103
July 9 v South China Athletic Assoc. (Hong Kong) at Carlaw Park, Auckland. Lost 3-5. Goals: Fleet 1, King 1, Sharp 1. Referee: R.H. Scott (Wellington). NZ: Stephenson, T. Cooper, M. Walker, D. Charlton (cpt), Laffey, Grootelaar, Sharp, Benge, R.A. King, K. Fleet, Steele Jr.

Selectors: R.A. Speed (Auckland), J.G. Shankie (Wellington) and G.W. Smith (Canterbury).

1956

A proposed South-East Asia tour in October and November 1956 involving games in Singapore, Malaya, Thailand, Hong Kong and Philippines fell through when satisfactory arrangements with the intended hosts were not concluded in time. However, 18 players were named for the tour before it was abandoned.
Goalkeepers: Ken Lander (Marist, Wellington), Terry Gavan (Point Chevalier, Auckland). Fullbacks: Jim Blair (Stop Out, Wellington), Peter Flynn (Shamrock, Canterbury), Max Walker (Eastern Union, Poverty Bay). Halfbacks: Dennis Charlton (Technical Old Boys, Canterbury), Tony Laffey (Western, Canterbury), Harry Selwood (Onehunga, Auckland), Dick Durant (Shamrock, Canterbury), Alan Preston (University, Wellington). Forwards: Gary Eccles (Point Chevalier, Auckland), Charlie Steele (Western, Canterbury), Ken Olley (Western, Canterbury), John Adams (Railways, Wellington), Arthur Forbes (King Edward Technical College Old Boys, Otago), Tom McNicholl (Onehunga), Arie Van Rooyen (Nomads, Canterbury), Dick Whittaker (Onehunga).
Selectors: J.G. Shankie (Wellington), R.A. Speed (Auckland) and G.W. Smith (Canterbury)

1957

104
June 22 v Eastern Athletic Assoc. (Hong Kong) at Basin Reserve, Wellington. Drew 1-1. Goals: McNicholl 1. Referee: M.T. Swain (Wellington). NZ: Stephenson, Flynn, Aird, McFarlane, Laffey (cpt), R.J. Durant, Steele Jr, D. Charlton, K. Poelman, McNicholl, Saunderson.

105
June 29 v Eastern Athletic Assoc. (Hong Kong) at Carlaw Park, Auckland. Won 2-1. Goals: Griffin 1, Poelman 1. Referee: A. Furse (Auckland). NZ: Stephenson, Flynn, Aird, D. Charlton, Laffey (cpt), McFarlane, Naidu, K. Poelman, Griffin, McNicholl, Whittaker.

106
July 27 v F.K. Austria at Eden Park, Auckland. Lost 1-7. Goals: McNicholl 1. Referee: R. Lund (Auckland). NZ: Stephenson, Flynn, Aird, D. Charlton, Laffey (cpt), McFarlane, Naidu, Higgins, Griffin, McNicholl, Whittaker.

107
August 3 v F.K. Austria at Athletic Park, Wellington. Lost 1-7. Goals: Griffin 1. Referee: D. Welham (Otago). NZ: Stephenson, Flynn, Juner, D. Charlton, Laffey (cpt), McFarlane, Eccles, Benge, Griffin, McNicholl, McCabe.

Selectors: J.G. Shankie (Wellington), R.A. Speed (Auckland) and G.W. Smith (Canterbury).

1958

108
August 16 v Australia at Basin Reserve, Wellington. Lost 2-3. Goals: Aird 1, Hume 1. Referee: M.T. Swain (Wellington). NZ: K. Hough, Lapwood, Aird, K. Armstrong (cpt), Van Den Broek, McFarlane, McCabe, Reid, Hume, Cuthill, Steele Jr.

109
August 23 v Australia at Carlaw Park, Auckland. Drew 2-2. Goals: Steele 2. Referee: R. Lund (Auckland). NZ: K. Hough, Lapwood, Aird, K. Armstrong (cpt), Van Den Broek, McFarlane, McCabe, McLaren, Hume, Kearns, Steele Jr.

110
August 26 v Waikato X1 at Seddon Park, Hamilton. Won 3-0. Goals: Armstrong 1, Hume 1, Steele 1. Referee: K. Davies (Waikato). NZ: K. Hough, Lapwood, F. Poelman, McLaren, Van Den Broek, McFarlane, Steele Jr, Kearns, Hume, K. Armstrong (cpt), McCabe.

111
August 31 v New Caledonia at Velodrome Georges Brunelet, Noumea. Won 2-1. Goals: McLaren 1, Steele 1. Referee: Captain Teste. NZ: K. Hough, Lapwood, F. Poelman, K. Armstrong (cpt), Van Den Broek, McFarlane, Steele Jr, Kearns, Hume, McLaren, McCabe.

112
September 7 v New Caledonia at Velodrome Georges Brunelet, Noumea. Won 5-1. Goals: Hume 3, Cuthill 1, Steele 1. Referee: Louis Trin. NZ: K. Hough, Lapwood, Laffey, K. Armstrong (cpt), Van Den Broek, McFarlane, Steele Jr, Reid (Kearns, sub), Hume, Cuthill, McCabe.

113
September 14 v New Caledonia at Velodrome Georges Brunelet, Noumea. Won 2-1. Goals: Hume 2. Referee: Andre Nakagawa. NZ: K. Hough, Lapwood, F. Poelman, K. Armstrong (cpt), Van Den Broek, McFarlane, Steele Jr, Kearns, Hume, McLaren, McCabe.

114
September 18 v Auckland at Blandford Park, Auckland. Drew 1-1. Goals: Hume 1. Referee: R. Haworth (Auckland). NZ: K. Hough, Lapwood, F. Poelman, K. Armstrong (cpt), Van Den Broek, McFarlane, Steele Jr (Cuthill, sub), Hume, McLaren (Laffey, sub), McCabe.

Selectors: J.G. Shankie (Wellington), R.A. Speed (Auckland) and G.W. Smith (Canterbury). Manager: R.A. Speed (Auckland).

1959

115
June 6 v Deportivo Saprissa (Costa Rica) at Carlaw Park, Auckland. Won 3-2. Goals: Wrathall 2, Bell 1. Referee: D. Welham (Otago). NZ: Callaghan, Lapwood, Laffey, Warrender (cpt), Leong, K. Armstrong, Bell, Wrathall, Van Rooyen, Kearns, Moynihan.

Selectors: J.G. Shankie (Wellington), R.A. Speed (Auckland) and G.W. Smith (Canterbury).

1960

116
September 5 v Tahiti at Stade de la Fautaua, Papeete. Won 5-1. Goals: Charlton 2, Raat 2, Bell 1. NZ: Callaghan, Middleton, McFarlane, Warrender (cpt), Kemp, K. Armstrong, Bell, Wrathall, E. Charlton, Raat, Moynihan.

117
September 8 v Tahiti Juniors at Stade de la Fautaua, Papeete. Won 8-0. Goals: Wrathall 2, McVey 2, Warrender 1, Charlton 1, Bell 1, Moynihan 1. NZ: Callaghan, Middleton, Rodger, Warrender (cpt), Kemp, McFarlane, Steele Jr, Wrathall, Raat (E. Charlton, sub), McVey, Moynihan (Bell, sub).

118
September 12 v Tahiti at Stade de la Fautaua, Papeete. Won 2-1. Goals: Charlton 1, Raat 1. NZ: Callaghan, Middleton, McFarlane, Warrender (cpt), Kemp, K. Armstrong, Bell, Wrathall, E. Charlton, Raat, Moynihan.

Selectors: J.G. Shankie (Wellington), R.A. Speed (Auckland) and G.W. Smith (Canterbury). Manager: G.W. Smith (Canterbury).

1961

119
June 5 v F.A. (England) X1 at Basin Reserve, Wellington. Lost 0-8. Referee: C. Dickie (Auckland). NZ: Whiting, Middleton, Leong, Warrender (cpt), Kemp, K. Armstrong, Eccles, Wrathall, Reid, Buller, R. Ormond.

120
June 10 v F.A. (England) X1 at Showgrounds, Auckland. Lost 1-6. Goals: McVey 1. Referee: A. Williams (Otago). NZ: Whiting, Middleton, Leong, Warrender (cpt), Kemp, K. Armstrong, Eccles, Inglis, Reid, McVey, R. Ormond.

Selectors: J.G. Shankie (Wellington), R.A. Speed (Auckland) and G.W. Smith (Canterbury).

1962

121
June 2 v New Caledonia at English Park, Christchurch. Won 4-1. Goals: McVey 2, Pugh 2. Referee: M.T. Swain (Wellington). NZ: Whiting, A. Evans, Leong, Wallace, Kemp, K. Armstrong (cpt), R. Ormond, Inglis, Pugh, McVey, Ritchie.

122
June 4 v New Caledonia at Basin Reserve, Wellington. Won 4-2. Goals: Armstrong 3, Ormond 1. Referee: A. Williams (Otago). NZ: Whiting, A. Evans, Leong, Wallace, Kemp, Rae, Eccles, Inglis, R. Ormond, K. Armstrong (cpt), Ritchie.

Selectors: G.W. Smith (Canterbury), R.A. Speed (Auckland), A. Kidd (Wanganui) and J. Welsh (Otago).

1964

123
January 27 v F.C. Basel (Switzerland) at Blandford Park, Auckland. Lost 1-4. Goals: Moore 1. Referee: C. Dickie (Auckland). NZ: Whiting, A. Evans, Leong, Lawson (K. Armstrong, sub), Kemp, Sudlow, Sefton, Inglis, Pugh (Moore, sub), R. Ormond (cpt), Torkington.

124
March 14 v Hong Kong X1 at Hong Kong. Lost 1-3. Goals: Moore 1. NZ: Whiting, A. Evans, S. Scott, Lawson, Kemp, Bilby, Russell, Inglis, Moore, R. Ormond (cpt), J. Ryan.

125
March 15 v Chinese Selection at Hong Kong. Lost 1-2. Goals: Moore 1. NZ: A. Stroud, A. Evans, Leong, Bilby, Kemp, Sudlow, Russell, R. Ormond (cpt), Moore, Sefton, Torkington. Sub: Inglis, S. Scott.

126
March 17 v Bangkok X1 at Bangkok. Lost 1-7. Goals: Moore 1. NZ: Whiting, A. Evans, Leong, Bilby, McBriar, Sudlow, Russell, R. Ormond (cpt), Moore, Sefton, J. Ryan.

127
March 20 v Shahim F.C. at Amajdieh Stadium, Teheran. Lost 1-5. Goals: Moore 1. NZ: A. Stroud, A. Evans, Leong, Lawson (Sudlow, sub), Kemp, Bilby, Russell, R. Ormond (cpt), Moore (Sefton, sub), Pugh (Inglis, sub), Torkington (J. Ryan, sub).

128
March 22 v Shahim F.C. X1 at Amajdieh Stadium, Teheran. Lost 1-4. Goals: Russell 1. NZ: Whiting, A. Evans (S. Scott, sub), Leong, Lawson, Kemp, Sudlow, Russell, Inglis, Moore, R. Ormond (cpt), Torkington.

129
March 28 v Karlsruher F.C. at Wildparkstadion, Karlsruher. Lost 1-4. Goals: Inglis 1. NZ: A. Stroud, A. Evans, Leong, Lawson, Kemp, Sudlow, Russell, R. Ormond (cpt), Moore (Inglis, sub), Sefton, J. Ryan.

130
March 30 v Nurnberg F.C. at Farbo Stadium, Nurnberg. Lost 1-2. Goals: Ormond 1. NZ: Whiting, A. Evans (S. Scott, sub), Leong, Lawson, Kemp, Bilby, Russell, Inglis, R. Ormond (cpt), Pugh (Moore, sub), Torkington.

131
April 8 v Bellinzona F.C. at Bellinzona. Lost 1-2. Goals: Ormond 1. NZ: Whiting, A. Evans, S Scott, Lawson, Kemp, Sudlow, Bilby, Inglis, R. Ormond (cpt), Pugh, Torkington.

132
April 9 v Grasshopper-Club at Sportplatz Hardturm, Zurich. Lost 1-3. Goals: Inglis 1. Referee: A. Buchel. NZ: Whiting, A. Evans, S. Scott, Lawson (Sefton, sub), Kemp, Sudlow, Russell (Pugh, sub), Inglis (Moore, sub), R. Ormond (cpt), Bilby, J. Ryan (Torkington, sub).

133
April 13 v F.A. (England) X1 at County Ground, Northampton. Lost 0-4. Referee: P. Bye. NZ: Whiting, A. Evans (Sefton, sub), S. Scott, Bilby, Kemp, Sudlow, Russell, Inglis, R. Ormond (cpt), Pugh, J. Ryan.

134
April 16 v England Amateurs at Dulwich Hamlet Ground, Dulwich. Lost 1-4 (Game abandoned due to conditions). Goals: Ryan 1. Referee: J. Finney. NZ: Whiting, Sefton, S. Scott, Bilby, Kemp, Sudlow, Moore, Inglis, R. Ormond (cpt), Pugh, J. Ryan (Torkington, sub).

135
April 20 v Nottingham, Forrest F.C. at City Ground, Nottingham. Lost 0-8. Referee: S.B. Stoakes. NZ: A. Stroud, Sefton, A. Evans, Bilby, Kemp, Sudlow, Russell, Inglis, Moore, R. Ormond (cpt), Torkington.

136
April 23 v Swindon Town F.C. at County Ground, Swindon. Lost 1-5. Goals: Moore 1. NZ: A. Stroud, A. Evans, Sefton, Lawson, Leong, Sudlow, S. Scott, R. Ormond (cpt), Moore, Pugh, J. Ryan (Torkington, sub).

137
April 26 v German-American League at New York. Lost 1-4. Goals: Sudlow 1. NZ: A. Stroud, A. Evans, Sefton, Lawson, Leong, Sudlow, S. Scott, R. Ormond (cpt), Kemp, Moore, Pugh (D. Torkington, sub).

138
April 29 v San Francisco United at Balboa Stadium, San Francisco. Won 5-2. Goals: Moore 2, Ormond 1, Evans 1, Ryan 1. Referee: Reynder. NZ: A Stroud, S. Scott, Leong, Bilby, Kemp, Sudlow, A. Evans, Inglis, Moore, R. Ormond (cpt), J. Ryan.

139
June 1 v S.C. Preussen Munster (Germany) at Newmarket Park, Auckland. Lost 0-6. Referee: C. Dickie (Auckland). NZ: Whiting, A. Evans, Gallagher, Bilby, Kemp, Sudlow, R. Ormond (cpt), Inglis, Raat, Cochran, B. Taylor.
Selectors: R.A. Speed (Auckland), J.G. Shankie (Wellington) and G.W. Smith (Canterbury).
Manager: J.I. Kershaw (Wellington). Assistant Manager: O. Hilton (Wellington). Liaison Officer: J. Smith (Wellington). Coach: K. Armstrong (Auckland). Medical Officer: Dr D.M. Saker (Wellington). Referee: C.B. Anderson (Canterbury).
The team that met Munster was selected by J.I. Kershaw, O. Hilton, R. Smith and J.G. Shankie.

1967

140
May 31 v Manchester United F.C. at English Park, Christchurch. Lost 0-11. Referee: R.W. Cullen (Canterbury). NZ: A. Stroud, W. Hunter, Lake, Gowans, McNab, Bilby (cpt), Rennie, Lamont, York, M. Burgess, Legg.

141
November 5 v Australia (Vietnam National Day Tournament) at Cong Hua Stadium, Saigon. Lost 3-5. Goals: Mears 1, Nemet 1, Shaw 1. Referee: Hong Duk Yong (South Korea). NZ: Siebert, Latimour, Lake, B. Turner, McNab (cpt), Rennell, Nemet, Mears, Shaw, Ferrier, Legg. Sub: E. Thomas, A. Gowans.

142
November 8 v Singapore (Vietnam National Day Tournament) at Cong Hua Stadium, Saigon. Won 3-1. Goals: Thomas 2, Turner 1. Referee: M. Sridaranop (Thailand). NZ: Siebert, Latimour, Lake, Gowans, McNab (cpt), Rennell, Nemet, B. Turner, E. Thomas, Caldwell, Mears. Sub: France.

143
November 8 v New Caledonia at Magenta Stadium, Noumea. Lost 0-4. NZ: Petersen, Wallace, Gillies, Kennedy, Habets, Bilby (cpt), Lamont, Kiss, Beck, Breslin, K. Ironside.

144
November 10 v Australia B at Magenta Stadium, Noumea. Lost 1-3. Goals: Breslin 1. NZ: Petersen, Wallace, Gillies, Kennedy, Habets, Bilby (cpt), B. Smith, Kiss, Martin, Breslin, K. Ironside.

145
November 10 v South Vietnam (Vietnam National Day Tournament) at Cong Hua Stadium, Saigon. Lost 1-5. Goals: Shaw 1. Referee: Luk Tat Sun (Hong Kong). NZ: Siebert, Latimour, Lake, Gowans, McNab (cpt), Rennell, Nemet, B. Turner, Shaw, France, E. Thomas. Sub: D. Taylor.

146
November 16 v Malaysia at Kuala Lumpur. Won 8-2. Goals: Shaw 3, Legg 1, Nemet 1, Ferrier 1, Mears 1, Turner 1. NZ: Siebert (Nuttridge, sub), Latimour, Lake, B. Turner, McNab (cpt), Rennell, Nemet, Mears, Shaw, France, Legg. Sub: Ferrier.

147
November 18 v West Australia at Perth. Won 5-2. Goals: Turner 2, Shaw 1, Gowans 1, Legg 1. NZ: Siebert, Latimour, Caldwell, Gowans, France (cpt), Rennell, Nemet, Mears, Shaw, B. Turner, Legg. Selectors: D.Wallace (Auckland), J.G. Shankie (Wellington) and G.W. Smith (Canterbury).

Officials for the Vietnam Tournament were: Manager: J. Cowie. Assistant Manager: G. Smith. Coach: J. Schwanner. Referee: R.E. McDonald (Otago). Officials for the New Caledonia Tournament were: Manager: G.L. Whyte. Assistant Manager: J.K. Smith. Coach: R.C. Carter. Referee: A. Williams (Otago).

1968

148
May 26 v Central League at Basin Reserve, Wellington. Won 10-2. Goals: Thomas 3, Mears 3, Latimour 1, Rennell 1, de Graaf 1, own goal 1. NZ: Siebert, Latimour, Lake (W. Hunter, sub), M. Ferguson, McNab (cpt), Rennell, Milne, de Graaf, E. Thomas, Mears, Legg.

149
June 5 v Cardiff City F.C. at Newmarket Park, Auckland. Lost 0-3. Referee: R.W. Cullen (Canterbury). NZ: Siebert, Latimour, Lake, Haydon, McNab (cpt), Wallace, Milne, B. Turner (M. Ferguson, sub), Breslin, Mears (de Graaf, sub), Legg.

150
September 17 v Fiji at Newmarket Park, Auckland. Won 5-0. Goals: Shaw 3, Haydon 1, Legg 1. Referee: L.W. Coffman (Auckland). NZ: Siebert, Latimour, W. Hunter, Wallace (cpt), M. Ferguson, Staines, E. Thomas, Pollard, Shaw, Haydon, Legg.

151
October 8 v New Caledonia at Newmarket Park, Auckland. Lost 1-3. Goals: Breslin 1. Referee: R. Rump (Auckland). NZ: Phillips (Siebert, sub), Latimour, G. Davis, Wallace (cpt), M. Ferguson, Staines, Breslin (Haydon, sub), Pollard, Shaw, Mears, Legg.

Selectors: D. Wallace (Auckland), J. G. Shankie (Wellington), and G.W. Smith (Canterbury). Coach: J. Schwanner.

1969

152
June 11 v F.A. (England) X1 at Newmarket Park, Auckland. Lost 0-5. Referee: L.W. Coffman (Auckland). NZ: Cutler (Phillips, sub), G. Davis, W. Hunter, Griffiths, A. Jeffery, Bilby (cpt), Francis (Bland, sub), E. Thomas, Guildea, Mears, Bruce.

153
July 25 v New Caledonia at Stade de Magenta, Noumea. Drew 0-0. Referee: Andre Nakagawa. NZ: Phillips, Latimour, W. Hunter (M. Jones, sub), Griffiths, McNab (cpt) (Moyes, sub), Bilby, de Graaf, Mears, E. Thomas, Guildea, Bland.

154
July 27 v New Caledonia at Stade de Magenta, Noumea. Lost 0-2. Referee: Gosse. NZ: Phillips, Latimour, M. Jones, Griffiths, Moyes, Bilby (cpt), de Graaf, Mears, E. Thomas, Guildea, Bland.

155
July 29 v New Caledonia at Stade de Magenta, Noumea. Lost 2-3. Goals: Bilby 1, de Graaf 1. Referee: Andre Nakagawa. NZ: D. Houghton, Latimour (M. Jones, sub), W. Hunter, Griffiths, Moyes, Bilby (cpt), de Graaf, Bruce, E. Thomas, Guildea, Mears (Legg, sub).

156
September 16 v Singapore at Jalan Besar Stadium, Singapore. Won 2-0. Goals: de Graaf 1, Mears 1. Referee: Ram Bishen Sing. NZ: Phillips, Latimour, W. Hunter, Griffiths, Moyes, Bilby (cpt), Bland, de Graaf, Guildea, E. Thomas, Mears.

157
September 18 v Jardines F.C. at Government Stadium, Hong Kong. Lost 1-4. Goals: de Graaf 1. NZ: Phillips, Latimour, W. Hunter, Griffiths, Moyes, Bilby (cpt), Bland, de Graaf, Guildea, E. Thomas, Mears (Legg, sub).

158
September 21 v Thailand X1 at Suphachalasai National Stadium, Bangkok. Won 3-0. Goals: Bilby 1, Guildea 1, Bland 1. NZ: Phillips, Latimour, W. Hunter, Griffiths, Moyes (M. Jones, sub), Bilby (cpt), Bland, de Graaf, Guildea, E. Thomas, Mears (Bruce, sub).

159
September 28 v Israel (World Cup) at Ramat-Gan Stadium, Tel Aviv. Lost 0-4. Referee: Nassiri (Iran). NZ: Phillips, Latimour, W. Hunter, Griffiths, Moyes, Bilby (cpt), Bland (Bruce, sub), de Graaf (Legg, sub), Guildea, E. Thomas, Mears.

160
October 1 v Israel (World Cup) at Ramat-Gan Stadium, Tel Aviv. Lost 0-2. Referee: Hassan (Iran). NZ: Phillips, Latimour, W. Hunter, Griffiths, Moyes (M. Jones, sub), Bilby (cpt), Bruce, Guildea, Bland, Mears, Legg.
A. Jeffery and D. Houghton were in the World Cup squad but neither played.

Selectors: D. Wallace (Auckland), J.G. Shankie (Wellington) and G. Evans (Canterbury). L. Brocic (Wellington) joined the selection panel for the World Cup matches following the death of Mr Shankie during the season.
Manager: J. Cowie. Assistant Manager: A.R. White. Coach: L. Brocic. Medical Officer: Dr M.B. Marshall.

1970

161
June 6 v Jardines F.C. (Hong Kong) at Newmarket Park, Auckland. Drew 0-0. Referee: T.G. Delahunty (Wellington). NZ: Curtin, W. Hunter, Lake, Pollard, Griffiths, Bilby, C. Campbell, E. Thomas, Watson, Lamont (cpt), Bland (de Graaf, sub).

Selectors: G. Evans (Southern), K. Armstrong (Northern) and T. McCavana (Central). Coach: J.B. Truman.

1971

162
July 10 v F.A. of Wales X1 at Newmarket Park, Auckland. Lost 0-1. Referee: T.G. Delahunty (Wellington). NZ: Morris, Lake, R. Armstrong, Bilby (cpt), Staines, Eliadis, Bland, Pollard, Brand, Lamont (de Graaf, sub), E. Thomas.

163
July 18 v New Caledonia at Stade de Magenta, Noumea. Lost 2-4. Goals: Hastie 1, Brand 1. Referee: Andre Nakagawa. NZ: Morris, Lake, Griffiths, France (cpt) (Bilby, sub), R. Armstrong, Hardman, Hastie (de Graaf, sub), Bland, Brand (J. Houghton, sub), E. Thomas, Tindall.

164
July 20 v New Caledonia at Stade de Magenta, Noumea. Lost 1-2. Goals: Tindall 1. Referee: Bataille. NZ: Jeram, Hastie, Lake (cpt), Griffiths, R. Armstrong, Hardman, Pollard, Bland, J. Houghton, de Graaf, Tindall (E. Thomas, sub).

Selectors: J.B. Truman (Wellington), K. Armstrong (Auckland), G. Evans (Nelson) and W. Berry (Otago).

Coach: J.B. Truman

A proposed trip to New Caledonia for the Oceania Cup tournament from October 30 - November 6 fell through when the New Caledonian organisers cancelled the event. The following players were selected to travel.
Goalkeepers: Tony Fleming (Christchurch United, Canterbury), Jack Nathu (Wellington City, Wellington).
Fullbacks: Gary Lake (Blockhouse Bay, Auckland), Keith Barton (Western Suburbs, Wellington), Iain Hastie (Mt Wellington, Auckland), Grahame Bilby (Wellington City, Wellington), Brian Armstrong (Mt Wellington, Auckland).
Halfbacks: Peter Eliadis (Eastern Suburbs, Auckland), Victor Pollard (Christchurch United, Canterbury), Bill de Graaf (Eastern Suburbs, Auckland).
Forwards: Geoff Brand (Stop Out, Wellington), Earle Thomas (Mt Wellington, Auckland), Malcolm Bland (Eastern Suburbs, Auckland), Iain Ormond (Blockhouse Bay, Auckland), Clive Campbell (Blockhouse Bay, Auckland), Dennis Tindall (Dunedin Suburbs, Otago).

1972

165
September 17 v New Caledonia at Basin Reserve, Wellington. Won 4-1. Goals: Ormond 3, Vest 1. Referee: T.G. Delahunty (Wellington). NZ: Morris, Sibley, Tillotson, Hastie, M. Ferguson, Vest (cpt), Tindall, B. Turner (P. Cameron, sub), D. Taylor (Brand, sub), Marley, I. Ormond.

166
September 30 v New Caledonia at Newmarket Park, Auckland. Won 2-1. Goals: Tindall 1, Ormond 1. Referee: L.W. Coffman (Auckland). NZ: Morris, Sibley (Ashurst, sub), Tillotson, Hastie, M. Ferguson, Vest (cpt), Tindall, Pollard, D. Taylor (Brand, sub), Marley, I. Ormond.

167
October 3 v West Australia at Lake Monger Velodrome, Perth. Won 3-2. Goals: Brand 1, Ormond 1, Vest 1. Referee: J. Allen. NZ: Curtin, Sibley, Tillotson, P. Cameron, Ashurst, Pollard, Tindall, B. Turner (M. Ferguson, sub), Brand, Vest (cpt), I. Ormond.

168
October 5 v Singapore B at Jalan Besar Stadium, Singapore. Won 2-0. Goals: Marley 1, Taylor 1. NZ: Morris, Hastie, Ashurst (Tillotson, sub), P. Cameron (Sibley, sub), M. Ferguson, W. Fleet (B. Turner, sub), D. Taylor (Tindall, sub), Pollard, Brand (I. Ormond, sub), Vest (cpt), Marley.

169
October 9 v Australia at Senayan Stadium, Jakarta. Lost 1-3. Goals: Vest 1. Referee: K. Kartadiredja. NZ: Morris (Curtin, sub), Sibley, Tillotson, Hastie, M. Ferguson, Pollard, Tindall (D. Taylor, sub), B. Turner (Ashurst, sub), Marley, Vest (cpt), I. Ormond.

170
October 11 v Indonesia at Senayan Stadium, Jakarta. Drew 1-1. Goals: Taylor 1. Referee: S. Haddade. NZ: Curtin, Sibley, Tillotson, Ashurst (W. Fleet, sub), Hastie, Pollard, D. Taylor, B. Turner, Brand (I. Ormond, sub), Vest (cpt) (Tindall, sub), Marley.

171
October 14 v New Caledonia at Stade de Magenta, Noumea. Lost 1-3. Goals: Tillotson 1. Referee: Andre Nakagawa. NZ: Curtin, Sibley, Tillotson (Pollard, sub), P. Cameron, M. Ferguson (cpt), W. Fleet, Tindall, B. Turner, D. Taylor (Vest, sub), Marley, I. Ormond.

Selectors: J.B. Truman (Wellington), K. Armstrong (Auckland), G. Evans (Nelson) and W. Berry (Otago). Manager: G.H. Moore. Coach: J.B. Truman. Doctor: M.B. Marshall.

1973

172
February 17 v Fiji (Oceania Cup) at Newmarket Park, Auckland. Won 5-1. Goals: Turner 1, Taylor 1, Brand 1, Bland 1, Vest 1. Referee: A. Nakagawa (New Caledonia). NZ: Curtin, Tillotson, Lake, Latimour, B. Armstrong, Tindall (Hardman, sub), Bland, B. Turner (Staines, sub), Brand, Vest (cpt), D. Taylor.

173
February 18 v Tahiti (Oceania Cup) at Newmarket Park, Auckland. Drew 1-1. Goals: Vest 1. Referee: P. Raman (Fiji). NZ: Morris, Sibley, R. Armstrong, M. Ferguson, B. Armstrong, Hardman, Tindall (Vest, sub), B. Turner, Marley, Staines (cpt), Bland (D. Taylor, sub).

174
February 21 v New Caledonia (Oceania Cup) at Newmarket Park, Auckland. Won 2-1. Goals: Marley 1, Latimour 1. Referee: B. Chaudet (New Hebrides). NZ: Morris, Tillotson, R. Armstrong, Latimour, Staines (cpt), Tindall, D. Taylor (Brand, sub), B. Turner, Marley, Vest (Hardman, sub), Bland.

175
February 23 v New Hebrides (Oceania Cup) at Newmarket Park, Auckland. Won 3-1. Goals: Bland 1, Hardman 1, Marley 1. Referee: P. Tahuaitu (Tahiti). NZ: Curtin, Sibley, Lake, M. Ferguson, Staines (cpt), Hardman, Brand, B. Armstrong (Tindall, sub), Marley, Vest, Bland (D. Taylor, sub).

176
February 24 v Tahiti (Oceania Cup) at Newmarket Park, Auckland. Won 2-0. Goals: Taylor 1, Marley 1. Referee: B. Chaudet (New Hebrides). NZ: Curtin, Tillotson, R. Armstrong, Latimour, Staines (cpt), Tindall (B. Armstrong, sub), D. Taylor, B. Turner, Marley, Vest, Bland.

177
March 4 v Australia (World Cup) at Newmarket Park, Auckland. Drew 1-1. Goals: Turner 1. Referee: Luk Tat Sun (Hong Kong). NZ: Curtin, Tillotson, Latimour, Staines (cpt), R. Armstrong, B. Turner, Vest, Tindall (B. Armstrong, sub), D. Taylor, Marley (Brand, sub), Bland.

178
March 11 v Indonesia (World Cup) at Sportsground, Sydney. Drew 1-1. Goals: Vest 1. Referee: K. Mahendran (Malaysia). NZ: Morris, Tillotson, Latimour, Staines (cpt), R. Armstrong, B. Turner, M. Ferguson (Tindall, sub), Randles, D. Taylor, Brand (Vest, sub), Marley.

179
March 13 v Iraq (World Cup) at Sportsground, Sydney. Lost 0-2. Referee: F. Alvarez (Philippines). NZ: Curtin, Sibley, Latimour, Staines (cpt), Lake, B. Turner, Tindall (Hardman, sub), Randles, D. Taylor (Bland, sub), Vest, Marley.

180
March 16 v Australia (World Cup) at Sportsground, Sydney. Drew 3-3. Goals: Tindall 2, Vest 1. Referee: K. Mahendran (Malaysia). NZ: Curtin, Tillotson, Latimour, Staines (cpt), R. Armstrong, B. Turner, Randles, Hardman (Sibley, sub), Tindall, Vest, D. Taylor (M. Davis, sub).

181
March 18 v Indonesia (World Cup) at Olympic Park, Melbourne. Lost 0-1. Referee: G. Suppiah (Singapore). NZ: Morris, Tillotson, B. Armstrong, Staines (cpt), R. Armstrong, B. Turner, Randles, Hardman (Brand, sub), Tindall, Vest, D. Taylor (Bland, sub).

182
March 24 v Iraq (World Cup) at Sportsground, Sydney. Lost 0-4. Referee: Kim Joo-won (South Korea). NZ: Curtin, Sibley (B. Turner, sub), Latimour, B. Armstrong, Lake, R. Armstrong, Vest, Tillotson, D. Taylor (Brand, sub), Staines (cpt), Bland.

183
August 12 v Iran at Newmarket Park, Auckland. Drew 0-0. Referee: T.G. Delahunty (Wellington). NZ: Dando, Tillotson, Griffiths, France (cpt), R. Armstrong, B. Turner (A. Smith, sub), Legg, Vest, E. Thomas, Boyland (Park, sub), D. Taylor.

Officials for the Oceania and World Cups were: Manager: C.J. Dempsey. Assistant Manager: R.A. Kelly. Coach: J.B. Truman. Physiotherapist: P. Heim.

1975

184
July 20 v China P.R. at Newmarket Park, Auckland. Won 2-1. Goals: Thomas 1, Taylor 1. Referee: A.T. Blackburn (Auckland). NZ: Jeram, Sibley, Griffiths, B. Armstrong, Park, Storer (B. Turner, sub), W. Fleet, D. Taylor, Weymouth (Legg, sub), E. Thomas (cpt), Mulgrew (Elrick, sub).

185
July 23 v China P.R. at Basin Reserve, Wellington. Drew 2-2. Goals: Thomas 1, Taylor 1. Referee: T.G. Delahunty (Wellington). NZ: Jeram, K. Barton, Griffiths, B. Armstrong, Park, B. Turner, W. Fleet, Legg (Storer, sub), Mulgrew, E. Thomas (cpt), D. Taylor.

186
July 26 v China P.R. at Queen Elizabeth II Park, Christchurch. Won 2-0. Goals: Thomas 2. Referee: R.E. McDonald (Otago). NZ: Nuttridge, Sibley, Griffiths, Elrick, Park, B. Turner (Storer, sub), W. Fleet, D. Taylor, Weymouth (Legg, sub), E. Thomas (cpt), Mulgrew.

187
October 4 v Indonesia X1 at English Park, Christchurch. Won 8-0. Goals: Thomas 4, Houghton 1, Park 1, Mulgrew 1, Ormond 1. Referee: R.N. Harries (Wellington). NZ: Jeram (Dando, sub), Sibley, J. Houghton, Elrick, Park, Storer, W. Fleet, D. Taylor, I. Ormond, E. Thomas (cpt), Mulgrew.

188
October 19 v China P.R. at Workers Stadium, Peking. Lost 1-2. Goals: Ormond 1. NZ: Jeram, Sibley, J. Houghton, Elrick, Park, Storer (B. Turner, sub), W. Fleet, D. Taylor, I. Ormond, E. Thomas (cpt), Mulgrew.

189
October 23 v Shantung at Athletic Stadium, Tsinan. Won 2-0. Goals: Taylor 2. NZ: Dando, Sibley, J. Houghton, Elrick, Park, B. Turner, Legg, D. Taylor, I. Ormond, E. Thomas (cpt), Mulgrew.

190
October 27 v Shanghai at Peoples Stadium, Shanghai. Won 1-0. Goals: Ormond 1. NZ: Jeram, Sibley, J. Houghton, Elrick, Park, Storer, Legg, B. Turner, I. Ormond, E. Thomas (cpt), Mulgrew (Weymouth, sub).

191
October 30 v Hupei at Peoples Stadium, Wuhan. Drew 1-1. Goals: Thomas 1. NZ: Jeram, Sibley, J. Houghton, Elrick, Park, B. Turner (Storer, sub), W. Fleet, D. Taylor, I. Ormond, E. Thomas (cpt), Mulgrew (Paddison, sub).

192
November 1 v Hunan at Peoples Stadium, Wuhan. Won 3-0. Goals: Ormond 1, Thomas 1, Mulgrew 1. NZ: Jeram (Dando, sub), Sibley, J. Houghton, Elrick, Park, Storer, B. Turner, D. Taylor, I. Ormond (Weymouth, sub), E. Thomas (cpt), Mulgrew.

193
November 5 v Macao at Macao. Drew 1-1. Goals: Mulgrew 1. NZ: Dando, Sibley, Elrick, Park (cpt), Tillotson, Storer (B. Turner, sub), W. Fleet, Legg, I. Ormond, Weymouth (E. Thomas, sub), Paddison (Mulgrew, sub).

194
November 9 v Singapore at Jalan Besar Stadium, Singapore. Drew 2-2. Goals: Houghton 2. Referee: G. Suppiah (Singapore). NZ: Jeram, Sibley, J. Houghton, Elrick, Park, B. Turner, W. Fleet (Storer, sub), D. Taylor, I. Ormond, E. Thomas (cpt), Mulgrew (Weymouth, sub).

195
November 11 v Singapore Kings Cup X1 at Jalan Besar Stadium, Singapore. Won 5-1. Goals: Thomas 2, Mulgrew 2, Park 1. Referee: Ong Eng Young (Singapore). NZ: Jeram, Sibley, J. Houghton, Elrick (Tillotson, sub), Park, B. Turner, W. Fleet, D. Taylor, I. Ormond (Weymouth, sub), E. Thomas (cpt), Mulgrew.

196
November 13 v Persebeya F.C. at Senayan Stadium, Jakarta. Won 2-0. Goals: Park 1, Weymouth 1. Referee: O. Soetedjo. NZ: Dando, Sibley, J. Houghton (cpt), Tillotson, Park, Storer (Legg, sub), W. Fleet, B. Turner, D. Taylor, I. Ormond (Paddison, sub), Weymouth.

197
November 15 v Persija F.C. at Senayan Stadium, Jakarta. Won 1-0. Goals: Weymouth 1. NZ: Jeram, Sibley, J. Houghton, Elrick, Park, B. Turner (Legg, sub), W. Fleet, D. Taylor, I. Ormond, E. Thomas (cpt) (Storer, sub), Weymouth (Tillotson, sub).

Manager: T.J. Killalea. Assistant Manager: G. Thomas. Coach: J.B. Truman. Doctor: M.B. Marshall.

1976

198
February 29 v Australia at Newmarket Park, Auckland. Lost 0-1. Referee: A.T. Blackburn (Auckland). NZ: Jeram, Sibley, J. Houghton, Elrick, Park, B. Turner, W. Fleet, D. Taylor (Storer, sub), I. Ormond, E. Thomas (cpt), Mulgrew.

199
March 2 v Australia at Olympic Park, Melbourne. Lost 1-3. Goals: Taylor 1. Referee: S.G. Mellings (Australia). NZ: Jeram, Sibley, J. Houghton, Elrick, Park, B. Turner, W. Fleet, D. Taylor, I. Ormond, E. Thomas (cpt), Mulgrew.

200
May 14 v Sunderland F.C. at Newmarket Park, Auckland. Lost 0-3. Referee: J.W. Cameron (Waikato). NZ: Jeram, Sibley, J. Houghton, Simeonoff, Park, B. Turner, Hobbs (Elrick, sub), D. Taylor, I. Ormond, E. Thomas (cpt), Davidson (Mulgrew, sub).

201
May 30 v Heart of Midlothian F.C. at Newmarket Park, Auckland. Lost 0-3. Referee: A.T. Blackburn (Auckland). NZ: Dando, Sibley, Simeonoff, Elrick, Park, B. Turner (cpt), W. Fleet, D. Taylor, I. Ormond (Davidson, sub), Weymouth, Mulgrew (E. Thomas, sub).

202
September 13 v Burma (President's Cup Tournament) at Municipal Stadium, Seoul. Won 2-0. Goals: Tindall 1, Malcolmson 1. Referee: Lee Woo-hyun (South Korea). NZ: Curtin, Sibley, J. Houghton, Elrick, Park, Tindall (Sumner, sub), B. Turner, D. Taylor, Weymouth (Mulgrew, sub), Malcolmson, E. Thomas (cpt).

203
September 16 v Indonesia (President's Cup Tournament) at Municipal Stadium, Seoul. Drew 0-0. Referee: Lee Woo-bong (South Korea). NZ: Curtin, Sibley, J. Houghton, Elrick, Park, Tindall, B. Turner, W. Fleet, D. Taylor, Malcolmson (Weymouth, sub) (Mulgrew, sub), E. Thomas (cpt).

204
September 18 v Thailand (President's Cup Tournament) at Municipal Stadium, Seoul. Won 3-1. Goals: Turner 2, Thomas 1. Referee: S. Kathiravale (Malaysia). NZ: Curtin, Sibley, J. Houghton, Elrick, Park, Tindall (Mulgrew, sub), Sumner, W. Fleet, D. Taylor, B. Turner (Dods, sub), E. Thomas (cpt).

205
September 21 v South Korea B (President's Cup Tournament) at Municipal Stadium, Seoul. Won 1-0. Goals: Mulgrew 1. Referee: P. Jayaram (Singapore). NZ: Jeram, Sibley, J. Houghton, Elrick, Dods, Simeonoff, Sumner, W. Fleet, Park (D. Taylor, sub), E. Thomas (cpt) (Tindall, sub), Mulgrew.

206
September 23 v South Korea A (President's Cup Tournament) at Municipal Stadium, Seoul. Lost 0-2. Referee: P. Jayaram (Singapore). NZ: Curtin, Sibley, J. Houghton (cpt), Elrick, Dods, Tindall (Simeonoff, sub), W. Fleet, D. Taylor, Weymouth, Sumner, Mulgrew.

207
September 25 v South Korea B (President's Cup Tournament) at Municipal Stadium, Seoul. Lost 0-1. Referee: S. Kathiravale (Malaysia). NZ: Curtin, Sibley, J. Houghton (cpt) (D. Taylor, sub), Elrick, Park, Simeonoff, Sumner, W. Fleet (Tindall, sub), Weymouth, B. Turner, Mulgrew.

208
September 28 v South Korea B at Daegu. Drew 1-1. Goals: Malcolmson 1. Referee: Park Jong-hwan (South Korea). NZ: Curtin, Dods, Sibley, Elrick, Park, Tindall, Sumner, D. Taylor (Weymouth, sub), Mulgrew, Malcolmson, B. Turner (cpt).

209
October 2 v New Caledonia at Stade de la Magenta, Noumea. Lost 1-2. Goals: Turner 1. NZ: Jeram, Dods, Sibley, Simeonoff, Park, Tindall (Sumner, sub), B. Turner, D. Taylor, Weymouth (Mulgrew, sub), Malcolmson, E. Thomas (cpt).

Manager: R.A. Kelly. Assistant Manager: M. MacKenzie. Coach: J.B. Truman. Physiotherapist: I. Sim.

1977

210
February 28 v Ba (Fiji) at Newmarket Park, Auckland. Won 5-2. Goals: Nelson 4, Sumner 1. NZ: Dando, Sibley, Griffiths, Elrick (cpt), R. Armstrong, Sumner, B. Turner (W. Fleet, sub), Lesbirel, Weymouth, Nelson, E. Thomas (G. Hough, sub).

211
March 5 v New Caledonia at Newmarket Park, Auckland. Won 3-0. Goals: Campbell 2, Hough 1. Referee: A.T. Blackburn (Auckland). NZ: Curtin, Sibley, J. Houghton (cpt), Elrick, Park, D. Taylor, W. Fleet, Lesbirel, C. Campbell, Nelson, G. Hough.

212
March 8 v New Caledonia at Newmarket Park, Auckland. Won 4-0. Goals: Nelson 2, Campbell 1, Taylor 1. Referee: L.W. Coffman (Auckland). NZ: Jeram, Sibley, J. Houghton (cpt), Park, R. Armstrong, B. Turner, Lesbirel, D. Taylor, C. Campbell, Nelson, Weymouth.

213
March 19 v Chinese-Taipei (World Cup) at Newmarket Park, Auckland. Won 6-0. Goals: Nelson 3, Campbell 1, Taylor 1, Weymouth 1. Referee: G. Suppiah (Singapore). NZ: Curtin, Sibley, J. Houghton, Elrick, R. Armstrong, B. Turner (W. Fleet, sub), Sumner, D. Taylor, C. Campbell, Nelson, Weymouth.

214
March 23 v Chinese-Taipei (World Cup) at Newmarket Park, Auckland. Won 6-0. Goals: Sumner 3, Nelson 2, own goal 1. Referee: H.S. Dhillon (Singapore). NZ: Curtin, Sibley (Park, sub), J. Houghton (cpt), Elrick, R. Armstrong, B. Turner, Sumner, D. Taylor, C. Campbell, Nelson, Weymouth.

215
March 27 v Australia (World Cup) at Sportsground, Sydney. Lost 1-3. Goals: Nelson 1. Referee: Chan Tam-Sun (Hong Kong). NZ: Curtin, Sibley, J. Houghton (cpt), Elrick, R. Armstrong, B. Turner, Sumner, D. Taylor, C. Campbell (Dods, sub), Nelson, Weymouth (Park, sub).

216
March 30 v Australia (World Cup) at Newmarket Park, Auckland. Drew 1-1. Goals: Nelson 1. Referee: Cheung Kwok-kui (Hong Kong). NZ: Curtin, Sibley, J. Houghton (cpt), Elrick, R. Armstrong, B. Turner, Sumner, D. Taylor, Dods, Nelson, Weymouth (Park, sub).

217
May 25 v Luton Town F.C. at Newmarket Park, Auckland. Won 3-2. Goals: Nelson 2, Malcolmson 1. Referee: R.N. Harries (Wellington). NZ: Curtin, Sibley, Young, Elrick (cpt), R. Armstrong, B. Turner, Sumner (W. Fleet, sub), Lesbirel, Dods, Malcolmson, Nelson.

218
May 26 v Luton Town F.C. at Basin Reserve, Wellington. Lost 2-3. Goals: Malcolmson 1, Nelson 1. Referee: A.T. Blackburn (Auckland). NZ: Curtin, Sibley, J. Houghton (cpt), Elrick, R. Armstrong, B. Turner, Sumner, D. Taylor, Dods, Malcolmson, Nelson.

1978

219
June 7 v England B at English Park, Christchurch. Lost 0-4. Referee: R.N. Harries (Wellington). NZ: Davie, Park, Sibley, Elrick (cpt), R. Armstrong, Dods (Cole, sub), B. Turner, Sumner, D. Taylor (Stamp, sub), E. Thomas, Nelson.

220
June 11 v England B at Basin Reserve, Wellington. Lost 1-3. Goals: Turner 1. Referee: W.K. Munro (Auckland). NZ: Jeram (Davie, sub), Dods, Sibley, Almond, Park, B. Turner (D. Taylor, sub), Cole, Sumner, Elrick (cpt), Nelson, E. Thomas (Stamp, sub).

221
June 14 v England B at Newmarket Park, Auckland. Lost 0-4. Referee: T.G. Delahunty (Wellington). NZ: Davie, Dods, Sibley (cpt), Almond, Park, B. Turner, Sumner, R. Armstrong, I. Ormond (Stamp, sub), Weymouth, Nelson (Elrick, sub).

222
September 11 v Iran (President's Cup Tournament) at Daegu. Lost 1-2. Goals: Simeonoff 1. Referee: Baek Bong-Ki (South Korea). NZ: Pickering, Sibley, Adam, Simeonoff, Elrick, B. Turner (cpt), Cole, Simonsen, Cresswell (Ten Broeke, sub), Nelson, Sumner.

223
September 13 v Morocco (President's Cup Tournament) at Busan. Lost 0-3. Referee: Maeng Kwang-Sup (South Korea). NZ: Pickering, Sibley, Elrick, Simeonoff, Cole, B. Turner (cpt), Sumner, Simonsen, Cresswell (N. Haines, sub), Nelson, Ten Broeke (M. Armstrong, sub).

224
September 15 v West Germany* (President's Cup Tournament) at Municipal Stadium, Seoul. Won 3-0. Goals: M. Armstrong 1, Ten Broeke 1, Sumner 1. Referee: T. Kibritjian (USA). NZ: Pickering, Sibley, Elrick, Adam, Cole, Simonsen, Sumner, Debenham, M. Armstrong, B. Turner (cpt), Ten Broeke.
*Eintracht Frankfurt F.C. XI represented West Germany.

225
September 27 v Selangor F.C. (Malaysia) at Kuala Lumpur. Lost 1-2. Goals: Cresswell 1. NZ: Gosling, Sibley, Elrick, Adam, Cole, Debenham (Simeonoff, sub), Simonsen, Cresswell (Ten Broeke, sub), Sumner, B. Turner (cpt), Nelson.

226
October 1 v Singapore at Singapore. Won 2-0. Goals: Simonsen 1, Nelson 1. NZ: Pickering, Sibley (N. Haines, sub), Elrick, Adam, Cole, Debenham (Simeonoff, sub), Simonsen, Cresswell, B. Turner, Sumner, Nelson.

Tour Manager: G.H. Moore. Manager: G.P. Bilby. Coach: J.B. Truman. Assistant Coach: T. Conley. Physiotherapist: I. Sim. Referee: T.G. Delahunty.

1979

227
May 11 v Norwich City F.C. at Newmarket Park, Auckland. Lost 1-4. Goals: Nelson 1. Referee: W.K. Munro (Auckland). NZ: Davie, Cole, Malcolmson, Elrick, Bright, Sibley (cpt), Almond (Cresswell, sub), Sumner, B. Turner (Paddison, sub), Nelson (D. Ormond, sub), Stamp.

228
June 13 v Australia at Newmarket Park, Auckland. Won 1-0. Goals: Ormond 1. Referee: T.G. Delahunty (Wellington). NZ: R.H. Wilson, Sibley (cpt), Malcolmson, Almond, Elrick, B. Turner, Sumner, Cole, D. Ormond (Stamp, sub), Nelson, Verweij.

229
June 29 v Fiji at Buckhurst Park, Suva. Won 6-0. Goals: Nelson 3, Rufer 1, Cole 1, Turner 1. NZ: R.H. Wilson, Sibley (cpt), Malcolmson, Elrick, Bright (Metzger, sub), Cole, B. Turner, Leijh, Stamp (D. Ormond, sub), S. Rufer, Nelson.

230
July 1 v Fiji at Churchill Park, Lautoka. Won 3-0. Goals: Malcolmson 1, Rufer 1, C. Turner 1. NZ: Davie, Sibley (cpt), Malcolmson, Elrick, Metzger, Cole, B. Turner (Bright, sub), C. Turner, D. Ormond, S. Rufer (Stamp, sub), Nelson.

231
July 26 v New Caledonia at Stade de Magenta, Noumea. Won 2-0. Goals: Nelson 1, Sumner 1. Referee: Andre Nakagawa. NZ: R.H. Wilson, Sibley (cpt), Malcolmson, Almond, Elrick, Cole (Stamp, sub), B. Turner, Sumner, D. Ormond (S. Rufer, sub), Nelson, Verweij (Bright, sub).
The trip to Fiji was followed by another to New Caledonia where two games were also due to be played however the first of these fixtures was cancelled due to heavy rain. NZ officials for both tours were: Tour Leader: D. McDonald. Manager: A. Egan. Coach: J. Adshead. Physiotherapist: D.W. Edwards.

232
October 2 v Al-Qadisiyya S.C. at Qadisiyya Stadium, Kuwait. Lost 1-2. Goals: Campbell 1. NZ: Davie, Sibley (cpt), Malcolmson, Almond, Cole, B. Turner, McDermid, Sumner (C. Turner, sub), C. Campbell (Jenkins, sub), Nelson (S. Rufer, sub), Verweij.

233
October 3 v Bahrain at Isa Town Stadium, Manama. Won 2-0. Goals: Campbell 1, Verweij 1. Referee: M.A. Khulgoon (Bahrain). NZ: R.H. Wilson, Sibley (cpt), Malcolmson (Adam, sub), Almond, Elrick, Cole, B. Turner (Bright, sub), Sumner, C. Campbell, S. Rufer (Nelson, sub), Verweij (C. Turner, sub).

234
October 5 v Al Ahli S.C. at Al-Ahli Stadium, Dubai. Drew 1-1. Goals: Almond 1. NZ: B. Turner, Sibley (cpt), Adam, Almond, Elrick, Cole, Sumner, C. Turner, C. Campbell (S. Rufer, sub), Nelson, Verweij (Malcolmson, sub).

235
October 8 v Bahrain at Isa Town Stadium, Manama. Won 2-1. Goals: B. Turner 1, Nelson 1. Referee: A.K.M. Abdul Reza (Bahrain). NZ: R.H. Wilson, Sibley (cpt), Adam, Almond, Elrick, Cole (Verweij, sub), Sumner, C. Turner, C. Campbell (S. Rufer, sub), Nelson, B. Turner (Jenkins, sub).

236
October 10 v Irish F.A. X1 at The Oval, Belfast. Lost 0-2. Referee: O. Donnelly (Northern Ireland). NZ: R.H. Wilson, Sibley (cpt), Adam, Almond, Elrick, C. Turner (McDermid, sub), Sumner, Bright, Nelson, B. Turner (Malcolmson, sub), Verweij (S. Rufer, sub).

237
October 12 v League of Ireland at Richmond Road, Dublin. Lost 1-2. Goals: B. Turner 1. Referee: J. Carpenter (Eire). NZ: R.H. Wilson, Sibley (cpt), Malcolmson, Almond, Elrick, B. Turner, Adam, Sumner, C. Campbell, Nelson, Verweij.

238
October 15 v England B at Leyton Stadium, London. Lost 1-4. Goals: Nelson 1. Referee: G.J.M. Geurds (Netherlands). NZ: R.H. Wilson, Sibley (cpt), Malcolmson, Almond, Elrick, B. Turner (C. Turner, sub), Sumner, Adam (Cole, sub), C. Campbell (S. Rufer, sub), Nelson, Verweij.

239
October 17 v Ipswich Town F.C. at Portman Road, Ipswich. Lost 0-1. Referee: B.A. Collings (England). NZ: Davie, Sibley (cpt), Adam (Malcolmson, sub), Almond, Bright, McDermid (Sumner, sub), C. Turner, Cole (B. Turner, sub), Jenkins (C. Campbell, sub), Nelson, Verweij (S. Rufer, sub).

240
October 22 v Norwich City F.C. at Carrow Road, Norwich, Lost 0-5. Referee: V. Roper (England). NZ: R.H. Wilson, Sibley (cpt), Malcolmson (C. Turner, sub), Almond, Elrick (Bright, sub), B. Turner (Cole, sub), Sumner, Adam, C. Campbell, Nelson, Verweij (S. Rufer, sub).

241
October 29 v Dundee F.C. at Dens Park, Dundee. Lost 1-8. Goals: Sumner 1. Referee: R.B. Valentine (Scotland). NZ: Davie (cpt), Sibley, Malcolmson, Almond, Elrick (McDermid, sub), C. Campbell, B. Turner, Cole, Nelson, Sumner, Verweij (C. Turner, sub).

Tour Leader: C.J. Dempsey.
Manager: J. Arnold.
Assistant Manager: A. Egan.
Coach: J. Adshead.
Physiotherapist: D.W. Edwards.

While the full New Zealand team was in Britain a B team was named to play in the Oceania Cup Tournament in New Caledonia from December 9-16 however this tournament was postponed. The players named were:
Goalkeepers: Frank Van Hattum (Manurewa, Franklin), Peter Moot (Christchurch United, Canterbury).
Fullbacks: James Margaritis (Christchurch United, Canterbury), Lee Stickland (Manurewa, Franklin), Ricki Herbert (Nelson United, Nelson), Garth Macleod (Blockhouse Bay, Auckland), Alex Metzger (Blockhouse Bay, Auckland), Michael White (Rongotai College, Wellington).
Halfbacks: Bill de Graaf (Mt Wellington, Auckland), John Leijh (Mt Wellington, Auckland), Keith Hobbs (North Shore, Auckland), Nigel Debenham (Dunedin City, Otago).
Forwards: Michael Groom (Hamilton, Waikato), Ken Cresswell (Nelson United, Nelson), Bill Harris (Diamond United, Wellington), Alistair Elder (Mt Roskill, Auckland), Mark Armstrong (Manurewa, Franklin).
Tour Leader: T.J. Killalea. Manager: J. Adshead. Coach: A. Jones. Physiotherapist: D.W. Edwards.

1980

242
February 19 v Fiji at Buckhurst Park, Suva. Drew 1-1. Goals: Elder 1. Referee: F. Nair (Fiji). NZ: R.H. Wilson, Sibley (cpt), Adam, Almond, Dods, C. Turner, Sumner, de Graaf (Hobbs, sub), Groom, M. Armstrong (Welch, sub), Elder.

243
February 21 v Fiji at Churchill Park, Lautoka. Won 2-0. Goals: Elder 2. NZ: Van Hattum, Dods, Stickland, Almond, R.W. Durant, C. Turner, Sumner, Hobbs (de Graaf, sub), Groom (M. Armstrong, sub), Welch, Elder.

244
February 25 v Tahiti (Oceania Cup) at Stade de Magenta, Noumea. Lost 1-3. Goals: Sumner 1. Referee: C. Bambridge (Australia). NZ: R.H. Wilson, Sibley (cpt), Adam, Almond, R.W. Durant, C. Turner, Sumner, de Graaf (Park, sub), Groom, Hobbs (M. Armstrong, sub), Elder.

245
February 27 v Fiji (Oceania Cup) at Stade de Magenta, Noumea. Lost 0-4. Referee: C. Bambridge (Australia). NZ: R.H. Wilson (Van Hattum, sub), R.W. Durant, Hobbs, Almond, Park, C. Turner, Sumner (cpt), Groom, Welch, Elder (de Graaf, sub), M. Armstrong.

246
February 29 v Solomon Islands (Oceania Cup) at Stade de Magenta, Noumea. Won 6-1. Goals: Armstrong 3, de Graaf 2, Groom 1. Referee: H.R. Naicker (Fiji). NZ: Van Hattum, R.W. Durant, Sibley (cpt), Almond, Park, C. Turner, Sumner (Elder, sub), Hobbs, Groom, de Graaf (Stickland, sub), M. Armstrong.

Manager: T.J. Killalea. Coach: J. Adshead. Assistant Coach: V. Mobley. Doctor: E. Grieve.

247
May 16 v Southern Region at English Park, Christchurch. Drew 1-1. Goals: Adam 1. Referee: A. Edwards (Canterbury). NZ: Van Hattum, Sibley (cpt), R.W. Durant, Almond (Adam, sub), R. Armstrong, Sumner, Boath (Groom, sub), Leijh, C. Campbell, Glubb, Wooddin.

248
May 18 v Central Region at Newtown Park, Wellington. Lost 1-2. Goals: Debenham 1. Referee: G.W. Fleet (Wellington). NZ: Van Hattum, Sibley (cpt), R.W. Durant, Adam, R. Armstrong, Sumner, Debenham, Leijh, Groom, Glubb (C. Campbell, sub), Wooddin.

249
August 20 v Mexico at McKinlay Park, Auckland. Won 4-0. Goals: B. Turner 2, Wooddin 1, G. Turner 1. Referee: W.K. Munro (Auckland). NZ: Van Hattum, Hill, Bright, Herbert, R. Armstrong, D. Ormond (C. Campbell, sub), Sumner (cpt), Mackay, G. Turner (Billot, sub), B. Turner, Wooddin (M. Armstrong, sub).

250
September 15 v Canada at Empire Stadium, Vancouver. Lost 0-4. Referee: W. Winsemann (Canada). NZ: Van Hattum, Hill, Herbert, Bright, R. Armstrong, D. Ormond, Sumner (cpt), Mackay, G. Turner (C. Campbell, sub), B. Turner, Wooddin (Adam, sub).

251
September 18 v Canada at Edmonton. Lost 0-3. Referee: D. Maglio (Canada). NZ: Van Hattum, Billot (Hill, sub), Adam, Herbert, R. Armstrong, D. Ormond, Sumner (cpt), Mackay (M. Armstrong, sub), C. Campbell, B. Turner, Wooddin (G. Turner, sub). Tour leader: C.J. Dempsey. Manager: J. Adshead. Coach: K. Fallon.

252
October 16 v Kuwait (Merdeka Tournament) at Merdeka Stadium, Kuala Lumpur. Won 5-1. Goals: Groom 2, Baxter 1, Taylor 1, de Graaf 1. NZ: Davie, Leijh, Sibley (cpt), Dunford, Strom, Baxter, de Graaf, C. Evans, D. Taylor, W. Rufer (Phelan, sub), Groom.

253
October 19 v South Korea (Merdeka Tournament) at Merdeka Stadium, Kuala Lumpur. Won 2-1. Goals: Groom 1, de Graaf 1. NZ: Davie, Leijh, Sibley (cpt), Dunford, Strom, Baxter, de Graaf, C. Evans, D. Taylor, W. Rufer (W. Harris, sub), Groom.

254
October 21 v Indonesia (Merdeka Tournament) at Merdeka Stadium, Kuala Lumpur. Drew 0-0. NZ: Davie, Leijh, Sibley (cpt), Dunford, Strom, Baxter, de Graaf, C. Evans, D. Taylor, Groom (Phelan, sub), W. Harris (Van Helden, sub).

255
October 24 v Burma (Merdeka Tournament) at Merdeka Stadium, Kuala Lumpur. Drew 1-1. Goals: Groom 1. NZ: Davie, Leijh (Masson, sub), Sibley (cpt), Dunford, Strom, Baxter, de Graaf, C. Evans, D. Taylor, Groom, W. Harris.

256
October 26 v Morocco (Merdeka Tournament) at Merdeka Stadium, Kuala Lumpur. Lost 0-3. NZ: Davie, Leijh, Sibley (cpt), Dunford (Phelan, sub), Strom, Baxter, de Graaf, C. Evans, D. Taylor, W. Harris, Groom.

257
October 28 v Thailand (Merdeka Tournament) at Merdeka Stadium, Kuala Lumpur. Drew 1-1. Goals: de Graaf 1.Referee: Ahmad Faraj (Kuwait). NZ: Davie, Leijh, Sibley (cpt), C. Evans, Strom, Baxter, de Graaf, D. Taylor, W. Harris, W. Rufer (Phelan, sub), Groom.

258
October 30 v Malaysia (Merdeka Tournament) at Merdeka Stadium, Kuala Lumpur. Lost 0-2. NZ: Davie, Leijh, Sibley (cpt), C. Evans, Strom, Baxter (Masson, sub), de Graaf, D. Taylor, W. Harris, W. Rufer (Phelan, sub), Groom.
Tour Leader: B. Cunningham. Manager/Coach: A. Jones. Assistant Manager: J. Houghton. Physiotherapist: M. Oram. Referee: W.K. Munro.

1981

259
April 25 v Australia (World Cup) at Mt Smart Stadium, Auckland. Drew 3-3. Goals: G. Turner 1, Wooddin 1, Sumner 1. Referee: G. Menegali (Italy). NZ: R.H. Wilson, Hill, Herbert, Almond, Dods, Mackay (Elrick, sub), Cole, Sumner (cpt), G. Turner, B. Turner (C. Campbell, sub), Wooddin.

260
May 3 v Fiji (World Cup) at Govind Stadium, Ba. Won 4-0. Goals: B. Turner 3, Cole 1. Referee: Othman Bin Omar (Malaysia). NZ: R.H. Wilson, Hill, Herbert, Almond, Dods, Mackay (C. Campbell, sub), Cole, Sumner (cpt), G. Turner, B. Turner, Wooddin (Malcolmson, sub).

261
May 7 v Chinese-Taipei (World Cup) at Municipal Stadium, Taipei. Drew 0-0. Referee: T. Asami (Japan). NZ: R.H. Wilson, Hill, Herbert, Almond, Dods, C. Campbell (Boath, sub), Sumner (cpt), Cole, B. Turner (Elrick, sub), Malcolmson, Wooddin.

262
May 11 v Indonesia (World Cup) at Senayan Stadium, Jakarta. Won 2-0. Goals: B. Turner 1, G. Turner 1. Referee: N. Ausukont (Thailand). NZ: R.H. Wilson, Hill, Herbert, Almond, Dods, Mackay (C. Campbell, sub), Cole, Sumner (cpt), G. Turner (Elrick, sub), B. Turner, Wooddin.

263
May 16 v Australia (World Cup) at Cricket Ground, Sydney. Won 2-0. Goals: Wooddin 1, G. Turner 1. Referee: G. Courtney (England). NZ: R.H. Wilson, Hill, Herbert, Almond, Dods, Mackay (Malcolmson, sub), Cole, Sumner (cpt), G. Turner, B. Turner (C. Campbell, sub), Wooddin.

264
May 23 v Indonesia (World Cup) at Mt Smart Stadium (Auckland). Won 5-0. Goals: G. Turner 2, B. Turner 1, Wooddin 1, Elrick 1. Referee: V. Graca Oliva (Portugal). NZ: R.H. Wilson, Hill, Herbert, Almond, Dods (Elrick, sub), Mackay, Cole, Sumner (cpt), G. Turner, B. Turner (C. Campbell, sub), Wooddin.

265
May 30 v Chinese-Taipei (World Cup) at Mt Smart Stadium, Auckland. Won 2-0. Goals: Wooddin 1, G. Turner 1. Referee: T. Boskovic (Australia). NZ: R.H. Wilson, Hill, Herbert, Almond, Dods, Mackay, Cole, Sumner (cpt), Boath (C. Campbell, sub), G. Turner, Wooddin.

266
August 16 v Fiji (World Cup) at Mt Smart Stadium, Auckland. Won 13-0. Goals: Sumner 6, G. Turner 2, B. Turner 2, Mackay 1, Cole 1, Wooddin 1. Referee: V. Getkaew (Thailand). NZ: R.H. Wilson, Hill (Bright, sub), Herbert, Almond, Elrick, Mackay, Cole, Sumner (cpt), G. Turner (Boath, sub), B. Turner, Wooddin.

Manager: J. Adshead. Coach: K. Fallon. Physiotherapist: D. Edwards.

267
September 1 v India (Merdeka Tournament) at Merdeka Stadium, Kuala Lumpur. Drew 0-0. Referee: Salah M. Karim (Iraq). NZ: Davie, Leijh (Masson, sub), Sibley (cpt), C. Evans, Strom, Marshall, de Graaf, Metzger, D. Taylor, McClure, Nelson.

268
September 4 v Malaysia (Merdeka Tournament) at Merdeka Stadium, Kuala Lumpur. Won 1-0. Goals: Taylor 1. Referee: Salah M. Karim (Iraq). NZ: Pickering, Leijh, Sibley (cpt), C. Evans, Strom, D. Taylor, Metzger, de Graaf, Cresswell, McClure, Nelson.

269
September 7 v Indonesia (Merdeka Tournament) at Merdeka Stadium, Kuala Lumpur. Drew 0-0. Referee: S. Shahid Hakeem (India). NZ: Pickering, Leijh, Sibley (cpt), C. Evans, Strom, Metzger, Scheirlinck, Cresswell, D. Taylor, McClure, de Graaf (Marshall, sub).

270
September 10 v United Arab Emirates (Merdeka Tournament) at Merdeka Stadium, Kuala Lumpur. Lost 0-1. Referee: Mohd Noor Saud (Malaysia). NZ: Davie, Leijh, Sibley (cpt) (Simeonoff, sub), C. Evans, Strom, Scheirlinck, Cresswell, Marshall (A. Brown, sub), D. Taylor, McClure, Nelson.

271
September 12 v Japan (Merdeka Tournament) at Merdeka Stadium, Kuala Lumpur. Won 1-0. Goals: Nelson 1. Referee: N. Chandra (Singapore). NZ: Davie, Leijh, Scheirlinck, C. Evans, Strom, Marshall, Metzger, Cresswell, D. Taylor, McClure, Nelson.

Tour Leader: W. Gendall. Manager: A. Jones. Assistant Manager: J. Houghton. Physiotherapist: M. Oram. Referee: G.W. Fleet.

272
September 24 v China P.R. (World Cup) at Workers Stadium, Beijing. Drew 0-0. Referee: T. Sano (Japan). NZ: R.H. Wilson, Dods (Hill, sub), Herbert, Almond, Elrick, Mackay, Cole, Sumner (cpt), G. Turner, B. Turner, Wooddin.

273
October 3 v China P.R. (World Cup) at Mt Smart Stadium, Auckland. Won 1-0. Goals: Herbert 1. Referee: V. Getkaew (Thailand). NZ: R.H. Wilson, Dods (Hill, sub), Herbert, Almond, Elrick, Mackay, Cole, Sumner, McClure, B. Turner, G. Turner (Boath, sub).

274
October 10 v Kuwait (World Cup) at Mt Smart Stadium, Auckland. Lost 1-2. Goals: Wooddin 1. Referee: H. Sudarso (Indonesia). NZ: R.H. Wilson, Hill, Herbert, Almond, Elrick, Mackay, Cole, Sumner (cpt), G. Turner (McClure, sub), B. Turner, Wooddin.

275
November 7 v Victoria at Olympic Park, Melbourne. Won 2-1. Goals: McClure 1, Adam 1. NZ: R.H. Wilson, Hill, Adam, Almond, Elrick (Dods, sub), Mackay (Simonsen, sub), Cole, Sumner (cpt), McClure, B. Turner, G. Turner.

276
November 10 v Geelong at Bell Park, Geelong. Won 3-1. Goals: G. Turner 2, Adam 1. NZ: Van Hattum, Hill, Herbert, Almond, Dods, Simonsen, Cole, Sumner (cpt), McClure (Adam, sub), B. Turner, G. Turner.

277
November 28 v Saudi Arabia (World Cup) at Mt Smart Stadium, Auckland. Drew 2-2. Goals: McClure 1, Herbert 1. Referee: A. Ithurralde (Argentina). NZ: R.H. Wilson, Dods, Herbert, Almond, Elrick, Mackay, Cole, Sumner (cpt), McClure (Malcolmson, sub), Wooddin, G. Turner (Boath, sub).

278
December 14 v Kuwait (World Cup) at Qadisiyya Stadium, Kuwait. Drew 2-2. Goals: Sumner 1, Rufer 1. Referee: H. Lund-Sorensen (Denmark). NZ: R.H. Wilson, Dods, Herbert, Almond, Elrick, G. Turner, Cole, Sumner (cpt), W. Rufer, B. Turner, Wooddin.

279
December 19 v Saudi Arabia (World Cup) at National Stadium, Riyadh. Won 5-0. Goals: Rufer 2, B. Turner 2, Wooddin 1. Referee: C. Corver (Netherlands). NZ: R.H. Wilson, Dods, Herbert, Almond, Elrick, Boath (Mackay, sub), Cole, Sumner (cpt), B. Turner (Malcolmson, sub), W. Rufer, Wooddin.

1982

280
January 10 v China P.R. (World Cup) at Jalan Besar Stadium, Singapore. Won 2-1. Goals: Wooddin 1, Rufer 1. Referee: R. Arppi Filho (Brazil). NZ: R.H. Wilson, Dods, Herbert, Almond, Elrick, Boath (Simonsen, sub), Cole, Sumner (cpt), G. Turner, W. Rufer (Adam, sub), Wooddin.

281
February 11 v Hungary at Mt Smart Stadium, Auckland. Lost 1-2. Goals: B. Turner 1. Referee: W.K. Munro (Auckland). NZ: R.H. Wilson, Hill, Adam, Almond (cpt), Elrick, Mackay, Cole, Boath, McClure (Cresswell, sub), W. Rufer, B. Turner (Malcolmson, sub).

282
February 14 v Hungary at Queen Elizabeth II Park, Christchurch. Lost 1-2. Goals: Rufer 1. Referee: G.W. Fleet (Wellington). NZ: Van Hattum, Hill, Adam, Almond (cpt), Elrick, Mackay (Bright, sub), Cole, Cresswell, McClure, Malcolmson (Simonsen, sub), W. Rufer.

283
May 8 v League of Ireland at Mt Smart Stadium, Auckland. Won 1-0. Goals: G. Turner 1. Referee: W.K. Munro (Auckland). NZ: R.H. Wilson, Hill, Herbert, Almond, Dods, McClure, Boath, Sumner (cpt), G. Turner (Cresswell, sub), W. Rufer, Wooddin.

284
May 9 v League of Ireland at International Stadium, Rotorua. Won 1-0. Goals: Rufer 1. Referee: J.W. Cameron (Waikato). NZ: Van Hattum, Bright, Adam, Malcolmson, Elrick (cpt), Mackay, Cresswell, Simonsen, G. Turner, B. Turner, W. Rufer (McClure, sub).

285
May 12 v League of Ireland at Childers Road, Gisborne. Drew 0-0. Referee: T.G. Delahunty (Wellington). NZ: Pickering, Hill, Herbert, Almond, Elrick, Mackay, McClure, Sumner (cpt), Cresswell (B. Turner, sub), W. Rufer, Wooddin (G. Turner, sub).

286
May 16 v League of Ireland at Caledonian Ground, Dunedin. Lost 1-2. Goals: McClure 1. Referee: R. Paterson (Otago). NZ: R.H. Wilson, Dods, Adam, Almond, Elrick, McClure, Boath (Cresswell, sub), Sumner (cpt), G. Turner, W. Rufer, S. Wooddin.

287
May 19 v League of Ireland at Surrey Park, Invercargill. Won 1-0. Goals: Rufer 1. Referee: L. Sharp (Southland). NZ: Van Hattum, Hill, Malcolmson, Almond (cpt), Elrick, McClure, Simonsen (G. Turner, sub), Cresswell, B. Turner, W. Rufer, Wooddin.

288
May 23 v Watford F.C. at Queen Elizabeth II Park, Christchurch. Lost 0-1. Referee: A.J. Edwards (Canterbury). NZ: Van Hattum, Hill, Herbert, Almond, Elrick (Dods, sub), McClure (G. Turner, sub), Boath, Cresswell, B. Turner (cpt), W. Rufer, S. Wooddin.

289
May 26 v Watford F.C. at Athletic Park, Wellington. Drew 1-1. Goals: Wooddin 1. Referee: G.W. Fleet (Wellington). NZ: R.H. Wilson, Dods, Malcolmson, Almond (cpt), Elrick (Mackay, sub), Cresswell, Boath, G. Turner, B. Turner, W. Rufer, S. Wooddin.

290
May 29 v Watford F.C. at Mt Smart Stadium, Auckland. Lost 0-2. Referee: W.K. Munro (Auckland). NZ: R.H. Wilson, Elrick, Malcolmson, Almond, Cresswell, Mackay, Boath, Sumner (cpt), G. Turner, W. Rufer, Wooddin.

291
June 15 v Scotland (World Cup) at Estadio La Rosaleda, Malaga. Lost 2-5. Goals: Sumner 1, Wooddin 1. Referee: D. Socha (USA). NZ: Van Hattum, Hill, Malcolmson (Cole, sub), Almond (Herbert, sub), Elrick, Mackay, Boath, Sumner (cpt), Cresswell, W. Rufer, Wooddin.

292
June 19 v U.S.S.R. (World Cup) at Estadio La Rosaleda, Malaga. Lost 0-3. Referee: Y.M. El-Ghoul (Libya). NZ: Van Hattum, Dods, Herbert, Boath, Elrick, Mackay, Cole, Sumner (cpt), Cresswell, W. Rufer, Wooddin.

293
June 23 v Brazil (World Cup) at Estadio Benita Villamarin, Seville. Lost 0-4. Referee: D. Matovinovic (Yugoslavia). NZ: Van Hattum, Dods, Herbert, Almond, Elrick, Mackay, Boath, Sumner (cpt), Cresswell (Cole, sub), W. Rufer (B. Turner, sub), Wooddin.

1983

294
February 22 v Australia at Mt Smart Stadium, Auckland. Won 2-1. Goals: Cresswell 1, Herbert 1. Referee: W.K. Munro (Auckland). NZ: Pickering, Elrick, Herbert, Boath (cpt), R. Armstrong, Mackay, Cole, G. Turner, Cresswell, Nelson, Metzger (Henry, sub).

295
February 27 v Australia at Olympic Park, Melbourne. Won 2-0. Goals: Cole 1, Adam 1. Referee: J. Johnston (Australia). NZ: Pickering, Elrick, Herbert, Boath (cpt) (Adam, sub), R. Armstrong, Mackay, Cole, G. Turner, Cresswell, Nelson (McClure, sub), Wooddin.
Tour Leader: R.H. Kerslake. Coach: A. Jones. Assistant Coach: K. Fallon. Physiotherapist: D.W. Edwards.

296
June 5 v South Korea 'Yukong' (President's Cup Tournament) at Municipal Stadium, Seoul. Lost 0-2. Referee: T. Kibritjian (USA). NZ: Pickering, D. Burgess, Herbert, Adam, Strom, Cole (Metzger, sub), Boath (cpt), Sumner (Henry, sub), Cresswell, Nelson, G. Turner.

297
June 7 v Ghana (President's Cup Tournament) at Municipal Stadium, Seoul. Won 2-0. Goals: Herbert 1, G. Turner 1. Referee: Park (South Korea). NZ: Pickering, D. Burgess, Herbert, Adam, Strom, Cole, Boath (cpt), Henry, Cresswell, Nelson (Verweij, sub), G. Turner.

298
June 9 v Sudan (President's Cup Tournament) at Stadium, Taegu. Drew 1-1. Goals: Metzger 1. Referee: Baek Bong-kee (South Korea). NZ: Pickering, D. Burgess, Herbert, Adam, Strom, Cole, Henry, Boath (cpt) (Masson, sub), Cresswell, Metzger, G. Turner.

299
June 11 v P.S.V. Eindhoven (Netherlands) (President's Cup Tournament) at Stadium, Pusan. Lost 0-3. Referee: T. Kibritjian (USA). NZ: Pickering, D. Burgess (Strom, sub), Herbert, Adam, Boath (cpt), Cole, Henry (C. Evans, sub), Sumner, Metzger, G. Turner, Cresswell.

Tour Leader: T.C. Gottermeyer. Coach: A. Jones. Assistant Coach: K. Fallon. Physiotherapist: M. Oram. Referee: W.K. Munro.

300
August 16 v Fiji at National Stadium, Suva. Lost 0-2. Referee: M. Singh (Fiji). NZ: Pickering, Elrick, Herbert, Boath (cpt), R. Armstrong, Mackay (Adam, sub), Cole, Sumner, Cresswell, G. Turner, Wooddin (McClure, sub).

301
August 18 v Fiji at Prince Charles Park, Nadi. Won 1-0. Goals: Cresswell 1. Referee: G. Kanna (Fiji). NZ: Pickering, Elrick, Herbert, Boath (cpt), R. Armstrong, Mackay (Adam, sub), Cole, Sumner, Cresswell, McClure, G. Turner.

302
September 25 v Japan (Olympic Tournament) at Mt Smart Stadium, Auckland. Won 3-1. Goals: Sumner 2, Boath 1. Referee: Lee Kok-leong (Singapore). NZ: Van Hattum, Elrick, C. Evans, Herbert, R. Armstrong, Mackay, Boath (cpt), Sumner, G. Turner, McClure (Tuaa, sub), Cresswell.

303
October 1 v Chinese-Taipei (Olympic Tournament) at Mt Smart Stadium, Auckland. Won 2-0. Goals: Boath 1, Turner 1. Referee: G. Kanna (Fiji). NZ: Van Hattum, Elrick (Cole, sub), C. Evans, Herbert, R. Armstrong (Groom, sub), Mackay, Boath (cpt), Sumner, G. Turner, McClure, Cresswell.

304
October 7 v Japan (Olympic Tournament) at National Stadium, Tokyo. Won 1-0. Goals: Sumner 1. Referee: Othman Bin Omar (Malaysia). NZ: Van Hattum, Herbert, C. Evans, Boath (cpt), Elrick, Mackay, Cole, Sumner, G. Turner, McClure (Tuaa, sub), Cresswell.

305
October 12 v Chinese-Taipei (Olympic Tournament) at National Stadium, Taipei. Drew 1-1. Goals: Boath 1. Referee: R. Reyes (Philippines). NZ: Pickering, Herbert (Groom, sub), C. Evans, Boath (cpt), Elrick, Mackay, Cole, Sumner, G. Turner, Tuaa, Cresswell (McClure, sub).

Tour Leader: B. Cunningham. Coach: A. Jones. Assistant Coach: K. Fallon. Physiotherapist: D.W. Edwards.

1984

306
March 31 v Malaysia at Basin Reserve, Wellington. Won 2-0. Goals: McClure 1, Turner 1. Referee: G.W. Fleet (Wellington). NZ: Pickering, Garland (D. Burgess, sub), Herbert, C. Evans, Elrick, Mackay, Cole, Boath (cpt), G. Turner, Groom (Birch, sub), McClure.

307
April 3 v Malaysia at English Park, Christchurch. Won 6-1. Goals: McClure 3, Boath 2, Turner 1. Referee: A.J. Edwards (Canterbury). NZ: Van Hattum, Herbert, C. Evans, Boath (cpt), Garland, Mackay (Tuaa, sub), Simonsen, Cole, G. Turner, McClure, Birch (de Jong, sub).

308
April 8 v Malaysia at Mt Smart Stadium, Auckland. Drew 0-0. Referee: J.W. Cameron (Waikato). NZ: Van Hattum, Herbert, C. Evans, Boath (cpt), Elrick, Mackay, Simonsen, Cole (Tuaa, sub), G. Turner, McClure, Groom.

309
April 15 v Saudi Arabia (Olympic Tournament) at National Stadium (Singapore). Lost 1-3. Goals: Herbert 1. Referee: T.H. Gurkan (Philippines). NZ: Van Hattum, Herbert, C. Evans, Garland, Elrick, Cole, Groom, Boath (cpt), Mackay, McClure, G. Turner (Tuaa, sub).

310
April 19 v Kuwait (Olympic Tournament) at National Stadium (Singapore). Lost 0-2. Referee: Chan Tam Sun (Hong Kong). NZ: Van Hattum, Herbert (cpt), Garland, C. Evans, Elrick, Groom, Simonsen, Cole, Mackay, McClure (Adam, sub), Tuaa (Birch, sub).

311
April 22 v South Korea (Olympic Tournament) at National Stadium, Singapore. Lost 0-2. Referee: J. Al-Sharif (Syria). NZ: Van Hattum, Herbert (cpt), Garland, C. Evans, Elrick, Cole, Simonsen, Groom (D. Burgess, sub), Mackay, McClure (Metzger, sub), Birch.

312
April 24 v Bahrain (Olympic Tournament) at National Stadium, Singapore. Lost 0-1. Referee: Ahmad Bash (Jordan). NZ: Van Hattum, Herbert, Garland, C. Evans, Elrick, Groom, Simonsen, Boath (cpt), Mackay, Birch (de Jong, sub), McClure (Metzger, sub).

Tour Leader: J. Arnold. Manager: A. Jones. Assistant Coach: K. Fallon. Physiotherapist: M. Butler.

313
June 9 v Glasgow Rangers F.C. at Mt Smart Stadium, Auckland. Lost 0-3. Referee: W.K. Munro (Auckland). NZ: Van Hattum, Garland, Herbert, Boath (cpt), Cresswell, W. Harris (Halford, sub), Mackay (Hagan, sub), Simonsen (C. Evans, sub), G. Turner, C. Walker, Wooddin.

314
October 18 v Fiji at Churchill Park, Lautoka. Won 2-1. Goals: Walker 1, Wooddin 1. Referee: P. Rampley (Australia). NZ: R.H. Wilson, Felton, Herbert, Byrne, Leijh (Dunford, sub), G. Turner, Sumner, Boath (cpt), McClure (Birch, sub), Wooddin, C. Walker.

315
October 20 v Fiji at National Stadium, Suva. Drew 1-1. Goals: Dunford 1. Referee: P. Rampley (Australia). NZ: Gosling, Felton, Herbert, Byrne, Dunford (Garland, sub), G. Turner, Sumner (cpt), Simonsen, Mackay, Wooddin, C. Walker (Birch, sub).

316
October 24 v Newcastle United F.C. at St James Park, Newcastle. Lost 0-3. Referee: A. Saunders (England). NZ: R.H. Wilson, Felton (Leijh, sub), Herbert, Byrne, Garland, G. Turner (McClure, sub), Sumner (W. Harris, sub), Boath (cpt), Mackay, Wooddin (Birch, sub), C. Walker.

317
October 29 v Reading F.C. at Elm Park, Reading. Won 2-1. Goals: Turner 1, Walker 1. Referee: D. Keen (England). NZ: Gosling, Garland, Herbert, Boath (cpt), Leijh, (Felton, sub), G. Turner, Simonsen (Sumner, sub), W. Harris (Mackay, sub), McClure, C. Walker, Birch (Wooddin, sub).

318
October 31 v Glasgow Rangers F.C. at Ibrox Stadium, Glasgow. Lost 0-5. Referee: K. Hope (Scotland). NZ: R.H. Wilson, Felton (Leijh, sub), Herbert, Byrne, Garland, G. Turner, Boath (cpt) (Sumner, sub), Simonsen (Mackay, sub), McClure (W. Harris, sub), C. Walker, Birch (Wooddin, sub).

319
November 5 v Leicester City F.C. at City Stadium, Leicester. Lost 1-4. Goals: Walker 1. NZ: Gosling, Dunford, Herbert, Byrne, Leijh, G. Turner, Sumner (W. Harris, sub), Boath (cpt) (Simonsen, sub), Mackay, C. Walker, Birch.

320
November 7 v Portsmouth F.C. at Fratton Park, Portsmouth. Lost 2-3. Goals: Mackay 1, Walker 1. Referee: A. Robinson (England). NZ: R.H. Wilson, Felton (Byrne, sub), Dunford (Herbert, sub), Garland, Leijh, Mackay (Sumner, sub), Simonsen (cpt), W. Harris (G. Turner, sub), McClure, C. Walker, Birch.

321
November 13 v England B at City Ground, Nottingham. Lost 0-2. Referee: D. Richardson (England). NZ: R.H. Wilson, Dunford, Herbert, Boath (cpt), Leijh (Garland, sub), Sumner, G. Turner, Simonsen (Byrne, sub), Mackay, C. Walker, Birch (W. Harris, sub).

Tour Leaders: J.W. Gendall and R. Husband. Coach: A. Jones. Assistant Coach: K. Fallon.

1985

322
May 18 v Newcastle United F.C. at Queen Elizabeth II Park, Christchurch. Lost 1-2. Goals: Sumner 1. Referee: L. Sharp (Southland). NZ: R.H. Wilson, Mulligan (Leijh, sub), Hobbs, Dunford, Cresswell, Cole (cpt), Sumner, Byrne, Henry, Hagan, C. Walker (Little, sub).

323
May 19 v Newcastle United F.C. at Basin Reserve, Wellington. Drew 2-2. Goals: Sumner 1, Walker 1. Referee: A.J. Edwards (Canterbury). NZ: Van Hattum, Cole (cpt), Hobbs, Dunford, Cresswell, Leijh (D. Edge, sub), C. Evans, Sumner, G. Turner, Little (C. Walker, sub), Hagan.

324
May 22 v Newcastle United F.C. at McLean Park, Napier. Lost 0-4. Referee: K. Wallace (Auckland). NZ: R.H. Wilson, Mulligan, Hobbs, Dunford, Cresswell, Cole (cpt), Simonsen, Byrne, Sumner, Hagan (Halford, sub), C. Walker.

325
May 25 v Newcastle United F.C. at Mt Smart Stadium, Auckland. Lost 2-3. Goals: Walker 1, own goal 1. Referee: J.W. Cameron (Waikato). NZ: Van Hattum, Mulligan, Hobbs, Dunford, Cole (cpt), Boath, Simonsen, C. Evans, Sumner, Hagan, C. Walker (Little, sub).

326
June 3 v Fiji at Links Avenue, Mt Maunganui. Won 5-0. Goals: Walker 3, Hagan 1, Little 1. Referee: G.W. Fleet (Franklin). NZ: Gosling, Mulligan, Hobbs, Dunford, Cole (cpt), Hagan (D. Edge, sub), Simonsen, C. Evans, Henry, Little, C. Walker.

327
June 5 v Fiji at Childers Road, Gisborne. Won 3-0. Goals: Walker 2, Sumner 1. Referee: J.W. Cameron (Waikato). NZ: Gosling, Mulligan (Little, sub), Hobbs, Dunford, Cresswell, Cole (cpt) (Henry, sub), Sumner, Byrne (C. Evans, sub), Simonsen, Hagan (Birch, sub), C. Walker.

328
June 7 v Fiji at McKinlay Park, Auckland. Won 2-0. Goals: Sumner 1, own goal 1. Referee: W.K. Munro (Auckland). NZ: Van Hattum, Mulligan (McClure, sub), Hobbs, Dunford, Cole (cpt), Simonsen, Sumner, C. Evans, Henry, Little (Birch, sub), Hagan.

329
September 10 v Otago at Caledonian Ground, Dunedin. Won 2-1. Goals: Dunford 2. Referee: D. Ritchie (Otago). NZ: Gosling, Mulligan, Hobbs, Dunford, Cresswell, Boath (cpt) (Cole, sub), Sumner (D. Edge, sub), C. Evans, G. Turner, C. Walker, Hagan (Henry, sub).

330
September 12 v Canterbury at English Park, Christchurch. Drew 1-1. Goals: Walker 1. Referee: A. Edwards (Canterbury). NZ: Van Hattum, Mulligan, C. Evans (Hobbs, sub), Dunford, Cresswell, Cole, Boath (cpt) (D. Edge, sub), Byrne, G. Turner, Henry (Sumner, sub), C. Walker.

331
September 21 v Australia (World Cup) at Mt Smart Stadium, Auckland. Drew 0-0. Referee: K. Hackett (England). NZ: Van Hattum, S. Rufer, C. Evans, Dunford, Cresswell, G. Turner, Sumner, Boath (cpt), D. Edge (Henry, sub), W. Rufer, C. Walker.

332
October 5 v Chinese-Taipei (World Cup) at Mt Smart Stadium, Auckland. Won 5-1. Goals: Sumner 3, Edge 1, Walker 1. Referee: C. Bambridge (Australia). NZ: Van Hattum, Mulligan, C. Evans, Dunford, Cresswell, Cole, Sumner, Boath (cpt) (Byrne, sub), G. Turner, C. Walker, D. Edge.

333
October 12 v Chinese-Taipei (World Cup) at Queen Elizabeth II Park, Christchurch. Won 5-0. Goals: Turner 2, Walker 2, Boath 1. Referee: D. Campbell (Australia). NZ: Van Hattum, Mulligan, C. Evans, Dunford, Cresswell, Cole, Sumner (Hagan, sub), Boath (cpt), G. Turner, C. Walker, D. Edge.

334
October 26 v Israel (World Cup) at Mt Smart Stadium, Auckland. Won 3-1. Goals: W. Rufer 1, Dunford 1, Walker 1. Referee: E. Mulder (Netherlands). NZ: Van Hattum, S. Rufer, C. Evans, Dunford, Cresswell, G. Turner, Cole (Sumner, sub), Boath (cpt), D. Edge (Hagan, sub), W. Rufer, C. Walker.

335
November 3 v Australia (World Cup) at Sportsground, Sydney. Lost 0-2. Referee: G.J.M. Geurds (Netherlands). NZ: Van Hattum, S. Rufer (Mulligan, sub), C. Evans, Dunford, Cresswell, Boath (cpt), Sumner (D. Edge, sub), Herbert, G. Turner, W. Rufer, C. Walker.

336
November 10 v Israel (World Cup) at Ramat Gan Stadium, Tel Aviv. Lost 0-3. Referee: D. Pauly (West Germany). NZ: Van Hattum, Mulligan, C. Evans, Dunford, Cresswell, McClure, Boath (cpt) (Sumner, sub), Byrne, D. Edge, Hagan, C. Walker.

1986

337
February 17 v U.S.S.R. X1 at Mt Smart Stadium, Auckland. Lost 0-1. Referee: K. Wallace (Auckland). NZ: Van Hattum, Mulligan, C. Evans, Dunford, T. Mason (Witteveen, sub), G. Turner (W. Harris, sub), Sumner, Boath (cpt), Cresswell, G. Brown, Hagan.

338
February 19 v U.S.S.R. X1 at Newtown Park, Wellington. Drew 1-1. Goals: Dunford 1. Referee: L. Sharp (Southland). NZ: Pickering, O'Neill (Mulligan, sub), C. Evans, Dunford, Cresswell, McClure, Sumner, Boath (cpt), G. Turner, G. Brown (W. Harris, sub), Hagan.

339
February 21 v U.S.S.R. X1 at Queen Elizabeth II Park, Christchurch. Lost 1-2. Goals: Dunford 1. Referee: A.J. Edwards (Canterbury). NZ: Pickering, Mulligan, C. Evans, Dunford, Cresswell, McClure, Sumner (Deeley, sub), Boath (cpt), Witteveen, G. Brown (W. Harris), Hagan.

340
February 23 v U.S.S.R. X1 at Park Island, Napier. Lost 0-2. Referee: J.W. Cameron (Waikato). NZ: Pickering, Mulligan, C. Evans, Dunford, T. Mason (Cresswell, sub), McClure (G. Brown, sub), Witteveen, Boath (cpt), G. Turner, Barkley, Hagan (Deeley, sub).

341
February 25 v U.S.S.R. X1 at Childers Road, Gisborne. Lost 2-4. Goals: Witteveen 1, Hagan 1. Referee: G.W. Fleet (Franklin). NZ: Schofield, Mulligan, C. Evans, Dunford, Cresswell, G. Turner, Witteveen, Boath (cpt), Probert (Barkley, sub), Hagan, W. Harris (McClure, sub).

342
September 17 v Fiji at Churchill Park, Lautoka. Won 4-2. Goals: Herbert 2, Evans 1, McGarry 1. Referee: M. Singh (Fiji). NZ: Gilgrist, Mulligan, C. Evans, Herbert, Brydon (Simpson, sub), McGarry, Boath (cpt), McClure, Chote (Witteveen, sub), Barkley, McClennan (de Jong, sub).

343
September 19 v Fiji at National Stadium, Suva. Won 2-1. Goals: Evans 1, Barkley 1. Referee: H.R. Naicker (Fiji). NZ: A.J. Stroud, Mulligan, Lund, C. Evans, Herbert, Simpson, Boath (cpt) (McGarry sub), Witteveen; McLennan (de Jong, sub), Barkley, McClure.

Tour Leader: B. Clement. Administration: N. Robinson. Coach: K. Fallon. Physiotherapist: D.W. Edwards.

344
October 25 v Australia (Trans Tasman Cup) at Mt Smart Stadium. Drew 1-1. Goals: Deeley 1. Referee: G.W. Fleet (Franklin). NZ: Van Hattum, Cole, Herbert, Dunford, Cresswell (Barkley, sub) (McGarry, sub), G. Turner, Boath (cpt), Witteveen, McClennan, Hagan, Deeley.

345
November 2 v Australia (Trans Tasman Cup) at Parramatta Stadium, Sydney. Lost 1-2. Goals: Deeley 1. Referee: G. Powell (Australia). NZ: Van Hattum, Mulligan, Herbert, Dunford (cpt), Cresswell, Cole, Boath (Barkley, sub), Sumner, McClennan (McGarry, sub), Hagan, Deeley.

1987

346
February 8 v Dynamo Minsk F.C. (U.S.S.R.) at Childers Road, Gisborne. Lost 0-2. Referee: G.W. Fleet (Franklin). NZ: Gosling, Mulligan, C. Evans, Herbert (cpt), Cresswell, McGarry (Henry, sub), D. Edge (Cole, sub), Boath, Brydon. W. Harris, Hagan (Barkley, sub).

347
February 11 v Dynamo Minsk F.C. (U.S.S.R.) at Newtown Park, Wellington. Lost 0-3. Referee: A.J. Edwards (Canterbury). NZ: Gosling (Finlayson, sub), Mulligan, C. Evans, Herbert, Cresswell (Brydon, sub), Cole, Boath, Dunford (Cpt), D. Edge (Barkley, sub), Hanson (McGarry, sub), Hagan.

348
February 15 v Dynamo Minsk F.C. (U.S.S.R.) at Links Avenue, Mt Maunganui. Drew 0-0. Referee: J.W. Cameron (Waikato). NZ: Van Hattum, Mulligan, C. Evans, Herbert, Cresswell, Boath, Cole, Dunford, Brydon (D. Edge, sub), McGarry, Barkley (Hanson, sub).

349
February 17 v Dynamo Minsk F.C. (U.S.S.R.) at English Park, Christchurch. Lost 0-2. Referee: L. Sharp (Southland). NZ: Gosling, Mulligan, C. Evans, Herbert, Cresswell, McGarry (Hanson, sub), Boath (Cole, sub), Dunford (cpt), Brydon (D. Edge, sub), Hagan, Barkley.

350
September 2 v Australia (Trans Tasman Cup) at Olympic Park, Melbourne. Drew 1-1. Goals: Ironside 1. Referee: C. Bambridge (Australia). NZ: Gosling, Mulligan, R. Ironside, C. Evans, Cresswell, Cole, Halligan, Dunford (cpt), D. Edge (McGarry, sub), Barkley, de Jong (Hagan, sub).

G. Schofield travelled with team to Australia but did not take the field. A. Deeley was also a reserve in Melbourne.

Tour Leader: N. Robinson. Coach: K. Fallon. Assistant Coach: E. Edge. Masseur: J. Hannah.

351
September 9 v Australia (Trans Tasman Cup) at Recreation Ground, Lower Hutt. Won 1-0. Goals: de Jong 1. Referee: G.W. Fleet (Franklin). NZ: Gosling, Mulligan (Boath, sub), R. Ironside, C. Evans, Cresswell, McGarry, Cole, Dunford (cpt), D. Edge, Hagan (Barkley, sub), de Jong.

G. Schofield travelled with team to Australia but did not take the field. A. Deeley was also a reserve in Melbourne.

352
November 7 v Western Samoa (Olympic Tournament) at Apia Park, Apia. Won 7-0. Goals: Ironside 3, Halford 1, McGarry 1, Halligan 1, Deeley 1. Referee: C. Bambridge (Australia). NZ: Gosling, Herbert, C. Evans, Dunford, Cresswell, McGarry (Barkley, sub), Halligan, D. Edge, Halford, de Jong (R. Ironside, sub), Deeley.

353
November 13 v Western Samoa (Olympic Tournament) at Western Springs Stadium, Auckland. Won 12-0. Goals: Hagan 4, McGarry 3, Deeley 3, Halford 1, Barkley 1. Referee: H.R. Naicker (Fiji). NZ: Gosling, Mulligan, C. Evans, Dunford (cpt), Cresswell, McGarry (Barkley, sub), Halligan, D. Edge, Halford, Hagan, Deeley (de Jong, sub).

1988

354
January 2 v I.F.K. Gothenburg (Sweden) at Domain, Tauranga. Lost 0-2. Referee: J.W. Cameron (Waikato). NZ: Schofield (Gosling, sub), Herbert, Boath, R. Ironside, Brydon (Zoricich, sub), Cole, Riley, D. Edge (K. Wright, sub), Tuaa (Barkley, sub), Hagan, de Jong.

355
January 5 v I.F.K. Gothenburg (Sweden) at Nelson Park, Hastings. Drew 0-0. Referee: G.W. Fleet (Franklin). NZ: Gosling, Mulligan, Herbert, C. Evans (cpt), Cresswell, McGarry (Cole, sub), Halligan, Halford, D. Edge, Hagan (C. Walker, sub), de Jong.

356
January 7 v I.F.K. Gothenburg (Sweden) at Athletic Park, Wellington. Won 2-1. Goals: Halford 1, Halligan 1. Referee: B. Tasker (Wellington). NZ: Gosling, Mulligan, Herbert, C. Evans (cpt), Cole, McGarry (Cresswell, sub), Halford (Brydon, sub), Halligan, D. Edge, Hagan (C. Walker, sub), de Jong.

357
February 21 v Young Brazil at Western Springs Stadium, Auckland. Drew 1-1. Goals: Walker 1. Referee: G.W. Fleet (Franklin). NZ: Gosling, Mulligan, Herbert, C. Evans (cpt), Dunford, McGarry (Cole, sub), Halligan, G. Turner, D. Edge, Nixon, C. Walker.

358
February 24 v Young Brazil at Queen Elizabeth II Park, Christchurch. Won 3-0. Goals: McGarry 2, Barkley 1. Referee: L. Sharp (Southland). NZ: Schofield, Mulligan, Herbert, R. Ironside, Dunford (cpt) (Cole, sub), McGarry, Halligan (K. Wright, sub), G. Turner, D. Edge, Nixon (Barkley, sub), C. Walker.

359
February 28 v Young Brazil at Recreation Ground, Lower Hutt. Lost 0-1. Referee: J.W. Cameron (Waikato). NZ: Gosling, Zoricich, R. Ironside, C. Evans (cpt), Brydon, McGarry (D. Edge, sub), Halford, Cole, K. Wright (Nixon, sub), Barkley, de Jong (C. Walker, sub).

360
March 1 v Young Brazil at Nelson Park, Hastings. Won 3-1. Goals: McGarry 1, Walker 1, Ironside 1. Referee: B. Tasker (Wellington). NZ: Schofield, Mulligan, Herbert, R. Ironside, Cole, G. Turner, Halford (Barkley, sub), Halligan (Brydon, sub), D. Edge, McGarry, C. Walker (de Jong, sub).

361
March 6 v Chinese-Taipei (Olympic Tournament) at Olympic Park, Melbourne. Won 1-0. Goals: Barkley 1. Referee: S. Takada (Japan). NZ: Gosling, Mulligan, Herbert (cpt), R. Ironside, Cole, McGarry, G. Turner, Halligan, D. Edge, C. Walker (Barkley, sub), de Jong (Nixon, sub).

362
March 9 v Israel (Olympic Tournament) at Hindmarsh Stadium, Adelaide. Lost 0-2. Referee: A. Snoddy (Northern Ireland). NZ: Gosling, Mulligan, Herbert, C. Evans (cpt), Cole, Halligan, G. Turner (de Jong, sub), R. Ironside, D. Edge (Halford, sub), McGarry, C. Walker.

363
March 13 v Australia (Olympic Tournament) at Football Stadium, Sydney. Lost 1-3. Goals: McGarry. Referee: H. Silva Arce (Chile). NZ: Gosling, Mulligan, Herbert, C. Evans (cpt), Cole, Halford, Halligan, R. Ironside, D. Edge (Barkley, sub), McGarry, Nixon (C. Walker, sub).

364
March 20 v Chinese-Taipei (Olympic Tournament) at Queen Elizabeth II Park, Christchurch. Won 2-0. Goals: McGarry 1, Halford 1. Referee: D. Syme (Scotland). NZ: Gosling, Mulligan, C. Evans, Herbert, Cole, McGarry, Halligan, R. Ironside (de Jong, sub), D. Edge, Little (Halford, sub), Hanson.

365
March 23 v Australia (Olympic Tournament) at Athletic Park, Wellington. Drew 1-1. Goals: McGarry 1. Referee: G. Santos (Switzerland). NZ: Gosling, Herbert, C. Evans, R. Ironside, Dunford (cpt) (Nixon, sub), Halford, Cole, Halligan, G. Turner, McGarry, de Jong.

366
March 27 v Israel (Olympic Tournament) at Eden Park, Auckland. Lost 0-1. Referee: B. Ulloa-Morera (Costa Rica). NZ: Gosling, Zoricich, C. Evans, R. Ironside, Herbert, Halford, Halligan, G. Turner (Mulligan, sub), Cole (D. Edge, sub), McGarry, Barkley.

367
June 21 v Saudi Arabia at Olympic Park, Melbourne. Won 2-0. Goals: McGarry 1, own goal 1. Referee: B. Upjohn (Australia). NZ: Gosling, Mulligan, Lund, Herbert, Dunford (cpt), McGarry, Halligan, Ferris, W. Wright, C. Walker (Sumner, sub), McClennan (Probert, sub).

368
June 23 v Saudi Arabia at Middle Park, Melbourne. Won 3-2. Goals: Lund 1, Wright 1, McGarry 1. Referee: B. Grant (Australia). NZ: Gosling (Finlayson, sub), Mulligan, Lund, Herbert (R. Ironside, sub), Dunford (cpt), McGarry, Halligan (Sumner, sub), Ferris, W. Wright, C. Walker, K. Braithwaite (McClennan, sub).

369
October 12 v Australia (Trans Tasman Cup) at Caledonian Ground, Dunedin. Lost 1-2. Goals: Ironside 1. Referee: L. Sharp (Southland). NZ: Gosling, Ferris, Lund, Herbert, Dunford (cpt), McGarry, Riley, Halligan, McClennan, de Jong (R. Ironside, sub), W. Wright.

370
October 16 v Australia (Trans Tasman Cup) at Queen Elizabeth Oval, Bendigo. Lost 0-2. Referee: C. Bambridge (Australia). NZ: Gosling, Mulligan, Lund, R. Ironside, Dunford (cpt), McGarry, Riley, D. Edge (Ferris, sub), Halligan (Hanson, sub), McClennan, W. Wright.
A.J. Stroud travelled with team to Australia but did not take the field. Tour Leader: R. Pelosi. Manager/Coach: K. Fallon.

371
November 14 v Fiji at National Stadium, Suva. Drew 1-1. Goals: Tuaa 1. Referee: G. Kanna (Fiji). NZ: Gosling, Mulligan, R. Ironside, Lund, Probert, McClennan, Ferris, Halligan (cpt), D. Edge, Hanson (Chote, sub), Carville.

372
November 17 v Fiji at Churchill Park, Lautoka. Lost 0-2. Referee: G. Ahmed (Fiji). NZ: Gosling, Mulligan, R. Ironside, Lund, Jacobs, Halligan (cpt), Tuaa (Ferris, sub), Probert, McClennan, Chote, Cossey (D. Edge, sub).

373
November 19 v Fiji at Govind Park, Ba. Lost 0-1. Referee: P. Chandra (Fiji). NZ: A.J. Stroud, Mulligan, R. Ironside, Lund, Jacobs, Ferris, Halligan (cpt), (Tuaa, sub), Probert, McClennan (Carville, sub), Hanson (Chote, sub), D. Edge (Cossey, sub).

Tour Leader: B. Clement. Coach: K. Fallon. Physiotherapist: R. Cashman.

374
December 11 v Chinese-Taipei (World Cup) at Newtown Park, Wellington. Won 4-0. Goals: Wright 1, McClennan 1, Barkley 1, Halligan 1. Referee: C. Bambridge (Australia). NZ: Gosling, Herbert (cpt), Lund, Jennison, Ridenton, Levy, Halligan, Riley (Debenham, sub), Barkley, W. Wright, McClennan.

375
December 15 v Chinese Taipei (World Cup) at Western Springs Stadium, Auckland. Won 4-1. Goals: McClennan 3, Wright 1. Referee: G. Power (Australia). NZ: Gosling, Herbert (cpt), Lund, Jennison (Dunford, sub), Ridenton, Levy, Halligan, W. Wright (Debenham, sub), Barkley, W. Rufer, McClennan.

1989

376
March 5 v Israel (World Cup) at National Stadium, Tel Aviv. Lost 0-1. Referee: S. Muhmenthaler (Switzerland). NZ: Gosling, Herbert (cpt), Lund, C. Evans, T. Mason, Halligan (Levy, sub), Riley, Dunford, Barkley, W. Rufer, McClennan (Witteveen, sub).

377
March 12 v Australia (World Cup) at Football Stadium, Sydney. Lost 1-4. Goals: Dunford 1. Referee: S. Takada (Japan). NZ: Gosling, Herbert (cpt), C. Evans, Dunford, T. Mason, Levy, Witteveen (Gray, sub), Riley, Halligan (Debenham, sub), Barkley, McLennan.

378
April 2 v Australia (World Cup) at Mt Smart Stadium, Auckland. Won 2-0. Goals: Dunford 1, Wright 1. Referee: M. Bin Singah (Singapore). NZ: Gosling, Ridenton, Herbert (cpt), Lund, T. Mason, W. Wright, R. Ironside, Dunford, Barkley (Halligan, sub), de Jong, McClennan (Levy, sub).

379
April 9 v Israel (World Cup) at Mt Smart Stadium, Auckland. Drew 2-2. Goals: Wright 1, Dunford 1. Referee: C. Buillet (France). NZ: Gosling, Ridenton (Halligan, sub), Herbert (cpt), Lund, T. Mason, W. Wright, R. Ironside, Dunford, Riley (Levy, sub), de Jong, Barkley.

1990

380
January 30 v Rotor Volgograd F.C. (U.S.S.R.) (Kings Cup) at Bangkok. Lost 1-2. Goals: de Jong 1. NZ: Finlayson, K. Wright, Dunford (cpt), Romijn, Ferris, McGarry, Kirk (Chote, sub), R. Ironside, Halligan, de Jong, Barkley (Carville, sub).

381
February 3 v South Korea (Kings Cup) at Bangkok . Lost 0-3. NZ: Finlayson, K. Wright, Dunford (cpt), Romijn, Ferris, McGarry, Chote (Jackson, sub), R. Ironside, Halligan, de Jong, Barkley (Carville, sub).

382
February 7 v Pyongyang F.C. (North Korea) (Kings Cup) at Bangkok. Lost 2-3. Goals: de Jong 1, Carville 1. NZ: Van Hattum, Ridenton (T. Edge, sub), Ferris, Dunford (cpt), K. Wright, McGarry, Jackson, R. Ironside, Halligan, de Jong, Carville.

383
July 18 v Moscow Lokomotiv F.C. (U.S.S.R.) at Western Springs Stadium, Auckland. Drew 1-1. Goals: Ironside 1. Referee: G.W. Fleet (Franklin). NZ: Gosling, Ferris, C. Evans, Dunford (cpt), Ridenton, McGarry, R. Ironside, Halligan, D. Edge, Barkley, Cotton (McClennan, sub).

384
July 22 v Moscow Locomotiv F.C. (U.S.S.R.) at Basin Reserve, Wellington. Won 2-1. Goals: Ironside 2. Referee: K. Wallace (Auckland). NZ: Gosling, Ferris, C. Evans, Dunford, Ridenton, McGarry, R. Ironside, Halligan, D. Edge, Barkley, Cotton (McClennan, sub).

385
July 28 v Moscow Locomotiv F.C. (U.S.S.R.) at Queen Elizabeth II Park, Christcurch. Lost 0-1. Referee: L. Sharp (Southland). NZ: Gosling, Ferris, C. Evans, Dunford, Ridenton, McGarry, R. Ironside, Halligan, D. Edge, Barkley (Laus, sub), Cotton.

386
August 16 v China P.R. at Recreation Ground, Lower Hutt. Won 2-1. Goals: Gray 2. Referee: G.W. Fleet (Franklin). NZ: Gosling, Ferris, Gray, Dunford (cpt), Ridenton, McGarry, R. Ironside, Halligan, D. Edge, G. Cameron, Barkley.

CHATHAM CUP FINALS 1923-90

1923
Seacliff (Otago) b YMCA (Wellington) 4-0
at Athletic Park, Wellington on 1 October. Referee: J.A. Leddy (Wellington). Goals: Hooper 2, Macdougall, Baxter.
SEACLIFF: Charlie Rivers; Jock Anderson, George Anderson; Bill Rogers, Hugh McKechnie, Bill Murray; Malcolm Macdougall, Reg Baxter, Bill Hooper, R. ("Tommy") Burns, Wattie Hanlin.
YMCA: Arthur Tarrant; W. Pearson, Les McGirr; George Wotherspoon, Bill Rarity, Charlie Trott; Les Smith, Edgar Phillips, George Campbell, Harry Hindmarsh, Charlie Ballard.

1924
Harbour Board (Auckland) b Seacliff (Otago) 3-1*
at Athletic Park, Wellington on 27 September. Referee: A.E. Wells (Wellington). Goals: Palmer, Margison, Heyes for Harbour Board; Simmons for Seacliff.
HARBOUR BOARD : Jack Batty; W. Mitchell, G.S. Brittain; J. Worthington, R.I. Bell, Dan Jones; J.H. Tocker, Bill Palmer, H.M. Margison, Murray Heyes, C. Drayton.
SEACLIFF: Charlie Rivers; George Anderson, Bill Murray; H. Cox, Alex Waugh, Bill Rogers; Malcolm Macdougall, W. Simmons, Bill Hooper, J. Baillie, Wattie Hanlin.

1925
YMCA (Wellington) b Seacliff (Otago) 3-2*
at Newtown Park, Wellington on 19 September. Referee: M. Thornley (Canterbury). Goals: Dempster 2, Halley for YMCA; Hanlin, Hooper for Seacliff.
YMCA: Bert Bentley; Horrie Prince, Les McGirr; Neil McArthur, W. Pearson, Charlie Trott; Billy Nicolle, Stewart Dempster, Charlie Ballard, George Campbell, Dave Halley.
SEACLIFF: R. Gwilliam; George Anderson, Bill Rogers; Alex Waugh, Wattie Cooper, Bill Murray; D. Milne, Malcolm Macdougall, Bill Hooper, Wattie Hanlin, J. Baillie.

1926
Sunnyside (Canterbury) b North Shore (Auckland) 4-2 at Basin Reserve, Wellington on 4 September. Referee: C. Kelly (Wellington). Goals: Trotter 3, Pickering for Sunnyside; Hipkins, Woolley for North Shore.
SUNNYSIDE: Jim Callaghan; H. Thompson, J. Simpson; Jim Wales, R. Purdie, W. Bond; Bob McLachlan, D. Sutherland, Archie Trotter, H. Pickering, W. Robson.
NORTH SHORE: Stewart Lipscombe; Len Colebourne, Peter Gerrard; Reg Baxter, Dick Bird, Dan Jones; L. Hipkins, Ces Dacre, George Jay, John Woolley, Jock Bradshaw.

1927
Ponsonby (Auckland) b Northern (Otago) 3-2 at Newtown Park, Wellington on 24 September. Referee: G. Jackson (Wellington). Goals: Hunter, Innes, Adshead for Ponsonby; McDowell, McTavish for Northern.
PONSONBY: H.Watts; T. Pickett, M. Williams; John Morrison, G. Wright, J. Mooney; Gerry Hunter, Clem Bell, Bob Innes, J. Tomilty, J. Adshead.
NORTHERN: A. McQuarrie; L. Coates, Jim Scoular; Alex Perry, Hugh Munsie, Reg Cherry; A. McDowell, Tom McHugh, A. McTavish, Tom McCormack, Rab McLean.

1928
Petone (Wellington) b Northern (Otago) 1-0 at Basin Reserve, Wellington on 25 August. Referee: G. Jackson (Wellington). Goals: Farquhar.
PETONE: Peter McVean; R. Steel, Syd Haines; William Farquhar, Jim Campbell, A. Stobbs; J. McKenzie, J. Irvine, Andy Leslie, J. Cameron, T. James.
NORTHERN: A. McQuarrie; L. Coates, Jim Scoular; Alex Perry, Hugh Munsie, J. Baird; A. McDowell, Tom McHugh, Tom Ruddiman, Tom McCormack, Rab McLean.

1929
Tramways (Auckland) b Seacliff (Otago) 4-0 at Basin Reserve, Wellington on 26 August. Referee: D. Stirratt (Wellington). Goals: Spencer 2, Bell, Williams.
TRAMWAYS: Jack Batty; J. McElligott, Ernie Simpson; Jack Tinkler, Jim Christie, Joe Fyvie; A. Spong, Clem Bell, Harry Spencer, Evan Williams, F. Lewis.
SEACLIFF: T. Jackson; George Anderson, Bill Rogers; Bill Murray, Hugh Munsie, A. Maxwell; J. McLaughlan, W. Simmons, Bill Hooper, Tom McCormack, Rab McLean.

1930
Petone (Wellington) b Western (Canterbury) 2-1 at Basin Reserve, Wellington on 6 September. Referee: A.E. Caisley (Wellington). Goals: Craig, Dodds for Petone; Falloon for Western.
PETONE: Peter McVean; Scott Brown, Syd Haines; H. Smith, Jim Campbell, J. Irvine; C. Baistow, W. Knox, Andy Leslie, J. Dodds, Dave Craig.
WESTERN: George Colville; Ted Colville, William Kelly; William Whittington, George Roberts, Albert Ellis; Frank Bridgens, Stan Ellis, Clarrie Falloon, Albert McMillan, Tom Nelson.

1931
Tramurewa (Auckland) b Nomads (Canterbury) 5-2* at Basin Reserve, Wellington on 12 September. Referee: F. Sanders (Wellington). Goals: Bell 3, Spong, H. Donaldson for Tramurewa; Wilson, Goode for Nomads.
TRAMUREWA: Jack Batty; Alex Donaldson, Ernie Simpson; J. Balloch, Jim Christie, J. Brown; Arthur Spong, Clem Bell, Harry Spencer, H. Donaldson, D. Mill.
NOMADS: L. Sharr: Chaplin, B. Streeter; J. Adams, C. Pickup, J. Thompson; C. Sharr, G. Goode, Smith, A. Wilson, H. Chapman.

1932
Marist (Wellington) b Millerton All Blacks (Buller) 5-0 at Basin Reserve, Wellington on 3 September. Referee: T. Plant (Wellington). Goals: Barton 3, Marshment, Kershaw.
MARIST: Pat Turkington; John Kelly, Jack Laracy; Tom Hindle, Dick Bird, Jack Duffy; Eddie Barton, Mick Condon, Tom Marshall, Jim Kershaw, Stan Marshment.
MILLERTON: "Wig" Campbell; Wally White, Jack Teichert; James Young, Tom Blyth, Tony Graham; Peter Taylor, Bobby Adam, Jim Blyth, Geordie Newman, Joe Cowan.

1933
Ponsonby (Auckland) b Millerton All Blacks (Buller) 2-1 at Basin Reserve, Wellington on 26 August. Referee: J. Sanderson (Wellington). Goals: Jepson, Innes for Ponsonby; Pollock for Millerton.
PONSONBY: Arthur Watson; Reg Haggett, Hue Stewart; John Morrison, Jock Grant, Eric Masters; Frank Ahern, Bob Innes, Jack Jepson, Archie Morrison, Alan Forman.
MILLERTON : Eric Smith; Bill Miller, Bill Longstaff; George Orman, Tom Blyth, Tony Graham; Peter Taylor, Charles Orman, Jim Blyth, Tom Pollock, Joe Cowan.

1934
Thistle (Auckland) b Thistle (Canterbury) 2-1 at Basin Reserve, Wellington on 15 September. Referee: G. Jackson (Wellington). Goals: Watson, Wood for Auckland Thistle; Adam for Canterbury Thistle.
THISTLE (Auckland): A. Gerrard; Jim McCosh, A. Williams; Wally Watson, George Wright, Peter Wiseman; Les Wood, Archie Dunsmore, L. Williamson, Dick Hislop, Murray Kay.
THISTLE (Canterbury): M. Mitchell; H. Johnston, G. Sutherland; J. Paton, Alex Sutherland, A. Walker; J. Simpson, D. Sutherland, J. Adam, J. Bruce, G. Walker.

1935
Hospital (Wellington) b Western (Canterbury) 3-1
at Basin Reserve, Wellington on 31 August. Referee: W.P. Smith (Otago). Goals: McGrory, Billy Woods, Gibb for Hospital; Gordon for Western.
HOSPITAL: Jack Wyatt; Bill Miles, L. Thompson; Joe Todd, Ernie Jeffery,Colin Simon; A. Gibb, W. McGrory, C. Webster, Billy Woods, J. Woods.
WESTERN: John White; Stan Cawtheray, John Henderson; Dick Henderson, Merv Gordon, Albert Ellis; Stan Ellis, Geoff Ellis, Gordon Smith, Bill White, Bill Ives.

1936
Western (Canterbury) b Thistle (Auckland) 3-2
at Basin Reserve, Wellington on 29 August. Referee: N.D. Brian (Wellington). Goals: Bill White 2, Ellis for Western; Angus 2 for Thistle.
WESTERN: John White; Stan Cawtheray, George Roberts; Dick Henderson, Merv Gordon, Albert McMillan; Bill White, Geoff Ellis, Gordon Smith, Bill Ives, Edward Hall.
THISTLE: Arthur Watson; Ron Stone, M. Williams; Peter Wiseman, George Wright, Wally Watson; Les Wood, Archie Dunsmore, Fred Angus, L. Williamson, Murray Kay.

1937
No competition.

1938
Waterside (Wellington) b Mosgiel (Otago) 4-0
at Basin Reserve, Wellington on 3 September. Referee: E.J. McQueen (Wellington). Goals: Sonny Ward 2, Walker, Janes.
WATERSIDE: Sid Ward; Pat Harris, Bob Bolton; Charlie Anderson, Fred Hazel, Bob Cocks; Colin McCarthy, Tom Walker, Sonny Ward, Alf Longbottom, Toby Janes.
MOSGIEL: A. Hall; R. Kitto,R. Steven; Alex Stenhouse, C. Skinner, A. Paull; G. Nicholson, W. Rogers, J. Skinner, A. Davidson, W. Steven.

1939
Waterside (Wellington) b Western (Canterbury) 4-2
at Basin Reserve, Wellington on 2 September. Referee: S. Doree (Canterbury). Goals: McCarthy 2, Longbottom, Sonny Ward for Waterside; Galbraith, R. Smith for Western.
WATERSIDE: Sid Ward; Allan Jordan, Bob Bolton; Joe Calder, Fred Hazel, Phil Traynor; Colin McCarthy, Tom Walker, Sonny Ward, Alf Longbottom, Toby Janes.
WESTERN: Peter Brooks; Stan Cawtheray, Albert McMillan; Charlie Anderson, Merv Gordon, George Roberts; Alan Almond, Roger Smith, Gordon Smith, Jack Smith, Harry Galbrath.

1940
Waterside (Wellington) b Mosgiel (Otago) 6-2
at Basin Reserve, Wellington on 24 August. Referee: J.W. Graham (Wellington). Goals: McCarthy 3, Sonny Ward, Walker, Longbottom for Waterside; Sharpe, Rogers for Mosgiel.
WATERSIDE: Sid Ward; Bob Watts, Bob Bolton; Joe Calder, Fred Hazel, Phil Traynor; Colin McCarthy, Tom Walker, Sonny Ward, Alf Longbottom, Toby Janes.
MOSGIEL: A. Hall; A. Johnstone, R. Steven; Alex Stenhouse, H. Mills, A. Sharpe; G. Nicholson, W. Rogers, J. Skinner, A. Davidson, W. Steven.

1941-44
No competition

1945
Western (Canterbury) b Marist (Wellington) 4-3*
at Basin Reserve, Wellington on 1 September. Referee: V. Wheeler (Wellington). Goals: Jack Smith 3, Druker for Western; Irvine, Price, own goal for Marist.
WESTERN: Alex Laing; George Graham, Alex Green; Charlie Anderson, Merv Gordon, George Roberts; Alan Almond, Joe Druker, Gordon Smith, Jack Smith, Ray Dowker.
MARIST: John Mallia; Jack Duffy, Norm Tarrant; Les Foley, Jack Porteous, Des Nunns; Pat Tilyard, Ray Nunns, G. Irvine, Henry Bell, Ray Price.

1946
Marist (Wellington) b Technical Old Boys (Canterbury) 2-1
at Basin Reserve, Wellington on 24 August. Referee: T.G. Chapman (Wellington). Goals: Hatchard, Bell for Marist; Thomas for Technical.
MARIST: John Mallia; Ces Nunns, Jack Duffy; Ron Gilding, Jack Porteous, Des Nunns; Pat Tilyard, Ray Nunns, Henry Bell, Jack Hatchard, Ray Price.
TECHNICAL: Ray Davey; Maurice Dean, Peter O'Malley; Ernie Harris, Vic Smith, Sid Goldsmith; Jim Cook, Henry Tullett, Don Grieve, Keith Lucas, Cyril Thomas.

1947
Waterside (Wellington) b Technical Old Boys (Canterbury) 2-1*
at Basin Reserve, Wellington on 23 August. Referee: J. Sanderson (Wellington). Goals: Bell, Janes for Waterside; Bailey for Technical.
WATERSIDE: Alex Healey; Pat Harris, Bob Bolton; Alf Scott, Phil Traynor, Bob Cullen; Toby Janes, Mick Powell, Wally Mildenhall, Tom Walker, Mark Bell.
TECHNICAL: Ray Davey; Maurice Dean, Peter O'Malley; Ernie Harris, Vic Smith, Jim Cook; Don Grieve, Reg Storer, Colin Bailey, Keith Lucas, Cyril Thomas.

1948
Technical Old Boys (Canterbury) b Waterside (Wellington) 2-0 at Basin Reserve, Wellington on 21 August. Referee: A. Aspen (Wellington). Goals: O'Malley, Thomas.
TECHNICAL: Ray Davey; Maurice Dean, Ernie Harris; Earl Mason, Vic Smith, Jim Cook; Don Grieve, John MacLennan, Colin Bailey, Peter O'Malley, Cyril Thomas.
WATERSIDE: Alex Healey; Pat Harris, Bob Bolton; Eric Wheatley, Phil Traynor, Bob Cullen; Joey Pledger, Tom Walker, Bob McKinley, Wally Mildenhall, Toby Janes.

1949
Petone (Wellington) b Northern (Otago) 1-0 at Basin Reserve, Wellington on 27 August. Referee: F. Callaghan (Wellington). Goals: Hewitt.
PETONE: Ben Savage; Bob Reid, Fred Peters; Bob Walker, John Blundell, John Jakens; Jim Russell, Dave McKissock, Wally Hewitt, Frank Naylor, Jim Gale.
NORTHERN: Jim Stephenson; Mick Ives, Bob McLean; Arthur Williams, Wally Meehan, Brian Walsh; Albie Jenkins, Ivan Walsh, Bill Berry, Norman McDonald, Bernie Cox.

1950
Eden (Auckland) b Technical Old Boys (Canterbury) 3-2* at Basin Reserve, Wellington on 2 September. Referee: W.M. Smith (Otago). Goals: Goddard, Jakens, Brewer for Eden; Thomas, Bailey for Technical.
EDEN: Bob King; Eric Kendall, Jack Wilson; Mack Butts, Jack Leonard, John Jakens; John Garrick, George Addis, Don Brewer, Norman Day, Peter Goddard.
TECHNICAL: Lindsay McKenzie; Maurice Dean, Ernie Harris; Vic Smith, Nelson King, Jim Cook; John MacLennan, Peter O'Malley, Colin Bailey, Keith Lucas, Cyril Thomas.

1951
Eastern Suburbs (Auckland) b Northern (Otago) 5-1 at Basin Reserve, Wellington on 8 September. Referee: A. Aspen (Wellington). Goals: King 3, Frogley, Anderson for Eastern Suburbs; McFarlane for Northern.
EASTERN SUBURBS: Jack Currie; Tim Cooper, Tom Wallace; Bob McLuckie, Jack Gisby, John Jakens; Jack Anderson, Andy Wallace, Reg King, Ken Fleet, Tony Frogley.
NORTHERN: Jim Stephenson; Mick Ives, Bob McLean; Arthur Williams, Wally Meehan, Brian Walsh; Albie Jenkins, Ivan Walsh, Bill Berry, Norman McDonald, Trevor McFarlane.

1952
North Shore United (Auckland) drew with Western (Canterbury) 1-1* at Basin Reserve, Wellington on 30 August. Referee: W.T. Dodd (Otago). Goals: Moyle for North Shore; Joseph for Western.
NORTH SHORE: Roy Gordon; Tom Chubb, Murray Best; Bill Bradshaw, Ray Hodgson, Ernie Barker; Herb Moyle, Les Wood, Alan Richards, Leo Hope-Ede, Mark Bell.
WESTERN: Jack Smith; Frank Bradley, J. Austin; John Longmuir, David Mackie, John White; Noel Joseph, Alex Davis, Ken Olley, Stan Eastham, Roger Smith.

1953
Eastern Suburbs (Auckland) b Northern (Otago) 4-3 at Basin Reserve, Wellington on 5 September. Referee: J.K. Wellwood (Wellington). Goals: King 2, Fleet, Murray Anderson for Eastern Suburbs; McFarlane 2, Boardman for Northern.
EASTERN SUBURBS: Peter Risbridge; Tim Cooper, Leo Twiname; Jack Anderson, Jack Gisby, Bob McLuckie; Don Kendrick, Andy Wallace, Reg King, Ken Fleet, Murray Anderson.
NORTHERN: Jim Stephenson; Dick Naus, Bob McLean; Jim Swift, Wally Meehan, Jim Johnston; Bill Boardman, Ivan Walsh, Bill Berry,Theo Berben, Trevor McFarlane.

1954
Onehunga (Auckland) b Western (Canterbury) 1-0 at Basin Reserve, Wellington on 4 September. Referee: P. George (Otago). Goals: McCullough.
ONEHUNGA: Tony Holt; Charlie Ackland, Eddie Alexander; Harry Precious, Jesse Bingham, Arne Rasmussen; Ernie Shepherd, Dave Weedall, Tom McNicholl, Rod McCullough, Gerald Textor.
WESTERN: Sam Guillen; Frank Bradley, Fred Haydon; Cliff Banham, Tony Laffey, Stan Ralph; Mike Shardlow, John Longmuir, Peter Cole, John White, Peter Saunderson.

1955
Western (Canterbury) b Eastern Suburbs (Auckland) 6-2 at Basin Reserve, Wellington on 3 September. Referee: R.H. Scott (Wellington). Goals: Saunderson 3, White, Davis, Ralph for Western; Anderson, King for Eastern Suburbs.
WESTERN: Jan Voogt; Fred Haydon, Mike Shardlow; John Longmuir, Tony Laffey, Stan Ralph; Peter Cole, Alex Davis, John White, Ken Olley, Peter Saunderson.
EASTERN SUBURBS: George Poulus; Tim Cooper, Leo Twiname; Bob McLuckie, Geoff Walker, Jim Connew; Bert Azzara, John Wrathall, Reg King, Ken Fleet, Murray Anderson.

1956
Stop Out (Wellington) b Shamrock (Canterbury) 4-1 at Basin Reserve, Wellington on 25 August. Referee: E.O. Mason (Otago). Goals: Sharp, Sergent, Schryvers, Benge for Stop Out; Fields for Shamrock.
STOP OUT: Dennis Hudson; James Neumann, James Blair; George Smith, Frank Jeromson, Henk Grootelaar; Derek Gentry, Fred Benge, Abram Schryvers, Jack Sharp, Brian Sergent.
SHAMROCK: Joe Callaghan; Tom Campion, Kevin O'Flaherty; Peter Fletcher, Peter Flynn, Dick Durant; Robert Nicholls, Jim Price, Ernie Fields, Cliff Banham, Brian Newsome.

1957
Seatoun (Wellington) b Technical Old Boys (Canterbury) 3-1 at Basin Reserve, Wellington on 31 August. Referee: C.G. Edwards (Auckland). Goals: Logan 2, Goddard for Seatoun; McAnulty for Technical.
SEATOUN: Bert Hiddlestone; William King, Ronald Jeffery; Jack Metcalf, Brian Fletcher, Keith Gibson; Neil Kerr, Robert O'Brien, Stanley Goddard, Ron Kearns, William Logan.
TECHNICAL: Keith Sanders; Colin Spinks, Maurice Dean; Dennis Charlton, Jim Hunter, Ian Drewitt; Albert Gardenbroek, Vic Smith, Ted Charlton, Andy McAnulty, Ernie Fields.

1958
Seatoun (Wellington) b Christchurch City (Canterbury) 7-1 at Basin Reserve, Wellington on 9 August. Referee: D. Welham (Otago). Goals: Donovan 6, Wright for Seatoun; Giblett for City.
SEATOUN: Bert Hiddlestone; William King, Gordon McClelland; Jack Metcalf, Brian Fletcher, Keith Gibson (Neil Kerr sub); Robert O'Brien, Raymond Wright, John Donovan, Ron Kearns, William Logan.
CHRISTCHURCH: Graeme Richards; Alex Juner, Tim Lynch; Tom Clackson, Malcolm Wild, Roy Herbert; A. McDonald, Alex Wilson, Peter Devine (Ken Giblett sub), Tom Munro, Doug Worthington.

1959
Northern (Otago) b North Shore Utd (Auckland) 3-2 at Basin Reserve, Wellington on 22 August. Referee: M.T. Swain (Wellington). Goals: Own goal, Berry, George Little for Northern; Middleton, Foulkes for North Shore.
NORTHERN: Jim Stephenson; Alex Young, Trevor McFarlane; Wally Boath, Theo Berben, Stan Forbes; Bill Berry, Ray Higgins, George Little, Duncan McVey, Phillip Little.
NORTH SHORE: Cliff Maynard; John Collins, Cliff Schmidt; Ken Armstrong, Derek Easto, Bill Bradshaw; Chris Foulkes, Tom Paterson, Alex Middleton, Peter Maynard, Peter Oden.

1960
North Shore Utd (Auckland) b Technical Old Boys (Canterbury) 5-3 at Basin Reserve, Wellington on 27 August. Referee: A. Williams (Otago). Goals: Lowndes 2, Armstrong, Paterson, Ryan for North Shore; Verham, Campbell, Charlton for Technical.
NORTH SHORE: Dick Ansley; John Collins, Graham Hankins; Ken Armstrong, Warwick Ward, Derek Easto; John Ryan, Tom Paterson, Alex Middleton, Tony Lowndes, Peter Oden.
TECHNICAL: Keith Flintham; Ian Graham, Kevin Rasmussen; Kevin Hendy, Richard Van Dalsum, Arthur Verlander; Malcolm Jones, Arthur Verham, Ted Charlton, William Shannon, John Campbell.

1961
Northern (Otago) b North Shore Utd (Auckland) 2-0 at Basin Reserve, Wellington on 26 August. Referee: C. Anderson (Canterbury). Goals: George Little, Campbell for Northern.
NORTHERN: Jim Stephenson; Alex Young, Trevor McFarlane; John Rae, Jim Ferguson, Stan Forbes; Bill Berry, Bruce Campbell, George Little, Duncan McVey, John Little.
NORTH SHORE: Alan Windsor; John Collins, Graham Hankins; Ken Armstrong, Warwick Ward, Derek Easto; John Ryan, Tom Paterson, Alex Middleton, Lotsy Polyanszky, Peter Oden.

1962
Technical Old Boys (Waikato) b Northern (Otago) 4-1 at Basin Reserve, Wellington on 1 September. Referee: C. Dickie (Auckland). Goals: Nevison 2, Feenstra, Jones for Technical; George Little for Northern.
TECHNICAL: Mel Clarke; Tom Henderson, Frits Poelman; Ray McLean, Arthur Leong, Charlie Caldwell; Klaas Poelman, Peter Feenstra, Paul Nevison, Jon Dekkers, Trevor Jones.
NORTHERN: Jim Stephenson; Alex Young, Trevor McFarlane; John Rae, Jim Ferguson, John Little; Bill Berry, Duncan McVey, George Little, Roger Kingsland, Phillip Little.

1963
North Shore Utd (Auckland) b Nomads (Canterbury) 3-1 at Basin Reserve, Wellington on 31 August. Referee: R.E. McDonald (Otago). Goals: Middleton, Maynard, McNicholl for North Shore; Muirson for Nomads.
NORTH SHORE: Arthur Stroud; John Collins, Robert Gore; Ken Armstrong, Warwick Ward, Derek Easto; Harold Russell, Tom McNicholl, Alex Middleton, Peter Maynard, Peter Oden.
NOMADS: Derek Chapman; Rean Cattle, Michael Rennell; Graeme McKenzie, David Simmonds, George Donaldson; Paul McParland, Doug Ennis, Robin Muirson, Tony Gowans, Graham Button.

1964
Mt Roskill (Auckland) b Technical Old Boys (Otago) 3-1 at Basin Reserve, Wellington on 5 September. Referee: T.J. Ward (Wellington). Goals: Geoff Cozens 2, Darby for Mt Roskill; Porteous for Technical.
MT ROSKILL: Tony Cozens; Ian Loudon, Michael Blanchette; Matt Gilmour, John Kemp, Michael Squires; Geoff Cozens, David Blanchette, Ray Darby, Kevin Orrell, Bruce Leuschke.
TECHNICAL: Blair Davidson; David Toner, Syd Duncan; John Kroon, Eric Smith, Brian Boomer; David Connor, Wene Parata, Bill Porteous, John Brown, John Paul.

1965
Eastern Suburbs (Auckland) b St Kilda (Otago) 4-1 at Basin Reserve, Wellington on 4 September. Referee: R.W. Cullen (Canterbury). Goals: Trefor Pugh 2, Legg 2 for Eastern Suburbs; Slinn for St Kilda.
EASTERN SUBURBS: Terry Moore; Bryan Pugh, Fred Dubber; Ken Armstrong, Tom NcNab, Paul Rennell; Gerald McCormack, John Wrathall, Trefor Pugh, Philip Rainer, John Legg.
ST KILDA: Malcolm Barnes; Alex Caldwell, Robert Dean; Adrian Jakobs, Bill Kennedy, Noel Cunningham; Clive Rennie, Brian Slinn, Tony Schraa, Dougal Downie, Brian Smith.

1966
Miramar Rangers (Wellington) b Western (Canterbury) 1-0 at Basin Reserve, Wellington on 3 September. Referee: L.W. Coffman (Auckland). Goals: Les Taylor.
MIRAMAR: Peter Whiting; Colin McIvor, Graham Taylor; John Bruce, Jack Barton, Colin Ward; Peter Priddey, Henry Greasley, Les Taylor, Stefan Billing, Geoff Clayson.
WESTERN: David Smith; Phil Frost, Terry Mann; Terry Haydon, David Almond, Tom Langan; Chris Martin, Martin Clements, Tony Treadwell, Alan Brooks, Derek Torkington.

1967
North Shore Utd (Auckland) b Christchurch City (Canterbury) 2-1 at Basin Reserve, Wellington on 2 September. Referee: D.W. Grant (Manawatu). Goals: Rimmer, Campbell for North Shore; Haydon for City.
NORTH SHORE: Dennis Mack; David Gerrard, Malcolm Graham; Terry Bell, John Parker, Don Jones; Bill Rimmer, Ian Campbell, Les Taylor, Peter Maynard, Brian Collins.
CHRISTCHURCH: Owen Nuttridge; Allen Westwood, Bill McKenna; Tony Gowans, Gwyn Evans, Brian Gowans; Chris Martin, Martin Clements, Robin Taylor, Terry Haydon, Franko Madrussan.

1968
Eastern Suburbs (Auckland) b Technical (Canterbury) 2-0 at Basin Reserve, Wellington on 7 September. Referee: J.S. Nicol (Nelson). Goals: Wrathall 2.
EASTERN SUBURBS: Kevin Harlock; Doug Law, Fred Dubber; Bill de Graaf, Tom McNab, John Staines; Gerald McCormack, Paul Rennell, John Wrathall, Ray Mears, John Legg.
TECHNICAL: Ian Marshall; Grahame Davis, Alex Hawthorn; Ken France, Graham Griffiths, Jim Chalmers; Adrian Daw, Bryce Wilkinson, Alan Caine (Peter Kay, sub), Stewart Squire, Kevin Pahi.

1969
Eastern Suburbs (Auckland) b New Brighton (Canterbury) 2-0 at Basin Reserve, Wellington on 6 September. Referee: T.G. Delahunty (Wellington). Goals: Wrathall, de Graaf.
EASTERN SUBURBS: Kevin Harlock; Ross Gisby, Fred Dubber; Philip Rainer, John Kroon, John Staines; Ray Mears, Bill de Graaf, John Wrathall (Doug Law, sub), Paul Rennell, John Legg.
NEW BRIGHTON: Derek Phillips; Jim Le Poidevin, Bill Doornenbal; Graeme McCann, Bill Chisholm, Des Duffy; Gavin Lewis, Graham Storer, Warren Quirke, Geoff Taylor, Keith Morgan.

1970
Blockhouse Bay (Auckland) drew with Western Suburbs (Wellington) 2-2* at Basin Reserve, Wellington on 5 September. Referee: J. Houston (Poverty Bay). Goals: Shaw 2 for Blockhouse Bay; Huntley 2 for Western Suburbs.
BLOCKHOUSE BAY: John Morris; Gary Lake, Carlo Fogarin; John Batty, Howard Bough, Mick Seed; Clive Campbell, Glen Root, Colin Shaw, Paul Codd, Iain Ormond.
WESTERN SUBURBS: Bruce Nicol; Keith Barton, Rean Cattle; John Conner Allan Jeffery, Tom Heptinstall; Barry Humphreys, John Young (Tom Davie, sub), Bruce Baker (Willie Winton, sub), Wayne Huntley, David Wallace.

replay
Blockhouse Bay b Western Suburbs 3-2 at Newmarket Park, Auckland on 12 September. Referee: J. Houston (Poverty Bay). Goals: Campbell, Ormond, Shaw for Blockhouse Bay; Baker, Humphreys for Western Suburbs.
BLOCKHOUSE BAY: Morris; Lake, Fogarin; Batty, Bough, Seed; Campbell, Root, Shaw, Codd, Ormond.
WESTERN SUBURBS: Nicol; Barton, Cattle; Conner, Jeffery, Heptinstall; Humphreys, Young, Baker, Huntley, Wallace.

1971
Western Suburbs (Wellington) b Wellington City (Wellington) 3-2* at Basin Reserve, Wellington on 11 September. Referee: E. Saker (Hawkes Bay). Goals: Wallace, Jeffery, Humphreys for Western Suburbs; Cameron, Beck for City.
WESTERN SUBURBS: Neil Palmer; Keith Barton, Rean Cattle; John Young, Allan Jeffery, John Conner; Tom Heptinstall (Gary Paddison, sub), David Wallace (Andy Polyanszky, sub), Bruce Baker, Barry Humphreys, Wayne Huntley.
WELLINGTON: Jack Nathu; Alan Westwood, Graeme McDowell; Grahame Bilby, Paul Cameron (Martyn Love, sub), Istvan Nemet; Henry Nauta, Will Ritchie, Julius Beck, Steven Bruce, Jim Ferrier.

1972
Christchurch Utd (Canterbury) drew with Mt Wellington (Auckland) 4-4* at Basin Reserve, Wellington on 2 September. Referee: R.W. Harries (Wellington). Goals: Dacombe 4 for Christchurch; Ron Armstrong 2, Turner, Thomas for Mt Wellington.
CHRISTCHURCH: Tony Fleming; Lawrie Blyth, Grahame Davis; Ken France, Graham Griffiths, Brian Hardman; Victor Pollard, Tom Randles, Graham Dacombe, Alan Marley, Ian Park (Stuart Cameron, sub).
MT WELLINGTON: Kevin Curtin; Tony Sibley, Ron Armstrong; Brian Armstrong, Iain Hastie, Nigel Ashurst (John Houghton, sub); Dennis Tindall, Brian Turner, Earle Thomas, David Taylor, George Lamont (Vivian Hope-Ede, sub).

replay
Christchurch Utd drew with Mt Wellington 1-1*
at English Park, Christchurch on 9 September. Referee: R.W. Harries (Wellington). Goals: Park for Christchurch; Tindall for Mt Wellington.
CHRISTCHURCH: Fleming; Blyth, Davis; Griffiths, France, Hardman; John Oliver (Trevor Blake, sub), Randles, Dacombe, Marley, Park.
MT WELLINGTON: Curtin; Sibley, R. Armstrong; Hastie, B. Armstrong, Tindall; Max Davis, Turner, Houghton (Thomas, sub), Lamont (Hope-Ede, sub), Taylor.

second replay
Christchurch Utd b Mt Wellington 2-1
at Newmarket Park, Auckland on 23 September. Referee: R.W. Harries (Wellington). Goals: Park, Marley for Christchurch; Ron Armstrong for Mt Wellington.
CHRISTCHURCH: Fleming; Blyth, Davis; Griffiths, France, Hardman; Pollard, Randles, Dacombe, Marley, Park.
MT WELLINGTON: Curtin; Sibley, R. Armstrong; Hastie, B. Armstrong, Ashurst; Tindall, Turner, (Davis,sub), Thomas (Taylor, sub), Houghton, Lamont.

1973
Mt Wellington (Auckland) b North Shore Utd (Auckland) 3-0 at Newmarket Park, Auckland on 1 September. Referee: A.T. Blackburn (Auckland). Goals: Taylor 2, Houghton.
MT WELLINGTON: Neville Siebert; Tony Sibley, Ron Armstrong; Barry DIckey, Iain Hastie, Nigel Ashurst; Vivian Hope-Ede (Max Davis, sub), Brian Turner, John Houghton, David Taylor, Bill de Graaf (Earle Thomas, sub).
NORTH SHORE: David Turner (Greg Titchener, sub); Eddie Donnelly, Don Mitchell; Michael Chubb, Geoff Payne (Keith Hobbs, sub), Don Jones; Adrian Elrick, Mick Seed, Martin Hill, Tony Burgess, Roger Stevens.

1974
Christchurch Utd (Canterbury) b Diamond Utd (Wellington) 2-0 at Queen Elizabeth II Park, Christchurch on 7 September. Referee: W.K. Munro (Auckland). Goals: Park, Hardman.
CHRISTCHURCH: Bill Weir; Graham Griffiths, Roy Drinkwater, Ken France, Lawrie Blyth; Brian Hardman, Tom Randles, Bill Amey; Kees Doornebal, Steve Sumner, Ian Park.
DIAMOND: Steve Pateman; Martyn Love, Sam Malcolmson, Duncan Hill, Harry Carrington; Michael Simeonoff, John Young, Ken Millar; Henry Nauta (David Farron, sub), Eric Lesbirel, Lou Adams.

1975
Christchurch Utd (Canterbury) b Blockhouse Bay (Auckland) 4-2* at Newmarket Park, Auckland on 13 September. Referee: J.W. Cameron (Waikato). Goals: Moran, own goal (Lake), Mulgrew, McNaughton for Christchurch; Farac, Shaw for Blockhouse Bay.
CHRISTCHURCH: Phil Dando; Lawrie Blyth, Graham Griffiths, Roy Drinkwater, Ian Park; Brian Hardman, Steve Sumner, Bill Amey; Kees Doornenbal (Mark McNaughton, sub), Norman Moran, Kevin Mulgrew.
BLOCKHOUSE BAY: John Morris; Gary Lake, David Cantley, John Batty, Warren Cantley; Duncan Ormond, Kevin Stratful, Colin Shaw (Willie Clark, sub); Gary Paddison, Mike Farac, Iain Ormond.

1976
Christchurch Utd (Canterbury) b Eastern Suburbs (Auckland) 4-0 at Queen Elizabeth II Park, Christchurch on 4 September. Referee: T.G. Delahunty (Wellington). Goals: Moran 2, own goal (Bell), McNaughton.
CHRISTCHURCH: Phil Dando; Trevor Reece, Graham Griffiths, Roy Drinkwater, Ian Park; Brian Hardman, Steve Sumner, Bill Amey; Mark McNaughton, Norman Moran, Kees Doornenbal.
EASTERN SUBURBS: Praven Jeram; Greg Sanford, Bill de Graaf, Stewart Carruthers, Tom Bell; Warren Fleet (John Haberla, sub), John Legg, Peter Lepper (Brent Stubbins, sub); Jack Schuurman, Gary Jenkins, Jim Nimmo.

1977
Nelson Utd (Nelson) b Mt Wellington (Auckland) 1-0 at Newmarket Park, Auckland on 10 September. Referee: J.C. Perkins (Wellington). Goals: Enoka.
NELSON: Keith Barrett; David Brydon, Kevin Fallon, John Slotemaker, Colin Chisholm; Keith Mackay (Peter Simonsen, sub), John Enoka, Charles Ure; David Powdrell, Eric James, Ken Cresswell.
MT WELLINGTON: George Yearbury; Glenn Dods, Tony Sibley, Stewart Carruthers, Ron Armstrong; Brian Turner, Paul Johnstone, Vivian Hope-Ede; Clive Campbell, Earle Thomas, Kevin Weymouth.

1978
Manurewa (Franklin) b Nelson Utd (Nelson) 1-0 at Trafalgar Park, Nelson on 3 September. Referee: R. de Raat (Auckland). Goals: Foster.
MANUREWA: Frank Van Hattum; Robert Leijh, Lee Stickland, David Bright, Stephen Lincoln; David Fifield, George Lamont, Peter Bryson; Chris Turner, Mark Armstrong, Bruce Foster.
NELSON: Owen Nuttridge; David Brydon, John Slotemaker, Roger Fitzgerald, John Enoka; Alex Smith (Keith Mackay, sub), Peter Simonsen, Ronald Kolk; David Powdrell, Eric James, Ken Cresswell.

1979
North Shore Utd (Auckland) b Mt Wellington (Auckland) 2-1 at McLennan Park, Papakura on 2 September. Referee: W.K. Munro (Auckland). Goals: Hobbs, Iain Ormond for North Shore; Leijh for Mt Wellington.
NORTH SHORE: Allan Gilgrist; Nigel Grantham, Wayne Hutchinson, Adrian Elrick, Duncan Cole; Ted Edwards, Keith Hobbs, Martin Jennison; Duncan Ormond, Kieron Hales, Iain Ormond.
MT WELLINGTON: Alex Davie; Ken Billot, Tony Sibley, Stewart Carruthers, John Leijh; Bill de Graaf, Warren Fleet (Rodney Weir, sub), Bill McClure; Clive Campbell, Keith Nelson, Kevin Weymouth.

1980
Mt Wellington (Auckland) b Dunedin City (Otago) 2-0 at Basin Reserve, Wellington on 7 September. Referee: G.W. Fleet (Wellington). Goals: Carruthers, McClure.
MT WELLINGTON: Alex Davie; Tony Sibley, Ricki Herbert, Ron Armstrong, Ken Billot (John Leijh, sub); Bill de Graaf, Stewart Carruthers, David Taylor; Clive Campbell, Brian Turner, Bill McClure.
DUNEDIN: Jim Taylor; David Munro, Paul Hillis, David Gibson, Bill Chisholm; Jim Wilson, Graham Carr, George Caird, Pat Berry; Gordon McDonald, John Russell.

1981
Dunedin City (Otago) b Mt Wellington (Auckland) 3-1 at Basin Reserve, Wellington on 22 August. Referee: N. Burt (Canterbury). Goals: Glubb 2, Wilson for Dunedin; McClure for Mt Wellington.
DUNEDIN: Jim Taylor; Paul Hillis, Matt Eggleston (Michael Reardon, sub), Terry Wilson, John Scholten, Malcolm Ferguson, John Russell, George Caird, Michael Glubb, Pat Berry, Graham Carr.
MT WELLINGTON: Alex Davie; Tony Sibley, Ricki Herbert, Chris Hill, Ron Armstrong; John Leijh, Warren Fleet (Ian Masson, sub), Glen Adam; Bill McClure, Keith Nelson, David Taylor.

1982
Mt Wellington (Auckland) b Miramar Rangers (Wellington) 1-0* at Basin Reserve, Wellington on 12 September. Referee: L. Sharp (Southland). Goals: Nelson.
MT WELLINGTON: Alex Davie; Ricki Herbert (Roger Collins, sub), Tony Sibley, John Price, Ron Armstrong; John Leijh, Nigel Debenham, David Taylor (Mark Slane, sub); Bill McClure, Keith Nelson, Alex Metzger.
MIRAMAR: Barry Pickering; David Burgess, Michael Simeonoff, Brent Pratt, Colin Chisholm; John Cameron, Peter Chote, Peter Bennie; Arthur Brown, Costa Leonidas, John Fashanu.

1983
Mt Wellington (Auckland) drew with Gisborne City (Poverty Bay) 2-2* at Childers Road, Gisborne on 18 September. Referee: A. Edwards (Canterbury). Goals: de Jong, Nelson for Mt Wellington; Walker 2 for Gisborne.
MT WELLINGTON: Bob Wilshire; John Leijh, Tony Sibley, John Price, Ron Armstrong; Alex Metzger (Eddie Gavigan, sub), Glen Adam (Tony Scheirlinck, sub), Nigel Debenham; Keith Nelson, Fred de Jong, Andy Willock.
GISBORNE: Don Finlayson; Ross Mackay, Kevin Fallon (Martin Kirsopp, sub), John Gillies, James Margaritis; Grant Turner, Sean Byrne, Martin Ryan, Paul Rosser (Richard Mulligan, sub); Colin Walker, Ken Cresswell.

replay
Mt Wellington (Auckland) b Gisborne City (Poverty Bay) 2-0 at McKinlay Park, Auckland on 20 September. Referee: A. Edwards (Canterbury). Goals: Price, Nelson.
MT WELLINGTON: Wilshire; Leijh, Sibley, Price, Armstrong; Gavigan (Metzger, sub), Adam, Debenham; Nelson, de Jong, Willock.
GISBORNE: Finlayson; Mackay, Fallon, Gillies, Margaritis; Turner, Ryan, Cresswell, Rosser; Jim Doherty (Mulligan, sub), Walker.

1984

Manurewa (Franklin) b Gisborne City (Poverty Bay) 2-1 at Mt Smart Stadium, Auckland on 13 October. Referee: K. Copeland (Otago). Goals: Sumner 2 for Manurewa; Cresswell for Gisborne.
MANUREWA: Rudi Feitsma; Paul Gemmell, Keith Garland, David Bright, John Price; Keith Mackay, Mike Groom, Steve Sumner, Kevin Hagan; Mark Armstrong, Kevin Birch (Paul Marshall, sub).
GISBORNE: Don Finlayson; Richard Mulligan, Sean Byrne, John Gillies, John Enoka; Paul McLoughlin, Peter Simonsen, Grant Turner, Ken Cresswell; Kevin Meacock, Colin Walker.

1985

Napier City Rovers (Hawkes Bay) b North Shore Utd (Auckland) 3-1 at Mt Smart Stadium, Auckland on 7 September. Referee: B. Tasker (Wellington). Goals: Clarke, Halford, Brown for Napier; Weymouth for North Shore.
NAPIER: Clive Holmes; Terry Milligan, Shaun Baxter, Stan Clark, Terry Parkin; Paul Halford, Karl Bauerfeind, Phil Jackson, Steve O'Donoghue; Harry Clarke, Greg Brown (Shane Clapperton, sub).
NORTH SHORE: Allan Gilgrist; Paul Loader (Ted Edwards, sub), Keith Hobbs, Lee Green, James Varney; Duncan Cole, Kevin Hagan, Allan Boath, Peter Henry; Brian McKeown, Barry Weymouth (Brian Mitchell, sub).

1986

1st Leg

Mt Maunganui (Bay of Plenty) b North Shore Utd (Auckland) 1-0 at Fuji Film Stadium, Auckland on 5 October. Referee: D. Fellows (Hawkes Bay). Goals: Ferris.
MT MAUNGANUI: Graham Wilson; Dave Anderson, Kevin Lothian, Alex Young, Merv Montgomery; David Pike (Graeme Smith, sub), Tony Ferris, Grant Proudman; Mike Haddleton, Noel Barkley, Richard Gray.
NORTH SHORE: Allan Gilgrist; Paul Loader, Brian Mitchell, Allan Boath, Chris Harding (Lee Green, sub); Robert Ironside, Duncan Cole, Terry Emms, Darren McClennan, Brian McKeown (Kim Wright, sub), Kevin Hagan.

2nd Leg

North Shore Utd b Mt Maunganui 4-1
at Links Road, Mt Maunganui on 12 October. Referee: D. Fellows (Hawkes Bay). Goals: Hagan, McClennan, Wright, McKeown for North Shore; Proudman for Mt Maunganui.
NORTH SHORE: Gilgrist; Harding, Cole Ironside, Green; Hagan (Mitchell, sub), Justin Worsley, Wright (Matthew Jackson, sub); Emms, McKeown, McClennan.
MT MAUNGANUI: Wilson; Anderson, Lothian, Young, Montgomery; Pike (Graham Beamer, sub) Ferris, Proudman; Smith (Haddleton, sub), Barkley, Gray.
North Shore won on aggregate scores 4-2

1987

1st Leg

Gisborne City (Poverty Bay) b Christchurch Utd (Canterbury) 5-1 at Childers Road, Gisborne on 4 October. Referee: K. Wallace (Auckland). Goals: Morrell 2, Nixon, Birch, Sumner for Gisborne; Verweij for Christchurch.
GISBORNE: David Reynolds; Richard Mulligan, Stan Morrell, John Gillies, Ken Cresswell; Kevin Birch, Steve Sumner, Brian Strutt, Sean Byrne; Kevin Meacock, Paul Nixon.
CHRISTCHURCH: Alan Stroud; Paul Hillis, Ceri Evans, Garry Lund, Kevin Calder; Paul Nicholls, Danny Halligan, Keith Braithwaite, Johan Verweij; John Hanson, Allan Carville.

2nd Leg

Gisborne City drew with Christchurch Utd 2-2
at Queen Elizabeth II Park, Christchurch on 11 October. Referee: K. Wallace (Auckland). Goals: Byrne, Strutt for Gisborne; Nicholls, Carville for Christchurch.
GISBORNE: Reynolds; Mulligan, Morrell, Gillies, Cresswell; Birch (Thomas Edge, sub), Sumner, Strutt, Byrne (Neal Phillips, sub); Meacock, Nixon.
CHRISTCHURCH: Stroud; Hillis, Evans, Lund, Calder; Nicholls, Halligan, Braithwaite, Verweij (Brent Berry, sub); Hanson, Carville.

1988

1st Leg

Waikato Utd (Waikato) drew with Christchurch Utd (Canterbury) 2-2 at Queen Elizabeth II Park, Christchurch on 22 October. Referee: R. Brown (Auckland). Goals: Tate, Bauerfeind for Waikato; Hanson, Verweij for Christchurch.
WAIKATO: Gary Dillistone; Lawrence Fitzpatrick, Brian Hayes, Dave Merritt, Chris Roberts; Lance Bauerfeind, Paul Gemmell, Darren Melville, Graham Jones; Steve Tate, Mark Cossey.
CHRISTCHURCH: Alan Stroud; Paul Hillis, Mike Fullen, Garry Lund, Kevin Calder; Paul Nicholls, Danny Halligan, Keith Braithwaite, Steve Sumner (Johan Verweij, sub); John Hanson, Allan Carville.

2nd Leg

Waikato Utd drew with Christchurch Utd 1-1
at Muir Park, Hamilton on 24 October. Referee: R. Brown (Auckland). Goals: Tate for Waikato; Braithwaite for Christchurch.
WAIKATO: Dillistone; Fitzpatrick, Hayes, Merritt, Roberts; Bauerfeind, Gemmell, Melville, Jones; Tate, Cossey.
CHRISTCHURCH: Stroud; Hillis, Fullen, Lund, Calder; Nicholls, Halligan, Braithwaite, Verweij (Sumner, sub); Hanson, Carville.
Waikato won on away goals 2-1

1989

Christchurch Utd (Canterbury) b Rotorua City (Bay of Plenty) 7-1 at Newtown Park, Wellington on 17 September. Referee: G. Cowie (Southland). Goals: McGarry 3, Braithwaite, Verweij, Fitzpatrick, Sumner for Christchurch; Zohs for Rotorua.
CHRISTCHURCH: Alan Stroud; Lawrence Fitzpatrick, Mike Fullen, Paul Hillis, Kevin Calder; Paul Nicholls, Danny Halligan, Steve Sumner, Johan Verweij; Michael McGarry, Keith Braithwaite.
ROTORUA: David Harris; Kevin Badcock, Maarten Van Hattum (Tim Manktelow, sub), Neal Phillips, Martin Gorry; David Wright (Sascha Viertel, sub), Shane Zohs, Kerry Bartlett, Callum Gorman; Keith Swansbury, Darrin Brown.

1990

Mt Wellington (Auckland) b Christchurch Utd (Canterbury) 3-3* at Basin Reserve, Wellington on 16 September. Referee: R. Woolmer (Franklin). Goals: Own goal (Verweij), Barkley, Armstrong for Mt Wellington; Carville 2, McGarry for Christchurch.
MT WELLINGTON: Grant Schofield; Dean Smith, Martin Jennison (Kelvin Sefton, sub), Michael Ridenton, Ron Armstrong; Eddie Gavigan (Terry Torrens, sub), John Leijh, Dave Witteveen, Steve O'Donoghue; Grant Lightbown, Noel Barkley.
CHRISTCHURCH: Alan Stroud; Lawrence Fitzpatrick, Michael Fullen, Johan Verweij, Kevin Calder; Michael McGarry, Danny Halligan, Michael Boomer, Julyan Falloon; Allan Carville, Keith Braithwaite.
Mt Wellington won on penalties 4-2

* Denotes extra time

CHATHAM CUP WINS

6 North Shore United
5 Eastern Suburbs, Christchurch United, Mt Wellington
4 Waterside, Western
3 Petone
2 Ponsonby, Tramways/Tramurewa, Marist, Seatoun, Northern, Manurewa
1 Seacliff, Harbour Board, YMCA, Sunnyside, Thistle (Auckland), Hospital, Technical Old Boys (Canterbury), Eden, Onehunga, Stop Out, Technical Old Boys (Waikato), Mt Roskill, Miramar Rangers, Blockhouse Bay, Western Suburbs, Nelson United, Dunedin City, Napier City Rovers, Gisborne City, Waikato United.

APPEARANCES IN FINALS

11 North Shore United
9 Western, Mt Wellington
8 Northern, Christchurch United
7 Technical Old Boys (Canterbury), Eastern Suburbs
5 Waterside
4 Seacliff
3 Marist, Petone, Gisborne City, Hospital/Western Suburbs
2 YMCA, Tramways/Tramurewa, Ponsonby, Millerton All Blacks, Thistle (Auckland), Mosgiel, Seatoun, Nomads, Christchurch City, Blockhouse Bay, Nelson United, Dunedin City, Miramar Rangers, Manurewa.
1 Harbour Board, Sunnyside, Thistle (Canterbury), Eden, Onehunga, Stop Out, Shamrock, Technical Old Boys (Waikato), Mt Roskill, Technical Old Boys (Otago), St Kilda, New Brighton, Wellington City, Wellington Diamond United, Napier City Rovers, Mt Maunganui, Waikato United, Rotorua City.

CHATHAM CUP WINS BY ASSOCIATION

26	Auckland
16	Wellington
11	Canterbury
4	Otago
2	Franklin
2	Waikato
1	Nelson
1	Hawkes Bay
1	Poverty Bay

MOST WINNERS MEDALS

6 Steve Sumner (1974, 1975, 1976, 1984, 1987, 1989)
5 Ron Armstrong (1972, 1980, 1982, 1983, 1990)

MOST APPEARANCES IN FINAL*

8 Tony Sibley, Ron Armstrong
7 Steve Sumner
6 Jim Stephenson, Bill de Graaf, John Leijh
* Losers medals were first presented in 1951

MOST GOALS IN FINAL

6 John Donovan (1958)
4 Graham Dacombe (1972)
3 Archie Trotter (1926), Clem Bell (1931), Eddie Barton (1932), Colin McCarthy (1940), Jack Smith (1945), Reg King (1951), Peter Saunderson (1955), Michael McGarry (1989).

RECORD VICTORY

Seatoun v Christchurch City (1958)	7:1
Christchurch United v Rotorua City (1989)	7:1

HIGHEST AGGREGATE SCORE

Waterside v Mosgiel (1940)	6:2
Western v Eastern Suburbs (1955)	6:2
Seatoun v Christchurch City (1958)	7:1
North Shore United v Technical Old Boys (1960)	5:3
Christchurch United v Mt Wellington (1972)	4:4
Christchurch United v Rotorua City (1989)	7:1

JACK BATTY MEMORIAL CUP

Presented to the player of the final, this trophy honours the late Jack Batty who was a member of the HMS Chatham and who won three medals himself with Harbour Board, Tramways and Tramurewa.
The trophy was donated by Jack's son, John Batty a medalist with Blockhouse Bay in 1970.
The winner receives a silver tray and four silver wine goblets as permanent mementos.

Winners have been:

1985	Greg Brown	Napier City Rovers	1988	Steve Tate	Waikato United
1986	Duncan Cole	North Shore United	1989	Michael McGarry	Christchurch United
1987	Dave Reynolds,	Gisborne City	1990	Michael McGarry	Christchurch United

NATIONAL SOCCER LEAGUE

PARTICIPANTS AND PERFORMANCES 1970 - 1990
FINISHING PLACES YEAR BY YEAR

NUMBER OF TEAMS	8	10	10	10	10	10	10	12	12	12	12	12	12	12	12	12	12	14	14	14	14
THE TEAMS	1970	1971	1972	1973	1974	1975	1976	1977	1978	1979	1980	1981	1982	1983	1984	1985	1986	1987	1988	1989	1990
AUCKLAND CITY	-	-	10	-	-	-	-	-	-	-	-	-	-	-	-	-	-	-	-	-	-
BLOCKHOUSE BAY	1	4	2	3	5	3	5	8	3	8	11	-	-	-	-	-	-	-	-	-	-
CAVERSHAM	-	-	8	10	-	4	3	12	-	-	-	-	-	-	-	-	-	-	-	-	-
CHRISTCHURCH UTD	3	3	3	1	2	1	8	3	1	2	7	6	7	5	3	9	4	1	1	6	3
COURIER RANGERS	-	-	-	-	-	-	-	-	5	11	-	-	-	-	-	-	-	-	-	-	-
DUNEDIN CITY	-	-	-	-	-	-	-	11	-	5	6	2	3	9	7	8	8	12	-	-	-
DUNEDIN SUBURBS	-	6	-	-	-	-	-	-	-	-	-	-	-	-	-	-	-	-	-	-	-
DUNEDIN TECHNICAL	-	-	-	-	-	-	-	-	-	-	-	-	-	12	-	-	-	-	-	-	-
EAST COAST BAYS	-	-	-	-	-	-	-	-	-	-	-	-	11	-	-	-	-	-	-	-	-
EASTERN SUBURBS	2	1	4	5	9	7	6	9	4	12	-	-	-	-	-	-	-	-	-	-	-
GISBORNE CITY	6	5	5	4	8	8	10	-	-	-	2	4	4	10	1	2	5	2	9	13	12
HAMILTON	-	-	-	-	-	-	-	4	10	-	8	9	10	-	-	-	-	-	-	-	-
HUNGARIA	7	-	-	-	-	-	-	-	-	-	-	-	-	-	-	-	-	-	-	-	-
HUTT VALLEY UTD	-	-	-	-	-	-	-	-	-	-	-	-	-	-	-	-	-	9	10	5	10
INVERCARGILL THISTLE	-	-	-	-	-	-	-	-	-	-	-	-	12	-	-	-	-	-	-	-	-
MANAWATU UTD	-	-	-	-	-	-	-	-	-	10	-	-	-	-	-	-	11	13	14	-	-
MANUREWA	-	-	-	-	-	-	-	-	-	4	3	7	9	1	4	10	12	10	12	9	5
MT ALBERT-PONSONBY	-	7	-	-	-	-	-	-	-	-	-	-	-	-	-	-	-	-	-	-	-
MIRAMAR	-	-	-	-	-	-	-	-	-	-	-	8	6	7	5	5	2	14	8	11	9
MT WELLINGTON	4	2	1	2	1	5	2	6	2	1	1	3	1	4	10	4	1	8	2	3	2
MT MAUNGANUI	-	-	-	-	-	-	-	-	-	-	-	-	-	-	-	-	-	4	3	2	7
NAPIER CITY ROVERS	-	-	-	-	-	-	-	-	-	-	-	-	8	8	8	12	-	6	4	1	6
NELSON UTD	-	-	-	-	-	-	-	7	7	6	12	-	-	11	11	6	10	11	13	-	-
NEW BRIGHTON	-	-	9	9	3	9	4	10	-	-	-	-	-	-	-	-	-	-	-	-	-
NEW PLYMOUTH O.B.	-	-	-	-	-	-	-	-	-	-	-	-	-	-	-	-	-	-	-	-	13
NORTH SHORE UTD	-	-	-	-	6	2	7	1	6	3	5	5	2	2	9	3	7	7	6	10	8
PAPATOETOE	-	-	-	-	-	-	-	-	-	-	-	-	-	3	2	11	6	5	11	14	-
RANGERS (CHRISTCHURCH)	-	-	-	-	-	-	-	-	-	-	9	12	-	-	-	-	-	-	-	-	-
STOP OUT	5	8	6	7	4	6	9	2	8	9	10	-	-	-	-	-	-	-	-	-	-
TAKAPUNA CITY	-	-	-	-	-	-	-	-	-	-	-	10	-	-	-	-	-	-	-	-	-
UNIVERSITY (AUCKLAND)	-	-	-	-	-	-	-	-	-	-	-	-	-	-	12	7	9	-	-	-	-
WAIKATO UTD	-	-	-	-	-	-	-	-	-	-	-	-	-	-	-	-	-	-	5	8	4
WAITAKERE CITY	-	-	-	-	-	-	-	-	-	-	-	-	-	-	-	-	-	-	-	4	1
WATERSIDE	-	-	-	-	-	-	-	-	11	-	-	-	-	-	-	-	-	-	-	12	14
WELLINGTON CITY	-	9	7	8	7	10	-	-	-	-	-	-	-	-	-	-	-	-	-	-	-
WELLINGTON DIAMOND UTD	-	-	-	6	10	-	1	5	9	7	4	1	5	6	6	1	3	3	7	7	11
WESTERN SUBURBS	8	10	-	-	-	-	-	-	-	-	-	-	-	-	-	-	-	-	-	-	-
WOOLSTON	-	-	-	-	-	-	-	-	12	-	-	11	-	-	-	-	-	-	-	-	-

NATIONAL SOCCER LEAGUE
FINAL TABLES

		HOME				AWAY				GRAND TOTAL				
1970	**Pl**	**W**	**D**	**L**	**F-A**	**W**	**D**	**L**	**F-A**	**W**	**D**	**L**	**F-A**	**Pts**
Blockhouse Bay	14	6	1	0	20-3	4	1	2	20-13	10	2	2	40-16	22
Eastern Suburbs	14	5	1	1	17-10	5	1	1	16-7	10	2	2	33-17	22
Christchurch Utd	14	5	0	2	22-13	4	2	1	18-13	9	2	3	40-26	20
Mt Wellington	14	4	1	2	18-18	3	2	2	17-15	7	3	4	35-33	17
Stop Out	14	2	2	3	14-17	2	0	5	11-21	4	2	8	25-38	10
Gisborne City	14	2	1	4	13-14	1	2	4	9-17	3	3	8	22-31	9
Hungaria	14	2	3	2	15-15	1	0	6	9-21	3	3	8	24-36	9
Western Suburbs	14	0	0	7	7-21	1	1	5	11-19	1	1	12	18-40	3
1971	**Pl**	**W**	**D**	**L**	**F-A**	**W**	**D**	**L**	**F-A**	**W**	**D**	**L**	**F-A**	**Pts**
Eastern Suburbs	18	5	3	1	21-10	7	1	1	30-13	12	4	2	51-23	28
Mt Wellington	18	8	1	0	30-6	3	2	4	21-16	11	3	4	51-22	25
Christchurch Utd	18	7	1	1	28-10	2	4	3	15-10	9	5	4	43-20	23
Blockhouse Bay	18	4	4	1	20-11	5	0	4	25-14	9	4	5	45-25	22
Gisborne City	18	6	1	2	28-16	2	4	3	10-17	8	5	5	38-33	21
Dunedin Suburbs	18	2	3	4	13-19	4	0	5	12-25	6	3	9	25-44	15
M.A.P.	18	2	2	5	12-18	2	2	5	8-14	4	4	10	20-32	12
Stop Out	18	2	3	4	12-21	1	3	5	13-24	3	6	9	25-45	12
Wellington City	18	3	2	4	11-20	1	1	7	10-30	4	3	11	21-50	11
Western Suburbs	18	2	1	6	8-23	1	4	4	10-20	3	5	10	18-43	11
1972	**Pl**	**W**	**D**	**L**	**F-A**	**W**	**D**	**L**	**F-A**	**W**	**D**	**L**	**F-A**	**Pts**
Mt Wellington	18	8	0	1	25-8	5	2	2	21-11	13	2	3	46-19	28
Blockhouse Bay	18	6	2	1	18-6	6	2	1	17-11	12	4	2	35-17	28
Christchurch Utd	18	6	3	0	22-9	6	0	3	20-14	12	3	3	42-23	27
Eastern Suburbs	18	5	3	1	23-13	4	1	4	19-15	9	4	5	42-28	22
Gisborne City	18	5	1	3	16-11	1	4	4	16-17	6	5	7	32-28	17
Stop Out	18	3	2	4	12-17	2	4	3	15-13	5	6	7	27-30	16
Wellington City	18	4	2	3	17-12	2	1	6	6-14	6	3	9	23-26	15
Caversham	18	4	2	3	14-17	1	1	7	11-26	5	3	10	25-43	13
New Brighton	18	1	3	5	14-20	0	2	7	9-25	1	5	12	23-45	7
Auckland City	18	1	1	7	12-30	1	2	6	9-27	2	3	13	21-57	7
1973	**Pl**	**W**	**D**	**L**	**F-A**	**W**	**D**	**L**	**F-A**	**W**	**D**	**L**	**F-A**	**Pts**
Christchurch Utd	18	8	1	0	24-6	5	2	2	14-5	13	3	2	38-11	29
Mt Wellington	18	5	1	3	23-12	5	0	4	17-9	10	1	7	40-21	21
Blockhouse Bay	18	4	2	3	13-13	5	1	3	12-9	9	3	6	25-22	21
Gisborne City	18	4	0	5	16-14	4	4	1	17-12	8	4	6	33-26	20
Eastern Suburbs	18	5	1	3	12-12	4	1	4	18-18	9	2	7	30-30	20
W.D.U.	18	5	2	2	16-14	3	2	4	5-13	8	4	6	21-27	20
Stop Out	18	3	2	4	17-14	4	1	4	15-14	7	3	8	32-28	17
Wellington City	18	4	1	4	16-12	2	1	6	13-21	6	2	10	29-33	14
New Brighton	18	4	2	3	14-15	1	1	7	11-28	5	3	10	25-43	13
Caversham	18	2	1	6	3-13	0	0	9	3-25	2	1	15	6-38	5
1974	**Pl**	**W**	**D**	**L**	**F-A**	**W**	**D**	**L**	**F-A**	**W**	**D**	**L**	**F-A**	**Pts**
Mt Wellington	18	5	3	1	17-10	7	2	0	27-9	12	5	1	44-19	29
Christchurch Utd	18	4	3	2	19-10	4	3	2	12-9	8	6	4	31-19	22
New Brighton	18	7	0	2	19-9	2	3	4	15-16	9	3	6	34-25	21
Stop Out	18	5	1	3	18-14	4	2	3	8-9	9	3	6	26-23	21
Blockhouse Bay	18	3	4	2	16-11	5	0	4	16-12	8	4	6	32-23	20
North Shore Utd	18	3	3	3	8-8	3	1	5	15-19	6	4	8	23-27	16
Wellington City	18	2	3	4	18-21	3	2	4	14-17	5	5	8	32-38	15
Gisborne City	18	3	1	5	11-18	2	2	5	10-17	5	3	10	21-35	13
Eastern Suburbs	18	4	1	4	16-19	1	2	6	7-26	5	3	10	23-45	13
W.D.U.	18	4	0	5	17-9	0	2	7	5-25	4	2	12	22-34	10

1975	Pl	W	D	L	F-A	W	D	L	F-A	W	D	L	F-A	Pts
Christchurch Utd	18	5	3	1	21-8	6	1	2	14-8	11	4	3	35-16	26
North Shore Utd	18	5	3	1	18-7	3	4	2	15-11	8	7	3	33-18	23
Blockhouse Bay	18	5	2	2	16-10	4	3	2	13-11	9	5	4	29-21	23
Caversham	18	2	6	1	11-7	2	4	3	10-12	4	10	4	21-19	18
Mt Wellington	18	4	2	3	10-8	3	2	4	9-11	7	4	7	19-19	18
Stop Out	18	5	2	2	11-8	2	2	5	11-16	7	4	7	22-24	18
Eastern Suburbs	18	5	2	2	15-14	2	1	6	9-19	7	3	8	24-33	17
Gisborne City	18	4	1	4	8-10	1	3	5	5-15	5	4	9	13-25	14
New Brighton	18	3	2	4	12-14	1	2	6	6-14	4	4	10	18-28	12
Wellington City	18	2	2	5	10-14	1	3	5	8-15	3	5	10	18-29	11

1976	Pl	W	D	L	F-A	W	D	L	F-A	W	D	L	F-A	Pts
W.D.U.	18	5	1	3	15-16	8	0	1	16-13	13	1	4	31-29	27
Mt Wellington	18	4	1	4	13-12	6	2	1	20-5	10	3	5	33-17	23
Caversham	18	6	2	1	25-11	2	4	3	15-15	8	6	4	40-26	22
New Brighton	18	4	1	4	13-14	6	0	3	18-13	10	1	7	31-27	21
Blockhouse Bay	18	4	2	3	13-10	2	3	4	11-12	6	5	7	24-22	17
Eastern Suburbs	18	2	4	3	14-13	4	1	4	17-19	6	5	7	31-32	17
North Shore Utd	18	3	1	5	16-16	3	3	3	12-13	6	4	8	28-29	16
Christchurch Utd	18	2	2	5	11-16	5	0	4	10-7	7	2	9	21-23	16
Stop Out	18	3	0	6	10-19	1	4	4	15-22	4	4	10	25-41	12
Gisborne City	18	1	3	5	9-19	2	0	7	12-20	3	3	12	21-39	9

1977	Pl	W	D	L	F-A	W	D	L	F-A	W	D	L	F-A	Pts
North Shore Utd	22	7	2	2	19-11	7	1	3	18-14	14	3	5	37-25	31
Stop Out	22	7	4	0	23-11	4	4	3	17-17	11	8	3	40-28	30
Christchurch Utd	22	6	4	1	19-9	3	5	3	13-8	9	9	4	32-17	27
Hamilton	22	4	5	2	18-11	5	4	2	23-11	9	9	4	41-22	27
W.D.U.	22	5	4	2	17-11	3	3	5	24-20	8	7	7	41-31	23
Mt Wellington	22	4	2	5	10-14	4	5	2	17-7	8	7	7	27-21	23
Nelson Utd	22	4	4	3	10-12	2	5	4	12-17	6	9	7	22-29	21
Blockhouse Bay	22	4	4	3	11-15	3	3	5	12-18	7	7	8	23-33	21
Eastern Suburbs	22	4	1	6	19-21	2	4	5	12-15	6	5	11	31-36	17
New Brighton	22	4	5	2	16-14	1	2	8	8-22	5	7	10	24-36	17
Dunedin City	22	3	4	4	11-13	2	3	6	8-17	5	7	10	19-30	17
Caversham	22	2	2	7	11-25	1	2	8	3-18	3	4	15	14-43	10

1978	Pl	W	D	L	F-A	W	D	L	F-A	W	D	L	F-A	Pts
Christchurch Utd	22	8	2	1	33-10	5	4	2	12-6	13	6	3	45-16	32
Mt Wellington	22	7	1	3	20-13	7	3	1	20-13	14	4	4	40-26	32
Blockhouse Bay	22	4	6	1	19-11	6	2	3	19-17	10	8	4	38-28	28
Eastern Suburbs	22	8	0	3	28-12	4	3	4	18-12	12	3	7	46-24	27
Courier Rangers	22	6	3	2	17-7	3	2	6	8-12	9	5	8	25-19	23
North Shore Utd	22	4	5	2	25-17	3	3	5	14-19	7	8	7	39-36	22
Nelson Utd	22	4	2	5	12-17	3	6	2	11-17	7	8	7	23-34	22
Stop Out	22	5	2	4	13-14	1	5	5	13-17	6	7	9	26-31	19
W.D.U.	22	3	5	3	12-14	3	0	8	15-31	6	5	11	27-45	17
Hamilton	22	3	1	7	14-21	4	1	6	19-22	7	2	13	33-43	16
Waterside	22	3	1	7	13-20	3	1	7	11-24	6	2	14	24-44	14
Woolston	22	1	3	7	5-17	3	1	7	13-21	4	4	14	18-38	12

1979	Pl	W	D	L	F-A	W	D	L	F-A	W	D	L	F-A	Pts
Mt Wellington	22	11	0	0	34-4	9	0	2	34-13	20	0	2	68-17	40
Christchurch Utd	22	6	3	2	26-12	4	3	4	21-18	10	6	6	47-30	26
North Shore Utd	22	6	1	4	17-12	4	3	4	20-17	10	4	8	37-29	24
Manurewa	22	7	2	2	24-12	2	4	5	9-16	9	6	7	33-28	24
Dunedin City	22	6	2	3	25-25	4	2	5	14-19	10	4	8	39-44	24
Nelson Utd	22	7	2	2	24-8	2	2	7	12-22	9	4	9	36-30	22
W.D.U.	22	4	4	3	15-19	3	3	5	8-15	7	7	8	23-34	21
Blockhouse Bay	22	4	3	4	15-20	2	3	6	16-21	6	6	10	31-41	18
Stop Out	22	3	4	4	18-17	2	3	6	9-18	5	7	10	27-35	17
Manawatu Utd	22	5	3	3	15-12	1	2	8	7-21	6	5	11	22-33	17
Courier Rangers	22	3	5	3	12-18	1	3	7	14-30	4	8	10	26-48	16
Eastern Suburbs	22	3	3	5	13-19	1	4	6	14-28	4	7	11	27-47	15

1980	Pl	W	D	L	F-A	W	D	L	F-A	W	D	L	F-A	Pts
Mt Wellington	22	9	1	1	26-5	6	4	1	27-14	15	5	2	53-19	35
Gisborne City	22	6	5	0	26-12	5	4	2	18-12	11	9	2	44-24	31
Manurewa	22	4	3	4	18-19	6	3	2	21-13	10	6	6	39-32	26
W.D.U.	22	5	4	2	15-10	4	4	3	16-16	9	8	5	31-26	26
North Shore Utd	22	8	0	3	19-9	3	2	6	9-18	11	2	9	28-27	24
Dunedin City	22	4	6	1	26-11	2	2	7	11-21	6	8	8	37-32	20
Christchurch Utd	22	4	4	3	23-17	3	2	6	11-16	7	6	9	34-33	20
Hamilton	22	5	4	2	14-10	2	1	8	12-26	7	5	10	26-36	19
Rangers	22	4	0	7	20-22	3	3	5	11-19	7	3	12	31-41	17
Stop Out	22	5	1	5	15-23	1	4	6	12-23	6	5	11	27-46	17
Blockhouse Bay	22	3	2	6	16-19	2	3	6	14-24	5	5	12	30-43	15
Nelson Utd	22	2	2	7	14-22	4	0	7	17-30	6	2	14	31-52	14

1981	Pl	W	D	L	F-A	W	D	L	F-A	W	D	L	F-A	Pts
W.D.U.	22	6	3	2	22-10	7	2	2	24-7	13	5	4	46-17	31
Dunedin City	22	8	2	1	26-10	5	3	3	17-16	13	5	4	43-26	31
Mt Wellington	22	8	1	2	32-5	5	2	4	18-11	13	3	6	50-16	29
Gisborne City	22	8	0	3	23-7	6	1	4	20-10	14	1	7	43-17	29
North Shore Utd	22	5	2	4	16-15	7	1	3	19-16	12	3	7	35-31	27
Christchurch Utd	22	6	2	3	15-8	1	7	3	8-11	7	9	6	23-19	23
Manurewa	22	4	2	5	18-15	5	1	5	23-17	9	3	10	41-32	21
Miramar	22	4	5	2	16-16	2	3	6	7-21	6	8	8	23-37	20
Hamilton	22	4	2	5	12-18	3	3	5	6-16	7	5	10	18-34	19
Takapuna City	22	1	4	6	10-26	3	3	5	16-21	4	7	11	26-47	15
Woolston	22	3	3	5	13-22	1	3	7	10-31	4	6	12	23-53	14
Rangers	22	0	4	7	4-22	0	1	10	6-30	0	5	17	10-52	5

1982	Pl	W	D	L	F-A	W	D	L	F-A	W	D	L	F-A	Pts
Mt Wellington	22	8	3	0	28-6	7	3	1	24-9	15	6	1	52-15	36
North Shore Utd	22	10	0	1	31-11	1	7	3	13-14	11	7	4	44-25	29
Dunedin City	22	7	3	1	14-5	3	4	4	16-16	10	7	5	30-21	27
Gisborne City	22	8	3	0	26-6	2	4	5	13-25	10	7	5	39-31	27
W.D.U.	22	7	3	1	19-7	1	5	5	10-16	8	8	6	29-23	24
Miramar	22	6	3	2	20-15	3	1	7	10-17	9	4	9	30-32	22
Christchurch Utd	22	3	5	3	15-13	2	6	3	12-13	5	11	6	27-26	21
Napier City Rovers	22	5	5	1	21-11	2	3	6	16-29	7	7	8	36-40	21
Manurewa	22	5	4	2	21-18	2	2	7	10-16	8	5	9	31-33	21
Hamilton	22	2	5	4	8-15	1	2	8	13-24	3	7	12	21-39	13
East Coast Bays	22	3	4	4	14-19	1	0	10	9-25	4	4	14	23-44	12
Invercargill Thistle	22	3	2	6	15-23	0	3	8	3-28	3	5	14	18-51	11

*Napier City Rovers 1 Manurewa 1 altered to 0-1 for rule infringement. Table adjusted to incorporate this alteration.

1983	Pl	W	D	L	F-A	W	D	L	F-A	W	D	L	F-A	Pts
Manurewa	22	7	3	1	27-9	6	2	3	19-14	13	5	4	46-23	44
North Shore Utd	22	10	1	0	30-10	0	5	6	10-17	10	6	6	40-27	36
Papatoetoe	22	3	3	5	13-19	7	2	2	16-8	10	5	7	29-27	35
Mt Wellington	22	5	3	3	18-11	4	2	5	13-15	9	5	8	31-26	32
Christchurch Utd	22	6	1	4	24-17	3	4	4	17-20	9	5	8	41-37	32
W.D.U.	22	5	3	3	15-8	3	5	3	14-17	8	8	6	29-25	32
Miramar	22	4	4	3	17-18	4	4	3	19-15	8	8	6	36-33	32
Napier City Rovers	22	4	5	2	13-9	4	1	6	16-17	8	6	8	29-26	30
Dunedin City	22	4	1	6	12-19	5	1	5	11-12	9	2	11	23-31	29
Gisborne City	22	4	4	3	15-13	3	3	5	12-16	7	7	8	27-29	28
Nelson Utd	22	6	1	4	15-11	2	2	7	13-23	8	3	11	28-34	27
Dunedin Technical	22	1	3	7	9-25	0	1	10	9-34	1	4	17	18-59	7

For 1983 and subsequent seasons, a win was worth 3 points and a draw 1 point.

1984	Pl	W	D	L	F-A	W	D	L	F-A	W	D	L	F-A	Pts
Gisborne City	22	8	3	0	27-4	7	3	1	32-12	15	6	1	59-16	51
Papatoetoe	22	5	4	2	18-11	5	3	3	17-15	10	7	5	35-26	37
Christchurch Utd	22	7	1	3	21-18	3	4	4	16-14	10	5	7	37-32	35
Manurewa	22	6	3	2	26-19	3	3	5	14-23	9	6	7	40-42	33
Miramar	22	6	3	2	23-17	2	4	5	17-29	8	7	7	40-46	31
W.D.U.	22	2	6	3	15-13	5	3	3	17-13	7	9	6	32-26	30
Dunedin City	22	4	2	5	21-18	4	2	5	13-22	8	4	10	34-40	28
Napier City Rovers	22	5	2	4	21-24	2	3	6	17-29	7	5	10	38-53	26
North Shore Utd	22	2	4	5	14-15	5	0	6	13-16	7	4	11	27-31	25
Mt Wellington	22	4	4	3	19-17	1	5	5	9-19	5	9	8	28-36	24
Nelson United	22	3	2	6	10-21	2	4	5	15-21	5	6	11	25-42	21
University	22	3	2	6	17-17	2	2	7	14-19	5	4	13	31-36	19

1985	Pl	W	D	L	F-A	W	D	L	F-A	W	D	L	F-A	Pts
W.D.U.	22	7	4	0	23-10	5	1	5	27-23	12	5	5	50-33	41
Gisborne City	22	6	1	4	24-15	5	4	2	17-11	11	5	6	41-26	38
North Shore Utd	22	8	2	1	25-11	3	2	6	22-22	11	4	7	47-33	37
Mt Wellington	22	5	5	1	28-17	3	3	5	12-13	8	8	6	40-30	32
Miramar	22	6	3	2	20-12	2	3	6	15-21	8	6	8	35-33	30
Nelson Utd	22	6	1	4	21-18	3	2	6	14-28	9	3	10	35-46	30
University	22	6	2	3	15-14	3	1	7	15-31	9	3	10	30-45	30
Dunedin City	22	6	1	4	24-16	2	4	5	10-22	8	5	9	34-38	29
Christchurch Utd	22	5	1	5	17-13	3	3	5	7-12	8	4	10	24-25	28
Manurewa	22	5	3	3	16-23	2	3	6	14-26	7	6	9	30-49	27
Papatoetoe	22	6	1	4	20-15	2	1	8	16-22	8	2	12	36-37	26
Napier City Rovers	22	3	4	4	21-20	2	1	8	15-23	5	5	12	36-43	20

1986	Pl	W	D	L	F-A	W	D	L	F-A	W	D	L	F-A	Pts
Mt Wellington	22	8	3	0	20-8	4	5	2	22-14	12	8	2	42-22	44
Miramar	22	4	6	1	19-14	8	1	2	26-13	12	7	3	45-27	43
W.D.U.	22	4	3	4	27-18	7	3	1	19-11	11	6	5	46-29	39
Christchurch Utd	22	5	4	2	18-10	6	2	3	20-12	11	6	5	38-22	39
Gisborne City	22	5	3	3	28-19	6	2	3	18-16	11	5	6	46-35	38
Papatoetoe	22	2	4	5	18-19	4	4	3	17-15	6	8	8	35-34	26
North Shore Utd	22	3	4	4	20-20	3	3	5	18-31	6	7	9	38-51	25
Dunedin City	22	4	1	6	25-23	2	4	5	13-17	6	5	11	38-40	23
University	22	4	1	6	17-24	1	6	4	13-24	5	7	10	30-48	22
Nelson Utd	22	4	3	4	14-17	1	3	7	14-30	5	6	11	28-47	21
Manawatu	22	4	2	5	16-18	1	3	7	14-28	5	5	12	30-46	20
Manurewa	22	3	3	5	13-18	2	1	8	14-24	5	4	13	27-42	19

1987	Pl	W	D	L	F-A	W	D	L	F-A	W	D	L	F-A	Pts
Christchurch Utd	26	11	0	2	32-12	7	4	2	28-12	18	4	4	60-24	58
Gisborne City	26	8	4	1	28-11	6	5	2	24-20	14	9	3	52-31	51
W.D.U.	26	8	3	2	25-13	7	2	4	27-22	15	5	6	52-35	50
Mt Maunganui	26	6	3	4	19-17	8	1	4	16-11	14	4	8	35-28	46
Papatoetoe	26	6	4	3	29-19	6	2	5	24-14	12	6	8	53-33	42
Napier City Rovers	26	6	4	3	23-18	5	3	5	18-21	11	7	8	41-39	40
North Shore Utd	26	6	4	3	24-13	4	5	4	17-15	10	9	7	41-28	39
Mt Wellington	26	7	4	2	31-19	4	2	7	25-29	11	6	9	56-48	39
Hutt Valley Utd	26	5	3	5	20-26	4	0	9	16-26	9	3	14	36-52	30
Manurewa	26	5	2	6	17-20	2	4	7	16-24	7	6	13	33-44	27
Nelson Utd	26	5	2	6	18-19	1	2	10	10-32	6	4	16	28-51	22
Dunedin City	26	4	1	8	15-24	2	3	8	17-37	6	4	16	32-61	22
Manawatu	26	1	4	8	12-28	3	5	5	18-22	4	9	13	30-50	21
Miramar	26	3	1	9	23-37	3	1	9	20-31	6	2	18	43-68	20

1988	Pl	W	D	L	F-A	W	D	L	F-A	W	D	L	F-A	Pts
Christchurch Utd	26	11	2	0	41-7	9	3	1	22-7	20	4	2	63-14	64
Mt Wellington	26	9	4	0	34-8	10	0	3	30-10	19	4	3	64-18	61
Mt Maunganui	26	9	2	2	26-14	7	4	2	26-20	16	6	4	52-34	54
Napier City Rovers	26	6	2	5	27-21	6	1	6	18-23	12	3	11	45-44	39
Waikato Utd	26	6	2	5	20-10	5	3	5	19-20	11	5	10	39-30	38
North Shore Utd	26	7	2	4	21-12	4	2	7	22-29	11	4	11	43-41	37
Wellington Utd	26	6	1	6	31-27	4	4	5	26-25	10	5	11	57-52	35
Miramar	26	6	3	4	29-17	4	2	7	18-27	10	5	11	47-44	35
Gisborne City	26	5	2	6	25-23	5	2	6	21-23	10	4	12	46-46	34
Hutt Valley Utd	26	5	2	6	15-19	4	4	5	13-15	9	6	11	28-34	33
Papatoetoe	26	4	2	7	14-23	5	2	6	13-20	9	4	13	27-43	31
Manurewa	26	5	1	7	20-29	1	3	9	12-40	6	4	16	32-69	22
Nelson Utd	26	2	4	7	12-25	2	0	11	12-32	4	4	18	24-57	16
Manawatu	26	1	3	9	13-34	3	1	9	17-37	4	4	18	30-71	16

1989	Pl	W	D	L	F-A	W	D	L	F-A	W	D	L	F-A	Pts
Napier City Rovers	26	8	4	1	33-18	8	3	2	24-18	16	7	3	57-36	55
Mt Maunganui	26	9	4	0	25-9	7	3	3	13-9	16	7	3	38-18	55
Mt Wellington	26	8	1	4	37-14	8	3	2	25-16	16	4	6	62-30	52
Waitakere City	26	8	3	2	28-16	7	2	4	23-19	15	5	6	51-35	50
Hutt Valley Utd	26	8	3	2	24-13	5	1	7	21-25	13	4	9	45-38	43
Christchurch Utd	26	7	2	4	26-16	5	4	4	22-17	12	6	8	48-33	42
Wellington Utd	26	6	0	7	20-20	6	4	3	22-18	12	4	10	42-38	40
Waikato Utd	26	3	7	3	19-18	5	4	4	12-13	8	11	7	31-31	35
Manurewa	26	5	3	5	15-16	4	3	6	19-22	9	6	11	34-38	33
North Shore Utd	26	3	3	7	20-28	4	1	8	26-31	7	4	15	46-59	25
Miramar	26	3	4	6	20-19	2	4	7	20-24	5	8	13	40-43	23
Waterside Karori	26	4	1	8	23-26	1	4	8	15-32	5	5	16	38-58	20
Gisborne City	26	4	3	6	16-25	0	3	10	10-41	4	6	16	26-66	18
Papatoetoe	26	1	3	9	12-28	2	2	9	14-33	3	5	18	26-61	14

Miramar Rangers 1 Christchurch Utd 1 altered to 0-1, Miramar Rangers 1 Hutt Valley 1 altered to 0-1, Gisborne City 2 Manurewa 2 altered to 0-2, all for rule infringements. Table adjusted to incorporate these alterations.

1990	Pl	W	D	L	F-A	W	D	L	F-A	W	D	L	F-A	Pts
Waitakere City	26	11	1	1	36-10	9	1	3	24-14	20	2	4	60-24	62
Mt Wellington	26	9	3	1	31-7	9	3	1	23-12	18	6	2	54-19	60
Christchurch Utd	26	8	3	2	29-15	7	1	5	21-17	15	4	7	50-32	49
Waikato Utd	26	6	3	4	21-20	8	2	3	23-11	14	5	7	44-31	47
Manurewa	26	6	5	2	19-12	4	3	6	19-20	10	8	8	38-32	38
Napier City Rovers	26	6	5	2	23-13	3	6	4	18-23	9	11	6	41-36	38
Mt Maunganui	26	7	1	5	31-17	2	4	7	9-21	9	5	12	40-38	32
North Shore Utd	26	5	2	6	17-16	3	4	6	17-22	8	6	12	34-38	30
Miramar	26	3	3	7	18-19	5	2	6	17-28	8	5	13	35-47	29
Hutt Valley Utd	26	5	1	7	13-20	3	4	6	11-20	8	5	13	24-40	29
Wellington Utd	26	5	3	5	18-19	3	2	8	16-35	8	5	13	32-52	29
Gisborne City	26	4	4	5	16-19	2	2	9	14-30	6	6	14	30-49	24
New Plymouth	26	2	2	9	12-26	3	4	6	16-21	5	6	15	28-47	21
Waterside Karori	26	2	5	6	15-22	1	3	9	7-25	3	8	15	22-47	17

NZFA TROPHIES

FOOTBALL ASSOCIATION TROPHY

In 1925 the New Zealand F.A. was the recipient of a very handsome trophy donated by The Football Association (England). For many years enquiries had been made regarding a visit from an English international team. These requests, while received with favour, could never be met but, as a gesture of goodwill, the parent body presented what was to become known as the English Trophy for competition amongst the major associations in the Dominion. Similar trophies were presented to the controlling bodies in Australia and Canada.

RESULTS

(Home team mentioned first)

1926

League System

Date	Game		Result	Referee	
3 Jul	Wellington	v Auckland	0:4	C. Kelly	W
17 Jul	Otago	v Wellington	4:3	W.P. Smith	O
7 Aug	Auckland	v Canterbury	9:2	A.E. Caisley	W
14 Aug	Wellington	v Canterbury	4:1	S. Wilson	W
28 Aug	Canterbury	v Otago	0:4	J. Stout	C
18 Sep	Auckland	v Otago	4:1	G. Cox	SA

	P	W	D	L	F	A	Pts
1. Auckland	3	3	0	0	17	3	6
2. Otago	3	2	0	1	9	7	4
3. Wellington	3	1	0	2	7	9	2
4. Canterbury	3	0	0	3	3	17	0

1927

League System

Date	Game		Result	Referee	
13 Aug	Auckland	v Wellington	3:1	E. Parkinson	A
20 Aug	Wellington	v Otago	2:4	G. Jackson	W
27 Aug	Canterbury	v Wellington	4:3	J. Jennings	C
3 Sep	Otago	v Auckland	1:2	W.P. Smith	O
10 Sep	Canterbury	v Auckland	1:1		
17 Sep	Otago	v Canterbury	1:3		

	P	W	D	L	F	A	Pts
1. Auckland	3	2	1	0	6	3	5
2. Canterbury	3	2	1	0	8	5	5
3. Otago	3	1	0	2	6	7	2
4. Wellington	3	0	0	3	6	11	0

1928

Challenge system introduced. Trophy held by Wellington subject to challenge.
(Auckland and Canterbury were to play the first match but when neither Association would guarantee the visitor's expenses, Wellington was asked if it would be a guarantor. Wellington accepted and invited Canterbury to be the first challenger as its expenses would be considerably smaller than those incurred by Auckland in travelling to Wellington.

Date	Game		Result	Referee	
11 Aug	Wellington	v Canterbury	7:4	A.E. Caisley	W
1 Sep	Wellington	v Auckland	0:3	B.T. Martin	W
8 Sep	Auckland	v Wellington	2:2	R.H. Parfitt	A
		1929			
20 Jul	Auckland	v Wellington	4:2	A.E. Parkinson	A
29 Aug	Auckland	v Wellington	4:2	J.W. Pikesley	R N
		1930			
5 Jul	Auckland	v Wellington	4:2	A.E. Parkinson	A
		1931			
13 Jun	Auckland	v Wellington	4:5	E. Parkinson	A

1 Aug	Wellington	v Otago	3:4	W.E. Watts	W
29 Aug	Otago	v Canterbury	3:2	W.P. Smith	O

1932

11 Jun	Otago	v Canterbury	3:1	F.G. Smith	O
2 Jul	Otago	v Wellington	2:2	W.P. Smith	O
6 Aug	Otago	v Auckland	2:2	A. Bowie	A

1933

10 Jun	Otago	v Wellington	5:4	F.G. Smith	O
224 Jun	Otago	v Canterbury	3:1	A. Bowie	A
26 Aug	Otago	v Auckland	1:2	W.P. Smith	O

1934

16 Jun	Auckland	v Otago	2:1	E.F. Miller	A
14 Jul	Auckland	v Wellington	2:2	A. Kyle	A
1 Sep	Auckland	v Canterbury	3:2	A. Firth	A

1935

15 Jul	Auckland	v Wellington	6:1	E. Marsh	SA
29 Jun	Auckland	v Otago	2:0	G. Shand	A

1936

6 Jun	Auckland	v Canterbury	1:2	E. Parkinson	A
5 Aug	Canterbury	v Otago	7:0	W.H. Moore	C

1937

2 Jun	Canterbury	v Wellington	8:3	J. Jennings	C
31 Jul	Canterbury	v Otago	4:1	L.E. Doherty	C
2 Oct	Canterbury	v Auckland	3:3	W.H. Moore	C

1938

20 Aug	Canterbury	v Wellington	4:3	C.G. Sweeney	C
27 Aug	Canterbury	v Otago	1:2	E.B. Harris	C

1939

17 Jun	Otago	v Auckland	2:5	J. Welsh	O
15 Jul	Auckland	v Wellington	3:2	C. Edwards	A
19 Aug	Auckland	v Wellington	6:1	A. Firth	A
23 Sep	Auckland	v Canterbury	4:3	C. Edwards	A

1940

6 Jul	Auckland	v Wellington	2:1	J.C. Sibbin	A
21 Sep	Auckland	v Canterbury	5:2	F.O. Green	A
5 Oct	Auckland	v Wellington	3:6	F.N. Marino	A

1941

28 Jun	Wellington	v Auckland	6:3	J. Houston	W
26 Jul	Wellington	v Canterbury	3:6	A. Aspen	W
20 Sep	Canterbury	v Otago	4:1	C. Hamilton	C

1942-43

No competition

1944

1 Jul	Canterbury	v Wellington	3:1

1945

8 Sep	Canterbury	v Wellington	2:2

From 1946 to 1953 the trophy was contested annually at a tournament on the Sovereign's Birthday.

1946

at Blandford Park, Auckland

1 Jun	Auckland	v Wellington	3:1	T.G. Gottermeyer	C
	Canterbury a bye				

3 Jun	Final Auckland v Canterbury	4:2	J. Sanderson	W

1947

at Caledonian Ground, Dunedin

31 May	Canterbury v Otago	7:2	V. Wheeler	W
	Auckland v Wellington	4:2	W.T. Dodd	O
2 Jun	3rd Place Wellington v Otago	6:0	T. Mathie	C
	Final Auckland v Canterbury	4:3	W.M. Smith	O

1948

at Basin Reserve, Wellington

5 Jun	Canterbury v Otago	3:0	R. Scott	W
	Wellington v Auckland	3:2	C.G. Sweeney	C
7 Jun	3rd Place Auckland v Otago	5:1		
	Final Canterbury v Wellington	5:4	J.H. Thomson	Wg

1949

at Showgrounds, Christchurch

4 Jun	Canterbury v Otago	7:2	E. Page	A
	Auckland v Wellington	3:2	M. Cassin	C
6 Jun	3rd Place Wellington v Otago	3:2	F. King	O
	Final Canterbury v Auckland	5:1		

1950

at Blandford Park, Auckland

3 Jun	Wellington v Canterbury	3:2	C. Edwards	A
	Auckland v Otago	10:2	T.C. Gottermeyer	C
5 Jun	3rd Place Otago v Canterbury	6:0	A. Aspen	W
	Final Auckland v Wellington	3:2	W.T. Dodd	O

1951

Tournament cancelled due to industrial trouble. To decide the Trophy winner, the two North Island teams were to meet, likewise the two South Island teams with the winners to play-off. Auckland decided it would not take part in the re-arranged competition.

4 Jun	Canterbury v Otago	2:4		
	Wellington a bye			
18 Aug	Final Wellington v Otago	6:3	*C.G. Sweeney	C

1952

at Basin Reserve, Wellington

27 Aug	Wellington v Auckland	4:2	I. Billcliff	C
	Canterbury v Otago	4:2	R. Lund	A
	3rd Place Otago v Auckland	4:3		
	Final Wellington v Canterbury (Trophy shared)	3:3	D. Welham	O

1953

at University Oval, Dunedin

31 May	Wellington v Canterbury	5:0	J. Mellor	A
	Auckland v Otago	3:1	M.T. Swain	W
2 Jun	3rd Place Otago v Canterbury	4:4	N. Williams	O
	Final Auckland v Wellington	4:2	L.J. Tointon	C

1954

Challenge system re-introduced.

5 Jun	Auckland v Bay of Plenty	3:3	J. Crooks	A
19 Jun	Auckland v Hawkes Bay	2:2	R.C. Innes	A
3 Jul	Auckland v Wellington	3:1	J. Smith	A
31 Jul	Auckland v Taranaki	7:1	C. Edwards	A
11 Sep	Auckland v Waikato	0:2	R. Lund	A

1955

18 Jun	Waikato v Manawatu	3:3	J. Smith	A

25 Jun	Waikato	v Auckland	2:4	M.T. Swain	W
23 Jul	Auckland	v Bay of Plenty	4:0	A. Mackie	A
27 Aug	Auckland	v Poverty Bay	8:2	J. Smith	A
17 Sep	Auckland	v Wellington	2:3	A. Mackie	A

1956

30 Jun	Wellington	v Canterbury	1:4*	I.D. Banks	W
	*Canterbury forfeited Trophy for using an ineligible player				
18 Aug	Wellington	v Waikato	2:1	R. Lund	A
1 Sep	Wellington	v Hawkes Bay	9:2	D. Welham	O
8 Sep	Wellington	v Auckland	1:2	I. Billcliff	C

1957

1 Jun	Auckland	v Poverty Bay	3:0	R.C. Innes	A
13 Jul	Auckland	v Canterbury	0:3	W. Austin	A
24 Aug	Canterbury	v Waikato	5:4	J. Davidson	C
28 Sep	Canterbury	v Otago	4:1	I. Billcliff	C

1958

31 May	Canterbury	v South Canterbury	6:1	L.J. Tointon	C
5 Jul	Canterbury	v Auckland	0:3	J. Davidson	C
27 Sep	Auckland	v Waikato	1:1	A. Furse	A

1959

13 Jun	Auckland	v Waikato	3:1	R. Brighton	A
1 Aug	Auckland	v Bay of Plenty	6:0	K. Davies	WK
26 Sep	Auckland	v Poverty Bay	1:3	B. Robertson	WK

1960

16 Jul	Poverty Bay	v Hawkes Bay	2:0		
6 Aug	Poverty Bay	v Auckland	1:2		
26 Sep	Auckland	v Bay of Plenty	5:2	C.H. Dickie	A

1961

12 Aug	Auckland	v Waikato	6:0	J. Cherrie	W
19 Aug	Auckland	v Bay of Plenty	6:0	K. Davies	WK
2 Sep	Auckland	v Poverty Bay	4:2	J.B. Hulton	WK
16 Sep	Auckland	v Otago	2:0	G. Baxter	HB

1962

4 Jun	Auckland	v Western Bay of Plenty	10:1		

1963

League system

1 Jun	Auckland	v Canterbury	9:2	J.B. Hulton	WK
3 Jun	Wellington	v Canterbury	4:0	E.J. Saker	HB
24 Aug	Auckland	v Wellington	2:2	L.W. Coffman	A

	P	W	D	L	F	A	Pts
1. Wellington	2	1	1	0	6	2	3
2. Auckland	2	1	1	0	11	4	3
3. Canterbury	2	0	0	2	2	13	0

1964

League System

1 Jun	Canterbury	v Wellington	0:3	R.E. McDonald	O
6 Jun	Wellington	v Auckland	1:6	J. Warren	M
7 Jun	Canterbury	v Auckland	0:0	T.J. Ward	W

	P	W	D	L	F	A	Pts
1. Auckland	2	1	1	0	6	1	3
2. Wellington	2	1	0	1	4	6	2
3. Canterbury	2	0	1	1	0	3	1

1965

Challenge system

11 Sep	Auckland	v Canterbury	1:1		

1966

Challenge system

21 Aug	Auckland	v Canterbury	5:1		
28 Aug	Auckland	v Wellington	2:1	P.S. Codd	A

1967

2 Leg knockout system

9 Sep	Wellington	v Auckland	4:1	J. Armstrong	W
	Canterbury	v Otago	5:1	N. de Meyer	C
16 Sep	Auckland	v Wellington	3:1	P.S. Codd	A
	Otago	v Canterbury	3:1	F. Anderson	O
23 Sep	Final Auckland	v Canterbury	2:0	W.K. Munro	A

1968-69

No competition

Trophy then awarded to winner of National League from its inception.

1970	Blockhouse Bay
1971	Eastern Suburbs
1972	Mt Wellington
1973	Christchurch United
1974	Mt Wellington
1975	Christchurch United
1976	Wellington Diamond United
1977	North Shore United
1978	Christchurch United
1979	Mt Wellington
1980	Mt Wellington
1981	Wellington Diamond United
1982	Mt Wellington
1983	Manurewa

Since 1984 when the National League winner was presented with a sponsor's trophy there has been no competition for the Football Association Trophy.

WINFIELD CHALLENGE SHIELD

In recognition of the Auckland Football Association's centenary celebrations, the Winfield company donated the Winfield Shield in 1987 for inter-association competition.

Auckland, as inaugural holder, accepted five challenges during the 1988 season, successfully repulsing four before bowing to Otago.

14 Associations have now had a chance to take the shield thanks to generous sponsorship from the Shield donors whose intention of encouraging a resurgence of interest in provincial football is being realised.

Date	Game	Result	Referee
	1988		
18 May	Auckland v Northland	6:0	E. Taylor
16 Jun	Auckland v Waikato	3:0	G. Fleet
13 Jul	Auckland v Franklin	4:2	S. De Boer
19 Aug	Auckland v Manawatu	3:2	G. Fleet
21 Sep	Auckland v Otago	1:3	R. Brown
	1989		
24 May	Otago v North Otago	2:0	G. Binney
21 June	Otago v South Canterbury	3:0	K. Hollebon
5 Jul	Otago v Southland	2:2	M. Fraser
19 Jul	Otago v Hawkes Bay	1:1	G. Cowie
23 Aug	Otago v Canterbury	1:2	A. McGregor
1 Nov	Canterbury v Nelson	4:0	R. Gallon
	1990		
9 May	Canterbury v Mid Canterbury	7:0	R. Anderson
13 jun	Canterbury v Taranaki	1:0	K. Jones
11 Jul	Canterbury v Franklin	4:0	H. Potter
26 Sep	Canterbury v Otago	1:0	D. Haase
10 Oct	Canterbury v Auckland	1:2	R. Gallon

JUNIOR NATIONAL CUP

Contested by teams comprising players under 18 years of age.

Year	Venue	Game	Result	
1945	Wellington	Marist (Well)	b. Mornington (Otago)	4:2
1946	Wellington	Marist (Well)	b. Technical O.B. (Canterbury)	3:1
1947	Wellington	Mornington (Otago)	b. YMCA (Auckland)	3:1
1948	Wellington	Auckland	b. Otago	7:0
1949	Dunedin	Otago	b. Wellington	2:1
1950	Auckland	Auckland	b Otago	4:1
1951	Christchurch	Wellington	b. Canterbury	2:1
1952	Wellington	Wellington	b. Southland	3:1
1953	Dunedin	Wellington	b. Otago	2:1
1954	Auckland	Auckland	b. Canterbury	7:0
1955	Christchurch	Auckland	b. Canterbury	5:3
1956	Auckland	Auckland	b. Canterbury	3:2
1957	No competition			
1958	Christchurch	Auckland	b. Canterbury	4:2
1959	Wellington	Wellington	b. Otago	2:2
1960	Dunedin	Otago	b. Wellington	4:3
1961	Wellington	Wellington	b. Otago	1:0
1962	Dunedin	Otago	b. Wellington	4:3
1963	Auckland	Auckland	b. Canterbury	6:2
1964	Christchurch	Canterbury	b. Wellington	4:0
1965	Wellington	Wellington	b. Otago	2:0
1966	Dunedin	Auckland	b. Otago	6:1
1967	Auckland	Auckland	b. Canterbury	6:3
1968	Christchurch	Auckland	b. Canterbury	3:2
1969	Auckland	Auckland	b. Franklin	4:3 *
1970	Dunedin	Auckland	b. Otago	2:1
1971	Wellington	Canterbury	b. Wellington	2:0
1972	Christchurch	Wellington	b. Canterbury	3:2
1973	Christchurch	Christchurch United	b. Papatoetoe	6:5
1974	Manurewa	Christchurch United	b. Manurewa	2:1
1975	Auckland	Christchurch United	b. Manurewa	1:0
1976	Christchurch	Christchurch Rangers	b. Manurewa	5:4
1977	Manurewa	Christchurch Rangers	b. Manurewa	3:2
1978	Christchurch	Christchurch United	b. Glenfield Rovers	3:0
1979	Wellington	Petone	b. Mt Wellington	1:0
1980-90	No competition			

**Age lowered to Under-16 this year only.*

AIR NZ CHALLENGE TROPHY

Inaugurated in 1975 with sponsorship from the national airline, the inter-city challenge series ran for two years before fading into oblivion.

Date	Game		Result	Referee	
1975					
6 Feb	Auckland	v Canterbury	1:0	L.W. Coffman	A
9 Mar	Auckland	v Wellington	4:0	A. Boniface	A
1976					
28 Mar	Wellington	v Auckland	0:0	L. Willmer	W

BROWN SHIELD

The Association Football Challenge Trophy, generally known as the Brown Shield, was donated in 1891 by Mr Robert Brown, a whisky merchant from Glasgow. It has a unique place in the history of the N.Z. Football Association as the original inter-association trophy but more significantly the gift was the motivating factor for the inauguration of the Association.

From 1892-1925 the Brown Shield was the premier award in domestic football but on the presentation of The Football Association Trophy the Shield was allocated for competition amongst the "minor' associations of the North Island and is still contested on that basis.

RESULTS

1892 at Christchurch

Wellington	v Canterbury	9:2
Otago	v Auckland	1:0
Wellington	v Otago	6:2

1893 at Wellington

Auckland	v Wellington	2:1
Otago a bye		
Otago	v Auckland	4:1

1894 at Christchurch

Canterbury	v Otago	3:1
Wellington a bye		
Canterbury	v Wellington	7:4

1895 at Auckland

Auckland	v Wellington	2:0
Ruahine a bye		
Auckland	v Ruahine	3:0

1896 at Dunedin

Auckland	v Otago	3:0
Wellington a bye		
Auckland	v Wellington	2:1

1897 at Wellington

Ruahine	v Wellington	2:0

1898 at Wellington

Wellingto	v Ruahine	6:1
Auckland	v Otago	3:1
Auckland	v Wellington	3:1

1899

No competition

1900 at Auckland

Auckland	v Wellington	6:1
Otago a bye		
Otago	v Auckland	1:0

1901

League system

Auckland	v Wellington	1.2
Otago	v Auckland	6:1
Wellington	v Auckland	1:0

Trophy awarded to Otago

1902

No competition

1903 at Wellington

Wellington	v Auckland	4:1
Otago	v Canterbury	2:1
Wellington	v Otago	2:1

1904-05

No competition

1906 at Taranaki

Taranaki	v Ruahine	4:1
Wellington	v Auckland	5:1
Wellington	v Taranaki	4:0

1907 at Auckland

Wellington	v Taranaki	6:1
Auckland a bye		
Auckland	v Wellington	3:1

1908 at Dunedin

Wellington	v Taranaki	4:0
Otago a bye		
Wellington	v Otago	4:2

1908 was the last year under Tournament rules. The Shield was then open to challenge with Wellington as winner of the 1908 tournament to receive the first challenge.

1909	Wellington	v Taranaki	5:2
	Wellington	v Canterbury	2:2
	Wellington	v Auckland	2:1
	Wellington	v Hawkes Bay	11:1
1910	Wellington	v Wanganui	7:1
	Wellington	v Otago	3:1
	Wellington	v Auckland	0:2
	Auckland	v Canterbury	2:3
1911	Canterbury	v Otago	4:1
	Canterbury	v Manawatu	3:0
	Canterbury	v Wellington	1:1
1912	Canterbury	v Poverty Bay	9:2
	Canterbury	v Wanganui	5:3
	Canterbury	v Wellington	2:6
1913	Wellington	v Otago	2:2
	Wellington	v Taranaki	5:2
	Wellington	v Canterbury	1:2
	Canterbury	v Manawatu	8:0
	Canterbury	v Auckland	3:1
1914	Canterbury	v Buller	3:0
	Canterbury	v Hawkes Bay	8:0
	Canterbury	v Wanganui	7:3
	Canterbury	v Otago	2:2
1915-17	No competition		
1918	Canterbury	v Wellington	1:0
	Canterbury	v Otago	3:2
1919	Canterbury	v Auckland	1:0
	Canterbury	v Otago	5:1
	Canterbury	v Wellington	0:1
	Wellington	v Wanganui	6:0
1920	Wellington	v Auckland	1:1
	Wellington	v Canterbury	4:1
	Wellington	v Poverty Bay	8:3
	Wellington	v Auckland	4:2
	Wellington	v Wanganui	3:1
1921	Wellington	v Wanganui	2:1
	Wellington	v Canterbury	4:2

	Wellington	v Auckland	0:2
	Auckland	v South Auckland	4:0
1922	Auckland	v South Auckland	6:1
1923	Auckland	v South Auckland	2:0
	Auckland	v Wanganui	10:1
	Auckland	v Wellington	2:0
	Auckland	v Manawatu	6:1
1924	Auckland	v South Auckland	3:2
	Auckland	v Canterbury	3:2
1925	Auckland	v North Auckland	3:1
	Auckland	v Wellington	6:1
	Wellington	v South Auckland	4:2

From 1926 the four main centres became ineligible to compete. South Auckland and Poverty Bay as the first two challengers that year met to decide the first holder under the new rules.

1926	South Auckland	v Poverty Bay	4:0
	South Auckland	v Manawatu	4:1
	South Auckland	v Wanganui	2:1
	South Auckland	v North Auckland	4:0
1927	South Auckland	v North Auckland	3:2
1928	South Auckland	v Hawkes Bay	1:1
	South Auckland	v North Auckland	3:1
1929	South Auckland	v North Auckland	3:0
	South Auckland	v Hawkes Bay	1:1
1930 No challenges			
1931	South Auckland	v North Auckland	4:2
	South Auckland	v Manawatu	3:2
1932	South Auckland	v North Auckland	1:2
1933	North Auckland	v South Auckland	2:2
1934-38	No challenges		

In 1938 Council decided the Shield should be returned to the national association, the North Auckland Association having gone into recess. The Shield was then awarded to Wanganui, the aim being to encourage participation by Associations in the lower half of the North Island.

1939	Wanganui	v Manawatu	2:7
1940	Manawatu	v Hawkes Bay	5:1
	Manawatu	v Wanganui	1:7
	Wanganui	v Taranaki	6:0
1941-45	No challenges.		

In 1946 a scheme was introduced whereby each eligible Association would have at least one game for the Shield. To facilitate this scheme the Shield became a knockout trophy with competitors being divided geographically to keep travel costs to a minimum. The Shield was contested under this format up to and including 1964. Results of finals in that period were:

Year	**Venue**	**Game**	**Result**
1946	Wanganui	Wanganui b. Poverty Bay	5:2
1947	Palmerston Nth	Manawatu b. Wanganui	9:2
1948	Wanganui	Wanganui b. Manawatu	5:0
1949	Palmerston Nth	Wanganui b. Manawatu	4:1
1950	Wanganui	Wanganui b. Manawatu	4:2
1951	New Plymouth	Rotorua b. Taranaki	5:2
1952	Hamilton	Waikato b. Manawatu	5:2
1953	Palmerston Nth	Manawatu d. Rotorua	3:3
1954	Hamilton	Waikato b. Manawatu	1:0
1955	Palmerston Nth	Waikato b. Manawatu	1:0
1956	Rotorua	BOP b. Wanganui	4:2
1957	Palmerston Nth	Waikato b. Manawatu	5:2
1958	Hamilton	Waikato b. Hawkes Bay	5:0
1959	Palmerston Nth	BOP b. Manawatu	5:3
1960	New Plymouth	Taranaki b. Poverty Bay	2:1
1961	Manawatu and Waikato were due to meet in final but as game was not played the Shield was not awarded.		
1962	Gisborne	Poverty Bay b. Wairarapa	9:0
1963	Gisborne	Poverty Bay b. BOP	5:3
1964	Gisborne	Franklin b. Poverty Bay	4:1

In 1965 the challenge system was re-introduced.

Year	**Game**		**Result**
1965	Franklin	v Waikato	2:3
1966	Waikato	v Bay of Plenty	2:1
	Waikato	v Franklin	1:1
1967	Waikato	v Bay of Plenty	1:5
1968	No challenges		
1969	Bay of Plenty	v Franklin	3:2
1970	Bay of Plenty	v Franklin	4:5
1971	Franklin	v Waikato	2:0
1972	No challenges		
1973	Franklin	v Waikato	4:2
	Franklin	v Northland	3:1
1974	Franklin	v Waikato	7:3
1975	Franklin	v Waikato	1:1
	Franklin	v Northland	1:4
1976	No challenges		
1977	Northland	v Franklin	2:1
1978 to 1987		No challenges	
1988	Northland	v Tongariro	8:3
1989	Northland	v Franklin	2:4
1990	No challenges		

THE PETER DAWSON CUP

This Cup was presented to the New Zealand Football Association in 1922 by Peter Dawson Ltd, distillers of Glasgow, following a tour of New Zealand by a director of the firm, Mr Peter Dawson. It was to be used for the purpose of fostering South Island football. Although all South Island Associations were eligible to challenge, high travel costs prevented anyone other than a close neighbour from doing so. After World War II the Cup was given over to "minor' Associations. This did boost the game in the smaller centres but eventually the travel became too heavy a burden once more and with the Buller and Westland Associations going into recess regular competition ceased.

RESULTS

Year	Game	Result
1922	Otago v Southland	3:0
1923	Otago v Southland	2:0
	Otago v Canterbury	2:1
1924	No competition	
1925	Otago v Southland	2:0
	Otago v South Canterbury	5:3
	Otago v Canterbury	1:3
1926	Canterbury v South Canterbury	4:0
	Canterbury v Buller	1:2
	Buller v Nelson	1:1
1927	No competition	
1928	Buller v Westland	0:2
1929	Westland v Nelson	4:0
	Westland v Canterbury	3:1
1930	Westland v Buller	1:0
	Westland v Canterbury	3:2
1931	Westland v Buller	3:1
	Westland v Canterbury	3:1
1932	Westland v Canterbury	3:2
	Westland v Buller	3:4
	Buller v Westland	1:1
1933	Buller v Westland	5:2
	Buller v Nelson	4:1
1934	Buller v Westland	5:3
1935	No competition	
1936	Buller v Nelson	3:1
	Buller v Westland	8:1
1937	Buller v Westland	2:1
1938	Buller v Westland	1:5
1939	Westland v Buller	4:2
	Westland v Buller	4:0
1940	Westland v Buller	5:1
1941-42	No competition - trophy returned to N.Z.F.A.	
1943	Buller v Canterbury	1:8
1944-46	No competition	

From 1947 through to 1961 the Peter Dawson Cup was contested on a knockout basis with teams divided geographically (north-west, south-east). Canterbury and Otago as "major" Associations did not participate.

Year	Venue	Game	Result
1947	Timaru	Southland b. Sth Canterbury	1:0
1948	Invercargill	Westland b. Southland	3:1
1949	Greymouth	Southland b. Westland	3:2
1950	Invercargill	Buller b. Southland (Decided on penalties)	2:2
1951	Westport	Southland b. Buller	4:3
1952	Invercargill	Southland b. Buller	3:2
1953	Nelson	Nelson b. Southland	6:3
1954	Invercargill	Southland b. Nelson	8:3
1955	Westport	Buller b. Southland	4:3
1956	Timaru	Sth Canterbury b. Nelson	4:2
1957	Nelson	Nelson b. Southland	2:0
1958	Invercargill	Southland b. Nelson	4:2
1959	Nelson	Nelson b. Southland	9:2
1960	Invercargill	Southland b. Marlborough	2:0
1961	Nelson	Nelson b. Southland	Default
1962-63		No competition.	
1964	Greymouth	Nelson b Marlborough	3:2
1965-68		No competition	
1969	Nelson	Nelson b Sth Canterbury	5:2
1970-80		No competition	
1981		Nelson b Southland	2:0
		Nelson b Sth Canterbury	2:1
1982-90		No competition	

ROTHMANS CUP

In 1962 Rothmans donated a trophy for an inter-club series featuring the local champions from Auckland, Wellington, Canterbury and Otago. Prize money went with the Cup. The series ceased after the second year of competition.

1962 Semi-Finals

	Eastern Suburbs (A)	v Northern (W)	2:2
	Northern (W)	v Eastern Suburbs (A)	2:4
	Eastern Suburbs won on aggregate		6:4
	Western (C)	v Northern (O)	0:4
	Northern (O)	v Western (C)	1:0
	Northern won on aggregate		5:0
Final			
	Eastern Suburbs (A)	v Northern (O)	0:2
	Northern (O)	v Eastern Suburbs (A)	1:2
	Northern won on aggregate		3:2

1963 Semi-Finals

	North Shore Utd (A)	v Diamond (W)	0:1
	Diamond (W)	v North Shore Utd (A)	2:6
	North Shore Utd won on aggregate		6:3
	King Edward T.C.O.B. (O)	v Nomads (C)	2:1
	Nomads (C)	v King Edward T.C.O.B. (O)	0:0
	King Edward T.C.O. B. won on aggregate		2:1
Final			
	North Shore Utd (A)	v King Edward T.C.O.B. (O)	3:1

THE INTER-ISLAND MATCH

Efforts to make the North Island and South Island match an annual fixture have never been very successful due to the high costs in assembling players. The first attempt foundered after two years. In 1946 the series was revived as part of a plan to stimulate interest in the code and a joint promotion at Lancaster Park with a rugby game as curtain-raiser to the inter-island match broke even. Unfortunately only the 1949 fixture at Auckland showed a profit and eventually the high cost of promotion resulted in the abandonment of regular fixtures.

The player most readily associated with the North v South match is Ken Fleet of Auckland who represented North Island five times between 1948 and 1953. Players who have appeared in four games are Phil Traynor and Ian Upchurch for the North Island; Vic Smith, Maurice Dean, Tom Gilchrist for the South Island.

RESULTS

Year	Venue	Result	Referee	
1920	Christchurch	North 3:2	G. Black	C
1921	Wanganui	Draw 4:4	W.G. Herd	WG
1933	Wellington	North 4:0	G. Jackson	W
1946	Christchurch	Draw 3:3	W.M. Smith	O
1948	Dunedin	Draw 2:2	D. Welham	O
1949	Auckland	South 2:0	R. Brighton	A
1950	Christchurch	South 4:1	C.G. Sweeney	C
1951	Wellington	North 4:1	J. Baxter	W
1952	Dunedin	North 3:2	W.T. Dodd	O
1953	Auckland	North 4:1	C. Edwards	A
1954	Christchurch	South 5:4	T.C. Gottermeyer	C
1956	Gisborne	South 3:2	A. Furse	A
1958	Wellington	Draw 2:2	G. Baxter	HB
1960	Auckland	Draw 4:4	T.J. Ward	W
1967	Christchurch	South 2:2	A. Williams	O

OFFICERS OF THE NEW ZEALAND FOOTBALL ASSOCIATION

President

George Rhodes	1893-1894
John Ross	1895
Hon. J.G. Ward	1896
Sir Robert Stout	1897-1900
Sir Joseph Ward	1901-1919
Hon C.P. Skerrett	1920-1928
Sir Charles Statham	1929-1933
Ernest Davis (Sir from 1937)	1934-1947
Walter Nash	1948-1953
J.C. Young	1954-1955
Hon. David Wilson	1956-1957
M.G. McInnes	1958-1959
R.A. Keeling	1960-1961
J. Meltzer	1962-1963
W.J. Arcus	1964-1965
F.G. Fullbrook	1966-1967
S.J. Guppy	1968-1969
L.J. Fisher	1970-1971
W.A. Fox	1972-1973
T.M. McGuigan	1974-1975
J. Cowie	1976-1977
L.R. Adams-Schneider	1978-1981
R.A. Kelly	1982-1985
Sir Robert Muldoon	1986-1987
C.J. Dempsey	1988-

It has been the custom since 1954 for the retiring president to assume the office of Immediate Past President.

Vice Presidents

L.C.H. Tripp	1894-1896
A. Heather	1894-1906
T.W. Maude	1894-1903
G. McLean	1895-1906
C.H. Izard	1897-1906
E.W. Andrews	1898-1903
- Jackson	1904-1905
Dr Johnston	1904
H.M. McDonald	1905-1906
C. Snow	1905-1906
- Stark	1905-1906
F.J. Courtney	1906-1955
- Cook	1906
E.E. Baume	1907-1909
C.H. Poole	1907-1910
J.G.W. Aitken	1907-1910
T.K. Sidey	1907-1912
J.F. Arnold	1907-1910
W. Carncross	1907-1921
Dr E.A. Walker	1907-1928
H.N. Holmes	1907-1911
P.L. Davies	1908-1934
S.W. Thornton	1908-1911
R. Heaton Rhodes	1909-1910
J.T. Hogan	1909-1910
J. Vigor Brown	1909-1910
A. Dillon	1909-1910
J.A. Hanan	1909-1910
R.B. Walker	1909-1910
C.E. Mackay	1910-1911
E.A. Blake	1911
C.C. Dacre	1912-1914
W. Rutherford	1912-1914
J. Ellis	1912-1914
H.J. McKeowen	1912-1925
H.G. Mayer	1912-1945
R. English	1912-1932
P.W. Barnett	1912-1913
C.E. Statham	1912-1928, 1934-35
J.J. Roberts	1912-1933
A.M. Mayers	1913-1926
J.C. Thomson	1912-1913
H.L. Godber	1914-1927, 1947-1953
C.P. Skerrett	1915-1919
W.J. Churchward	1915-1921
R.M. Chadwick	1915-1925
S. Myers	1915-1922
W.D. Ramsay	1914-1933
G.W. Fowlds	1914-1929
W.F. Stent	1915-1922
E. Ritson	1918-1925
W. Munckton	1918-1933
W.F. Sleeman	1919-1920
A.E. Wells	1919-1939
E.W. Harvey	1920
J.A. Nash	1922
L.A. Stapleton	1922-1925
L. Shewan	1922
A.G. Barnett	1922
J.D. Marks	1924-1934
E. Beckett	1924
J. McKinnon	1924-1929
A. Bolton	1924
E. Davis	1924-1933, 1948-1961
A. Menzies	1924-1931
H.J. Duncan	1924-1949
R.B. Bunt	1929-1949
W.G. Herd	1924-1947
A. Williams	1924-1945
J.C. Young	1924-1953, 1958-1961
F.G. Radford	1925-1935
A. Whatman	1925-1929
W. Adams	1925-1928
A. Scott	1925
C.F. Ward	1925, 1947-1951
H.S.W. King	1925-1938
J. Mason	1925
C.F. Wildish	1925-1928
W. McIntyre	1927-1949
T. McLaren	1927
G.W. Bagrie	1927
C.H. Bascand	1928-1931
W.H. Connor	1928
H.A. Young	1928
W. Robertson	1929-1939
W. Duncan	1929-1943
J.B. McCallum	1930-1936
J.M.A. Ilott	1930-1973
M.G. McInnes	1930-1957, 1962-1972
G. Dickinson	1931-1933
G. Cox	1931-1951
C. Lawrence	1931
D.E. Brown	1931-1955
N. McDougall	1932-1936
H.I. Graves	1932-1971
F.M. Ritchie	1933-1951
J. Simpson	1933-1951

E.R. Grace	1934-1958
R.G. Riding	1934-1951
T. Ruddiman	1934-1940
A.W. Sinclair	1935-1958
H. Gribble	1935-1964
E.J. Anderson	1937-1951
J.A. Robb	1937-1951
J.E. Jones	1937-1960
J.N. McFarlane	1937-1951
F.T.H. Bell	1937-1951
R.E. Selby	1938-1953
F.W. Mead	1938-1972
G. Littlejohn	1938
T. Smith	1938
W.G. Bryce	1939-1955
P. Mackenzie	1943-1952
L.W. Sturmey	1944-1980
F. Sanders	1945-
H.H.A. Renai	1945-1956
J.M. Ollier	1946-1953
W.B. Hicks	1946-1956
M. Heyes	1946-1979
G.C. Ballantyne	1946-1983
E.L. Hope	1947-1951
H.J. Hall	1947-1959
H. Ward	1947-1967
W. Wallace	1947-1951
A. Bell	1947-1951
W. Black	1948-1951
D. Wilson	1948-1955, 1960-1976
D.E. Hansen	1948-1951
J. Meltzer	1950-1961, 1966-1976
E.J. McQueen	1950-1980
J. Robertson	1960-1951
J.M. McLean	1953-1966
W.L. Wilson	1955
T.E. Thompson	1955-*
K. de Maus	1956-1969
W.P. Smith	1956-1982
M. Gordon	1957-1959
J.C. Sibbin	1957-1969
W.J. Arcus	1959-1963
W.A. Fox	1959-1971, 1976-*
F.G. Fullbrook	1959-1965, 1970-1984
H. Lock	1959-1968
J. Smith	1961-*
A.P. Neesham	1961-1967
W. Nash	1956-1969
G. Baxter	1962-*
B.S. Connor	1962-1975
G.A. Leary	1962-*
J.G. Shankie	1962-1969
W. Hawthorn	1964-1980
R.A. Keeling	1964-*
T.W. Dick	1966-1981
R. Higgs	1967-*
R. Speed	1967-*
A. Kyle	1967
T.G. Wells	1967-*
J.K. Smith	1969-1972
L. O'Rorke	1969-1971
C.R. Wilkins	1968-1988
D.C. Seath	1970-*
A.V. Cooper	1972-*
E.A. Harris	1972-*
J. Welsh	1974-1975
J. Dalziel	1974-*
J. Cowie	1974-1975
G.L. Whyte	1974-*
G. Smith	1974-1988
L.J. Fisher	1974-1976
T.M. McGuigan	1981-*
C.J. Dempsey	1981-1987
A.R. White	1981-*
D.A. MacDonald	1981-*
M.B. Starling	1981-*
T.J. Killalea	1982-*
E. Gould	1983-*
G. Te Au	1983-*
J. Arnold	1985-*
T.C. Gottermeyer	1985-*
A.K.K. Ross	1986-*
D. Romeril	1986-1988
E. Thompson	1988-*
R. Douglas	1989-*
R.M. Irvine	1990-*
R.A. Kelly	1990-*
I. Paton	1991-*

** Denotes current vice-president*

Life Members

	Elected	Deceased
F. Campbell	1933	1944
B.L. Salmon	1933	1935
J.J. Roberts	1934	1946
F. Sanders	1947	1951
L. Munro	1949	1965
G. Cox	1952	1967
B.T. Martin	1953	1959
W.B. Hicks	1957	1960
J.C. Young	1962	1966
J.I. Kershaw	1962-*	
W.J. Arcus	1966	1966
M.H. Webley	1966	1967
K. de Maus	1967	1969
G. Jackson	1967	1983
S.J. Guppy	1971	1982
J. Cowie	1976-*	
C.J. Dempsey	1988 *	

** Current Life Member*

Secretary

T.W. (Thomas) Maude	1892
A.M. (Alex) Henderson	1893-1897
F.J. (Frederic) Courtney	1898-1905
H.G. Bell	1906
B.L. Salmon	1907-1924
L.O. Atkinson	1925-1927
A. (Alf) Willianms	1928-1945
W.B. (Bill) Hicks	1945-1952
W.J. (Bill) Arcus	1953-1959
S.C. (Steuart) Goodman	1960-1964
T. (Terrence) Sanders	1965-1968
G.H. (Graham) Moore	1969-1972
S.C. (Steuart) Goodman	1973-1980

Secretary-General

G. (Gwyn) Evans	1981-1987
J. (John) Arnold	1987

Executive Director

P.G. (Paul) Cunningham	1988-1990
T.N. (Noel) Robinson	1990-

Treasurer

A.E. Gibbs	1893-1905
R.H. Nagle	1906-1907
G. Uren	1908
L. White	1909-1910
J.M. Ollier	1910-1911
W.M. Matheson	1911-1913
A.C. Kerr	1913-1916
B.L. Salmon	1917-1919
H.I. Graves	1920-1928
W.L. Wilson	1929-1953
J. Cowie	1954-1965

From 1966 the position of Treasurer was combined with that of Secretary.

Council Members 1891-1924

In this period Council comprised delegates from affiliated associations. When the number of associations increased to the point where delegate system was becoming unwieldy, a nine-member council was brought in.

The following is a list by Association, and in chronological order, of most of the delegates who served on the Council up to and including 1924, Alongside the Association name is the year the particular Associationfirst sent a delegate.

Auckland (1891)
J.R. Gibbons
- Ridings
J. Smith
W.F. Sloman
G.F. Brodie
J.M. Ollier
A.F. Newbold
T. McLaren
P. Rose
Buller (1894)
W.W. Bain
W. Allison
Bush (1894)
A.J. Abbott
Canterbury (1891)
L.C.H. Tripp
- Turnbull
C.T. Jones
B.L. Salmon
L. White
W.R. Perks
W.G. Bryce
Hawkes Bay (1908)
P.A. Cornish
T. Shields
H.J. McKeowen
J. Ince
Manawatu (1909)
W. Duncan
A. Varney
Marlborough (1910)
H.J. Yeoman
R. Hutcheson
C. Shapcott
Nelson (1921)
F. Sanders
North Auckland (1922)
S. Jardine
Otago (1891)
P.D. Leslie
- McMillan
R.H. Nagle
G. McNair
R.F. Mackay
C.F. Martin
C.E. Fordham
C.F. Ward
Poverty Bay (1910)
W.J.H. Reynolds
H.J. Buck
South Auckland (1922)
H.J. Yeoman
South Canterbury (1912)
A.J. Hyder
Southland (1904)
P. McWhannell
H.G. Mayer
H. Waters
W.E. Wells
H.J. Salmon
A. Menzies
H.M. McGirr
Taranaki (1906)
G.L. Mackie
A. Dickson
W. Auld
W.J. Ferkins
R. Downie
Wairarapa (1922)
W.S. Walls
R.Y. Walls
Wanganui (1909)
F. Campbell
Wellington (1891)
A.M. Henderson
- Todd
J.J. Roberts
A. Williams
F. O'Connell
J. McCrorie
C.F. Ward
R.Y. Walls
H.D. Warner
Westland (1922)
M.J. Hayward

Council Members 1925-1991
(Alphabetical Order)

	Years on Council	
Anderson, E. Ted	1	1957
Arnold, J. John	9	1978-86
Barton, E.J. Eddie	8	1951-58
Bede, Bro.	1	1943
Beldham, J. John	1	1983
Bilby, G.P. Grahame	7	1974-80
Boyden, K. Ken	1	1971
Bryce, W.G.	20	1925-38 1940-45
Burton, F. Fred	5	1958-62
Campbell, F. Frank	18	1925-33, 1936-44

Cassian, Bro.	1	1942
Chapman, G.F. Garry	1	1961
Chapman, W.A. Bill	8	1945-52
Cherry, R. Ron	1	1973
Clement, B. Bevan	7	1984-*
Connor, B.S. Bert	16	1945-60
Costello, A.J.	3	1946-48
Cowie, J. Jack	14	1950-53, 1966-75
Cox, D. Davis	4	1985-88
Cunningham, B. Bryan	12	1978-86, 1988-*
Cutler, F.W.	1	1945
Dacre, J.C. Jack	3	1953-54, 1965
de Krey, H. Harry	6	1967-72
Dempsey, C.J. Charlie	23	1965-1987
Denley, J. John	9	1982-*
Dick, J.H.	3	1939-41
Dick, T.W. Tom	6	1944-49
Dobbie, K.G. Keith	4	1975-78
Dods H.A. Harry	10	1974-75, 1982, 1984-*
Duncan, W.	1	1935
Dunning, J.E. John	1	1975
England, I. Ivan		1971-72
Ewing, J.L.	1	1936
Fenton, D.L. Dennis	2	1989-*
Flett, A. Alan	1	1953
Fraser, A. Alan	2	1977-78
Fraser, M. Malcolm	2	1935-36
Fox, W. Bill	1	1970
Gavin, C. Cyril	5	1973-77
Gendall, J.W.D. Ian	4	1962-65
Gendall, J.W. Warwick	12	1979-*
Godber, H.L. Harry	10	1928-37
Goodman, S.C. Steuart	2	1966-67
Gottermeyer, T.C. Trevor	17	1968-84
Gould, E. Ernie	9	1970-73, 1975-79
Graham, P.W. Peter	6	1965-70
Graves, H.I.	1	1931
Guppy, S.J. Syd	9	1959-67
Hall, C.	5	1946-50
Harris, E.A. Ernie	17	1957-68, 1981-85
Harrison, A. Arthur	14	1945-48
Hayburn, R. Ralph	4	1979-82
Henke, R. Rene	2	1977-78
Hicks, W.R. Bill	10	1938-44, 1953-55
Hilton, A. Arthur	4	1976-79
Hilton, O. Otto	8	1957-64
Hipkins, J. John	6	1970-75
Hollis, E.	10	1937-46
Houston, J. Jock	7	1946-52
Houston, S.	1	1948
Hullena, R.V. Bob	6	1969-74
Husband, R. Rod	4	1982-85
Hyder, A.J.	8	1925-32
Jackson, G. George	24	1949-51, 1953-73
Jenkins, J. Jack	1	1983
Johnston, W.G. Warren	1	1969
Kavanagh, R.H. Bob	8	1969-76
Kean, J.J. Mack	8	1949-56
Kelly, R.A. Ron	10	1968-77
Kennedy, A. Allan	2	1989-*
Kershaw, J.J. Jim	16	1949-64
Kerslake, R.H. Ray	5	198-84
Killalea, T.J. Terry	17	1969-81, 1987-*
Killick, P. Perce	5	1968-70, 1974-75
Kleyne, P. Peter	6	1970, 1972-76
Lamont, D. David	4	1985-88
Lothian, J. Jim	3	1933-35
Lyon, W.J.	1	1936
MacDonald, D.A. Dave	13	1969-81
McDonald, E. Ewan	2	1987-88
MacKenzie, M. Maurice	9	1970-78
Mackenzie, P. Peter	4	1936-39
McQueen, E.J. Ted	1	1948
Mackie, F.	3	1932-23
Mann, T. Terry	2	1989-*
Martin, B.T.	16	1937-52
Meltzer, J. Jack	9	1952-60
Milburn, J.A. Jack	14	1926-39
Mills, D.T. Don	3	1970-72
Montgomery, H.J. Hugh	2	1987-88
Munro, L. Leo	7	1942-48
Munro. L. Leo	1	1978
Munro, W.K. Bill	1	1991-*
Norman, M. Mike	2	1977-78
Ollier, J.M.	8	1934, 1935, 1940-45
O'Rorke, L. Larry	7	1965-71
Osten, P.D. Peter	4	1966-69
Pacey, S. St an	1	1968
Paton, I. Ian	17	1974-90
Paynter, M. Michael	3	1986-88
Pelosi, R. Rod	6	1985-*
Renai, H.H.A.	17	1928-44
Rigby, T.J. Trevor	5	1968-69, 1972-74
Roberts, J.J.	2	1925-26
Roberts, G. Gavin	2	1968-69
Robinson, T.N. Noel	5	1986-90
Romeril, D.E. Doug	3	1965-67
Rose, P.	2	1925-26
Ross, A.K. Keith	12	1973-84
Salmon, G.L.	11	1925-35
Sanders, F. Frank	21	1925-45
Sharp, B.	1	1961
Shankie, J.G. John	19	1947, 1949-61, 1965-69
Shedden, S.C.	5	1932-36
Smith, G.	1	1946
Smith, I. Ian	6	1975-84
Smith, J. Jack	2	1965, 1967
Smith, J.K. Jim	15	1954-68
Smith, P. Peter	2	1976-77
Smith, R.S. Bob	11	1956-66
Smyth, F.M.	1	1948
Starling, M.B. Mike	7	1972-78
Storey, L. Lorraine	1	1991-*
Te Au, G. George	11	1971-81
Thomas, G.L. George	10	1968-77
Titheradge, R. Roy	3	1963-65
Vaney, W.J.	14	1935-48
Varney, A. Arthur	6	1925-30
Vizard, A. Arthur	1	1971
Walker, C.	2	1947-48
Wallace, D.R. David	1	1975
Walls, J.R. Sr	15	1933-47
Walls, J.Y. Jr	4	1945-48
Ward, T.J. Terry	1	1974
Webley, M.H. Max	9	1949-57
Wells, A.E. Albert	1	1925
White, A.R. Ron	6	1968-73
White, J. John	1	1973
Whyte, G.L. Gordon	8	1961-68
Wildman, G. Gerry	3	1976-78
Wilkins, C.R. Charlie	15	1953-67
Willis, A.R.	2	1944-45

Willman, B.W. Brian	1	1978
Young, J. John	2	1975-76
Zewald, J. Jack	2	1966-67

*Current Council Member

Chairman of Council

A. Varney	1925-27
F. Campbell	1928-33
B.L. Salmon	1934-35
J.A. Milburn	1935-38
F. Campbell	1939-44
F. Sanders	1944
L. Munro	1945-48
T.W. Dick	1949
B.S. Connor	1950-54
J. Meltzer	1955
B.S. Connor	1956-58
J.I. Kershaw	1959-63
R.S. Smith	1964-66
J. Cowie	1967-74
R.A. Kelly	1975-78
T.J. Killalea	1978-81
C.J. Dempsey	1982-87
J.W. Gendall	1988-

National Coach

Ken Armstrong	1957-64
Lou Brocic	1965-66
Juan Schwanner	1967-68
Lou Brocic	1969
Barrie Truman	1970-76
Wally Hughes	1977-78
John Adshead	1979-82
Allan Jones	1983-84
Kevin Fallon	1985-88
John Adshead	1989
Ian Marshall	1990-

INDEX
(Applies to text section)

* Denotes name appearing in caption on full colour page